Studying and working in France

To Jenny, Joan and Anne

Studying and working in France

A student guide

Russell Cousins,
Ron Hallmark and Ian Pickup

Manchester University Press
Manchester and New York

Distributed exclusively in the USA and Canada by St. Martin's Press

Copyright © Russell Cousins, Ron Hallmark and Ian Pickup 1994

Published by Manchester University Press
Oxford Road, Manchester M13 9NR, UK
and Room 400, 175 Fifth Avenue, New York, NY 10010, USA

Distributed exclusively in the USA and Canada
by St. Martin's Press, Inc., 175 Fifth Avenue, New York, NY 10010, USA

British Library Cataloguing-in-Publication Data
A catalogue record for this book is available from the British Library

Library of Congress Cataloging-in-Publication Data
Cousins, Russell.
   Studying and working in France : a student guide / Russell
Cousins, Ron Hallmark, and Ian Pickup.
       p.   cm.
   Rev., updated, and expanded ed. of: Student guide to French
universities
   Includes bibliographical references and index.
   ISBN 0–7190–4220–8 (pbk.)
   1. Foreign study—France—Handbooks, manuals, etc.
   2. Universities and colleges—France—Handbooks, manuals, etc.
   I. Hallmark, Ron.   II. Pickup, Ian.   III. Cousins, Russell.   Student
guide to French universities.   IV. Title.
LB2376.3.F8C68   1994
370.19′62′0944—dc20   94–12626

ISBN 0 7190 4220 8 *paperback*

Photoset in Linotron Ehrhardt
by Northern Phototypesetting Co Ltd, Bolton

Printed in Great Britain
by Bell & Bain Ltd, Glasgow

Contents

Introduction

This *Guide* is a substantially revised, updated and expanded version of the authors' *Student Guide to French Universities*. The original volume was aimed primarily at British students planning a period of study-residence in France. This new edition seeks to broaden its focus in two distinct ways. It is now geared towards all anglophone students, including those from North America and Australasia. At the same time it offers advice to those young people who wish to spend a limited period of residence in France, other than by way of full-time study: students who have been nominated to a post of language assistant in a school, college or university, or who are to undertake a work placement in France. The book will therefore provide practical help and information for those opting for a GAP year (see Glossary), for undergraduates fulfilling course requirements, for students improving their command of the French language in the workplace or in an educational institution, or, indeed, for all those who need practical advice when planning for an extended stay in France.

The *Guide* will, quite naturally, be of particular help and interest to those modern languages undergraduates intending to study at French universities; much of the information given, however, is not restricted to language courses: the nature and role of universities in France is placed in a wider context; the range of academic awards, the halls of residence and information on individual French universities are but three of the more general topics which are treated.

The increasing co-operation between institutions of higher education throughout and well beyond the European Community is to some extent attributable to the adoption by the Council of Ministers of the COMETT, ERASMUS and LINGUA schemes and, more recently, of joint proposals for EC-US exchanges. These initiatives have encouraged formal links which simplify administrative arrangements and which lead to jointly-approved programmes of study. This has undoubtedly facilitated the transition from the British to the French system for many UK undergraduates and will doubtless do likewise for North American and other students. However, so many aspects of life in French universities (and, indeed, in French society in general) differ from those in the corresponding institutions in other countries, that even students who are to benefit from the many advantages which accrue from an Inter-University Cooperation Programme will find much practical help and guidance in this volume.

The *Guide* may be used in two ways: as a source of general information on French universities (their courses and administrative procedures), work placements and assistantships, and also as a source of answers to specific queries (the range of disciplines on offer in a particular university, or the meaning of an abbreviation, for example). Chapters 1–2 outline the place which universities occupy in higher education in France and examine course patterns. Chapter 3 sets out various accommodation possibilities, including, in particular, the work of the different CROUS (the regional equivalents of the Accommodation and Welfare Offices in the UK). Chapter 4 outlines work opportunities in France (work placements, assistantships and vacation jobs). For those contemplating study during their residence in France, Chapters 5–6 offer practical guidance relating to administrative and registration procedures and life in the student community in France. Chapter 7 prepares all anglophones for their return home and for their reintegration in the home-based study programme. The detailed description of French universities which follows in Part III, provides specific information about the principal French universities, together with notes on the major features of the relevant towns and surrounding area.

Finally, the Glossary and abbreviations (including acronyms), though not exhaustive, goes well beyond the terminology specific to any one discipline so as to include the academic, administrative, practical and everyday expressions which are likely to be encountered both before and during study-residence or a work placement in France.

For the benefit of non-linguists, key French terms are italicised in brackets after their English equivalents, when these are first introduced in the main body of the text.

The universities included in Part III are, generally, the ones with which the authors have had regular contact for a number of years in their capacity as 'Year Abroad' tutors for Birmingham undergraduates (BA,

BCom, BSocSc, BSc, LLB) spending one month, six months or, more normally, a full academic year at a French institution of higher education as a compulsory part of their undergraduate course. The authors are indebted to the many students – past and present – who have supplied them with a wealth of information which they themselves would have found it difficult, if not impossible, to obtain. Whilst every effort has been made to ensure that the information is correct at the time of going to press, it will be appreciated that it is difficult, if not impossible, to guarantee the lasting accuracy of every detail, given the speed with which changes, and indeed reforms, are being implemented in higher education in France.

The authors are also most grateful for the help and co-operation afforded by the CNOUS, whose many publications supplied facts and figures unobtainable elsewhere. They are similarly indebted to the various CROUS and *Scolarités* which kindly updated and supplemented the information supplied in the original version of this work; to the Ministère de l'Education Nationale and to the Service Culturel of the French Embassy in London for providing the text of key legislation and other essential information. Special thanks are due to those colleagues on both sides of the Channel, especially those from ERASMUS networks, whose constructive criticisms and suggestions concerning the original manuscript have proved invaluable. Whilst it must be reiterated that the *Guide* is to a large extent based on the authors' experience of sending modern languages undergraduates to France (and this, of necessity, limits their perception of the organisation and teaching of other disciplines), they are hopeful that this volume will serve a useful purpose for the large numbers of students who will make their way to *la belle France* in order to pursue their studies, to undertake a work placement, or, more generally, simply to improve their knowledge of its language, people and culture.

Russell Cousins	University of Birmingham
Ron Hallmark	October 1993
Ian Pickup

Part I
Background information

1
Universities: their role in higher education in France

Foreign students going to France, especially if they intend to enter the French university system, will have a fuller understanding of their French counterparts if they know about their educational background and the choices they have already made. French eighteen-year-old secondary-school pupils (*lycéens*) armed with their school-leaving certificate (*baccalauréat*) and wishing to pursue their studies to a higher level in the public sector are faced with a number of possibilities. The vast majority (something in the region of 60 per cent of those taking the *bac d'enseignement général* and a significant proportion of those taking the *bac technologique*) will decide to take up their automatic right to register at a university. Others will stay on at the *lycée* and enrol for courses (*classes préparatoires*) which lead to the highly competitive and selective alternative system of the Grandes Ecoles and the Ecoles Spécialisées. Yet others will attempt to secure one of the increasing number of places in the advanced technical-training departments of the *lycées* (*sections de techniciens supérieurs*) which, after two years, lead to the award of the *Brevet de Technicien Supérieur* (BTS).

The French university system differs in many respects from that of the UK and the USA, and perhaps most fundamentally in terms of access: whereas in British and American universities, entry is selective and, in some cases, fiercely competitive, French universities are open to all holders of the *baccalauréat* (*bacheliers*). Alongside the universities, the Grandes Ecoles train civil servants, engineers and senior administrative and management personnel for the public and private sectors, industry and commerce. These latter establishments already admit foreign students and the numbers of such students spending a period of study-residence in them will no doubt increase, given the proliferation of exchange agreements both within the EC and beyond. However, the vast majority of foreign students who wish to study in France will undoubtedly continue to register in French universities. It is for this reason that, in terms of study possibilities, this *Guide* will focus in the main on the universities, whilst placing them in the broader context of higher education in France.

1.1   The universities: a brief historical note

French universities have a long and venerable history. The earliest amongst them date from the thirteenth century: Paris (1211), Toulouse (1229) and Montpellier (1289). The Church, of course, exercised a virtual monopoly on education more or less to the time of the Revolution, but, as with so many other aspects of French society, the framework of the present educational system was established by Napoleon. For administrative purposes France was divided into *académies*, each one headed by a representative of the central authority, the *recteur*, and this administrative structure still persists today. However, Napoleon's concept of the university – l'Université Impériale – is no longer valid. Whereas the Emperor defined the university as the education system in its totality, incorporating the *écoles primaires*, the *lycées* and the *facultés*, subsequent changes have narrowed the use of the term to post-*baccalauréat* institutions of higher education.

For all practical purposes, the beginnings of French universities, as we now find them, can be traced back to the education reform act (*loi d'orientation*) which emerged from the social and political upheavals of 1968. It was the untenable situation in the *facultés* that was a major determining factor in the events of that year. Overcrowding had reached unprecedented levels: in many instances, the lecture rooms simply could not accommodate the numbers of students enrolled. At Nanterre, for example, the university, which had been built to cater for some 2,000 students, was faced with some 20,000 registering in October 1967. Staffing provision was manifestly inadequate. The hopelessly adverse staff-student ratios exacerbated even further the impersonal relations between teacher and taught which had always been a feature of the system. It is against this background that the student body raised a number of fundamental issues concerning the nature of the curriculum, the functioning of the various *facultés*, and indeed the very relationship between the universities and society at large.

Out of all this unrest emerged the parliamentary legislation on higher education which was passed in November of that year and which, viewed retrospectively, is to be seen as a watershed in the history of French universities.

1.2　The universities: *la loi d'orientation de l'enseignement supérieur du 12 novembre 1968*

This law, initiated by General de Gaulle and the then Ministre de l'Education Nationale, Edgar Faure, led to a radical reorganisation of the French university system. The hundred or so faculties, loosely grouped together as universities (one for each of the twenty-three *académies*) were abolished and replaced by seventy-one new-style universities and a small number of outposts (*centres universitaires*). The various *facultés* and their constituent departments therefore ceased to exist (though it is curious to see how the term *faculté* is still used in certain contexts today) and were replaced, as the main subdivisions of a university, by *unités d'enseignement et de recherche* (UER). The latter could correspond in their focus either to a traditional discipline (UER d'Anglais) or to a faculty (UER de Médecine et de Pharmacie) or even to a grouping of related disciplines (*thème d'études*) (UER des Sciences de l'Environnement). The underlying aim of the UER − as the name suggests − was the essential linking of teaching and research activities in higher education, two of the three basic functions (*missions*) of the universities, as laid down in the Act. The third, *la formation de l'homme* (the development of human potential), also marked a radically new departure in its extension of interest beyond the purely intellectual side of the personality.

The fundamental principles informing the *loi d'orientation* were autonomy, participation and *pluridisciplinarité* (multi-disciplinary structures). Autonomy, as enshrined in the Act, gave the universities and their constituent *unités d'enseignement et de recherche* the power to determine their own internal structures. They were to be run by committees or councils (*conseils*) composed of elected representatives from the student body, and the administrative and ancillary staff, in addition to the teaching and research staff. The highest elected body − the *Conseil d'Université* − incorporated a number of distinguished outside members who were prominent in the life of the region. Autonomy also applied to academic matters: the *conseil* of each UER was given the power to lay down its own programme of studies, research activities, teaching methods and modes of assessment. Decisions on these various matters had, however, to be made within the framework of a number of predetermined criteria (*règles communes*) for the validation of the standard national diplomas (see Chapter 2). Autonomy extended to financial matters: monies and other resources provided centrally were placed under the control of individual establishments, which were responsible for their own budgets, but, again, within the limits and guidelines imposed nationally.

The second fundamental principle – participation – is already evident in the existence of the various *conseils* referred to above, and is to be seen as a direct consequence of the events of May 1968. For the first time, students were given the right to vote their own representatives on to the relevant *conseils*. Elections amongst the teaching and research staff encouraged self-determination at every level. Members of the *Conseils d'Université* held ballots to elect their own representatives at regional and national level.

The third principle underpinning the *loi d'orientation* – *pluridisciplinarité* – was designed to break down the rigid, historically-based faculty distinctions between individual areas of study. It was also intended to diminish the formidable power that was traditionally placed in the hands of the faculty *professeurs*, who controlled all aspects of their own academic subjects. The new universities, though they might well have a dominant focus, were to be established as multi-disciplinary structures, combining wherever possible arts and letters with science and technology. Hence in a university such as Rennes II, an arts-dominated institution, the UER Littérature, the UER Langues, Littératures et Civilisations Etrangères, were combined with the UER Géographie et Aménagement de l'Espace, the UER Psychologie, Sociologie et Sciences de l'Education and the UER des Sciences et Techniques.

Since 1968, French universities have been in a constant state of change and evolution: successive Ministers of Education seem determined to leave as their legacy their own *loi* with its new initiative or focus. But despite subsequent legislation, the determining principles and global structures of the *loi d'orientation* subsist, along with the democratisation which is such a salient feature of this Act. The other main piece of legislation, however, which has determined the shape of the university system is the so-called *loi Savary* of January 1984. Indeed, the importance of this Act has been recently re-emphasised by events in the legislative process. Attempts in July 1993 by the new right-wing government to allow universities to apply for exemption from certain of its provisions (in particular those referring to the internal structures of university government and financial arrangements) were quashed by the Conseil Constitutionnel.

1.3 The universities: *la loi du 26 janvier 1984 (loi Savary)*

This controversial Act, which underwent significant modifications before ratification, applied not only to the universities but also to the whole range of institutions of post-*baccalauréat* education (notably the Ecoles Normales (as they were then), the Instituts Universitaires de Technologie (see Chapter 2.3) and the Grandes Ecoles d'Ingénieurs). One of the major inspirations behind the Act was the current concern regarding graduate employment prospects and the appropriateness of qualifications in relation to the world of work. In terms of university structures, there was to be a basic change of nomenclature: the Act replaced the *unités d'enseignement et de recherche* with *unités de formation et de recherche* (UFR), thereby placing much more emphasis on training (*formation*). In the same vein should be seen the increase in the number of professionally-orientated *maîtrises*. Access to such programmes was available on a competitive basis to those who had successfully completed the first two years of university study and obtained the appropriate qualification, the *Diplôme d'Etudes Universitaires Générales* DEUG). Moreover, the *loi Savary* increased the participation in university councils of representatives of industry and regional government.

Another major problem which the legislation was devised to address was the high drop-out rate which has always been a marked feature of the open-access system of French universities, especially during the first two years of study. Savary's reform sought to reduce this unfortunate wastage of human resources. The legislation accentuated the relationship between undergraduate study and professional activities in society at large by introducing greater emphasis on orientation and counselling (the DEUG *rénové*). Progressive specialisation directed students towards a specific subject strand (*filière*) which became increasingly career-orientated. Consultation with course tutors was designed to assist choices with regard to aptitudes and likely employment prospects. There were soon clear indications that, where adopted, this had gone some way towards having the desired effect.

From the moment when they were granted their own autonomy, the universities took to heart their right to determine their own constitution and structures. This appeared to include even the choice as to whether or not they would accept reforms proposed by central government. By the end of 1986 about half of the universities had failed to implement the new measures incorporated in the Act. Any adoption of the DEUG *rénové*, for example, entailed the signing of a contract with the Ministère de l'Education Nationale. Alongside more traditional course structures and awards there coexisted new-style diplomas. When Lionel Jospin became Minister of Education after the socialist victory in the General Election of 1988, he found universities in many and varied states of 'reform'. He therefore asked the Directeur des Enseignements Supérieurs to explore ways of standardising structures in accordance with the legislation in force, and in particular with the provisions of the *loi Savary*.

Despite the controversies to which it gave rise, particularly in so far as it confirmed selective entry to certain areas of higher education (courses within the Instituts Universitaires de Technologie (IUT), or in Medicine and Pharmacy for example), the 1984 Act continued to guarantee the right of all *bacheliers* to 'free' higher education. This has long been considered to be a fundamental republican right and has been guarded jealously by successive generations in the face of all perceived encroachments. Above all else, it was this issue which provoked the massive demonstrations in December 1986. The threat of greater selectivity discerned in the proposed *loi Devaquet*, together with provisions for large increases in registration fees (*droits d'inscription*), brought both *lycéens* and students in their hundreds of thousands on to the streets of Paris and other major university centres and led to the withdrawal of the bill and the resignation of the minister concerned. Similar unrest was generated by the perception of the same threat in Lionel Jospin's initial proposals for radical change in the early years of university courses (*la rénovation des premiers cycles*). The net result has been the continuation of the policy of open entry. Registration fees remain nominal and student enrolment continues at a high level in comparison with the UK: in 1992–93, there were some one and a quarter million students following university courses and the number is set to increase for the foreseeable future. Recent debates on education have highlighted the fact that, in terms of the percentage of the twenty to twenty-four year olds receiving education, France still lags behind the United States, Canada, Sweden, West Germany and Japan. Given French society's needs for an increasingly well-qualified workforce, two ambitious targets were set: 80 per cent of the relevant age group at *baccalauréat* level by the year 2000 and two million students in higher education by the early twenty-first century.

1.4   The Grandes Ecoles and Ecoles Spécialisées

The Ecoles have an extremely important role to play in France and one which marks them out as radically different from any institution of higher education in the UK. Their role, as previously stated, is to train top civil servants, engineers, senior administrative and management personnel for the public and private sectors, industry, commerce and the armed forces. To give a precise definition of the Ecoles is almost impossible because of their diverse nature and function. Whilst some are attached to universities and share their teaching staff, others are separate entities with their own specialist teachers. A high proportion of the Ecoles Supérieures de Commerce are sponsored by local Chambres de Commerce et d'Industrie. The curriculum in the different Ecoles is in many instances determined by the exigencies of the relevant outside professional bodies. Entry is competitive and highly selective, and is achieved either by means of special examinations or by meeting tough requirements in terms of qualifications already obtained. Access to the Grandes Ecoles d'Ingénieurs or the Ecoles Normales Supérieures, for example, follows two years of intensive, post-*baccalauréat* study in the *classes préparatoires aux grandes écoles* in the *lycées*.

The number of students enrolled (less than 60,000) is small by comparison with the million and a quarter in universities. The influence exercised by the Ecoles, however, is enormous. The distinguished Ecole Nationale d'Administration (ENA), for instance, admits only about 160 students per year, but from amongst their ranks have come a whole galaxy of prominent figures in French public life: four French Prime Ministers of recent years, Fabius, Chirac, Rocard and Balladur, and Presidents Pompidou and Giscard d'Estaing, were all former students (*énarques*), as were eight ministers in Rocard's first government.

In historical terms, the notion of the specialist Grandes Ecoles dates from the aftermath of the Revolution of 1789 and was reinforced in the nineteenth century by the needs created by the industrial revolution. The Convention (1792–95) established the Ecole Polytechnique, the Ecole Normale Supérieure, the Conservatoire des Arts et Métiers and the Conservatoire de Musique. The Ecole Polytechnique, for example, remains semi-military in character and is a major training ground for the upper echelons of the armed forces as well as for senior engineering personnel employed in government service. It provides an intensive two-year scientific programme, conducted at a very high level, which enables its students to further their studies at a prestigious *grande école d'application* in their chosen field of study (e.g. l'Ecole Nationale Supérieure des Mines, l'Ecole Nationale Supérieure des Ponts et Chaussées (Civil Engineering) or l'Ecole Nationale Supérieure des Télécommunications, etc.). The Grandes Ecoles are primarily associated with Science and Engineering, and there are in excess of 170 such establishments that are empowered to award an engineering diploma (*diplôme d'ingénieur*). However, there are others which specialise in the Humanities, for example, l'Ecole des Chartes and l'Ecole Nationale Supérieure des Bibliothécaires which train archivists, palaeographers and librarians for the major state libraries; others in Administration, such as l'Ecole Nationale d'Administration referred to above, l'Institut National d'Administration Publique and the various Instituts d'Etudes Politiques; yet others in Business Studies, e.g. l'Ecole des Hautes Etudes Commerciales and the growing number of Ecoles Supérieures de Commerce et d'Administration des Entreprises; not to mention the many establishments which provide training for their students in the different agricultural disciplines or prepare them for careers in the arts . . . The list is very long indeed.

Special mention should, however, be made of the Ecoles Normales Supérieures (ENS) which are four in number and whose primary function is to train scientific researchers, university teachers, a limited number of senior secondary teachers and, more generally, top civil servants, local government officials and management personnel for the public sector. All candidates for places in one of the ENS are obliged to sign an undertaking to work for the State for a minimum of ten years; once admitted, they assume the status of trainee civil servants (*fonctionnaires stagiaires*) and receive a salary (8,000F net per month) throughout their four years in the establishment.

The Grandes Ecoles and Ecoles Spécialisées mentioned above award their own *diplômes*, the high status of which reflects the reputation of the institution concerned. This reputation is a function of the competition for entry, the level and duration of study (usually three years after the two years of intensive preparation spent in the *classes préparatoires*), and the posts and salaries offered to their graduates, factors which are constantly analysed and published by the media and especially by the relevant professional bodies.

In this chapter we have placed French universities in the broader spectrum of higher education in France. The diversity of provision should not blind us to the fact that only a very small percentage of *bacheliers* (or *bachots* as students refer to them) attend the Grandes Ecoles; it is the university system which caters for the majority of post-*baccalauréat* students. It is to this that we shall now turn our attention.

2
Courses in French universities

It is the purpose of this chapter to explain the organisation of French universities in terms of their course patterns, their grouping of disciplines, the duration of studies and the qualifications which may be obtained. This will be done by means of an analysis of global structures and, in the main, in relation to national diplomas. Information on courses in individual universities is to be found in Part III.

In many areas of study, academic programmes in French universities are organised somewhat differently from those found in universities in the UK and the USA, for example. It is therefore important to be familiar with course structures and with the level required. A number of anglophones studying in France will follow courses for foreign students (many of which take place in the vacations). Students who fall into this category will find the following information useful in terms of general orientation. However, this chapter will be of particular benefit to students registering for the whole, or an integral part, of a national diploma.

It is, perhaps, important to emphasise first of all the status of the *diplômes nationaux*. French universities award national diplomas whose levels are indicated in relation to the number of years of post-*baccalauréat* study involved (e.g. *Bac + 2, Bac + 4*). These awards are sanctioned centrally by the Ministère de l'Education Nationale and are to be perceived as having the same status, whichever university was attended, and any suspicion of an attempt to call into question this notion makes hackles rise, as was demonstrated yet again as recently as the summer of 1993. The universities' national diplomas mark them out as being different from the Grandes Ecoles, each of which, as explained in the previous chapter, confers its own diploma. Universities have the right to offer, in addition to the *diplômes nationaux*, their own *diplômes*

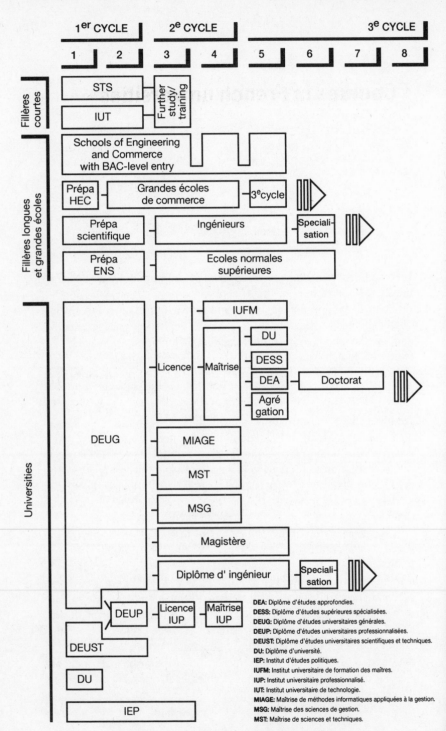

Figure 1 The pattern of higher education in France

d'université – awards which are not sanctioned by the Ministry centrally but which have been created to satisfy a specific need. The Université Stendhal (Grenoble III), for example, registers students from its foreign ERASMUS partners for the *Diplôme d'Université d'Etudes Européennes Intégrées (ERASME) Premier ou Deuxième Cycle*. It is the phrase *diplôme d'université* which immediately signals the 'localised' nature of the award. The word *cycle* takes us on to one of the main functions of this chapter: an analysis of the organisation of courses into their various groupings and levels.

2.1 Organisation of studies: the classical pattern

Various attempts have been made since the *loi d'orientation* of 1984 to reform what might be termed 'the classical pattern' of higher education in the universities. The most recent of these, initiated by Lionel Jospin during his time as Ministre de l'Education Nationale – and carried through, with modifications, by his successor, Jack Lang – envisages considerable changes to the pattern described below. It is clear that, as from the beginning of the academic year 1993–94, the procedures we are about to elucidate will no longer apply in some disciplines in some universities. What is not clear, however, in the current climate of government change and consequent austerity policies, is how long it will take for the new arrangements to be extended to all UFR. The initial reaction of the new right-wing government of 1993 was to put a brake on the process, and to seek to associate its generalisation with the renewal of the quadrennial contracts between individual establishments and the Ministry. Two systems will, therefore, coexist for some time but as many foreign students will continue to operate under the already-existing course structures, it is to these that attention will first be given. The new provisions will be described below.

University study in France has for some time been organised in three successive and sequential tiers (*cycles*), the first two of which last for two years each, the third of which is more or less open-ended. The *premier cycle* is designed to offer a grounding in university study and an introduction to the methodology pertaining to individual disciplines. It leads to the award of the first-level national diploma, the *Diplôme d'Etudes Universitaires Générales* (the DEUG) a qualification which, until the application of Lang's reform, could be taken in some thirty subject areas: *Droit* (Law), *Sciences Economiques, Lettres et Arts, Communication et Sciences du Langage, Sciences Humaines, Théologie, Sciences des Structures et de la Matière* (DEUG A), *Sciences de la Nature et de la Vie* (DEUG B),

Sciences et Techniques des Activités Physiques et Sportives (STAPS), *Soins* (Health Care), etc. Though the DEUG leads towards specialisation, it has always been multi-disciplinary in nature and composed of some units which are obligatory, some units with a limited choice, and others offering a 'free' choice. A DEUG *de Géographie* in Toulouse, for example, has entailed the study of Economics, History, Mathematics and a modern language, as well as the basic units in Geography and optional elements available in any area of study taught in the university.

An alternative award made at the end of the *premier cycle*, the DEUST, will be examined below under 2.3. However, by obtaining either of these diplomas, the student is qualified to proceed to the next level of study.

The *deuxième cycle* comprises the *licence* (after one year of further study (*Bac* + 3)) and the *maîtrise* (after two years (*Bac* + 4)). The underlying aim is to offer a progressively increasing degree of specialisation in a subject area, while maintaining elements of choice, as in the *premier cycle*. The *licence* corresponds roughly to the Bachelor's degree in the UK, and the *maîtrise* to the Master's, though these analogies are somewhat misleading, given differences of course organisation and the nature of study. The *maîtrise* looks forward to the third stage in that it always includes a mini-dissertation (*mémoire*) on a specialist topic which the student researches and documents independently.

The *troisième cycle* corresponds to the postgraduate area in the UK. The first year of study leads to the award of the *Diplôme d'Etudes Approfondies* (DEA), itself an essential methodological preparation and qualification for those wishing to embark upon a doctoral thesis (*doctorat*). Traditionally in France, particularly in the Humanities, the *Doctorat d'Etat* was a *magnum opus*, a definitive statement on a subject area, which could take up to twenty years to complete. This has been replaced by a somewhat more modest thesis, whose main function is to demonstrate research capability. The creation of a single pattern for the *doctorat* is intended to bring France's requirements more into line with the initial research qualifications of other countries, in particular her European partners and the United States.

Courses in the first two *cycles* of the 'classical pattern' invariably comprised a certain number of constituent units, usually known as *unités de valeur* (UV) (or sometimes as *certificats* in the *deuxième cycle*). In any given year of any given course, some of the units would be obligatory (UV *obligatoires*), some would be drawn from a limited range of choices (UV *optionnelles*) and yet others from an unrestricted range of possibilities (UV *libres*). Nomenclature has varied from university to university: a

UV might be referred to as an *élément*, a *module* or a *matière*. Not all UV necessarily had the same status within the course: their individual weightings were defined in terms of *coéfficients* or *unités de compte* (UC). The award of an individual diploma depended in principle on the successful completion of all the elements prescribed: compensation between *unités de valeur* was normally not allowed. Assessment was generally by a variable mixture of coursework marks (*contrôle continu*), mid-session tests (*partiels* or *devoirs sur table*), and end-of-year examinations (*examens de fin d'année*). In some cases it was possible to pass a UV simply on the basis of coursework marks and mid-session tests. Some examinations or tests operated on an 'open book' basis. End-of-session examination papers were commonly of four hours' duration and oral presentations were standard in many disciplines.

2.2 The need for reform

Of the issues that have fuelled debate on the French university system over the last twenty-odd years, none has been more prominent than, on the one hand, the relationship between academic qualifications and professional needs and, on the other, the drop-out rate among students, particularly during the *premier cycle*. It has often been felt that 'classical' university studies were too long and too abstract in many fields and did not do enough to prepare students for employment. This feeling was accentuated in the difficult times of the mid-1970s and 1980s, and again in the 1990s, when unemployment became only too pressing a reality. Alongside this problem there was an acute awareness of the changing needs of society in terms of qualified manpower to meet the demands of the technological revolution. Various attempts have therefore been made to diversify the qualifications available. These measures have entailed both the provision of shorter, two-year diplomas in specialist technological areas and a modification of aspects of traditional course structures.

2.3 Professional orientation: *études courtes*

The Instituts Universitaires de Technologie (IUT) were created in 1966 with the aim of training high-level technical staff for industry or the tertiary sector. They provide a two-year, highly intensive course (thirty-two 'contact hours' per week) which leads to the award of a *Diplôme Universitaire de Technologie* (DUT) in one of twenty-one relatively specialised areas (for example, *Génie Mécanique et Productique, Génie Thermique et Energie, Informatique, Information-Communication* and

Techniques de Commercialisation). As they were conceived from the outset as a preparation for the world of work, courses in the seventy-two IUT entail obligatory industrial placements (*stages en entreprise*). What marks out the IUT as different from the rest of the university system at the immediate post-*baccalauréat* stage is that entry is selective and competitive. Unlike the Ecoles, however, they have no special entrance examination; selection is made on the basis of academic record and interview.

The IUT have proved to be extremely popular with students and employers: in 1992 there were about ten applicants for each place. In the ambitious scheme launched in 1990, the *Plan Universités 2000,* which was designed to cater for up to 500,000 extra students in the following five years, the Ministry gave priority status to a more widespread and even distribution of IUT throughout France. Fifty thousand new places were to be made available by 1995, especially in the Paris region and in medium-sized towns in the provinces where no university establishment existed previously.

The IUT are separate institutions within the university framework. As from 1984, already-existing UER/UFR were enabled to incorporate a similar, two-year professionally-orientated diploma – the *Diplôme d'Etudes Universitaires Scientifiques et Techniques* (DEUST). Although parallel to the DEUG and acceptable as its equivalent for purposes of further study, the DEUST was especially set up to provide a practical qualification. It was designed to reflect the needs of local and regional specialisms in terms of industry, commerce, leisure activities and the arts; indeed the various DEUST licensed by the Ministry called upon the active participation in the teaching process of the relevant personnel from the professional sectors involved. Examples of such courses were *Formation aux Métiers de l'Eau* (Lyon I), *Droit des Assurances* (Poitiers) or *Profession Immobilière* (Toulon).

The new development represented by the DEUST would not appear to have burgeoned in any major way. The most obvious innovation in relation to the technological society is the institution of a new DEUG, the *DEUG de Technologies industrielles.* Precisely at the moment when the number of categories of the DEUG was being reduced by the Ministry, in the name of simplication of the system, this extra category was added by a decree of 17 June 1992. What most obviously distinguishes it from the DEUST is the fact that it is not conceived as a two-year diploma preparing students for the world of work. Rather, it is intended as a preparation for more advanced study within the framework of the new Instituts Universitaires Professionnalisés (see below), and for the training of technologically-qualified teachers and engineers. A significant feature of the course – initially available in only four centres – is that it seeks to familiarise students, from the outset, with the industrial application of new technologies.

2.4 Professional orientation: *études longues*

The introduction of professional orientation into the universities has not simply been a question of encouraging *études courtes* (as the above shorter courses are known) or modifying the pattern in the early stages of courses. Over the years, many attempts have been made to adapt the content of the 'classical' four-year strands (*études longues*) to the needs of society as perceived by the government of the day. The earliest of these attempts concerned the *deuxième cycle* and led to the creation of the *maîtrises professionnalisées*: the *Maîtrise de Sciences de Gestion* (MSG), the *Maîtrise d'Informatique Appliquée à la Gestion* (MIAGE) and the *Maîtrise de Sciences et Techniques* (MST). These two-year diplomas, developed alongside the more traditional and academic *Licence/Maîtrise* pattern, appear to have succeeded in fulfilling their initial aim of bridging the gap between the universities and subsequent professional activity. They attracted large numbers of highly-qualified candidates, so that selection at entry proved to be severe. At Nancy II, for example, only 81 out of 368 candidates were admitted during the first three years of the MSG course (1985–88). For the MST, on average, only one out of ten candidates was successful in obtaining a place. Applications could be made only by holders of the DEUG or its equivalent; candidates had also to be in possession of a *certificat préparatoire* before being allowed to register on the first year of the course.

Instruction on the above *maîtrises professionnalisées* is highly intensive and involves direct contact with industrialists and other outside specialists, both on the course and during industrial placements. The MST in particular offers a flexible formula covering a wide range of specialisms: there are more than seventy in Science and Computing, nearly fifty in Arts and Social Sciences and about the same number in Law, Economics and Business Studies.

While on the subject of professionally-orientated qualifications developed in the *deuxième cycle*, some mention should be made of the *magistères*. These 'superdiplomas', introduced in 1985, have fulfilled a similar function by means of three years of study for an even more stringently-selected group of DEUG-holders. With the number of such courses initially increasing every year (in 1988 there were ten new MST and fifteen new *magistères* licensed by the Ministry), the diversification of opportunities at this level was further enhanced. At the time, the impression was that 'la professionnalisation des deuxièmes cycles va bon train', even if the groups of students involved remained relatively small in comparison with total figures: in 1989, slightly over 3,000 MST and just over 2,000 MSG and MIAGE diplomas were awarded. The process was even extended to the research area with the introduction into the *troisième cycle* of the *Diplôme d'Etudes Supérieures Spécialisées* (DESS).

Two creations of the Jospin *régime* confirmed the determination of the Ministry to prepare university students in a more appropriate fashion for the world of work: the Instituts Universitaires Professionnalisés (IUP), and the Instituts Universitaires de Formation des Maîtres (IUFM). The latter were part of the Minister's response to the need to raise the profile of the teaching profession and thereby meet the challenge of recruiting teachers in sufficient numbers for the end of the century. Intended to provide a common training for teachers of all levels, the IUFM take in students at the *Bac* + 3 level (as from 1994–95, in principle, *Bac* + 2) and prepare them for the national competitive recruitment examinations, whilst enhancing their classroom experience. Financial inducements in the form of teaching allowances (*allocations d'enseignement*) paid over two years were introduced to increase the numbers enrolling. Four pilot schemes were launched in 1990, and the system was extended, not without some difficulty, to establish one such institution per academy in 1991.

The IUP select candidates at the end of the first year of university study and confer upon them an alternative executive qualification (*titre d'ingénieur-maître*) at the end of three further years. Twenty-three such institutions opened within the universities in 1991, and considerably more in 1992. The number of students involved increased four-fold during that period – from 2,000 to 8,000. Distinctive features of the programmes include the reliance for 50 per cent of the teaching – in the long term – upon industrial practitioners, and the encouragement of a large element of industrial experience for the students, on occasion extending to the creation of genuine sandwich courses. The portmanteau title of *ingénieur-maître* should not mislead anglophones: it embraces, in addition to a standard range of scientific and technological specialisations, various areas of general and special administration (such as *administration publique et privée*), commercial and general management (e.g. *commerce international, gestion hôtelière et touristique*), and communication studies (e.g. *sciences de l'information et communication, documentation dans l'entreprise*).

Early indications are such that the hostility of the right-wing government elected in 1993 might call into question the continued health – if not the existence – of both the IUFM and the IUP . . .

It should not be thought, however, that attempts to nudge university 'long' courses in the direction of a greater awareness of the needs of an appropriately-trained workforce have been largely restricted to the final years of study. Since the early 1980s, efforts have been made to influence course content and structures at all levels and in all disciplines. The *loi Savary*, referred to in the previous chapter, sought to incorporate into the early years of all courses, as part of the reform of the *premier cycle*, elements of career counselling and, on occasion, of preliminary employment orientation (*préprofessionnalisation*). Even Arts students committed to the pursuit of as long-established an academic discipline as Lettres Modernes – the language and literature of France – were caught up in this trend and were required to follow courses which sensitised them to the potential career outlets of their chosen *filière*. This approach was later reinforced by the socialist government's proposals for induction courses for all students.

Moreover, new course patterns were instituted as variants of traditional strands. Multi-disciplinary, professionally-orientated programmes were developed, such as *Administration Economique et Sociale* (AES) and *Mathématiques Appliquées et Sciences Sociales* (MASS) and *Langues Etrangères Appliquées* (LEA). 'Classical' courses for modern linguists, for example, essentially entailed, and still entail, the study of one foreign language and its civilisation and culture (*Langues et Civilisations Etrangères/Langues Vivantes Etrangères* (LCE/LVE). This was not ideal for the needs of the contemporary business world, hence the introduction of new applied modern languages courses, LEA, which combined, together with the study of *two* European languages, elements of Economics, Marketing, Accounting, Management and Business Studies. In common with the professionally-orientated courses examined above, LEA programmes also created links with the business world and prescribed work placements. On occasion, a period of study-residence in the country of one of the target languages was also compulsory.

2.5   Reducing the failure rate

The second major concern which, for the last decade or so, has strongly influenced thinking on French universities – indeed, on the French educational system as a whole – is the need to reduce the failure rate (*le combat contre l'échec scolaire*), or as Lionel Jospin, during his term of office as Minister of Education, put it, the need to increase the success rate (*le combat pour le succès scolaire*). Mass enrolment in the universities has masked an underlying reality: the low success rate, particularly during the *premier cycle*. Estimates have indicated that, depending on disciplines and locations, somewhere between 30 and 60 per cent of students embarking on first-year courses do not reach the *deuxième cycle*, and action has been taken in an attempt to reduce this wastage. It is primarily in this context that the various attempts made over the last ten years to reform the *premiers cycles*, and especially the DEUG, are to be seen.

A major problem was perceived to be that of newly-arrived students, perhaps away from home for the first time and in an unfamiliar, impersonal institution in which it was easy to become isolated and demoralised. In the 1980s, the solutions suggested included the transfer, in some cases, of the early years of study to the less hostile environment of smaller local centres (*délocalisation en antennes universitaires*), as well as emphasis on individual tutorial support, academic counselling and orientation. The most recent proposals, implemented by Jack Lang but modelled to a large extent on Jospin's ill-fated initiative, have much in common with these earlier attempts at reform as regards tutoring and other forms of support. This time, however, the starting-point was the need to make the system more comprehensible, through the reduction of the number of DEUG from an allegedly bewildering thirty or so to about ten.

To sustain interest and to improve motivation, it is considered essential that those entering the system find their way on to the course best suited to their individual talents. With this in mind, the newcomer is to be taken through a period of induction before being initiated into the working methods of the relevant discipline. Students choose a major area of study (*la majeure*) and subsidiary or minor units (*les mineures*). This structure is designed to preserve flexibility of choice and to permit change of path in the event of failure at any time during the early stages of the course. Back-up for information and counselling is offered by the Services (Communs) Universitaires d'Information et d'Orientation (S(C)UIO). Methodological and personal tutoring (*le tutorat*) will be given by selected senior students of at least *maîtrise* level employed for this purpose.

The scheme prescribes a structure in which broadly-based *modules* replace the old, highly-specialised UV, each one of which was an obligatory hurdle. Success in between six and twelve such modules, depending on the discipline followed, will lead to the award of the

DEUG. Moreover, these new course units act as transferable credits: once passed, they remain valid (*capitalisables*) in the event of partial failure and can be used in further attempts at the same diploma or can be counted towards the achievement of a related qualification.

Further reassurance is offered to students in terms of examination arrangements. Gone are the days when individual academics had it within their power to determine the success or failure of a given candidate on a given course. Henceforth, a panel of three examiners (*jury*) will have to agree results and communicate them to the examinees. Moreover, students have a right of access to their scripts and to an interview at which the reasons why the mark was awarded are given. Resits (*examens de la deuxième session*) are guaranteed and must take place at least two months after the initial examination.

When a reform of the DEUG was proposed in 1984, some universities and fields of study were slow or reluctant to adopt it. However, those that did – particularly in the sciences – produced encouraging figures as to its effectiveness: at Lyon I, the success rate in the first year of the DEUG in *Sciences des Structures de la Matière* increased from 32 per cent before implementation of the new pattern to 60 per cent afterwards; at Orsay (Paris XI), more than two out of every three students achieved a DEUG or DEUST diploma in June 1987. What is more, the chances of a *bachelier* reaching the *deuxième cycle* increased from 46.1 per cent in 1987 to 54.7 per cent in 1990. It remains to be seen what the outcome of the changes in the pipeline will be . . .

2.6 Courses for foreign students

So far we have concentrated on the French university system in terms of its provision for French nationals – or for those students from abroad who are suitably qualified in their own system, and in their mastery of the French language, to be assimilated into the same courses. It should, however, be made clear that universities in France have always seen it as part of their mission to provide courses in French language and civilisation for non-French speakers. As distinct from the UK, for example, where such provision is for the most part firmly in the hands of the private sector, State education in France has always assumed responsibility for the dissemination to non-francophones of the national language and culture. There are many reasons for this: some are historical, and are to do with the status of French as a major diplomatic and commercial language; others relate to co-ordinated efforts to protect the French language against the hegemony of English. At all events, the extent of the provision is impressive in terms of both level and variety of formulae. There are short courses (four weeks, six weeks, eight weeks, etc.) run during Easter and, more commonly, summer vacations. In addition, universities, through their specialist units (Institut d'Etudes Françaises pour Etudiants Etrangers, Département d'Enseignement du Français Langue Etrangère (DEFLE), or Département d'Etudes Françaises pour Etrangers (DEFE) for instance) provide courses throughout the academic year designed to accommodate a range of needs at a variety of levels. There are courses for complete beginners, as there are for advanced learners; courses for students with a special interest in Commerce, Economics or Law and refresher courses for foreign nationals who teach French; short, intensive courses to enable those whose French is limited or rusty to follow standard courses in French universities and year-long programmes leading to the award of nationally-recognised diplomas.

The three main university diplomas concerned are: the *Certificat Pratique de Langue Française* (*1er degré*), the *Diplôme d'Etudes Françaises* (*2e degré*) and the *Diplôme Supérieur d'Etudes Françaises* (*3e degré*). These State-approved awards were created by decree in 1961; they entail increasing levels of difficulty, though there are no academic pre-requisites in the case of the first two listed. A good basic knowledge of language and culture is required for entry to the *Certificat* course. The diploma comprises an introduction to the methodology of courses in higher education and offers various options dealing with the cultural, economic and political life of France. To qualify to take the advanced diploma, candidates must be in possession of the *Diplôme d'Etudes Françaises* and have the *baccalauréat* or its equivalent. The course pre-supposes a knowledge of the exercises and working methods of the French university system; holders of this award may apply for exemption from the first year of the *premier cycle* in *Lettres Modernes* or LCE/LVE.

Alongside these awards, there exist two *diplômes nationaux* created by decree in 1985; the *Diplôme Elémentaire de Langue Française* (DELF) and the *Diplôme Approfondi de Langue Française* (DALF). These two diplomas operate on a modular basis. Candidates may follow the course in its entirety or take as little as one module at a time. There is no academic prerequisite for the DELF, but candidates for the DALF must be in possession of the DELF or provide evidence that they have reached a standard which corresponds to its sixth and final unit. The DELF is designed to give candidates a level of linguistic and cultural competence which will allow them to live successfully in a French-speaking environment. The level specified for the DALF is that which will enable candidates to cope adequately with the demands of a university course.

Whereas, in general, higher education in France is 'free', courses for foreign students are more commercially priced (typically anything between 4,000F and 12,000F for the year 1992–93). For further information on courses for foreign students, see the detailed university entries in Part III. The Association pour la Diffusion de la Pensée Française (ADPF) publishes each year, on behalf of the Ministère des Affaires Etrangères, comprehensive guides to both summer and termtime courses for foreign students (see Bibliography).

2.7 Planning the way ahead

The above portrayal of course patterns in French universities may appear over-optimistic. By placing emphasis upon bright, new initiatives in keeping with the demands of a rapidly changing society, by suggesting ways in which endemic problems are being tackled, we have undoubtedly played down the fundamental problems which continue to plague the system. When Lionel Jospin took over the Ministry in 1988, universities had for a number of years been starved of resources, in terms both of capital investment and of the provision of adequate staffing. Buildings in particular had in many instances suffered and fallen into a state of neglect: one of the first actions of Jospin was to release funding for refurbishment. Given the increasing numbers of enrolments in the *premier cycle*, lecture rooms could not accommodate the students registered; the provision of office space for staff was woefully inadequate, thereby rendering consultation with students difficult. If student numbers were to be doubled by the early twenty-first century, an even more vast and costly building programme had to be embarked upon than was launched in January 1990. The 200,000m^2 of additional room space and the extra 400 million francs provided could do little more than hold the pass in the short term.

Announced in the summer of 1990, amidst great solemnity, as an innovative partnership between national and local government, the *Plan Universités 2000* set out to provide the necessary material environment for an extra 500,000 students over the next five years. The funding (some 32 billion francs), shared more or less equally between Paris and the local and regional authorities (*les collectivités territoriales*) on a contractual basis, was to pay for a massive programme of construction and refurbishment. Seven new universities, and 50,000 new IUT places, were included. University libraries were to be made more accessible and their collections enhanced. A major increase in the provision of places in residences and restaurants was planned – not to mention the repair, redecoration and updating of existing facilities. Towns and regions were asked to present their proposals to the Ministry, so that the appropriate contractual arrangements could be entered into. For the first time, local authorities were given the opportunity to be involved in the provision for higher education in their areas.

In his turn, Jack Lang injected a certain note of urgency into the process with the crash programme he instituted under the name of *Campus Eté 1992* which sought above all to improve the quality of life on the seven most dilapidated university sites and included a major refurbishment for many more. Regions came forward with their building plans and works were put in train. In the short term, the situation apparently started to get better.

As early as 1989, attempts were made to improve the lot of university teachers: those in post were better rewarded and, in addition, money was found to create significant numbers of extra posts (1,474 *enseignants chercheurs* in 1992 and a further 2,252 were written into the budget for 1993). What is more, overall figures for teaching staff in higher education had already risen from 42,830 in 1989 to 48,248 in 1991.

Despite this major investment in buildings and manpower for higher education that Jospin was able to achieve in the early years of his term of office, it must remain open to question as to whether it was ever sufficient to solve the accumulated problems of the French university system. To take one precise example, staff-student ratios had risen, in the years before he came to power, to levels which were difficult to reconcile with the pass rate he aimed for; the global average had risen to 1:23 but was as bad as 1:50 in some universities and in some disciplines. Given the rapid increase in student numbers, the new measures were slow to make an impact. In an interview published in 1991, Claude Allègre, Jospin's higher education guru, conceded that the global average remained at 1:22, and suggested that a solution to this problem lay in reducing a failure rate which inflated the number of people in the *premier cycle* unreasonably. Other problems signalled by academic and administrative staff – such as the non-availability of rooms of the right size and in sufficient numbers for the new tutoring arrangements – were not resolved.

An additional complicating factor was the election of a government of a different political persuasion in March 1993. The initial reaction of François Fillon, the new Ministre de l'Enseignement Supérieur et de la Recherche, was to accept the thrust of the projected reforms, but to seek to delay their implementation. He pressed ahead with them, none the less, when it was suggested to him that they might be implemented without further resource implications. That he could proceed on such a basis is in itself worrying.

François Mitterrand made education the priority of his second term as President, and subsequent socialist legislation confirmed this (*Loi No. 89–486 du 10 juillet 1989 sur l'éducation, Article premier* – 'L'éducation est la première priorité nationale'). Under Jospin, the Ministère de l'Education Nationale made an initial response to the challenge. To bring about the necessary improvements in higher education, it was argued, would require a massive increase in the proportion of national resources devoted to it. The stance of the government elected in 1993, given its commitment to a policy of defending a strong franc and to the reduction of public expenditure, must raise doubts as to whether the political will exists to carry through this ambitious policy of public investment.

Part II
Practical advice

3
Accommodation and welfare services

Many students will be accustomed to finding provision made for their non-academic needs – food, lodging, welfare, sport, and leisure – by their home institution. Each university or college runs its own halls of residence, student restaurants, lodgings office and welfare services (under whatever name). Each has, and operates, its own sports facilities. In each academic institution there is a Students' Union, which often duplicates 'official' provision in some of these areas with its own back-up services (for eating and welfare, for instance) as well as promoting a vast array of clubs and societies to cater for a wide spectrum of political, cultural, sporting, and leisure interests.

This is not the situation in French universities. They remain, very definitely, institutions of learning, devoted to the pursuit of teaching and research. Historically, there has been no equivalent in France of Students' Unions with their own premises and their general social and leisure commitments. Those student organisations which do exist tend to be national and political, concerned with educational policy and practice, and with the nomination of candidates for election to the various representative governing bodies within universities and associated institutions; or, on the other hand, local and specialised, formed for the promotion of a single activity (*associations sportives, associations culturelles*, etc.). Hence, responsibility for provision for the practical needs of student living is vested in an outside, government-funded body which operates on a national scale, the Oeuvres Universitaires.

3.1 The role of the CROUS

In their present form the Oeuvres Universitaires date from 1955. They were instituted by legislation to replace earlier, less formally-structured services aimed at providing for the welfare of students, in particular those which initially sought to rationalise and co-ordinate the work of student associations. The Oeuvres are administered through a national centre in Paris, 28 regional centres, that is to say one per *académie*, and 11 local centres. The Centre National des Oeuvres Universitaires et Scolaires (CNOUS) defines general policy, allocates to the regional centres the government funding which it receives for this purpose, and performs a general supervisory, co-ordinating and facilitating function. The Centres Régionaux des Oeuvres Universitaires et Scolaires (CROUS), located in the main academic centre of each *académie*, mount the various services offered to students, while the Centres Locaux des Oeuvres Universitaires et Scolaires (CLOUS) fulfil the same function in other university towns. Though a Centre Local is always dependent upon its tutelary CROUS, it may well enjoy a definite measure of independence, including control of its own allocation of funds. Finally, to bring their services more directly to a widely-dispersed student body, the CROUS also operate a system of sub-offices or outposts in other academic centres (*antennes*).

From the outset, the Oeuvres were entrusted with the mission of 'improving living and working conditions for students'. The amounts of public money they receive are impressive: in 1992 they were allocated almost 1,300 million francs in State subsidies. These resources constitute the main input of *aides indirectes* into higher education (as distinct from the *aides directes* which are made available to the most needy students in the form of grants). Such sums are used to provide subsidised meals, cheap accommodation and a range of other social and cultural services throughout France and her *Départements d'Outre-Mer* (DOM); that is to say Guyane, Martinique, Réunion, Guadeloupe and St Pierre et Miquelon. Given the size and importance of the operation, it is perhaps not surprising that the Oeuvres were placed under the joint aegis of the Minister responsible for higher education and the Minister in charge of the budget. The Oeuvres are, however, proud of their democratic structures, which ensure that the governing bodies (*conseils d'administration*) of both the CNOUS and the CROUS reflect the views of students. Elected representatives of student para-political organisations sit alongside academics, administrators, other grades of staff and outside personalities. The *Conseil d'Administration* of the CNOUS is chaired by a direct nominee of the minister responsible for higher education, while the regional equivalent is chaired by the relevant *recteur d'académie*, who also rejoices in the title of Chancelier des Universités.

To complete this outline of student welfare provision, it should perhaps be stressed that the clientele of the Oeuvres Universitaires et Scolaires is by no means restricted to those studying in the universities or the Grandes Ecoles. It embraces groups from many other sorts of institutions (*écoles d'infirmières* or *classes préparatoires aux grandes écoles*, for example). In fact, the condition of entitlement to its services is that the beneficiary should 'be registered in an institution (or a section of an institution) of higher education recognised as qualifying for the system of *Sécurité Sociale Etudiante*'. In the past, it was necessary for each student to establish this entitlement by obtaining a separate CROUS card, which had to be presented regularly for specific transactions, such as when buying subsidised meal tickets, or at the entrance to restaurants. Now, however, the student card issued by the academic institution itself, appropriately counterstamped, admits holders to the full range of services.

3.2 Student restaurants

It is as a purveyor of economical meals in the *Resto-U* that the CROUS makes its biggest impact on the vast student body in France. The number of meals served – 75 million in 1991 – bears witness to this, as do the crowds that throng the student restaurants at lunchtime (and, to a lesser extent, in the evening) or sit over coffee in the adjoining *cafétéria*. The source of attraction consists very largely, of course, in the state subsidy which kept the price of a three-course traditional meal in 1992–93 down to 12F. Nevertheless, on this basis the *Resto-U* provides a focus for students gathering in unaccustomed numbers.

During the first twenty or so years of the Oeuvres, only the 'traditional' meal was served in CROUS restaurants. Consisting as it did of an entrée, a main course of fish or meat garnished with vegetables, potatoes or pasta, and a choice of cheese or dessert, each menu was deemed to correspond fully to the nutritional needs of a balanced diet. In contributing a subsidy equal to 50 per cent of the cost of producing such a meal – as used to be the case – government facilitated healthy eating for the students, at a price consistent with the policy of 'free' higher education for all *bacheliers*. The proportion of the cost represented by the State subsidy has declined but still remains an important element. The price of the meal ticket continues to be fixed nationally; each increase is inevitably contested by students and their representatives. Feelings often run high!

Tickets are available to the holders of appropriate student cards in a book of ten (*un carnet*), and may be obtained from sales points in restaurants during opening hours. The vast majority of 'traditional' restaurants are self-service, so that students select their courses from the range on offer in exchange for a ticket. However, access to the *Resto-U* is not restricted to those registered locally and entitled to eat at the cheap rate. Other groups may be authorised to use the facilities if they pay a higher, non-subsidised rate (the *tarif passager*), which is determined by the *Conseil d'administration* of the CROUS concerned, and may therefore vary fron one *académie* to the next.

In the late 1970s, the Oeuvres became aware that the 'traditional' meal was losing its popularity. Financial stringency made it difficult to maintain quality as the Oeuvres were squeezed between reduced income from subsidies and a 'national' ticket price which did not rise quickly enough to compensate fully for increased costs. Tastes and eating habits were changing, to some extent in the light of new 'gastronomic' possibilities, or considerations of 'health' and 'slimming'. Equally, as academic timetables became more cramped, and free hours during the day less predictable, a visit to the student restaurant for a 'full' meal, with the associated time spent queuing, was less manageable or enjoyable. The Oeuvres were losing custom to other forms of eating houses, especially to fast food outlets or *cafés-brasseries* established in the vicinity of the place of study. The CROUS responded by increasing the nature and range of meals and snacks on offer (*la restauration diversifiée*). Many pilot schemes, and a good deal of investment, have produced a situation where students can find in 'official' catering the same possibilities that are available in the private sector: a better quality 'single course' meal for the standard ticket (with the possibility of buying side dishes for cash); higher-priced, but still economical, full meals; grills, pizza parlours, 'chip shops', fast-food restaurants, and a whole range of different snack bars, including French and Viennese pastry counters . . . not to mention the *restaurants médico-sociaux*, which make special provision for students with particular dietary needs.

Much has also been done to take business to the customers, by creating outlets for light meals and snacks in university buildings or in halls of residence, and by varying opening hours to cater for students in a hurry at whatever time of the day they are hungry or 'free' to eat. Under the new arrangements, it is often possible to pay cash rather than having to obtain meal tickets. Moreover, serious attempts have been made to produce attractive settings for new restaurants, and to improve the décor in the older outlets, so as to create a more congenial atmosphere and thus win back clients.

Most of the meals and snacks provided by the Oeuvres are sold in the

229 restaurants which they operate directly. However, to provide for some groups of customers who may study or work in establishments some distance from these – 18+ *sections* in *lycées*, for example (*classes préparatoires*, STS, etc. – see Chapter 1.4), or hospitals or *grandes écoles* – there is a system of *restaurants agréés*, which in 1991 numbered 430. This means that restaurants located in the relevant institutions can be linked to the local CROUS on a contractual basis, thus enabling their students to avail themselves of the same benefits.

Not surprisingly, opinions vary as to the quality of the food served. In any case, this is bound to be a matter of individual taste. There is no doubt, however, that the *Resto-U* represents good value for money. It is difficult, not to say impossible, to cater for oneself at the price. The annual volume of business is ample evidence of this, as are the queues which form at peak hours. Indeed, it was the crowding, and the very French approach to 'queueing', which often formed the principal disincentive to using the restaurants. In order to address this problem, the *Plan Universités 2000* incorporated the provision of some 50,000 extra places in student restaurants, together with a speeding up of the service. The *repas traditionnel* is still going strong, and continues to be the most common formula; but with the increased range of possibilities represented by *la restauration diversifiée*, the Oeuvres have tried to adapt to changing habits and to tempt all palates. Foreign students who, unlike most of their French counterparts, are often resident at weekends will surely appreciate the services offered. For this group, too, there is the added attraction that the *Resto-U* is one of the few places where they may encounter French students in large numbers. Hence it may well provide the lucky break that leads to initial contacts and the beginnings of integration.

3.3 CROUS accommodation

The second major concern of the Oeuvres is to assist students to find somewhere to live. This entails, in the main, providing places in their own halls of residence (or in hostels with which they have an agreement (*foyers agréés*)), allocating rooms in cheap municipal flats (*habitations à loyer modéré*) or bed-sitters (*studios*) or acting as honest broker for private citizens who are prepared to let to students.

The problem of accommodating some one and a quarter million students might at first appear to be immense but, fortunately, the situation is not quite so dire. It is traditional in France for students to enrol at one of the 'local' universities and about half of those following courses continue to operate from the family home, when it is within reach, thus reducing demand upon lodgings. Nevertheless, some idea of the difficulties that remain can be derived from the position of foreign students. France, ever proud of its policy of open access for all nationalities, and still conscious of its close ties with former colonies, is currently host to more than 131,500 foreign students. The total capacity of the accommodation directly under the control of the Oeuvres is, however, some 137,000 places and very considerable strain is placed on the facilities of some towns. Toulouse, for example, is, after Paris, the second university town in France in terms of student numbers (well over 80,000) and, in 1992, the local CROUS had only 7,296 rooms in halls in the town.

Until the recent developments discussed below, the accommodation provided in halls of residence tended to follow a similar pattern throughout France. With the exception of some older residences which antedated the creation of the Oeuvres Universitaires, it consisted largely of single rooms which were relatively small, but well appointed, and equipped with the standard furniture and fittings – desk, bed, chairs, adequate cupboard space – and a hand basin with hot and cold water. Showers, toilets and minimal kitchen facilities were available on each corridor, or on each level. The rooms were grouped into multi-storey blocks (on average some 150 rooms per block) and the blocks combined to make up a residence to accommodate somewhere between 300 and 1,000 students. Workrooms, television or meeting rooms and games areas were not entirely forgotten; but there was no sense in which French halls were designed to foster the deliberate community spirit or social dimension of British halls or of colleges elsewhere. Rather, they were conceived as an inexpensive base around which students could organise their lives.

Traditional-style halls were built mainly in the early years of the Oeuvres, and were financed by State capital grants or loans. Rents are therefore low, for only the running costs of the buildings fall upon the student residents. Since these costs can vary from region to region, there is no standard, national charge as in the case of the restaurants, and in 1992–93 monthly payments varied between roughly 600F and 700F. However, this represents only about half the average cost of comparable private accommodation, with the result that pressure upon rooms is very great, and only the applicants in greatest need are admitted. All applications are considered by a joint committee, where membership is divided between student representatives and CROUS officials. The criteria for admission take account of academic success and the financial circumstances of candidates and their families, with applicants from the lowest income groups having priority. Between 12 per cent and 15 per cent of the rooms available are occupied by foreign students.

Direct public finance for the building of such residences eventually dried up, at which point the Oeuvres had to look to other alternatives. A major new building effort was, however, launched within the context of the *Plan Social Etudiant* signed in 1991. In partnership with local and regional authorities, the CROUS set out to build accommodation for 30,000 extra students, between 1991 and 1995, at an average rate of 6,000 per year. In the event, these projections were surpassed in the first three years, during which some 25,000 new places were made available. Moreover, to take account of changing expectations in the student community, the CROUS have, in recent years, concentrated on the building of study-bedrooms, with their own cooking and bathroom facilities (*studios*). Some existing residences, based upon the standard 9m^2 per room, have been converted to this formula. Rent for such enhanced accommodation is obviously higher and often payable over twelve and not nine months; greater access to housing subsidies, available under the terms of the same plan, reduces monthly payments to amounts comparable to those paid in traditional residences.

Over the years, financial stringency had also necessitated economies on maintenance, with the effect that halls had become somewhat run-down. In 1988, the Socialist administration released money to remedy this situation. The effort has been continued with the effect that much of the peeling paint has been covered, many of the cracked walls have been repaired and missing lavatory seats have been been replaced. On balance, a room in hall, if it can be obtained, remains probably the most convenient and certainly the cheapest accommodation option for the foreign student. Apart from any other consideration, acceptance for a place in hall guarantees not only that the student will be housed during the period of study-residence but also that this is known before departure.

In some towns, the CROUS has, for a number of years, been able to offer places in inexpensive flats (HLM). These can take the form of individual bed-sitters, or, more probably, flats with up to four or five bedrooms. Single students are each allocated a room, while the lounge, kitchen and bathroom facilities are shared. The CROUS is responsible for providing basic furniture, and for essential day-to-day maintenance. The monthly charges reflect the rent plus any supplementary service costs that have to be paid to the owners of the HLM (often the town council).

It is more usual for this form of accommodation to be used to house students who have their own families. However, in some instances – Besançon for example – flats are allocated on a single-sex basis to groups of individuals, with the CROUS taking the opportunity at the same time to mix nationalities. The application and admissions procedure is the same as for rooms in hall. However, students who find themselves placed in HLM would be well advised to establish exactly what costs are covered by their monthly payments, and whether there are any other bills for which they are liable, such as heating, lighting or indeed the local residence tax (*taxe d'habitation*) which is levied on all residents on 1 January.

For the moment, it would seem that future expansion of CROUS-controlled accommodation will be in terms of flats or *studios*. Partly as a result of contact with their German counterparts (the Deutsches Studentenwerk), the CROUS were already following this path before the *Plan Social Etudiant* was mooted. Legislation in 1985 gave the local CROUS reservation rights in the case of any HLM development built on land owned by the Ministère de l'Education Nationale. In such cases, the CROUS could become the principal tenant and sublet flats to students. Moreover, a special legal dispensation allowed student sub-tenants, for the first time, to qualify for a housing subsidy (*aide personnalisée au logement* – APL) which was not available to student occupants of older HLM blocks. In this way, rents for accommodation in modern, well-appointed flatlets could be kept within reasonable bounds. Such properties had, and still have, of course, to conform to the standards applied to modern HLM developments.

In fact, increased student access to housing subsidies has encouraged a number of private enterprises to enter the market and to build blocks of inexpensive flatlets or *studios* which are affordable, because they qualify if not for APL then at least for ALS (*allocation logement à caractère social*). This allowance has been available, since January 1992, to EC students living in all forms of qualifying accommodation, both private and CROUS-controlled. Examples of such private enterprises catering for a student clientele are Eurostudiomes and Réside Etudes.

3.4 Private-sector accommodation

For the benefit of students who are unable to get into 'official' student accommodation, each CROUS runs a lodgings office (*service de logement en ville*) with an extensive list of names and addresses of private citizens who are prepared to let to students. This information may be consulted by callers who have then to do the telephone- and leg-work themselves and come to some arrangement with their prospective landlords.

However, faced in more recent years with a growing accommodation crisis, the various CROUS have been anxious to stress that their role in this respect is a more active one than simply as disseminators of information. Publicity campaigns have been mounted, often using the local media, with a view to raising awareness of the problem, in an effort to increase the amount and range of private accommodation made available to students. Counselling services have been set up for both intending landlords and student tenants, where each can be apprised of rights and obligations prior to the conclusion of any agreement. Sample contracts have been drawn up for fixed-term leases. Even inexpensive insurance policies are available to cover both parties for associated risks (*multirisques habitation*).

For the foreign student who is looking for independence or is weary of 'institutionalised living', private accommodation may at first sight seem an attractive option. The idea of having one's 'own place' is very appealing. However, the advantages must be weighed against the obvious shortcomings. In the first place, living in private accommodation will almost always prove to be more expensive, even much more expensive if, for any reason, ALS is not available. There may also be advantages in living in an outgoing, hospitable French family, and in being able to capitalise on such total immersion from a linguistic and cultural point of view. It may indeed be possible to find offers whereby a family will reduce, or even waive, rent in exchange for duties around the house. However, in such circumstances, the relationship can often change; and there remains the problem of reconciling the duties concerned with the demands of the university course being followed.

In almost all other circumstances it will be found that rents in the private sector are much higher than in CROUS accommodation. The great disadvantage of living 'in town', however, is that rooms cannot be found until you are on the spot. The CROUS address file is available only in the local office. Landlords and landladies in practice insist on dealing face to face with prospective tenants. Hence, unless there is the opportunity – and the money available – for an early expedition to the university town in question, the student will be faced with the daunting prospect of arriving in France at the beginning of the academic year without any definite arrangements for accommodation. There then ensues the tedious and often disheartening task of organising temporary accommodation (at whatever cost) and of trudging the streets in search of rooms that are still available. Only too often, there is the frustration of discovering that, whatever efforts are made to keep lists up to date, addresses given out as vacant are no longer on offer. To be in a foreign town without 'a home' is stressful, and hardly likely to encourage a sense of integration or to get the period of study-residence off to a good start.

Whatever form of accommodation is ultimately chosen, the local CROUS is the most obvious agency to work through. In addition to its own considerable holdings, and its accommodation lists and files, it maintains links on a more or less formal basis with other bodies which run hostels in the public and private sectors. Sometimes it is possible to refer applicants to these, or at least to provide information on them; hence, on occasion, rooms have been made available in young workers' hostels (*foyers des jeunes travailleurs*) or details have been given of hostels run by religious organisations – especially for women. Only in Paris is there a major student accommodation development which does not fall under the auspices of the Oeuvres, namely the very distinctive Cité Internationale Universitaire de Paris (see Part III, under *Paris*).

Other useful alternatives to using the services of the CROUS to find somewhere to live are: the regional CIJ or CIDJ (Centre d'Information (et de Documentation) Jeunesse), which often posts addresses on display boards (see Part III, entries under relevant university towns; the local Centre d'Information sur l'Habitat, whose address can be obtained from the Association Nationale pour l'Information sur le Logement (ANIL), which can be found in Part III under *Paris*; various student-organised agencies, which are largely based in the Paris region and often charge a registration fee; the relevant columns of the local press, particularly free newspapers; if you have access to it, the *Minitel* system (see Glossary) where you can call up one of the many relevant information services; and, finally, private accommodation and estate agencies (*agences immobilières*). In all cases, care must be taken to establish in advance the fees potentially involved. The *Minitel* system, in particular, can prove to be very expensive and should be used sparingly. Private agencies will invariably charge a fee, which can be as much as two months' rent.

3.5   Other CROUS services

It is also to the CROUS that students turn in the first instance for advice and help with many other, non-academic aspects of student life. Its information services, for example, act as a useful complement to the universities' own Services Universitaires d'Information et d'Orientation

(SUIO). Questions may relate to administration procedures (academic and civil), financial aid, part-time jobs or leisure activities in the area. All the CROUS act as correspondents for the revitalised Organisation pour le Tourisme Universitaire (OTU), which has its headquarters in Paris. They are therefore in a position to offer access to cheap travel facilities by rail, sea and air (see Chapter 6.8), not to mention the holiday packages and excursions which the OTU organises each year for students individually or in groups. In addition, each CROUS helps students find temporary jobs. Its relevant section – Emplois Temporaires Etudiants (ETE) – seeks to assist students who are in search of part-time paid employment, either out of necessity, or in order to have greater financial independence.

Among many facets of the work of the CROUS, three deserve special mention: their role as a cultural stimulus, their social welfare facilities, and the special duties they have with respect to scholarship-holders from certain countries abroad.

Each CROUS receives a budget specifically for cultural activities and in recent years the sums involved have been dramatically increased – some 3.5 million francs in 1992 and 6 million francs in 1993. This budget is designed to cover many activities, including the dissemination of information on theatre, concert and sporting programmes and the funding of clubs run by student groups in halls of residence. The latter usually come under the aegis of Joint Committees made up of CROUS officials and student representatives (*conseils de résidence paritaires*). Their number and continuing health vary enormously from residence to residence – and even from year to year – as a function of student drive and competence. However, here and there one can find book and record libraries, cine- and video-clubs, photographic dark-rooms, theatrical groups, etc., and sometimes, too, there are sports facilities (e.g. tennis courts) in the proximity of the halls. Moreover, in twelve university centres (Bordeaux, Caen, Dijon, Grenoble, Lille, Nantes, Paris, Poitiers, Reims, Rennes, Toulouse and Versailles) there are Cultural Centres (Maisons d'Activités Culturelles) which have special funding, and offer a broad range of activities (cinema, theatre, fine arts, music, dance, etc.).

It is under the same heading that many CROUS arrange inexpensive trips and excursions. For the most part these take place at weekends, or during holiday periods, and seek to explore some aspect of the local region, or the country at large. They are particularly popular with foreign students, hence the groups on these occasions acquire a distinctly cosmopolitan flavour. Equally, efforts are made to organise 'international' evenings, when national student communities can make a contribution in terms of their own cultural heritage, or when some French festival can be celebrated in traditional style.

Until recently, the activities mentioned above more or less covered the 'cultural' input of the CROUS. As from the academic year 1988–89, however, a new scheme, Culture-Action, was launched, whereby students could apply to the Oeuvres for funding for projects they themselves wished to promote. Applicants had to be able to show that they had obtained contributions in kind or by way of funding from other sources – national agencies, local or regional government, or business sponsorship schemes, for example. The role of the CROUS (in addition to furnishing whatever financial resources may be approved) was to provide advice and support at each stage of the project. Given the funds available for the purpose, the scheme represents an interesting stimulus to student initiative.

Student counselling is an equally important task of the Oeuvres. Each regional centre has its team of 'social workers' (*assistant(e)s de service social*) who are available for consultation, not only at the CROUS headquarters, but also, on a less frequent basis, on university premises, in residences and other student workplaces. Obviously, to be able to address the problems that arise, the social counsellors have to work closely with a wide range of outside bodies in the field of general health and welfare. Individual cases, however, often involve colleagues in other departments of the CROUS, particularly over matters of accommo-dation, employment or financial hardship.

Financial help in an emergency can be obtained, in the form of either a grant or a repayable interest-free loan, from the Fonds de Solidarité Universitaire (FSU). Most of the funding for this purpose is provided by the State in the form of an annual allocation to the CNOUS, which then apportions it between the twenty-eight CROUS. Some regional centres, however, are able to supplement State provision with monies from other sources, such as local councils. Applications for help from the fund are processed by the social service team, and submitted for approval to a CROUS committee. To deal with crises, however, each *assistant(e) social(e)* is empowered to make available up to 500F from the fund immediately. It is repeatedly stressed that any help received from the FSU is intended to relieve a particularly difficult set of temporary circumstances, and cannot be seen as a contribution to regular funding. Nevertheless, in a system where a limited number of students are supported by grants, applications are numerous, particularly at the beginning of the academic year, when the outlay involved in preparing for the session – or the late receipt of monies from other sources – may cause particular problems. In 1991, some 10,000 grants were made, totalling more than 11.5 million francs, and 4,500 loans (more than 4.75 million francs).

One aspect of student welfare which has only recently fallen within the purview of the Centres Régionaux is the payment of student grants to French nationals. This was traditionally administered by the staff of the *rectorat* of the *académie*. The provisions of the *Plan Social Etudiant* envisaged a massive increase in the number and size of grants, so that within a few years one student in four would become a grant-holder. The application procedures have, at the same time, been simplified: the student is now required to submit to the CROUS a single application form – the *dossier social unique* – which encompasses the whole range of financial aid available. It is anticipated that, by the beginning of the academic year 1994–95, the system will be established in all the CROUS.

3.6 CROUS provision for scholarship-holders

The Oeuvres have for some considerable time been responsible for foreign students holding French government awards (*boursiers du gouvernement français*) and certain other foreign nationals whose governments have agreements with France (*boursiers des états étrangers*). This role begins before the *boursiers* arrive in France. Officials of the CNOUS place the students in an appropriate establishment of higher education, informing them of the terms and conditions of the award, and organising any language or other preliminary training necessary to ensure maximum benefit from the educational experience in France. Provision is made for their reception in Paris and onward travel to their ultimate destination. Groups of such students are often given short induction courses in the capital.

Once the *boursiers* arrive in their university towns, it falls to the local CROUS to ensure they are 'successful in integrating academically, socially and culturally in France'. This means far more than the automatic provision of student accommodation, induction, payment of the grant, and help with administrative arrangements and formalities. Throughout the course of study, contact is maintained with appropriate academic supervisors, and reports on progress are issued at regular intervals. Information is sent back via the CNOUS to the relevant grant-awarding Ministry or foreign government, together with any special recommendations for action to overcome difficulties encountered or to modify or enhance the original academic programme. Moreover, with the financial backing of the Ministère des Affaires Etrangères, each CROUS organises for the benefit of such students a full programme of activities, designed to introduce them to different aspects of the business, social and cultural life of France. Here, the Service d'Accueil des Etudiants Etrangers (SAEE) at the CROUS has a crucial role to play.

By comparison with the provision made for the million and a quarter other university students in France, such solicitude as to the academic and social well-being of the 13,500 foreign *boursiers* amounts to real red-carpet treatment. One reason for such lavish attention may, however, be seen in the increasing importance given to maintaining contact with such 'priority' students once they have returned to their own countries. A national project has been launched, the *Programme d'Echanges avec les Anciens Stagiaires Etrangers* (PEGASE), which aims to perpetuate links with foreign nationals who have completed an academic or practical placement in France. Information, based initially upon the returns such students make at the end of their period of residence – which include indications of future career plans – is collected and collated by the CNOUS, the operational hub of the programme. The scheme operates through French embassies abroad.

3.7 Sport and medical facilities

It would be wrong to give the impression that student welfare is the exclusive preserve of the Oeuvres Universitaires. As laid down in the *loi d'orientation*, each university – or locally-based group of universities – has its Service d'Accueil des Etudiants Etrangers (SAEE), its Service (Inter)Universitaire de Médecine Préventive (et de Promotion de la Santé) (SUMP, SIUMP or SUMPPS) and its Service Universitaire des Activités Physiques, Sportives et de Plein Air (SUAPS). The SAEE is an obvious starting-point for new arrivals from abroad, for help with registration and administrative procedures; the SUMP offers free medical care in some circumstances, and has social workers who provide counselling; and the SUAPS is responsible for organising and publicising programmes of activities. In the case of university sport, however, the principal motive force remains, in general, the long-standing student organisations, the *associations sportives*, which exist within individual institutions. A governing body in Paris, the Fédération Nationale du Sport Universitaire (FNSU) operating through twenty-five regional offices, co-ordinates local, regional, national and even international fixtures in some thirty sports.

3.8 Looking to the future

When all is said and done, however, it is the Oeuvres Universitaires which have been given the task of 'improving living and working conditions for students'. It is undoubtedly the agency through which the government finances, in some measure, the non-academic side of student life, in particular through providing subsidised meals for all, and subsidised accommodation for those most in need. It is tempting to see this provision, given student numbers, as a partial substitute for an expensive, more extensive system of individual grants: *aide indirecte* instead of generalised *aide directe*. Even under the ambitious plans announced by the socialist government in the early 1990s, only one in four students was to be a grant-holder.

Over the years, the Oeuvres themselves have had to meet the challenge of re-defining their aims and objectives. Once the initial period of building restaurants and residences was over, and public capital investment more or less dried up, they were faced with the danger of becoming passive managers of ageing and even obsolescent facilities and systems. In the event, they sought new approaches, even in times of financial stringency. The huge influx of students in the 1980s strained resources to the absolute limit – and perhaps even beyond. The massive extent to which provision fell behind needs was fully recognised in the 1989 Act (*Loi No. 89–486 du 10 juillet 1989*):

> Dans l'enseignement supérieur, le retard pris dans le domaine des capacités et des conditions d'accueil ... impose un effort à moyen et à long terme en matière ... de constructions universitaires: locaux pédagogiques et de recherche ... installations sportives, logements et restaurants pour les étudiants.

Incorporated in the Act was the Observatoire de la Vie Etudiante whose function was to collect information relevant to all aspects of student life ('études, vie matérielle, sociale et culturelle'). The work of this body, on which student organisations are represented, is designed to facilitate decision-making with regard to the full range of student entitlements (restaurant and accommodation provision, health care and State aid).

It was to meet the deficiencies so clearly identified in the late 1980s that the Ministry launched two ambitious schemes – *Plan Universités*

2000 and the *Plan Social Etudiant.* These measures, taken by the socialist government in the wake of the Act, have in the short term alleviated the material problems that for so long beset French campuses. The crisis reached such proportions that commentators compared conditions in 1990 with those obtaining in 1968 (see, for example, Frédéric Gaussen in *Le Monde*, 19 January 1990).

At the beginning of the academic year 1993–94, two questions continue to loom large in the debate on welfare provision in the French higher education system. Adequate funding for some two million students by the year 2000 was always going to imply a massive national investment. Despite Jospin's success in achieving a major increase in the national budget for higher education, it was always questionable as to whether the financial targets could be met. The first question, therefore, which must be asked is: what will be the ongoing attitude adopted by the new right-wing government, which is looking to make cuts in public expenditure? Over the last five years, the tendency has been to pass at least a proportion of the bills down the line, from national to regional and local government. Whether it was a question of providing new academic buildings or residences, or of increasing grants or loans to students, the Ministry has been anxious to involve the regions and the towns in financing new developments. The second question, therefore, which has to be addressed is: how justified is the Ministry in assuming that regional and local government is an endless source of funding when it comes to making good the shortfall in national allocations?

4
Working in France

Many foreign students spending time in France will not enrol full-time on university courses but will seek some form of employment. Some will work for short periods during vacations; others will take a 'gap year'; a small number of graduates will be appointed to lecteurships in higher education (see section 4.7). But the most common alternatives to study will come in the form of a work placement or an assistantship. Each option involves its own procedures but there are steps common to all of them.

If your work experience in France is organised through an established scheme or exchange, some of the obvious formalities will be completed for you. But, in order to work in France, you will in all cases need to acquire various documents and to consider how best to present yourself to potential employers.

4.1 Documentation

The most obvious document required by all aliens is a passport, preferably one that is valid for the full duration of your stay. UK citizens should note that the British Visitor's Passport is not acceptable for working in France. Proof of student status will, in addition, bring many benefits. It can be provided either through possession of a current student card from your home institution or, preferably, an ISIC card. The latter is available from local student travel offices at a cost of £5 (US $15) on production of evidence of student status and a passport-size photograph. For EC nationals a work permit (*carte de travail*) is not necessary; they may spend up to three months in France looking for a job; other foreign nationals are required, in theory, to have obtained a job, an entry visa (*visa de (long) séjour*) and a work permit before leaving for France. American students with adequate French can, however, take advantage of a scheme organised by CIEE, New York, which enables them to seek employment in France for up to three months, once they are armed with a temporary permit (*autorisation provisoire de travail*). Many French employers and agencies are reluctant to consider foreign nationals who do not have a social security number. This can take some time to obtain, so forward planning will pay dividends.

Once you are in France, it will be necessary to obtain a residence permit (*carte de séjour*) from the local authorities. This is particularly important if you intend to stay and work for more than three months. Initial application should be made either to the Préfecture or to the police station (*commissariat*), where you will be asked to provide evidence that you can support yourself (a couple of thousand francs in your bank account or proof of possession of valid credit cards should suffice). Once your application has been accepted, you will be presented with an interim acknowledgement of your application (*attestation de demande de résidence*), prior to being granted the actual document at a later appointment, and most agencies and employers will be happy to take you on under these conditions. As part of the documentation process, you may well have to acquire certification of your civil status (*fiche d'état civil*), which is available from the local town hall (*mairie*), or from your Embassy. An essential document for this – and other purposes – is a certified copy and translation of the long form of your birth certificate (*acte de naissance copie et traduction certifiées conformes*) and Chapter 5.1 contains suggestions as to how these may be most economically obtained. You will also need your work contract, three passport photographs and proof of accommodation.

4.2 Making an application

Approaches to potential employers should be made in terms of a CV, or résumé, and covering letter.

The CV should, if possible, be typed and fitted on to a single sheet. Neatness and clarity of layout are of paramount importance. As qualifications are regarded as hyper-important in France, care should be taken to include dates and full titles of all diplomas already obtained and of any further awards in the pipeline. While hobbies and leisure activities might be considered as less important, all skills and experience relevant to work activities (e.g. driving licence, etc.) should be included. Be careful to ensure the absolute accuracy of the information you provide; subsequent corroboration may be sought. You will find a model

CV in French in part 3 of the Appendix (p. 297).

Covering letters – or indeed letters of acceptance of any post – should, however, be handwritten (*lettres manuscrites*). It will be considered more polite, and is often requested in advertisements because French employers commonly have recourse to graphologists when recruiting staff. The covering letter is your opportunity to orientate the information given in the CV towards the requirements of the particular job.

The question of the language to be used in these communications is a delicate one. Specialists in French will quite naturally make their applications in that language and couched in the appropriate formal French terminology (e.g. *je me permets de poser ma candidature*). It is, however, recommended that even advanced learners have them checked by a native speaker. This might be the ideal opportunity to seek the help and advice of a French exchange student or colloquial assistant in your own institution, in which case you might offer the same favour in return. Non-specialists should not raise false expectations of their competence in French and might be better advised to apply in English; this at least demonstrates proficiency in their native tongue which may well be the key to some jobs.

4.3   Tax and health insurance

You will need to investigate the tax position carefully. If you are appointed as a language assistant in a school, or in a university, for instance, you will probably be exempt from tax in France and your home country for up to two years in the job. A Double Taxation Agreement between the United Kingdom and France, for example, means that British assistants are exempt from French income tax for this period; and while sums earned abroad are in general liable for UK income tax, normally a 100 per cent deduction is allowed to returning assistants and no UK tax will be levied.

If you discover that you are liable for French income tax, you should be aware that the financial year is the calendar year, and that tax is paid a year in arrears; that is to say that French employees pay off their tax bill in the course of the following year, either in three instalments, or monthly. If you take up a job in France for the first time, therefore, you will not be required to pay tax until the September after the end of the first tax year worked. You should, however, register with the local tax office (*centre des impôts*) soon after arrival, and will be asked to submit a tax return for each year (*feuille de déclaration de revenus*).

Anyone working in France will, in all probability, be affiliated auto-matically to the French health and welfare scheme (*sécurité sociale*) for which contributions will be deducted from salary. This will qualify you for medical care only in terms of the French system, which needs to be supplemented to give 100 per cent cover (see Chapter 5.3). The most obvious way of obtaining full cover is to take out a 'top-up' policy with a private insurance company (e.g. a *mutuelle*), for which you will be eligible through your employment. Ultimately, it is up to you to check your health care status with your employer. It is also important to remember that you will not be insured for health risks during your move to France, or during the period while you are looking for work or during the first month or so of your employment. Independent arrangements are, therefore, to be recommended (see Chapter 5.4). Further information on Social Security arrangements for those moving within the EC is to be found in leaflets SA29 and SA30, obtainable from the Department of Health and Social Security, Overseas Group (for address see part 5 of the Appendix).

4.4   Vacation work

Though there has traditionally been a range of casual jobs available to students during the summer months in France, the continuing high level of unemployment has reduced the number of opportunities. For the well-organised and persistent, however, there are still possibilities which will enable you to experience French life while eeking out a basic existence. The service industry offers perhaps the most openings: there is a regular demand for hall or night porters, waiting staff, receptionists, chambermaids or kitchen helps in hotels. Bar work is also a fairly common, if not particularly remunerative, form of vacation work. Posi-tions are more readily available for those who already have two years' experience in hotel and catering work (see Appendix, part 5). Other popular options include jobs as supervisors, entertainers or couriers on campsites; as support staff on activity holidays or courses (*moniteurs/ monitrices* in *colonies de vacances*, or *animateurs/animatrices* on vacation study courses). French employers require applicants to have good French and to acquire the appropriate qualification (the *brevet d'aptitude aux fonctions d'animateur* (BAFA)), which will entail attendance at an appropriate fee-paying training programme in the Paris region (see Appendix, part 5); some employers will reimburse the fee but, in any case, as a qualified monitor you will certainly recoup your outlay.

Many female students work as an *au pair* (most employers prefer them to males) and this particular form of work can be arranged in advance through a specialist agency in the UK, which will, however, charge a fee for its services. There are also agencies in France (see Appendix, part 5). Work is for a minimum of three months and for a maximum of twelve (or possibly eighteen). Employers are required to obtain a work contract (*accord de placement au pair d'un stagiaire aide-familial* or *contrat de travail de stagiaire professionnel*). Non-EC nationals will need the contract, together with a certificate of enrolment in a language course for foreign students when they apply for the long-stay visa. Details of terms and conditions of *au pair* work are given in the leaflet *Au Pair Posts in France*, obtainable from the Visa Section of the French Embassy.

Casual summer work can still be found in labour-intensive farmwork, though modern methods have greatly reduced the need for unskilled labour. Fruit-picking, haymaking or grape harvesting (*les vendanges*) may prove to be attractive propositions, especially since it is possible to move from region to region as the various crops need to be harvested throughout the summer months. This type of work is, however, physically demanding and often involves long hours or work in variable weather conditions. Seasonal workers should receive the national minimum wage (the *Salaire Minimum Interprofessionnel de Croissance* or SMIC) which is roughly 30F per hour.

Charity and voluntary work (such as archaeological digs and conservation projects) can also be arranged through the agencies listed by the Central Bureau for Educational Visits and Exchanges in its publication *Working Holidays* (see Bibliography).

Non-EC students anxious to find vacation work in France must do so under the aegis of a government-approved organisation and are required to have a work visa. Full-time North American students who are US citizens, are at least 18 years of age and have a minimum of two years' French at college may take advantage of the CIEE scheme referred to above.

If you are already a student in an affiliated institution, it may be possible to find a placement through specialist organisations such as the International Association for the Exchange of Students for Technical Experience (IAESTE) or the Association Internationale des Etudiants en Sciences Economiques et Commerciales (AIESEC). The former is devoted to finding placements in the technical and managerial fields whilst the latter is more business orientated. Posts are difficult to obtain and are exchanged internationally; as reciprocity is the key factor, you stand a better chance of finding employment if you yourself are able to locate a job offer for someone from France. Remuneration will take the form of living expenses rather than salary. Most placements are for a maximum period of twelve weeks' duration, though exceptionally they may be for a whole year or more.

4.5 The 'year out'

It is becoming increasingly common for British school-leavers to inter-calate a year abroad between the end of sixth-form study and their entry into higher education. This has many advantages: the broadening of horizons, the cultivation of a sense of independence and personal responsibility, perhaps even the opportunity to accumulate savings for the expensive years ahead.

Provided that it is spent in a constructive manner, the 'year out' is usually appreciated by University Admissions Tutors who welcome the greater maturity the experience brings. Even in the case of non-linguists, a prolonged stay in France opens up new linguistic and cultural perspectives.

The idea of finding paid employment may initially seem daunting. There are, however, a number of options available to the adventurous. It may be possible to organise a placement for yourself, especially if you have contacts in France – say, through a previous school exchange or pen-friend. Be aware, however, that French employers prefer to recruit applicants whom they can interview. For those who are unable to make use of contacts, it is possible to place advertisements in national and regional newspapers or to write letters of application by the hundred. This method is, however, unlikely to produce a high rate of return. If you have no obvious way of breaking into French networks, it is probably wise to look to one of the professional organisations which specialise in finding temporary work in France.

An easier, if somewhat more expensive, way of arranging your stay is to go through an agency which caters specifically for students inter-calating a year between school and university. An obvious example in the UK is the GAP scheme. To register for this, you must be at least eighteen years of age when you take up your apppointment and apply as soon as possible in your final year of study at school (preferably before Christmas), enclosing a registration fee of £20. Successful applicants pay a £375 placement fee in two instalments: £50 (non-returnable) on acceptance of a position, and £325 two months before departure from the UK. Appointees must find their own travel expenses, and organise their insurance and medical cover.

There are only about thirty placements in France and these are in the social or welfare sector, dealing with the deprived or homeless. The work is challenging and good spoken French is essential. The most fluent speakers may seek placements of three or six months' duration caring for the mentally handicapped. Full board and accommodation are provided together with pocket money.

For those looking to spend only part of the year working abroad, seasonal opportunities exist. Jobs in the Alps Agency, for example, organises hotel work in Europe for German or French speakers for three to four months, beginning in either December or June. For those more interested in an academic placement, the Central Bureau for Educational Visits and Exchanges handles vacancies for junior language assistants in French secondary schools for a period of six months, beginning in January. These are an abbreviated form of the English Language Assistantships in Schools and Colleges Abroad, described in section 4.6 below. Applicants must be eighteen to twenty years of age and have an A level (or its equivalent) in French. There is a registration fee of £5 and applications must be made by the first week in June. Although travel costs are not remitted, board and lodging together with a monthly allowance are provided.

4.6 Teaching assistantships in secondary education

The assistantship scheme is long established, and many students look to it as a way of enhancing their command of the French language and familiarity with the target culture. Particularly for those intending to pursue a career in teaching, a year in a French secondary school environment offers a unique opportunity to gain classroom experience. Being an English Language Assistant forms an integral part of many British degree programmes in which French is a major component. For those undergraduates who choose to, or are required to, spend a year in France as an *assistant(e)*, there are several steps which need to be taken. UK students of French who are in course will receive the appropriate form from their Year Abroad Tutor or Director of Studies, and should return their duly completed applications, together with any fee payable, via their academic sponsor. All candidates should normally be under 30, and in all cases must be native speakers of English and have completed at least two years in higher education. As in the case of junior language assistantships, the scheme is administered by the Central Bureau for Educational Visits and Exchanges, whose December deadline for submission must be respected. US candidates who are interested in participating in the scheme should contact the Institute of International

Education, US Student Program Division, and request the current edition of *Fulbright and Other Grants for Graduate Study Abroad* (see Bibliography).

Most postings will inevitably be in the provinces. Although candidates may express preferences to be posted to a specific region of France, and to a particular type of school, it is not always the case that these can be accommodated. Successful applicants are appointed to serve from the beginning of October to the end of May; notification of posting will be sent direct from France, usually some time between June and August, though occasionally the certificate of appointment (*arrêté d'affectation*) does not arrive until late September. However, once you have learned in April that your application has been forwarded to France (and this means that you are virtually certain to be offered an assistantship), you should plan ahead and assemble administrative documents essential to your stay abroad, together with material you will wish to draw upon for your classes.

The essential documents you will require are those covered above in section 4.1 (valid full passport, equipped with visa in the case of non-EC nationals, a certified copy and translation of the full form of your birth certificate, ISIC card and, once established in France, a *carte de séjour*; non-EC nationals may also need a work permit). Given your new status in the French educational system, you will be entitled to the *carte professionnelle* which permits free entry to art galleries, museums and so on.

As you will be responsible – in the school or schools in which you will be working – for up to twelve hours per week of conversational English, with pupils with a wide range of ability and attainment, pedagogical material will take different forms. Immediately prior to taking up your appointment, you will be expected to attend the induction course run by the Ministère de l'Education Nationale in conjunction with the Centre Régional de Documentation Pédagogique (CRDP) in the *académie* in which you will be working. However, by that time you will already be in France, without easy access to informal documentation so readily available at home. Everyday written and visual material relating to your personal background (maps, posters, notices, timetables, advertisements, postcards, slides, photographs, newspaper cuttings, comics and magazines, mail order catalogues and so forth) is easily collected with a little forethought and for little or no outlay. Tapes of popular and folk music are a particularly valuable resource. Learning the rules of a few verbal games will stand you in good stead and lead to stimulating classes in which all can be encouraged to participate. Once you are in post, you can also draw on the material made available by the British Council (see Part III, 16), particularly when you have ascertained what gaps there are in the local resources. Contacting your predecessor, where possible, either through your school(s) or national agency, will enable you to acquire further insights and practical advice based on first-hand experience. You should, however, remain open-minded until you are in a position to judge for yourself; preconceptions or false expectations can militate against your own integration into a new society and this society's acceptance of you.

You may well be offered accommodation by the school or through a member of staff, in which case this should become clear in response to your letter confirming your acceptance of the appointment. If accommodation is not provided and you are thrown back on your own resources, you should follow the procedures outlined in Chapter 6.2. You should also remember that set-up costs are involved and that not all assistants receive their first salary cheque at the end of October. You should, therefore, have access to enough money to see you through the first two months. You will, of course, need to open a bank account soon after your arrival so that your salary can be paid by cheque or credit transfer (for advice on banking arrangements, see Chapter 5.5). In order to make possible the automatic payment of your salary cheque, you will need to provide the school authorities with your banking details in the form of an individual identification number (*relevé d'identité bancaire* or RIB).

Experience shows that the transition from home or undergraduate life to what, in many instances, may well be a very different setting can be problematic on both personal and academic grounds. Finding yourself initially alone in a strange town, away from friends and a familiar environment, will be a new situation for most, which they will have to learn to cope with. Settling into a room or flat, building a new life, forming new acquaintances and establishing a working routine all take time. As a student, you will have been used to relating mainly to people of your own age; now, as a language assistant, you have a somewhat ambiguous status, closer in age to your pupils but responsible to older colleagues. Though the teaching staff will doubtless welcome you, you should not expect to be treated immediately as an equal by them; nor should you expect automatic respect in the classroom. It would be wrong to assume that French schools are organised along the same lines as those you attended during your own secondary education, or, indeed, that they share the same ethos. Initially, no doubt, you will be perplexed by the internal hierarchy – the role of the *concierge* and of the school secretary, for example. Similarly, the awe in which are held the head of the *lycée* (*proviseur*) or the bursar (*intendant(e)*) may come as some surprise to you. You should also be aware that your French colleagues, like their university counterparts, will tend to be present in school only during their timetabled hours, and not at other times. Despite recent attempts by the Ministère de l'Education Nationale to promote a more rounded approach to personal development in schools, you will not find the same range of extra-curricular activities, or the same commitment to them, as at home.

Your predecessor may or may not have left a good impression, and your reception will undoubtedly be coloured by that. You may inherit a group of ready-made friends or you may have to overcome negative preconceptions about *les anglophones*. A temptation which is to be resisted, in the long term, is to associate only with other English-speaking assistants. Although this is understandable for support in the early weeks, it will ultimately inhibit your language development and social integration. Your most likely peer group will probably consist of the young, part-time auxiliaries employed to maintain discipline, the *surveillant(e)s* (known familiarly as *pion(ne)s*). Under the control of the *surveillant(e) général(e)* – the *surgé* – they are often self-supporting students still in higher education. If you are in a *lycée*, you may well also encounter other groups of the same age, such as those engaged in post-*baccalauréat* studies: the STS (see Glossary) or *classes préparatoires* (see Chapter 1.4).

While you are coming to terms with this new social environment, you will simultaneously be attempting to find your feet in an unfamiliar teaching situation. You may well have apprehensions about discipline, class sizes and being at a linguistic disadvantage, if it comes to having to explain in French points which might arise during your conversation classes in English. It is quite natural to experience self-doubt as to your abilities as a teacher. You may also be asked to carry out duties which go beyond those you had anticipated, such as correcting exercises, covering for absent colleagues and, as a native speaker of English, giving the language teachers the benefit of your 'authoritative' advice on usage. You will, quite naturally, be expected to be an expert on all matters relating to your own country, its civilisation and culture, and documentation provided by such bodies as the Central Bureau and the British Council will be helpful in this respect. Above all, when drawn into cultural comparisons between France and your home country, do not cast yourself in the role of the superior foreigner, dismissive of indigenous practices and values.

As time goes by, you will grow in confidence and become more at ease in your French environment and, more specifically, with your various colleagues. In the classroom, your developing awareness of group dynamics will make you increasingly effective and respected as a teacher. You yourself will have to experiment with topics and adapt them to your individual style. Previous assistants have found that topics such as family life, food, housing, social relationships, national customs, pop music and travel lead to animated discussions. The British royal family, the American presidency and Hollywood seem to arouse endless curiosity!

At the end of the year, you will doubtless emerge with the impression that the gains far outweigh the losses: you will have learned much more about yourself and the way in which you interact with other people of all ages. You should certainly be a more resilient, self-sufficient person. You may even have had the opportunity to define more clearly your likely career path, certainly as regards the teaching profession. And, despite the apparent disadvantage of being paid to *be* anglophone, you will have arrived at a much greater understanding of French society from within.

4.7 Teaching assistantships in higher education

As distinct from assistantships, where there are national schemes through which all individuals may apply, *lecteur/lectrice* appointments are, in the main, arranged on an annual or biennial exchange basis between universities in France and the UK or the US. For those graduates appointed to lecteurships, some of the initial difficulties of integration will be familiar as a result of undergraduate experience. Colloquial assistants in higher education are, however, often in much the same quandary as school assistants *vis-à-vis* their new academic colleagues and duties, and will need some time to acclimatise to their responsibilities. As in any new teaching situation, you should clarify in advance the precise nature of your commitments. Within the academic department to which you are attached, there will certainly be a full-time colleague whose role will include supervision of *lecteurs/lectrices*, and whom you should consult.

Workloads will inevitably differ, from language laboratory supervision to the occasional lecture and marking of scripts. You may be given the opportunity to discuss preferences in the light of your perceived aptitudes. Be prepared to face very large classes in which it will be impossible to replicate the style of work you are used to in oral classes in your home institution. Although your contractual maximum number of contact hours is likely to be around twelve, you may be offered additional work (*heures supplémentaires*), perhaps even in a neighbouring institution, for which you will be paid extra. As classes can begin at eight in the morning and go on until nine in the evening, you may consider trying to achieve, by agreement, a certain grouping of hours, particularly if you wish to pursue your own studies in parallel. In many cases you will be given a programme to follow, but not necessarily one which covers all your assignments. It is wise, therefore, to plan ahead and take with you the sort of easily collectable teaching materials described above. One particular point to bear in mind is that you may well be unaccustomed to presenting English grammar formally. Keen linguists in France will undoubtedly quiz you on moot points of English or American usage and you should be armed with a reputable English grammar book (see Bibliography for suggestions).

4.8   Work placements/internships

Work placements/internships (*stages*) are often arranged in one of two principal ways: either by your home institution, as the recognised format of the obligatory period of residence abroad specified for your study programme; or by the French educational institution to which you have been attached. You may, however, be required or encouraged to show initiative by finding your own placement and making your own detailed arrangements. Students who have already defined the kind of work they wish to undertake in terms of their career development may well achieve a better match in this way.

Obtaining employment independently will be an arduous and frustrating task. Given the French habit of operating through networks of relationships, it could be to your advantage to make use of any existing contacts you may have, or have available through family, friends, or any educational establishments you have attended. If, of course, you have ever worked – even briefly during vacations – for a company which has links with France, you may be able to exploit this connection. Should none of these avenues be open to you, it will be a question of using standard reference sources to identify appropriate firms and of writing speculatively. Do not neglect the resources of libraries, career services and those newspapers and periodicals which carry European advertisements. French friends may be able to help you by the information available on their *Minitel* system (see Glossary). IAESTE and AIESEC (see above) may be able to help you within their respective specialist areas, if your institution is an affiliated member. In the US, CIEE is the major agency for internships.

You should bear in mind that firms may be reluctant to employ students with little or no training in the job-specific skills. On the other hand, French companies do have a commitment to training and you may be fortunate enough to make contact with a firm that wishes to benefit from the presence of an anglophone, or requires short-term technical input to a project. At all events, once you have secured an offer of employment, it will doubtless be necessary to seek the approval of your home institution before you finally commit yourself contractually.

If arrangements are made for you by your course administrator, it is likely that an appropriate contract will have been negotiated on your behalf. If left to your own resources, make sure the proposed terms of employment include the following: a detailed job description, an indication of place, duration, dates of employment, gross salary and benefits, including holiday entitlement, if appropriate. Your home institution will wish to be satisfied that the job proposals amount to more than an opportunity for linguistic immersion but also extend and hone the skills developed by the course you have been following. Your eventual contract should make provision for a supervisor within the firm and facilitate any required visits by your tutors.

Once you begin your placement, you will need to be aware of the ethos that prevails in French firms. Though it is obviously dangerous to generalise, it is often the case that the hierarchy manifests itself in a more stringent fashion. Do not be surprised if the head of your company appears somewhat remote, with attitudes that oscillate between the patronising and the authoritarian. Always use formal terms of address (for example, the *vous* form, *Monsieur, Madame*, and appropriate titles: *Monsieur le Directeur/Madame la Directrice*). At the beginning and end of the day – and not only when you are introduced for the first time, and on taking your leave at the end of your placement – remember to shake hands with fellow employees. Smart appearance is essential, as you will rapidly discover in the presence of your dress-conscious colleagues. In the office or workplace, keep relationships on a formal, businesslike footing until exchanges of a more social or personal nature are initiated by others. Conversations which do not involve work are likely to centre, in the first instance, on the current state of health of the person speaking to you (the French equivalent of the British fixation with the weather). Within the firm, always deal with your immediate superior, unless instructed to do otherwise. When dealing with another organisation, contact someone of equivalent status to yourself. When entrusted with a specific task, discharge your duties punctiliously, and then ensure, discreetly, that it is clear that you have fulfilled your brief.

Expect working hours to be long. Starting times may be earlier and you could be expected to stay longer than you anticipated at the end of the day. Lunch breaks are, however, probably more flexible. It is important that you keep good time and fit in with the working practices you observe during the first few days of your placement. French firms attach a great deal of importance to the notion of a harmonious working relationship among their staff. When recruiting independently, they will regard this as one of the most crucial factors in the selection of new personnel and you would be well advised to avoid making classic mistakes such as: presuming, as a degree student schooled in the latest theoretical approaches, that you know better than long-standing practitioners; trying to foist on your French colleagues the notion that your British or American methods are innately superior; reacting insensitively to perceived cultural divergences by assuming that 'we're all the same really'!

Whatever situation you find yourself in, you should not lose sight of the fact that your placement is designed to benefit you in terms of career development, both personal and academic. You should try to assess your suitability, in the long term, for any of the styles and categories of work with which you come into contact. Heightened self-evaluation and the development of the ability to work with others are key by-products of work experience. One way of charting your progress is to keep a written record of your day-to-day experiences. This will, in any case, be invaluable when you come to produce the report normally required at the end of traineeships.

The work experiences outlined in the preceding pages vary greatly, from a menial vacation job to full-time sandwich training with commercial or professional organisations. No matter what the nature and scope of the employment you have undertaken, when the moment comes to say goodbye, you will in all probability be reluctant to recognise that a unique chapter in your life has come to an end. You must now resume your studies in surroundings which are no longer so familiar as they were, having left behind so many new-found friends. The real value of the benefits of this experience will only be apparent in retrospect.

5
Studying in France: what to do before you go

If your period of study-residence, work placement or assistantship in France is to be successful, preparations must be made well in advance. For those undertaking work placements and assistantships, most preparatory steps have been outlined in the previous chapter. However, you may well find the general advice which follows of further help, particularly if you envisage signing up for university courses as part-time students. What follows focuses in the main on the needs of those about to become full-time students in France, as they will not normally be able to profit from the advice of workmates and colleagues.

Students who arrive in a French town without having completed the necessary paperwork before departure are likely to fall foul of the relevant authorities and to have problems in finding accommodation. It is with this in mind that the following advice is offered.

Even if your home-based institution has a written agreement which simplifies registration procedures and makes clearly-defined concessions, you will still have to prepare the ground meticulously. Students who do not enjoy the benefits of an inter-university agreement will find that they have even more to do in advance. This will involve taking a number of steps, all designed to ensure that you are eventually enrolled for the right course, that you enjoy full student status and that you have somewhere to live.

The length of your study-residence in France and the type of course you are to follow there will determine what these steps are and just how far in advance you need to prepare for your stay. Your choice of French university may be pre-determined by your own university or college, but for those of you with a 'free' choice, Part III is designed to help you to make up your mind: it complements what was said in Chapter 2 by giving you details of the principal French universities. We recommend that you make this choice before embarking on any of the practical preparations which we set out below. You are therefore advised to consult all available documentation provided by your institution (course and CROUS handbooks, tourist information for the town concerned etc.); informal discussion with students returning from France and with tutors responsible for the year abroad is another frame of reference which will help you to decide. It ought to be pointed out at this juncture that, despite its obvious attractions, studying in Paris as a foreigner has its undeniable drawbacks: in addition to the requirement that students enrolling in the *premier cycle* for a national diploma must have been domiciled in the capital for at least one year prior to registration, it is also the case that the cost of living is much higher than in the provinces and the cosmopolitan atmosphere is less representative of French life as a whole.

5.1 Pre-registration formalities

For British students intending to register in the *premier cycle* for part (or even the whole) of a nationally-recognised French qualification the very first step will be to obtain a *dossier de demande d'inscription préalable* from the French Embassy in London. This normally has to be done towards the end of the first semester of the session prior to your departure. The *dossier* will, for most students, constitute their first encounter with a form to be completed in French. The experience can be a testing one, but it must be realised from the outset that, in the French system, personal details, often going far beyond those required by British 'bureaucracy', for example, will have to be given every time you fill in a form (e.g. mother's maiden name, date of birth of siblings). You must take this and other forms seriously and provide all the information requested; if you do not, your application will either be returned to you or – and this is more likely – be consigned to the wastepaper basket. Form-filling is rather tiresome but in the long term the effort you put into it will be worthwhile; and in any case the information needed can be given painlessly, once you have mastered a few (recurring) terms and the abbreviations in common use in French university life (see Glossary).

The *dossier de demande d'inscription préalable* requires you to give details of your academic career to date, to state precisely the course for which you wish to register (diploma, *cycle*, year of study); it also asks you to list two French universities in your order of preference. Unless intending applicants, their parents or spouses can fulfil the stringent residential qualifications obtaining in the *académies* of the Paris region

(Paris, Créteil, Versailles), they may not include any of the Paris universities in their list of choices. The completed *dossier* with the supporting material required (long birth certificate, five international reply coupons (*coupons-réponse internationaux*) and two self-addressed envelopes, in addition to a certified translation of the national qualification which allows access to higher education in your own country) must be returned to the issuing office by the deadline stipulated (15 March, for those who have not applied for an assistantship). With the *dossier* you will have received notification of a compulsory test of your competence in French. This test will form an integral part of the application process. Provided that you have reached an acceptable standard in this test and your existing qualifications meet course requirements (and that you have furnished all the information requested!), there is a good chance that you will be accepted by your preferred university. If you were for any reason to be turned down by your first choice, your application would be forwarded to the university named as your second choice. Should you be rejected by both universities, you may appeal against this decision to the Ministère de l'Education Nationale.

If you are a specialist student of French in a UK institution of higher education, there exists a *dossier spécial Grande-Bretagne* which may be obtained through your home Department and which simplifies the above procedures. Production of the full range of documents itemised above is deferred until a later stage and the compulsory language test is waived. In the case of all students using the *dossier spécial*, it is the British institution concerned which will forward it to the relevant first-choice French university.

Students applying for a second registration, or to enter at a higher level than the *premier cycle*, are not required to submit a *demande d'inscription préalable*. They themselves should contact the university of their choice between February and July, to establish registration requirements, which will vary from university to university depending on the nature of the course.

It will take some time – even two or three months – before you hear whether or not your application has been successful. Once you know that you have been accepted by the university of your choice, the next stage will be to carry out the necessary registration procedures, and part of this process can sometimes be completed before you leave for France. Your first step will be to accept the offer of a place; a deadline will have been specified for this (usually 31 July) and it is wise to send a photocopy of your French acceptance slip together with your own letter of acceptance (see part 1 of the Appendix for a sample letter). Registration proper will then be completed either by correspondence or – as is more likely – once you arrive in France at the beginning of the academic year (see Chapter 6.2). If you wish to apply for admission to anything other than the first year of the course (for example if you are to register for the second year of the DEUG *par équivalence*), you will need to request the necessary dispensation (*équivalence* or *aménagement d'études*) and part 2 of the Appendix provides sample letters for these purposes. It is prudent to start this process immediately upon receipt of your acceptance slip. Write to the Registry (*Bureau de Scolarité*) of your chosen university (see Part III for the university address), requesting the relevant form. Complete this and return it with the necessary documentation providing details of your academic career right up to the results of your latest end-of-year examinations in your own institution. Assuming an appropriate level of competence in French, if you have completed two years of undergraduate study on an Honours course in a comparable discipline in Britain, for example, you may expect to be credited with the equivalent of the first year of the *premier cycle*; a BA (Hons) degree should enable you to enter at post-DEUG level; a very good BA (Hons) degree may permit access to a *maîtrise*.

This brings us on to the question of documentation. We have already mentioned the fact that details of your academic career will be deemed important throughout the registration process. You will also have to establish your nationality and civil status on more than one occasion. It is advisable, before you take leave of your home institution, to obtain more than one set of certified photocopies (*copies certifiées conformes*) and, where appropriate, similarly certified translations of the following documents: your academic qualifications to date (in the UK, for example, O level/GCSE and A level certificates) and birth certificate (long form); your student card and passport; authentification of any higher education examination successes (first and/or second year of undergraduate study or first degree certificate); proof of your status as a grant- or scholarship-holder (e.g. a Local Education Authority grant or a British Academy Postgraduate Studentship).

Certification of your higher education examination results, together with details of all courses followed, will be particularly valuable where you wish to establish your status for *équivalence* purposes. The more complete this part of the documentation, the more detail given of course content, the easier you will find it to support your claim. Many students fail to take with them such records of their academic achievements and it is often the case that they do not find registration as painless a process as those who are able to produce a fuller academic profile.

Two final points ought to be made regarding the documents you take with you. In the case of certified copies, the relevant French authorities will normally accept documentation provided by your home institution (stamped *copie certifiée conforme* and countersigned). In the case of certified translations, however, the official line is that only documents authorised by an approved French diplomatic or consular agent are acceptable. In practice, where regular contacts have been made between institutions over a period of years, certified translations provided by your year abroad tutors under a recognised signature will usually suffice.

So much for the paperwork relating to your academic career. You will also need to obtain a medical certificate, with an appropriate French translation, dated less than three months prior to your departure. This should not entail a full medical examination but will simply testify that you are medically fit to live in the student community and to participate in sporting activities (*apte aux sports*). However, it will not excuse you from the compulsory first-year medical examination which some French universities require after your arrival.

Do not forget to take with you to France the originals of all the documents listed; your secondary education certificates are particularly important as they are *titres admis en équivalence du baccalauréat* and should therefore give you an automatic right to register. Some officials may need to check that they actually exist. **However, with all these documents, there is one golden rule: never surrender an original document (unless required to do so by the police); hand over to university officials only authenticated photocopies of documents.** Moreover, always keep one photocopy of everything listed above in reserve. Should you need additional copies while in France, it is worth remembering that main post offices have photocopying facilities.

For those of you who are to follow courses for foreign students (*cours pour étrangers*) or vacation courses (normally the *cours d'été* which take place in July, August or September – see Chapter 2.6 and Part III), many of the above formalities will not apply. If you are to follow courses specially designed for foreign students, the chances are that your own institution has already established its own procedures; but even where this is the case, you will still have to justify your academic and civil status once you are in France. The more complete the paperwork you take with you, the easier registration formalities will be once you arrive.

Candidates for a *cours d'été* should ensure that their application form is completed and returned to the university in question in good time, and certainly well before the deadline set. Places on these courses are often limited and, once they are full, students will be turned away. Though registration procedures are greatly simplified, it is essential to plan ahead and to make sure that you are fully informed of requirements (e.g. compulsory language test on arrival) and of periods of study, which may last for only two or four weeks but which may clash with holiday plans. Check prior to your departure for France whether or not you are obliged to take the examinations which sanction your course and what certification, if any, is required by your home institution. In the UK, where such courses are compulsory, the costs incurred will normally be met, wholly or in part, by your university or college.

Vacation courses tend to be presented as packages which include accommodation and even trips to places of interest in the surrounding area. Accommodation for students spending part or the whole of an academic session in France presents greater difficulties.

5.2   Applying for a room in a *résidence universitaire*

Finding somewhere to live is, then, another exercise which has to be planned well in advance of your departure for France. Experience shows that private accommodation is considerably more expensive than a room in a French hall of residence (*résidence universitaire*). The possibility of a flat or *studio* in town may seem very tempting, but such accommodation, which can only be obtained after your arrival in France, usually brings with it high rents, hidden service costs (*charges*) and the likelihood of isolation. Such drawbacks make life in the *cité universitaire* much more attractive. We give advice on life in a French *résidence* in Chapter 6. Although there may be disadvantages, we advise students embarking on a period of study in France to apply for a room in a hall.

Many of the private hostels which form a viable alternative to a *résidence* are run under the aegis of religious denominations, though in principle they are open to students of all persuasions. Some in addition offer full- or half-board. Full lists of hostels in your area are available from the local CROUS or the Centre (Régional) d'Information (et de Documentation) Jeunesse (CIJ, CIDJ or CRIDJ). Individual university entries in Part III give the relevant addresses and telephone numbers, and list some hostels and private sector accommodation.

As previously stated, the CROUS set aside only 12 per cent or so of their rooms for foreign students, and there is therefore considerable pressure on places available. It may well be, however, that your own institution has an inter-university agreement which includes help in finding somewhere to live within close proximity of your chosen French university. Whether or not this is the case, your CROUS application forms will, in all probability, be obtained for you by your home-based tutors. If no such arrangements are made, you will have to obtain a form direct from the relevant CROUS office. The date when application forms become available varies considerably, but at all events you should send for an application form (*dossier de demande d'admission en résidence universitaire*) in February (even though you will not at this stage have heard if you have been accepted by the corresponding university!). If you do not receive an immediate reply, this is often because the *dossiers* themselves are not yet available. Always remember to enclose an international reply coupon with any correspondence sent to the CROUS.

Application forms vary greatly – in layout and length – from one CROUS to another but however long or short the form, always ensure that you give all the information required. Careful perusal of the instruction sheet(s) can save time – particularly where it transpires that the information requested concerns French nationals only (separate application forms for overseas students are not normally provided). If a particular section or part of a section is not applicable, do not forget to delete these sections (*rayer les mentions inutiles*). It will also be necessary on occasion to adapt the form, designed for French students, to give an account of your academic record and personal circumstances as a foreign national. As in the case of the *dossier d'inscription préalable*, forms which are returned to France incomplete may be ignored. It is particularly important to take note of the list of supporting documents (*pieces à joindre au dossier*), which are likely to include some – even all - of the certificates mentioned above, a number of passport photographs and self-addressed envelopes (your permanent home address with your country of origin in French), together with international reply coupons and a photocopy of your passport or student card.

Many CROUS authorities will only let their rooms to students who are staying for a full academic year. You may have to undertake to pay for your room for nine months and put down a deposit (*caution*) against breakages or unpaid rent. This is normally equivalent to one month's rent. Students staying for only six months will still find it cheaper to pay for a full academic year rather than to rent private accommodation (often let, in any case, on a yearly basis). Many authorities require that you give evidence of financial solvency. If you enjoy grant-holder status (which under the UK system includes those who receive fees only from the public purse), a certificate confirming this (an *attestation de bourse*) is most helpful, as indeed it is when you apply for a residence permit (*carte de séjour*) after your arrival in France. Even if you are able to provide such a certificate, you may still need the signature of a financial guarantor on a form headed *engagement de caution personnelle et solidaire*. The guarantor can in some cases be a parent or guardian; an authorised agent of your university or college is sometimes preferred. For some French CROUS, the guarantor has to be someone who is resident and salaried in France, in which event you should ask your home institution what arrangements they have made to cover this. Further evidence of financial solvency is sometimes requested in the form of a statement of earned income of a parent or guardian; in the UK, Form P60 for employees or a chartered accountant's statement for the self-employed is perhaps the best means of providing this. You will also have to supply a certified translation together with an indication of the exchange rate used to arrive at the amounts quoted. It ought to be borne in mind that students from less privileged backgrounds are treated as priority candidates.

Some CROUS offices require you to send one month's rent (approximately 650F) prior to your departure; if this is not the case, the sum in question – plus the *caution* mentioned above – is payable on arrival, before you are allowed to take possession of the room allocated to you. Rooms are available from 1 October; if you intend to arrive before that date, you should ask for a *chambre passagère*, for which you will be charged as much as double the term-time rate on a prorata basis. For further information on general procedures once you arrive in France, see Chapter 6.1.

5.3 Health and personal insurance for visitors to France

It is absolutely essential that during your stay in France you are fully insured against the risk of illness and accident. The French Health Care system (*Sécurité Sociale*) is very different from its British and American counterparts in a number of respects: standard cover is for up to approximately 75 per cent of allowable medical expenses only; the patient pays the sum involved and then reclaims it from the local Caisse Primaire d'Assurance Maladie (see Chapter 6.7). Although France and the UK, for example, have formal reciprocal agreements regarding health care, this is not the case for all countries, particularly those outside the EC. It is as well to check your status before departure to France. Medical costs in France are high: if you had an accident and were covered for only 75 per cent of medical expenses, you could be faced with an impossibly large bill. UK residents travelling abroad for short periods can obtain from their local DHSS office a cover note giving access to necessary medical treatment in certain countries, including France (Form E111).

Students who are following vacation courses or working for short periods in vacations have no other choice than to take out a private insurance policy prior to departure, as described below. Those staying for more than three months need to consider making different arrangements. Anyone on a long-term employment contract in France, including language assistants, should expect to be covered by a combination of the French Health Care system and a 'top-up' policy from a relevant *mutuelle* (see Chapter 4.3). UK students staying for more than three months may apply to the DHSS Benefits Directorate, Overseas Branch, in Newcastle upon Tyne for a long-stay form. However, this does not offer 100 per cent cover; and the official position appears to be that 'as a general rule, persons going to study in France are required to contribute to the French Social Security Scheme for medical benefit purposes' unless they are in France under an EC co-operation programme such as ERASMUS. It is none the less advisable to obtain, where possible, an E111 form and it is even more important that you are properly covered for any sporting activities you may wish to engage in. We list below various ways in which students may obtain full health insurance cover, indicating the advantages and disadvantages of each method.

Sécurité Sociale Etudiante

- Advantages: this is normally available on registration (though not usually for vacation courses) and, as it is the basis of French health care for students, it offers all the advantages of the local system. If you are eligible (i.e. a full-time student and under 26), it costs 865F per year. If you are over 26 you must either produce a certificate of insurance taken out in your home country (with a translation certified by a French diplomatic or consular agent) or else subscribe to insurance in France, which may be three or four times more expensive.
- Disadvantages: *Sécurité Sociale Etudiante* offers in the region of 65–80 per cent cover, depending on the nature of the claim, **for health care only, in terms of the French system.** It is therefore absolutely necessary to supplement it, and student policies such as those provided by the Mutuelle Nationale des Etudiants de France (MNEF) or local equivalents affiliated to the Union Nationale des Sociétés Etudiantes Mutualistes Régionales (USEM) are designed specifically to do this. If you use this method, you must remember that it covers

health care only; you may well consider taking out additional insurance for other risks (see below). UK grant-holders, registered on compulsory, full-time courses in France, may apply for reimbursement from their Local Education Authority for health cover.

E111 with a 'top-up' French student policy (MNEF, etc.)

- Advantages: the special E111 form – if it is issued to you -is available free of charge.
- Disadvantages: some French universities will not accept E111, particularly as the form may not specify the period of validity.

Private insurance policies

- Advantages: if you or your family already subscribe to a private health care scheme, you may already be covered at no extra cost. If, on the other hand, you take out a policy with a private insurance company, such as Endsleigh in the UK, it will give you not only health insurance, but also cover for your journey to and from France, for your personal valuables, loss of cash, etc. Personal items are occasionally stolen from French residences, and should this happen, the Endsleigh – and other - policies are particularly helpful. **If you choose an alternative method of health insurance, it is still possible to obtain from private insurance companies, or from travel agents and so on, an insurance policy which covers travel, cash and cheques and also personal valuables.**
- Disadvantages: private health care schemes may have an unreasonably low ceiling for treatment abroad; do check the provisions carefully. A new private policy may be relatively expensive and those eligible for reimbursement of the premium will find that the Local Education Authority will pay back only the health care part, which may be as little as 40 per cent. There is usually an excess on such policies, which means that you are liable for the first £25 (or so) of any claim. You could find, therefore, that if you had a series of different minor illnesses, you would have to pay for all medicaments prescribed. **Some French universities refuse to accept Endsleigh (or equivalent) policies and insist that you make the requisite payments under the *Sécurité Sociale Etudiante* system.**

Whatever you decide, make sure that you have 100 per cent cover for health care for the entire period of residence in France. For those of you staying for the whole, or even just part, of the academic year, the advantages of the French insurance system are compelling; but if you opt for this method of health care insurance, additional travel insurance and cover for personal effects and cash should be obtained before you leave your country of origin.

5.4 Other insurance

Once in France, you may consider it prudent to obtain insurance for fixtures and fittings in your room; insurance to cover civil liability might also be considered and is indeed required by some CROUS. If you plan to take a car, you will of course need to consult your insurance broker or company about the extent of your cover, bearing in mind the length of your stay. It will most likely be the case that an existing policy will have to be renewed in the course of the year. At that point, weigh up the relative advantages of renewal at home, or a French policy for the remainder of your stay. Try your local *mutuelle* for advice, though, on all matters of insurance, information is available from the Centre de Documentation et d'Information de l'Assurance (CDIA) in Paris (see Glossary).

5.5 Financial arrangements

Another area where advance planning is essential is that of finance. Wage-earners in France, including *assistant(e)s*, will need a bank account into which their salary can be paid. As a UK student, whether or not you benefit from a Local Education Authority award (which is enhanced for study-residence in France – classified as a 'high-cost' country), you will need to make arrangements to have your grant cheque or parental contribution available once you have arrived in the French town or city of your choice. A short-term (or for some students, long-term) solution, within Europe, is to obtain a Eurocheque Encashment Card and an adequate supply of Eurocheques. The advantage of this is that students splitting an academic year between two European countries do not have to worry about changing their banking arrangements in mid-year. They can cash cheques obtained in the UK in a very large number of French banks with a minimum of formalities. It should be pointed out, however, that, contrary to claims made by the relevant banks in the UK, passports are very often required as evidence of identity for each transaction; students who become known in a particular bank can sometimes avoid having to comply with this requirement. The disadvantages of this solution are (i) that the Eurocheque scheme is costly if less than the maximum amount of money (currently 1,400F) is drawn, which means that it is often necessary to keep a large amount of money on your person or in your room; (ii) that if you lose your cheques or your card, replacements will take longer to arrive than if you have a 'local' bank account; (iii) that your Eurocheque Encashment Card might expire at the end of the calendar year when you still have six months of study-residence to complete. It would then be necessary to ensure you collect your new card from your home at Christmas or to have it forwarded to you in France by registered post.

If you have a credit card account in your home country, or a direct payment card (or ATM card), it is possible to obtain notes in French currency from cash dispensers (*distributeurs de billets*) displaying the appropriate sign by using your card and your PIN number. There is a small transaction charge for each operation, but the rate of exchange is more favourable than the tourist rate. In the case of a direct debit card, the advantages are that there are no interest charges (provided your account is within the agreed limits) and that your credit balance can be topped up by willing – or even unwilling – parents! Do remember, however, that, in the case of credit cards, the debt will attract interest at the usual rate, unless you pay it off promptly.

If you decide to open a French bank account, you will have to make arrangements with your bank manager at home for the transfer of funds to you in France; your choice of bank is best left until after your arrival, so that you can establish for yourself which is the most convenient. The choice may be influenced by the advice given by your predecessors from your home institution; efficiency and even the types of account available vary tremendously from bank to bank and from town to town. Traveller's cheques offer a short-term solution but they are not recommended as the sole resource for students whose period of study-residence is a complete academic year. Money brought in the form of traveller's cheques can, however, be used to open a bank account abroad. Whatever solution you choose, you must bear in mind that, when you first arrive in France, you will need to have large sums of money at your disposal – often in cash – in order to complete registration formalities and to make the initial payments required for private accommodation, or by the local CROUS office.

Long delays may occur in the transfer of funds from whatever source (Local Education Authority Awards, Scholarships, grants, etc.) if you do not make appropriate arrangements for the cheque to be paid to you before your departure, or to your home, so that your parents can forward it to your bank (addressed to the Manager, with clear instructions as to the account it is to be paid into). Equally, you should remember that it is a civil offence in France to be overdrawn in a current bank account without the prior consent of your branch manager. Some arrangement whereby, in an emergency, you can draw on funds at home is therefore to be recommended.

5.6 **Travel arrangements**

The only other arrangements which now remain concern travel. If you find that one or two friends or fellow-students are intending to register in the same French university, it is advantageous to travel together, so as to deal with the necessary formalities as a group and to be mutually supportive. When making your travel plans, do take account of term dates in France: you may need to be in France before the end of September to register; the vacations between terms one and two and two and three are of about two weeks' duration; and, in addition, you will have a mid-year break in February. Check that any return ticket you purchase will still be valid when you are able to travel back. Equally, the end of the autumn term and the beginning of the spring term coincide with peak periods for travel, so that plans have to be made well in advance. Check that your passport will be valid for the duration of your stay and allow ample time for renewal if necessary. Do not forget your driving licence: even if you are not taking a car, you may wish to hire one during your stay; and, in any case, it is useful as an alternative form of identification.

Personal circumstances will vary greatly: some year abroad students can allow themselves the luxury of air travel (despite the luggage restrictions involved); others will enjoy the benefits of having their own car. The vast majority of UK students will travel either by train or by coach. Always seek the advice of more than one travel agent, as student concessions such as those offered by Eurotrain or Eurolines can often save you a lot of money.

It is probable that you will need to take a considerable amount of luggage with you for your stay in France. It is worth bearing in mind, for instance, that although the weather may be extremely mild when you leave home, temperatures will drop significantly by the end of the first term, particularly in the east and the north of France. A good supply of flexible, adaptable clothing, including, obviously, several sweaters and appropriate waterproofs, is recommended.

Getting your belongings to France can also be a problem. For those travelling from the UK, a convenient solution is to register cases or a trunk as passenger-accompanied luggage at Victoria Station or at your local station. Should you choose the second of these options, it will be necessary for you to arrange to carry out the required customs formalities at Victoria. Unaccompanied luggage takes longer to arrive and will be charged at the higher rates applicable to rail freight. To send it by air freight may well be prohibitive. Those of you fortunate enough to be able to travel by car will clearly have fewer problems.

5.7 Things to take with you

Whilst it is to be hoped that you will adapt fully to the French way of life, and not, like some tourists, take with you every conceivable item you may wish to utilise (including the kitchen sink!), some essentials, carefully selected, will save heartache and unnecessary expense. First consider your accommodation: if you are in hall, take posters, maps, photographs, postcards, etc. to brighten up your room (with the necessary Blu-Tack for fixing). Spare bed-linen is often recommended too, especially if you prefer a change more frequently than the regulation once per month. A bed-cover, or even a simple rug, will make you feel more at home. At all events, it is a good idea to take a sleeping bag with you.

A personal radio/stereo system will provide entertainment; do not, however, bother to pack portable televisions as the French system is incompatible with most others. If you are taking electrical appliances, such as hair-dryers or travel irons, have them checked and if necessary replugged before you go. You will not be popular if a faulty appliance fuses all the lights in your corridor, flat or lodgings. An international adaptor might be a useful investment. Tea- and coffee-making equipment is probably best left until arrival. Mini-boilers, for example, tend to be cheaper in France. Books are heavy, but you will be well advised to take with you your essential reference works and dictionaries. One final point: many students find a pack of cards, portable board games, etc., a great source of comfort during the potentially difficult period of adaptation.

If you are to be housed in an HLM, try to check in advance what is provided: you may need to supply more bedding and a wider range of kitchen utensils. Assess carefully what you can reasonably take with you and what you will have to buy after your arrival. If you are likely to be looking for private accommodation, it will be even more difficult to ascertain your needs.

Should you be accustomed to certain medicines or toiletries (e.g. creams or cosmetics), take a supply with you as they (or their equivalent) will undoubtedly be much more expensive in France. If you favour particular proprietary brands for common ailments, such as colds, headaches or stomach upsets, etc., you may not find them in France. Tea, instant coffee and UK-produced confectionery are more expensive there too.

If you heed all the advice given in this chapter, you should encounter no major difficulties on arrival. You will, though, need time to adapt to life in a French community. For those on work placements, hints on how best to do this were given in Chapter 4; for those pursuing full-time academic courses, more detailed advice on registration procedures and on student life in general is given in the next chapter.

6

Studying in France: what to do when you get there

In Chapter 5 we described the procedures for applying to your preferred university. By June at the latest you will have heard whether or not you have been accepted and, if you have, whether it is by your first- or second-choice university. After confirming in writing your acceptance of the place offered (see part 1 of the Appendix for a sample letter) you must next take steps to register. In some universities the first stages of the registration process can be initiated by post, but, in the majority of cases, formal registration can only be completed in person during one of the periods specified, in July or, more conveniently for applicants from abroad, towards the end of September.

Once you arrive in your university town, what steps will you need to follow, and in what order? Your first concern will no doubt be accommodation, as you will need a base whilst you complete the necessary administrative and academic arrangements. Before you embark on this, leave your heavier luggage at the Left Luggage Office (*consigne*) at the railway station (*gare SNCF*) or coach station (*gare routière*). Do remember, however, to keep all essential papers with you.

6.1 Taking up CROUS-controlled accommodation

If you have applied for a place in a CROUS-controlled *résidence universitaire*, and if your home institution has some kind of ongoing arrangement, you may well have received confirmation that a room has been reserved before your departure. In this case you will have been required to send a letter of acceptance, usually together with a deposit (see Chapter 5.2). Even if you have been successful in obtaining a room, you may hear nothing further about your application until you arrive at the CROUS offices, where you will be informed which of the halls you are to be offered. At all events you should plan your journey so that you arrive during normal French office hours, preferably early in the morning, since you may well find that your local CROUS closes for lunch, and again by 16.00 hours, in many cases. Should you arrive after the office has closed, then you will need to find an inexpensive hotel, or even a room in the local Youth Hostel (*auberge de jeunesse*), for the first night (see individual entries in Part III). Once you have found out in which hall you have been given a place, you should go directly to the main office there (*secrétariat de direction*) to complete the necessary formalities, pay a month's rent and a *caution* (unless you have already done so), and, if required, sign an agreed inventory of the contents of your room. You may be offered a choice of room. In this case, avoid, where possible, the ground floor (which can be noisy and give rise to security problems) and the proximity of communal facilities (potentially noisy and noisome). Acceptance of a place in hall implies a readiness to abide by a number of basic rules concerning disturbances, the admission of guests, and the maintenance of your room in an acceptable condition. If you arrive before 1 October, you will be required to pay the temporary daily rate (*tarif passager*), which can be as much as double the monthly rate *pro rata*.

For many students in the UK and the USA, hall is the hub of their social life. They will have come to expect a good level of accommodation, communal meals for residents only, and a wide range of other facilities, such as a bar, a common room with newspapers and magazines, a TV room and games rooms. Informal entertainment, such as discos, films and plays, is regularly organised alongside more formal events such as dinners and balls. Resident Hall Tutors are on hand for consultation in case of personal problems.

French students' perceptions of hall are governed by a different set of expectations. More likely than not, they live within the region and will return home on Friday, dirty washing in their bags, only to return for courses the following Monday. In other words, French halls often have a deserted atmosphere at weekends and rarely does the same sense of community exist or develop in French residences, where the general ethos is more functional. The communal facilities are minimal, though there will probably be a TV room and a games area. Each floor usually has a kitchenette with one or two hot-plates, but pots and pans must be provided by residents, and there may not be a fridge. Do not expect a laundry room, though there is sometimes a drying area, which may not be totally secure, and an iron can often be borrowed from the *concierge*. Though perfectly adequate and usually well heated, the individual study-bedrooms are small and fairly basic. Use the personal possessions you have brought with you to brighten your room and to make it more welcoming. Do, however, check where you are allowed to fix material to the wall and by what method. A lamp, radio/personal stereo, and any covers you have brought with you will make your room more homely. Unfortunately, standard British or American plugs will not fit French sockets, so you must either buy an international adaptor or fit new plugs to appliances, including razors, hair-dryers, etc. Incidentally, hall regulations normally forbid domestic electrical appliances in study-bedrooms, although the use of such appliances is very common. At all events, be careful not to overload the circuits. It is advisable to proceed with caution: a sympathetic relationship with the cleaner on your floor (*femme de chambre*) is worth its weight in gold.

Rooms used to be cleaned daily during the week; this is now less common. Bed-linen is changed once a month, so you may find additional bedding useful. In general, French students are in the habit of going to bed much earlier and of getting up correspondingly earlier in the morning than their counterparts from some other countries. This pattern is in part explained by classes starting at eight in the morning, an hour which is often purely hypothetical for British students used to a different routine. Even if you want to have a lie-in (*faire la grasse matinée*), your *femme de chambre* may well insist on emptying your waste-paper basket, either as a matter of duty, or to make sure you are living within the rules!

The rules about noise are often strict, and visiting foreign students would be well advised to establish with their immediate neighbours (not forgetting those above and below) what is acceptable. The most common source of complaint relates to activities after 22.00 hours, when even relatively restrained conversation can give offence. Any disturbance after hours will almost certainly bring you into unpleasant confrontation with the night porter (*veilleur de nuit*), and may well be reported. Equally, the French are often shocked by the amount of alcohol consumed by their foreign visitors. In particular, drinking large quantities of table wine at improvised parties is frowned upon, and both discretion and moderation should be exercised in this respect. Taken together, the twin problems of noise and alcohol-related rowdiness generate most ill-feeling and often set back the process of integration. These aspects of behaviour give rise to mutual incomprehension and the strength of reactions produced highlights cultural differences where least expected.

Even if you are not successful with your application for a place in a traditional hall, you may be offered the possibility of alternative accommodation administered by the CROUS: either a *studio* in one of the new blocks (normally leased for twelve months only), or a room in an HLM, or in a private hostel with which the CROUS has an arrangement (see Chapter 3.3). Any one of these formulae might make you eligible for a housing subsidy, either the *allocation personnalisée au logement* (APL) or the *allocation de logement à caractère social* (ALS).

The key to entitlement to APL is not only the level of your personal resources and the duration of the lease, but particularly the nature of the building concerned: its age and the standards to which it is built or renovated are important factors, as are the contractual arrangements between the owner and the State. It is possible to ascertain whether this benefit is potentially available before signing a lease. However, since January 1992 EC students living in all forms of qualifying accommodation, both private and CROUS-controlled, and who are not entitled to draw APL, have been able to take advantage of a new form of benefit, the ALS, which operates on an individual basis.

Application for either ALS or APL should be made to the local Caisse d'Allocations Familiales (CAF). The following documents will be required: a full-year residence permit (*carte de séjour*), a rent receipt (*quittance*) bearing your name, and proof of your student status in France, for example your student card (*carte d'étudiant*). Once the completed dossier has been submitted to the CAF, there may be a delay of two months or more before any reimbursement is forthcoming, during which period the full rent will have to be paid. Such reimbursements are, however, usually back-dated and it is important therefore to keep accurate records of rent payments from day one. As this benefit generously allows a rebate of up to 50 per cent of monthly rent, its continued existence in its present form must be in doubt, given the austerity measures mooted by the French government in 1993.

Rent for CROUS-controlled accommodation other than rooms in traditional residences will be significantly more expensive, but receipt of either of the above benefits will reduce the cost considerably. However, as explained in Chapter 3.3, students living in an HLM are subject to the local residence tax (*taxe d'habitation*). You should therefore ask at the CROUS whether this charge has been incorporated into the monthly rental payments or is levied separately.

6.2 Taking up private-sector accommodation

Should you prefer the greater independence of living in privately-rented accommodation, you will probably have to accept considerably higher living costs, but you may still benefit from one of the housing subsidies described above. Again the CROUS will offer advice on this. It is also the CROUS, or one of the other organisations referred to in Chapter 3.4, that will be able to provide you with recommended addresses or names of reliable agencies. If you go through an agency you must expect to pay commission on the rental agreement. In your budgeting, you should therefore allow for a deposit of one or two months' rent (*dépôt de garantie*) as well as possible connection charges for gas/water/electricity if you are in property without a resident landlord.

If you decide upon a furnished room in a private house, or an independent flat or bed-sitter, make sure you have understood the terms of your arrangement or lease (*bail*) and what services are included in the monthly rental, which is usually payable in advance. Check what notice is required to terminate your agreement (*la résiliation du bail*), legally three months, but as little as one month under certain circumstances. It is more than likely that you will be asked to provide a financial guarantor (*caution*), possibly a credit-worthy French resident or institution. As a tenant, you are legally obliged to be insured for accidental or criminal damage and civil responsibility. Before moving in, take time to check meticulously the existence and condition of all items listed in the the landlord's inventory (*état des lieux*), noting carefully any obvious wear and tear. It is in your interests not to be rushed over this as, when you leave, you will be required to make good any further damage and breakages. Where appropriate, you should also read the utility meters in the presence of your landlord or his representative and ensure that a written record is kept. This is equally the opportunity to determine what extra charges you will be liable for: some landlords make an additional levy for heating, lighting, cleaning, linen and sometimes for baths or showers. Others may allow you to share a kitchen and some may even provide breakfast. It is advisable to clarify the owner's attitude towards guests and whether there are particular rules about noise.

Before entering into a tenancy, try to discover the nature of the neighbourhood. A seemingly quiet district may be a noisy commuter route first thing in the morning, or be frequented by dubious characters after dark. It is clearly essential that there should be convenient links with your place of study. It is worth remembering that provincial bus services often stop as early as 20.30 hours. The monthly rent for a single room with cooking facilities varies between 1,300F and 2,000F in the provinces, two or three times the price of a place in hall. In Paris you must think in terms of perhaps double these amounts, unless you are very lucky in finding a relatively inexpensive attic room (*chambre de bonne*)! Finally, if you are sharing with others, reach a clear understanding about shared bills, particularly the telephone.

In the event of a serious legal dispute over your tenancy, you should contact by registered letter the Commission Départementale de Conciliation through the Préfecture of the *département* in which you are resident. This service is free of charge, but should only be used as a last resort.

6.3 Registration (*inscription administrative*)

The registration process may well appear to you needlessly bureaucratic and frustratingly time-consuming. Bear in mind that every year many thousands of would-be French students have to go through exactly the same procedures. You will not be given, nor should you expect, special treatment. The corollary of the more open French system is the need to establish credentials, and you will consequently need a number of administrative and academic documents (see Chapter 5.1), and a considerable degree of patience. Office staff are often over-stretched at peak periods, and temporary helpers drafted in may not always be completely familiar with every foreign student's qualifications. Time is needed to check carefully the academic, financial and legal status of each applicant. At all events, you should ensure that you have with you on all occasions your full sheaf of documents (including originals) provided by your home institution (see Chapter 5.1). It is most annoying to be turned away and to be unable to complete part of your registration for want of a single piece of paper.

To minimise delays, the process is usually broken down into two stages, as you will soon discover. In the first instance you should report to the Registry specified (*bureau de scolarité*) at the time indicated on the form confirming your place in your selected discipline (*Lettres Modernes, Langues Etrangères Appliquées*, etc.). Take this document, together with all the required academic and administrative papers, and arrive early in the day to avoid lengthy queues. You may be able to complete initial registration on the spot, or you may receive a provisional enrolment form and a dossier to complete, together with an appointment for full registration at a later date. Your provisional enrolment certificate will enable you to buy meal tickets from the CROUS and to qualify for student reductions. Unless there is an agreement with your home university to waive fees, you should allow about 650F for registration, and be prepared for additional library fees and other miscellaneous charges. Cheques are not usually accepted and you should have the amount needed in cash, though for security reasons some universities require payment by a money order (*mandat*) purchased from a post office. You should also have about a dozen black and white passport-size photographs, full-face, bare-headed, together with three large stamped and self-addressed envelopes. These will be used to inform you of examination dates, and possibly medical examinations.

It may be that, before your registration is confirmed, you are required to establish your legal status in France by obtaining a residence permit (*carte de séjour temporaire*), valid for the year and obtainable from the local Préfecture. (Students from North America or Australasia, however, will already have armed themselves with a *visa de long séjour* prior to their arrival in France, in which case they must confirm this by registering with the appropriate authorities.) To obtain a residence permit, you will have to produce proof of your financial status either as a Local Education-tion Authority grant-holder or a self-supporting student with adequate income. You will also need to furnish evidence of health insurance in whatever form you have chosen (see Chapter 5.3). You should be prepared to pay your subscription to the *Sécurité Sociale Etudiante* scheme as part of the registration process.

In order to proceed to a level of study other than the first year of a given course, you will have to provide a full academic profile indicating all the main and subsidiary elements already completed in your home programme. If, for example, you wish to enter the second year of the *premier cycle*, you will need to prove that you can pass straight into this year by demonstrating that you have successfully completed a requisite period of study at your own institution. The information contained in your profile is considered by a validating committee (*commission des équivalences*) which considers individual cases on their merit. If you have not already taken steps prior to your departure to obtain the necessary *équivalences* (see Chapter 5.1), you should do so immediately. Should you miss the official dates, the validation of your application may be delayed by several weeks. During this period, you may well find yourself in a state of considerable uncertainty, without any guarantee as to the level at which you will ultimately be allowed to study, or you may even be placed temporarily in the first year of your chosen subject (*filière*).

6.4 Enrolment (*inscription pédagogique*)

When you have completed formal registration, you will now need to confirm the courses you intend to follow by enrolling for them individually.

You will no doubt have received advice from your home institution on the general pattern of study and perhaps even the specific units you are recommended to take. However, to establish the full range of courses available in any given year, it is advisable to buy the current academic handbook (*Guide pédagogique, Guide de l'étudiant, plaquette*, etc.). These are often published only at the last minute and may be hard to find. If you have difficulty in obtaining a copy, or, indeed, in understanding course structures and requirements, do not hesitate to consult the Service Universitaire d'Information et d'Orientation (SUIO). When you have acquired the relevant information, you may find that, by comparison with previous years, some courses have been withdrawn. If you are enrolled for a specific diploma such as the DEUG, make sure you have understood the requirements, in particular the requisite number of UV, or UC, or *modules*, and the examination procedures. You are likely to be required to follow a number of obligatory courses, others from a restricted range and yet others from an open list (for an outline of study programmes, see Chapter 2.1). However, you will soon discover that popular courses fill up very quickly or that others have to be ruled out because of timetable problems. You should therefore always have in reserve a number of alternatives. In most universities, there are briefing meetings or induction courses for new students, to explain more fully course structures, the range of elements on offer and methods of assessment such as *partiels*, *contrôle continu* and *examens de fin d'année*. You should make every effort to attend such meetings. In order to do so, you will need to make regular visits to the UFR concerned to consult notice-boards. It is also very useful to make contact with departmental secretaries, as they may well be able to speed up the operation. Use spare time to familiarise yourself with the layout of buildings.

Since you will most likely have to enrol for each course separately and in person, you should be fully prepared beforehand. The process itself will doubtless appear chaotic, as it often works on a first-come-first-served basis and may well be completed for all courses in a single day. You should therefore arrive in good time at the designated rooms, have passport-size photographs ready to attach to the completed course form, and then move on quickly to other rooms to repeat the exercise for the other units you intend to follow.

Lectures and classes may not start for a further couple of weeks or so, and you should continue to check departmental notice-boards regularly to confirm the time and location of your chosen courses, as these may be altered for administrative or other reasons. During this period you can wisely begin your preparation by reading the prescribed works indicated in the handbook, and by testing out library resources both on campus and elsewhere in the town. Municipal libraries are often a useful additional resource (see Part III for local addresses).

6.5 Adapting to French patterns of study

Libraries
University libraries in France are not organised on the same basis as those in the UK. One of the most obvious differences is that probably only a few dictionaries and general reference works (*usuels*) will be available on open shelves, and it is not possible to browse before making your final choice. If you wish to take out a book you must first note the reference in the library catalogues, fill in a request form, and hand this together with your library card to the librarian. Your request will be checked and the work, if available, will be fetched from the stacks. Borrowing time may be limited to hours or days rather than the whole term, and the number of volumes you may borrow at any one time will also be small. The amount of working space within the library is also likely to be restricted in comparison to that found in British or American libraries. You will probably find, however, that departmental libraries give you easy access to essential works.

Lectures and seminars
In the first few weeks at least, lecture theatres (*amphithéâtres*) and seminar rooms are likely to be bursting at the seams, and you should arrive in good time to secure a reasonable place. Do not expect the individual attention and small group work which is a feature of the British system. For many students unfamiliar with French pedagogical practice, and perhaps a little uncertain in their comprehension, following lectures and taking notes will initially be a bewildering experience. The detailed approach to textual analysis, or the insistence on background and exegesis, may be a new experience for students of literature, for example, who are perhaps used to a more general survey approach. Equally, in the practical classes – *travaux dirigés* (TD) – the rigorous structures applied to essay work, or the strict methodology expected in an *exposé* or a *commentaire de texte* may appear dauntingly severe. A great deal of time and effort will be saved if students familiarise themselves as soon as possible with methodological approaches in French universities. There are two obvious ways of achieving this: attend the induction courses for new students referred to above, or sign up for a module such as *techniques d'expression écrite et orale*.

Work required of the student will vary from course to course. You should expect to produce for each unit two or three assessed pieces (essays, commentaries, seminar papers) in the year, though for language courses there will be more regular amounts of work and possibly weekly exercises, most of which will be prescribed in the form of oral preparation for class discussion. Methods of assessment will differ. In France, all exercises are marked out of 20. Do not be surpised to find the full numerical mark range used uncompromisingly. French marking conventions are more or less as follows: *Excellent*, 18+; *Très Bien*, 16+; *Bien*, 14+; *Assez Bien* 12+; *Passable*, 10+; and anything below this is *Insuffisant*! Formal assessment will be either by coursework (*contrôle continu*), half-year exams (*partiels*) in January or February and/or full examinations in May/June (*examens de fin d'annee*). For the formal examination process, separate registration is usually necessary.

6.6 Settling down and making contacts

It is not unusual to feel a little homesick during the first few weeks, especially if you are experiencing life in a foreign country for the first time. There will even be occasions when you may begin to doubt the wisdom of committing yourself to an academic year in France. Such feelings are especially common when the initial excitement of discovering a different town has worn off and there is, as yet, no established pattern to your new life. Weekends in particular are likely to be low points, since so few French students remain in residence. You should seek to use the time positively by going out for the day, perhaps exploring the region or visiting friends. The Tourist Office, the Centre d'Information Jeunesse (CIJ) or the Service des Activités Culturelles at the CROUS will provide useful information on local opportunities. If you do feel particularly low, you should arrange to consult an *assistant(e) social(e)* at the CROUS (see Chapter 3.5), or in extreme circumstances there is a telephone helpline, SOS Amitié (see Part III for the local number).

Getting to know French people informally is not always easy and the means to achieve this goal are not particularly self-evident. In most universities, the Service d'Accueil des Etudiants Etrangers (SAEE) at the CROUS will provide contacts with welcoming French families and, in a number of towns, organisations such as the Alliance Française or the municipal *accueil* exist to foster cultural links and the integration of foreign students. Outside these formal structures you will find that shared interests in sport, religion or a cultural activity are often the way to establish a disinterested relationship with your French peer group, either in the university or in the wider community. The Maisons des Jeunes et de la Culture (MJC), which exist in many towns, provide such opportunities.

Do not expect French students, who will in the majority of cases already have a network of friends, to take to you without a reasonable effort on your part. Becoming involved with a drama group (French or English), a choir (religious or lay), a sports club, a church or a political society will provide an arena where you can be seen to make your personal contribution, and eventually your 'foreignness' will become secondary as mutual interest becomes the primary bond. If you simply hang around in groups sentimentalising about your friends back home and drifting into negative comparisons about French and English life-styles, you are unlikely to endear yourself to the inhabitants of your (temporarily) adopted country, and you will conform to the worst example of the stereotypical, inward-looking British exile regretting the loss of Empire.

Throw yourself into a French way of life. Join in regional activities, read the local newspaper, listen to the local radio station, show an interest in the issues which concern your neighbours, provide yourself with topics of conversation. Check regularly the CROUS programme of activities. These range from subsidised theatre trips and concerts through guided visits to local places of interests (*châteaux*, art galleries, vineyards, etc.) to more expensive excursions such as skiing weekends. It goes without saying that you will wish to sample the delights of your new town. You will naturally want to try cafés, restaurants and student bars for yourself, perhaps share the French love of the cinema, and you will be tempted by the potential pleasures of the nightclubs. But here a word of caution: French nightclubs/discotheques can be very expensive and for females occasionally little more than a forum for an exercise in self-defence.

For those of you living in self-catering accommodation, the local markets are a cheap source of fresh produce. As elsewhere, super-markets, and much more particularly hypermarkets on the outskirts of town, are usually much better value than local corner shops. If you own a car, petrol is considerably cheaper at the hypermarket, and the savings you make will more than pay for the journey.

6.7 Medical matters

As we have outlined above, general medical insurance is essential and, if you intend to participate in sporting activities, further insurance will be required. If you have not taken the precaution of providing yourself with full insurance cover as described in Chapter 5.3, you will have to take the necessary steps on arrival. *Sécurité Sociale Etudiante* and an optional top-up scheme (MNEF for example) can be obtained at registration.

Consulting a doctor or dentist
Should you require medical advice or treatment, try in the first instance the University Health Centre (Service de Médecine Préventive), if only because it is free. However, you may well encounter long delays, and because the service works primarily by appointment, you should not rely upon it in an emergency. You may prefer to consult a local doctor or dentist, in which case the recommendation of fellow students is often invaluable. Keep a record of the telephone number in case you need to make contact urgently. Ensure that the practitioner of your choice is *conventionné*, that is to say that the work will be carried out according to the agreed scale of national charges within the French health insurance scheme. You should expect to pay about 100F for a visit to a GP (*médecin généraliste*), 130F to see a specialist and 200F for a psychiatric consultation. Higher charges apply for home visits and treatment on Sundays and public holidays, while emergency night calls carry a further supplement. After your consultation, the doctor or dentist should provide you with a signed statement of the treatment carried out (*feuille de soins*). This will allow you to claim a refund on charges and on the medicines prescribed.

The system works in this way. The chemist will return your prescription with your medicines. The medicine containers have stamps (*vignettes*) which give the cost of the product. Stick these in the space reserved on the *feuille de soins*, which you sign and date. If you are operating in terms of E111, send or take this together with your prescription and *feuille de soins* to the local sickness benefits office (Caisse Primaire d'Assurance Maladie). You will first be given a statement itemising the refund to which you are entitled and subsequently the amount itself. You will receive about 70 per cent of the doctor's or dentist's fees and between 40 and 70 per cent of most prescribed medicines. Some medicines marked with a triangle are not recognised for refunds. If you are operating in terms of *Sécurite Sociale Etudiante* (with or without a top-up policy), you should send to the Caisse Primaire or Mutuelle office through which you agreed to be paid, documents establishing your entitlement to benefits (*sécurité sociale* and/or *mutuelle*), together with the *feuille de maladie* and/or the *feuille de soins*. If you have

Sécurité Sociale Etudiante cover with one of the top-up policies already mentioned, you can normally expect to be reimbursed 100 per cent. Private insurance policies will be subject to their own terms and conditions, but doubtless you will be required to present a full record of receipts and supporting documentation.

Remember to inform doctors you consult in France of any regular medication you are taking, including the contraceptive pill, since drugs prescribed for treatment may interact and produce unexpected and undesired side-effects.

Hospital treatment

If you require out-patient treatment, you must pay and then claim a refund in the same way as when you visit a doctor. If your illness requires in-patient treatment, you will receive a certificate. The hospital authorities will forward the *avis d'admission-prise en charge* form, confirming you are undergoing treatment, to the appropriate local sickness benefits office. Provided you receive treatment in an approved hospital, 80 per cent or more of the costs, depending on the cover you have taken out, will be refunded directly to the hospital. You will have to find any balance and, in some cases, a fixed daily hospital charge (*forfait hospitalier*).

Contraception, AIDS, etc.

Should you require contraception, discuss this with a member of the University Health Centre. With the spread of AIDS (*le* SIDA), about which the French government is justifiably most concerned, condoms (*préservatifs*) are now more readily available from street dispensers, often located outside chemists' shops (*pharmacies*). You should remember that there are other circumstances in which you might put yourself at risk: tatooing, ear-piercing and acupuncture are regarded with some suspicion by a number of American authorities.

6.8   **Further practical advice**

Personal safety

Regrettably, sexual harassment is not uncommon and many female students will decide to carry small defensive gas canisters (*bombes lacrymogènes*) or screech alarms for use against potential aggressors. Avoid dubious areas of the town or campus and be particularly vigilant if returning after dark. Poorly-lit areas near telephone boxes are often the favourite haunt of 'flashers'. Mixed groups are less likely to receive unwanted approaches than one or two females together. In hall, it is a wise precaution always to lock your door, even if you are only away for a short time, and never advertise your absence by leaving notes for friends on the door. Before taking showers, you may consider it sensible to check that you are the only occupant, as Peeping Toms may be lurking. Invite into your room only people you are sure of, as the invitation may be misconstrued. Equally, advertisements on open notice-boards offering English lessons to paying clients may result in unwanted responses!

Sadly, hitch-hiking has become a risky business and you would be well advised to think carefully before accepting a lift. Be on your guard against pickpockets and handbag snatchers. If you do lose personal papers, credit cards, etc., register the fact immediately with the police, otherwise your insurance claim may be invalidated. In any case, it is always worthwhile making a note of important details such as the numbers of your passport, *carte de séjour*, student registration card, insurance documents, credit cards, etc., in case of loss or theft. Another useful precaution, in case of emergency, is to register with your nearest Consulate. The above advice may seem negative or unduly alarmist, but experience has shown that vigilance and common sense can eliminate potential threats to your personal safety in just about all the circumstances you are likely to encounter.

Travel

During your period in France you may wish to visit friends, get to know other regions or perhaps, during holiday periods, cross into one of the adjoining countries. As a student in France you can obtain significant reductions on travel costs. To this end there exists the Organisation pour le Tourisme Universitaire (OTU) which is often found in the offices of the local CROUS. You can benefit from charter travel through SATA (Student Air Travel Association – Association Etudiante pour les Transports Aériens). The office also delivers the BSE (Billet Scolaire Etudiant), the BIJ (Billet International Jeune), BIGE (Billet Individuel de Groupe Etudiants) and the SNCF Carrissimo ticket. The BIJ ticket entitles you to a reduction of up to 25 per cent for travel outside France and the Carrissimo, for which a subscription is necessary, offers discounts of 50 per cent during off-peak periods (*périodes bleues*) and 20 per cent at certain other times (*périodes blanches*). In both cases students must be under 26. One of the delights in France is to travel by the high speed train – the TGV (*train à grande vitesse*) – but do remember that for each journey you need to book a seat reservation in addition to purchasing the standard ticket. Alternatively, once you have settled and feel confident enough to look to other ways of travelling about the country, you might try one of the bona fide student organisations for shared car travel. There is often a subscription and a contribution to basic costs.

Telephones

To ring home you dial: the French international access code (19); then the country code (e.g. 44 for the UK, 1 for the USA or 61 for Australia); then your area code, which may vary slightly from its internal form (e.g. Birmingham is 021 within the UK, and 21 from outside); and finally your domestic number. Thus to telephone Birmingham (UK), you dial: 19–44–21 followed by the subscriber's seven-digit number. If you are telephoning internally in France, from one province to another, dial the eight-figure number (the regional code plus the subscriber's number). If you are telephoning from Paris to the provinces, dial 16, wait until you hear a dialling tone and then enter the subscriber's eight-figure number. If you are telephoning from the provinces to Paris and *la région parisienne*, dial 16, then 1 (the Paris code), then the subscriber's eight-figure number (which will begin with 3 or 4). If you are telephoning from one Paris number to another, simply dial the eight-figure number. An increasing number of telephone boxes take only phonecards (*télécartes*). They may be purchasd in 50 or 120 units at a cost of 40F or 100F respectively at Post Offices, railway stations and selected *tabacs* (which also sell postage stamps). Cheap rates for all calls apply at certain periods; check your *télécarte* or the information sheet in the telephone box (*cabine*) for details. If, from within France, you need to consult the telephone directory (*annuaire*) for any metropolitan area, this may be done at your local post office by using the Minitel system (*annuaire électronique*). The system provides its own instructions on the screen; you simply type in the information required.

Emergency numbers remain standard throughout France: Police 17, Fire 18, Medical Emergencies (SAMU) 15; other numbers for the local Ambulance Service can be found in telephone boxes. Further local emergency numbers relating to individual university towns are given in Part III. It is a good idea to keep a list of these about your person.

One further word of advice: think carefully about the time at which you telephone French families. As a general rule, it is considered impolite to interrupt at meal times and to intrude on privacy after 21.30. Your acquired appreciation of cultural mores will enable you to judge what is, or is not, acceptable. If phoning between countries, do not forget the differences in time zones: even your parents may not appreciate a well-meaning call at 3 a.m.!

Making the most of your student status
Although goods and services in France often cost more than in the UK and the USA, you can frequently make savings by virtue of your student status. Apart from the significant reductions to be obtained on public transport (local buses, coaches, trains and even air travel (see above)), there are usually special rates for cinemas, theatres, concerts and nightclubs, though there may be restrictions as to days or times when these are available. Local leisure facilities, such as swimming pools, tennis courts, ice-skating rinks, etc., can be enjoyed at preferential rates, as well as many tourist attractions, including museums and art galleries (*musées*). **Remember, you must always produce your student card to prove your entitlement to these concessions.** Often local businesses, such as hairdressers, fashion shops and occasionally restaurants, will tempt you with discounts, though of course the reduction does not necessarily ensure good value for money. If you wish to hire sports or leisure equipment, such as skis or bicycles, always check first to see if there is a student rate. Finally, several major national newspapers and periodicals offer students discounts for a regular subscription.

7
Returning and reintegrating

Your study-residence, assistantship or work placement has come to an end. For many, particularly those who have spent a full academic year in France, it will be a moment of regret and apprehension: regret at leaving behind a life-style you have come to enjoy, friendships you have formed, another self in another place; apprehension too at starting a new course or returning to a university where former friends may have already graduated, where new lodgings will have to be found, where finals may loom. There are practical steps to be taken.

7.1 Academic matters

No doubt your home university will have required some form of certification that you have followed courses assiduously and have made progress in your chosen disciplines. The record of your performance in examinations during the year, whether in *partiels, examens de fin d'année*, or by *contrôle continu* (see Chapter 6.4), will be available from *Scolarité* but do not assume that you will automatically receive results, particularly if you leave France before their publication. Take a stamped, self-addressed envelope (permanent address) to the appropriate *Scolarité* with a request that your results should be forwarded to you. For those of you benefiting from an ERASMUS award, for example, certification of a satisfactory performance is essential. Without such proof, you may be required to reimburse your grant.

Many universities also require report forms (*attestations*) to be completed by individual course tutors and, here again, it is your responsibility to ensure that this happens. You should endeavour to see your tutors a couple of weeks before regular classes come to an end, to explain what is required of you. If you leave this step any later, you may find that your tutors are unavailable. When a course runs for only the first half of a year, you should ensure completion of certification at the equivalent period in the semester. There is no guarantee that you will be able to contact your tutor as the end of the year nears. You may at the same time need to remind your tutor tactfully that written exercises have not as yet been returned and that these are necessary for your portfolio.

For those involved in a work placement there is often an end-of-year report (*rapport de stage*) to complete for your home university which will complement the report to be forwarded by the company for which you have been working. You should respect the submission dates given to you by your university.

7.2 Leaving your accommodation

Whether you have been living in a hall of residence, school flat or private accommodation, there are a number of formalities to complete and commonsense courtesies to observe.

CROUS-controlled lodgings

If you have spent your year in a hall, you should give the *directeur/directrice* and/or the CROUS proper notice of the date you intend to leave, especially if it is slightly earlier than anticipated. Make sure, too, that your rent has been fully paid for the agreed period. You may, of course, have a *caution* to reclaim, though often this is used to pay the last month's rent. If there is an inventory (*état des lieux*) to be checked, ensure that this is carried out at the appropriate moment. You may wish to stay on in the region beyond the end of the academic year, and in many cases it will be possible to retain your room, though this will be at the non-subsidised *tarif passager* rate. The CROUS often finds it administratively convenient to place successive years of students from particular universities in the same hall, provided that your own stay has been a harmonious one.

By the end of the year you will no doubt have acquired various domestic items, such as pots and pans; a helpful *femme de chambre* will usually agree to store them for the use of others – perhaps even students from your home institution. Politeness does matter in fostering relationships and short notes to the *directeur/directrice* and *femme de chambre* marking your appreciation will not be out of place. Leave a good impression: it will help others next year. Sadly, students from a particular year who have been less than reasonably behaved have sometimes prejudiced the possibility of subsequent groups enjoying similar accommodation.

Private lodgings

If you have spent the year in privately-rented accommodation, you will have many more formalities to complete. Apart from agreeing the inventory with your landlord or his/her agent, you will have to make sure that appropriate notice is given for the termination of the lease (*bail*) and that services such as telephone, gas, electricity and water have been metered correctly and that bills and any relevant charges have been paid. If your tenancy has been trouble-free – for you and your landlord – bear in mind students from your home institution coming out the following year. You may well be able to pass on your accommodation and spare them many anxious hours if not days of searching and uncertainty.

7.3 Reporting back

During your stay in France you will have built up a considerable amount of invaluable local wisdom to pass on to future students. Doubtless those planning to come to 'your' French university, school – or even firm – will have already initiated contact, but even if this is not the case, you can put your individual experiences down on paper. Advise them about cafés and nightclubs – and particularly those to avoid! Point out places of interest, offer basic information about how to get by, pass on the name of a particularly friendly person at the Faculté or the CROUS, of a good doctor or dentist, indicate a helpful bank, convenient shops and sports clubs or societies which you have found to be particularly welcoming. Send back to your home university town guides, a copy of the CROUS guide, course booklets – indeed, any information that is more readily available on the spot – so that newcomers, facing choices for their year abroad, have the most up-to-date details possible. An honest evaluation of courses, in terms of content, organisation, and quality of teaching will enable other students to make more informed decisions. Reflect too on how you think arrangements might have been improved for your own year. A report to your year abroad tutor will be helpful for the planning of subsequent periods of study-residence or work placements.

There may well be French counterparts going to your home university or region the next academic year, although it is unlikely, perhaps, that the individuals concerned can be identified before your return home. However, if in the course of the year you have been approached by interested students, try to remain in contact so that you can welcome them on arrival and – perhaps – even offer them help over accommodation and integration into their new environment.

7.4 Financial matters

Occasionally students are tempted to retain their French bank accounts in the firm belief that they will return to France regularly or, indeed, permanently. However, even when the anticipated return takes place, it is not necessarily to the same part of the country and, given the parochial nature of some regional French banks, it is perhaps better to close your account and start again, should the need arise.

You must, of course, take the necessary steps to close your account. Accounts which are left open but which are not used will simply attract unwelcome charges. The procedure for closing down an account will vary from bank to bank and even branch to branch. It is important, however, to verify that all transactions have been completed; forgotten and unpresented cheques create problems once the account has been closed.

For those in receipt of a salary, or of subsistence expenses, the account must not be closed until final payments have been received; or alternatively, arrangements should be made for money to be transferred to your home bank account. Do bear in mind that charges will be levied.

7.5 Travel arrangements

As a student you should be able to take advantage of special deals in terms of travel, though to benefit from these, you may have to book well in advance. Without realising it, you will have doubtless acquired a number of additional items – ski equipment, perhaps? – which will now have to be transported back home. If your luggage has become too difficult to manage yourself, you can always send it via SERNAM (see Glossary). Since January 1993, the customs arrangements between France and other EC countries have become less restrictive, but you should remember that there are still a number of prohibited items, e.g. tear gas canisters (*bombes lacrymogènes*) are still illegal in the UK. Students returning to lands further afield – the USA or Australasia, for instance – should remember to check their own customs regulations. It is worth bearing in mind that student reductions on educational materials make purchases of course textbooks, pens, folders and so on an attractive proposition.

7.6 The year ahead

Academic matters
At some point during your year in France, you will have been made

aware that a fresh academic session awaits you on your return. A new set of reading lists will advise you of the books and materials you need, and it goes without saying that texts for the French specialist will not only be more readily available in France but considerably cheaper. Though paperback editions are, more often than not, stocked by university bookshops, critical editions and critical guides may have to be ordered. Similarly, if your field of study includes film, you will find a good range of video cassettes in all FNAC outlets, though it should be remembered that unless you have access to a multistandard player to cope with the current French SECAM system, films in colour will only reproduce for the time being in black and white. CDs recorded by French singers are relatively expensive but often unavailable outside the country. A sub-scription (*abonnement*) to a favourite newspaper or magazine will keep you in contact with trends in French culture and developments in the contemporary language. Offering to exchange equivalent material with a keen anglophile is clearly a cheaper way of doing this.

Accommodation

Before the end of your year in France, it would be prudent to consider your accommodation arrangements for the following session. Applying for a place in a hall of residence, university flat or searching for private accommodation should not be left to the last moment. Arrangements must be made in accordance with the deadlines specified. In recent years the number of students accepted at UK institutions, in particular, has put increasingly severe pressure on accommodation resources. In your year away the pressure may well have increased even more.

Reinsertion

Settling down again – perhaps to the serious business of preparing for final examinations – may not be easy. Many students who happily integrated into French student ways find that a period of rehabilitation is necessary. Fond memories of the home university may not match up to reality. Friends will have moved on, the campus may not look the same, freshers will doubtless seem like escapees from kindergarten. As you organise your own reinsertion into your home-based course, spare a thought for those students from France who may be joining your own department or another part of the university. A moment's reflection will recall the difficult, disorientating experiences of the first days at the French university, when a friendly face made a world of difference. You can now be that face for the new arrivals. Help them to settle in with practical advice. Now that you have first-hand knowledge of both educational systems and/or of work experience in both countries, you are in the privileged position of being able to explain the differences in practice and to give them the benefit of your wisdom. Encourage your visitors to join in the activities of one or more of the many campus-based social clubs, which are not so common in France; invite them out for the occasional meal or theatre trip; in short, unveil the mysteries of the student subcultures. Why not invite them to speak in French on some aspect of life in France, where their personal experiences and reflections would no doubt be of interest and benefit to their hosts and make them feel more appreciated. Strange though it may seem, giving of your time to your opposite numbers will enable you to reintegrate more easily.

And soon the cycle will start again. As students who have already completed a period of study-residence or work in France, you may soon be placed in the position of advising inexperienced and potentially anxious students where they should spend their year abroad. Although the vast majority of students will have enjoyed a profitable year, your own experience may not have been perfect; indeed, it may have been less than you had hoped for, but in your advice and assessment try to distance yourself from purely negative reactions. Remember to temper your necessarily limited perceptions with those of others in order to provide a more rounded and balanced view of your period in France. Your perspectives on your stay will have already changed, and will go on changing; the perspectives and expectations of those following in your footsteps will, in the first instance, depend to a large degree on your briefing.

Part III
French universities and their towns

Figure 2 France: the metropolitan *académies* and major university towns

French universities and their towns

The reasons for choosing a particular university in France are many and varied. There is a wide range of options, but the student's ultimate choice is often determined as much by the academic programme on offer as by a town's geographical setting and its leisure facilities. This part of the *Guide*, therefore, sets out to provide information on individual universities, their courses, the town and the surrounding area.

For those spending a full academic year in France, the main disciplines of each university are outlined together with more detailed information for students of modern languages. The list of institutions, though not exhaustive, offers the student a considerable choice. Universities are presented alphabetically under the more readily recognised town names rather than according to their official nomenclature; hence, the Université Michel de Montaigne, for example, is to be found under Bordeaux where it is situated. Paris poses a special problem: it would be unrealistic to attempt to describe in detail the seventeen universities situated in the region, or, indeed, to account for all the attractions and facilities of the French capital. The universities and their disciplines have all been listed but detailed descriptions are given only of the Institut Britannique de Paris and the Cité Internationale de Paris.

Finding suitable accommodation usually comes a close second after deciding on a particular course of study and for this reason details of both CROUS-controlled and private-sector accommodation are provided for each university town.

For those seeking to spend a short period of study-residence in France – perhaps a vacation, a single semester, or some part of a 'gap year' – the information on courses for foreign students will be more appropriate. These programmes are listed separately and are supplemented by details of the diplomas which can be obtained, accommodation possibilities and leisure activities.

Each entry contains a selection of useful addresses and telephone numbers for those looking for the town's administrative offices; the Mairie, the CAF, the Préfecture, etc., as well as the nearest British and American consulates. Also given is general information on theatres, cinemas, museums and art galleries as well as sporting and other leisure facilities. These listings are restricted to the most well known and more complete information should be sought from the local Centre d'Information Jeunesse (CIJ), the various Maisons des Jeunes et de la Culture (MJC), the CROUS or the Tourist Office. Similarly the hotels and restaurants given in the entry are no more than a convenient first list for the student or visitor with no knowledge of the town. It should be added that much of the information on restaurants, sporting and leisure facilities has been been provided by students of the University of Birmingham who were spending a full academic year in the town concerned. The restaurants included were chosen for their value for money and ambiance. While every attempt has been made to ensure that the information, including the price bands for hotels and restaurants, is correct it will be understood that these are often subject to rapid change.

It will quickly become apparent that familiarity with the acronyms given and defined in the Glossary or explained even more fully in the text (see Index) is essential. For reasons of space and ease of usage, the full title of common administrative offices has not been spelled out in full so that the local Caisse Primaire d'Assurance Maladie or Caisse d'Allocations Familiales will be given respectively under their acroynms of CPAM and CAF. Similarly the common emergency telephone numbers (Fire 18; Police 17; Ambulance 15) have not been indicated, but local alternatives have been given where appropriate.

1 Aix-en-Provence

The universities and their disciplines

Université de Provence (**Aix-Marseille I**): lettres et sciences humaines, sciences exactes et naturelles.
Centre Saint Charles, 3 place Victor Hugo, 13331 Marseille Cedex 3. Tel: 91 10 60 60. Fax: 91 50 13 00
SUIO:
- (sciences): same address and telephone number, ext: 335
- (lettres et sciences humaines): 29 avenue Robert Schuman, 13621

Aix-en-Provence Cedex 1. Tel: 42 59 99 30, exts: 300 and 302

Aix-Marseille II: sciences économiques, sciences exactes et naturelles, géographie, formations de santé, technologie, formations en éducation physique et sportive.

Jardin du Pharo, 58 boulevard Charles Livon, 13284 Marseille Cedex 7. Tel: 91 39 65 00. Fax: 91 31 31 36

SUIO: same address and telephone number, exts: 265 and 268. Additional centres for sciences économiques: 14 avenue Jules Ferry, 13621 Aix-en-Provence Cedex *and* Campus universitaire de Luminy, Grand Hall 163, avenue de Luminy, 13288 Marseille Cedex 9. Tel: 91 41 41 60 *or* 91 26 05 09

IUT: avenue Gaston Berger, 13625 Aix-en-Provence Cedex 1. Tel: 42 26 57 23

Aix-Marseille III: droit et sciences politiques, économie, sciences exactes et naturelles, comptabilité, transports, technologie.

3 avenue Robert Schuman, 13628 Aix-en-Provence Cedex 1. Tel: 42 17 27 18. Fax: 42 64 03 96

SUIO (droit et économie): same address. Tel: 42 59 29 84

IEP: Institut d'Etudes Politiques, 25 rue Gaston de Saporta, 13100 Aix-en-Provence. Tel: 42 21 15 90

University libraries
- Droit, Economie et Sciences, 3 avenue Robert Schuman. Tel: 42 59 01 00
- Lettres et Sciences Humaines, chemin Moulin de Testas. Tel: 42 27 30 59
- Sciences Economiques, 14 avenue Jules Ferry. Tel: 42 33 48 90

Courses for languages undergraduates

LEA offers the following modern foreign languages: Arabic, Chinese, English, German, Greek, Italian, Portuguese, Russian and Spanish.

In *Lettres Modernes*, there are courses in French language, literature and civilisation from the medieval period to the twentieth century. There is a similar pattern of course choices for the following language-based studies: Arabic, Catalan, Chinese, Czech, English, German, Modern Russian, Serbo-Croat and Turkish. To these may be added American Studies, Latin American Studies, Comparative Literature, Ethnology, History, History of Languedoc, Art History, Archaeology, Music, Philosophy, Psychology, Sociology, Literary Theory, Critical

Approaches, General and Applied Linguistics, Media and Communication Studies, History of the Cinema, Film Analysis, Critical Approaches to Film Analysis, Contemporary Drama, Phonetics, Psycholinguistics and Sociolinguistics, Creole, Regional French Studies, Esperanto and Latin.

Courses for foreign students

Full-year courses

Service Commun d'Enseignement du Français aux Etudiants Etrangers (SCEFEE), Université de Provence, 29 avenue Robert Schuman, 13621 Aix-en-Provence Cedex 01. Tel: 42 59 22 71. Fax: 42 20 64 87

Students, who must be aged at least 18, take a placement test on arrival. Teaching is in groups of 15–20. Courses lead to the award of the DELF and the DALF. Students must arrange their own accommodation.

Institut d'Etudes Françaises pour Etudiants Etrangers (IEFEE), 23 rue Gaston de Saporta, 13625 Aix-en-Provence Cedex.
   Tel: 42 23 28 43. Fax: 42 23 02 64

Courses for the full academic year are organised by Aix-Marseille III. Students must be aged 18 or over. There are three levels of study: beginners', intermediate and advanced. Courses, based on groups of 10–15 students, focus on language acquisition, literature and aspects of French civilisation and can lead to the award of university diplomas in these areas. Accommodation is usually with families or in rented rooms.

Vacation courses

Courses are run in the summer months by both Aix-Marseille I and Aix-Marseille III (for addresses, telephone and fax numbers see above).

Aix-Marseille I caters for students of all levels. Students must be at least 18 and a placement test on arrival determines the course level. For beginners, there is an audio-visual course, and for students at more advanced levels, courses on the language, literature, cinema, theatre and *cuisine* of France. Courses are for two or three weeks in July and August. Accommodation is in university halls. Extra-curricular activities include guided tours of Provence towns, concerts, dances and free access to sporting facilities. The following qualifications can be obtained: *Certificat de Langue Française* (from elementary to advanced levels), *Certificat de Langue et de Littérature Françaises* (from beginners' to advanced levels).

Aix-Marseille III provides three levels of tuition in spoken and written French. Students must be at least 18 and a placement test on arrival determines the course level. At beginners' and intermediate levels, there is emphasis on grammar and pronunciation, with regular sessions in language laboratories. At the more advanced level, course work also includes textual analysis. Courses are held in June, July and September, and accommodation can be arranged in single or double rooms.

CROUS

Cité Abram, avenue Benjamin Abram, 13621 Aix-en-Provence Cedex.
   Tel: 42 16 13 13
OTU: same address. Tel: 42 27 76 85
SAEE: Cité Universitaire les Gazelles, avenue Jules Ferry, 13621
   Aix-en-Provence. Tel: 42 26 33 75

CROUS-controlled accommodation
There is accommodation for approximately 3,000 students in halls close to the university campus. All halls are mixed. To apply for a room, you should write in the first instance to the SAEE (for address, see above).
● Les Gazelles, avenue Jules Ferry. Tel: 42 26 33 75 (939 rooms)
● Cuques, traverse de Cuques. Tel: 42 26 47 52 (1,236 rooms)
● Arc de Meyran, avenue Gaston Berger. Tel: 42 26 58 28 (321 rooms)
● L'Estellan, avenue Maréchal Leclerc, ZUP. Tel: 42 59 09 38 (497 rooms)
For married students there are a few one-bedroomed flats in HLM.

CROUS restaurants
A traditional three-course meal is provided at all restaurants.
● Arts et Métiers (CRENSAM), cours des Arts et Métiers.
● Cuques, traverse de Cuques.
● Les Fenouillères, avenue Gaston Berger.
● Les Gazelles, avenue Jules Ferry.
At Les Gazelles there is also a small cafeteria for pizzas, sandwiches, pastries, etc.

Private-sector accommodation

● Résidence Le California, Espace Beauvalle, 2 rue Jean Andréani, 13084. Tel: 42 27 65 11. Fax: 42 27 65 14

• Les Floridianes, 24 boulevard Charrier, 13090. Tel: 42 37 23 23.
  Fax: 42 64 00 18 (64 flats)

Privately-run hostels

Foyer St Thomas de Villeneuve, 40 cours des Arts et Métiers, 13100.
  Tel: 42 23 37 21 (Females; 21 rooms)
If you are looking for accommodation in September, the Tourist Office
will provide addresses. Write to Le Service de Logement Etudiant,
Office du Tourisme, 13100 Aix-en-Provence.

The town and its surrounding area

A prosperous town of 130,000 inhabitants, Aix lies within easy reach of
Marseille and the Mediterranean resorts. The university dates from
1413 and there are over 40,000 students registered at Aix campuses. As
the historic capital of Provence, the town has a rich architectural heritage with fine civic buildings and a number of elegant seventeenth- and
eighteenth-century town houses. Aix is justly famous for its old quarter
and le Cours Mirabeau, a beautiful tree-lined avenue with attractive
fountains. Buildings of note include the Cathédrale de Saint-Sauveur,
the Bibliothèque Méjanes, the Pavillon Vendôme and the Palais de
Justice. Among the artists and writers associated with Aix and its region
are J.-B. Van Loo, François-Marius Granet, Paul Cézanne, Victor
Vasarely, Louise Colet, Emile Zola and St-John Perse. A culturally
active town with several cinema screens, theatres and a *conservatoire*, Aix
hosts international film, dance and music festivals. The countryside
around Aix, with its archaeological sites, is of particular interest and
beauty. Areas to visit include the valley of the River Durance, the
Luberon Mountains, Lake Bimont, the Sainte Victoire Mountain and
the nearby Gorges du Verdon. There are several reputable local wines
and the Côtes d'Aix-en-Provence now enjoys VDQS status. Calissons
d'Aix are a celebrated delicacy made from marzipan. Aix can be reached
by the A8 motorway and a local rail network links the town with
Marseille, which has a TGV service to Paris.

Tourist information

Office Municipal du Tourisme: 2 place du Général de Gaulle, 13100.
  Tel: 42 16 11 61. Fax: 42 16 11 62

Hotels

A room with breakfast in one of the following will cost between 200F and 350F.

- Hôtel de France, 63 rue Espariat. Tel: 42 27 90 15. Fax: 42 26 11 47 (near the town centre)
- Hôtel du Casino: 38 rue Victor Leydet. Tel: 42 26 03 95. Fax: 42 27 76 58 (near the town centre)
- Le Moulin, l avenue Robert Schuman. Tel: 42 59 41 68. Fax: 42 20 44 28 (a few minutes from the university and the CROUS)

Youth Hostel

3 avenue Marcel Pagnol. Tel: 42 20 15 99 (bed and breakfast 63F; take no. 12 bus from La Rotonde to Vasarely)

Restaurants

There is a wide choice of restaurants in the pedestrianised old quarter of Aix. Here is a selection:

- Le Carillon, 8 rue Portalis (menus from 47F; Mondays-Fridays)
- La Laetitia, 25 rue Van Loo. Tel: 42 27 15 64 (menu 60F)
- Le Palatino, 1 bis cours Mirabeau. Tel: 42 26 86 54 (menus at 55F and 88F)

If self-service restaurants are preferred, try:

- Le Flunch, place de la Rotonde. Tel: 42 27 25 22
- Le Quick, 30 cours Mirabeau. Tel: 42 26 01 85

Leisure facilities

Theatre

- Théâtre des Ateliers, 28 place Miolis. Tel: 42 38 10 45
- Théâtre Municipal, 17 rue de l'Opéra. Tel: 42 38 44 71
- Théâtre 108, 37 boulevard A. Briand. Tel: 42 21 06 70
- Théâtre de La Fonderie, 14 cours St Louis. Tel: 42 63 10 11
- Théâtre Prévert, 24 boulevard de la République. Tel: 42 26 36 50

Cinema

Reduced rates are available on Mondays and Wednesdays, and Mondays to Fridays with a student card.

- Cézanne, 21 rue Goyrand Prolongé. Tel: 42 26 04 06 (9 screens)
- Mazarin, 6 rue Laroque. Tel: 42 26 99 85 (3 screens; shows foreign language films)

- Renoir, 24 cours Mirabeau. Tel: 42 26 05 43 (3 screens)
- Studio Keaton, 45 rue Manuel. Tel: 42 26 86 11 (closed Wednesdays)

Museums and art galleries
- Atelier Cézanne, 9 avenue Paul Cézanne. Tel: 42 21 06 53 (6F; closed Tuesdays)
- Fondation Saint John Perse, Espace Méjanes, 8–10 rue des Allumettes. Tel: 42 25 98 85 (free; open Tuesdays, Wednesdays and Fridays)
- Fondation Vasarely, avenue Marcel Pagnol-Jas de Bouffan. Tel: 42 20 01 09 (20F; closed Tuesdays)
- Musée Paul Arbaud, 2a rue du Quatre Septembre. Tel: 42 38 38 95 (10F; closed Sundays)
- Musée Granet, place Saint Jean de Malte. Tel: 42 38 14 70 (7F; closed Tuesdays)
- Musée d'Histoire Naturelle, 6 rue Espariat. Tel: 42 26 23 67 (7F)
- Musée des Tapisseries, 28 place des Martyrs de la Résistance. Tel: 42 23 09 91 (5F; closed Tuesdays)
- Musée du Vieil Aix, 17 rue Gaston de Saporta. Tel: 42 21 43 55 (10F; closed Mondays)

Maisons des Jeunes et de la Culture
- Bellegarde, 37 boulevard A. Briand. Tel: 42 21 06 70
- Jacques Prévert, 24 boulevard de la République. Tel: 42 26 36 50
- Office Municipal des Jeunes, 1 avenue Camille Pelletan. Tel: 42 26 29 65

Sports
To make use of university facilities, you should go to the Bureau des Sports. You will need your student card, two photographs, and a medical certificate (translated into French if necessary) indicating your fitness for sport. There is a registration fee of 25F.
FNSU: 33 boulevard de la Corderie, 13007 Marseille. Tel: 91 54 14 11
Municipal swimming pool: Piscine Yves Blanc, route du Tholonet. Tel: 42 62 44 37 (student reductions)
Le Club Espace 13: 27 boulevard A Briand. Tel: 42 26 26 58 (keep fit centre; student reductions)

Useful addresses

Main post offices:
- 2 rue Lapierre. Tel: 42 27 68 00 (near the Tourist Office)
- place de la Mairie. Tel: 42 23 44 17 (in the old quarter)

Commissariat: 10 place Jeanne d'Arc. Tel: 42 26 04 81

Mairie: place de l'Hôtel de Ville. Tel: 42 25 95 95

Municipal library: Bibliothèque Méjanes, Espace Méjanes, 8–10 rue des Allumettes. Tel: 42 25 98 84

Bookshops:
- La Mazarine, 11 rue Montmajour
- Librairie Makaire, 2 rue Thiers
- Librairie de Provence, 31 cours Mirabeau
- Librairie des Vents du Sud, 7 rue Maréchal Foch
- Librairie de l'Université, 12 rue Nazareth
- Librairie Goulard, 37 cours Mirabeau
- Paradox Bookstore, 2 rue Reine Jeanne (large stock of English books)

CAF: 2 cours des Minimes. Tel: 42 26 53 46

CIJ: 37 bis boulevard Aristide Briand. Tel: 42 96 03 76

EDF-GDF: 68 avenue St. Jérome. Tel: 42 37 91 91

Centre Américain, 409 rue Jean Paul Coste. Tel: 42 38 42 38

Centre Franco-Américain de Provence, 9 boulevard Jean Jaurès. Tel: 42 23 23 36

Nearest British Consulate (Marseille): 24 avenue du Prado, 13006 Marseille. Tel: 91 53 43 32. Fax: 91 37 47 06

Nearest US Consulate (Marseille): 12 boulevard Paul Peytral, 13286 Marseille. Tel: 91 54 92 00. Fax: 91 55 09 47

Street market: place de Verdun (in front of the Palais de Justice; Tuesdays, Thursdays and Saturdays)

Supermarket near halls: Super Casino, rue St Jérôme

Health care

BAPU: Cité Les Gazelles, Pavillon 7. Tel: 42 38 29 06 *or* 91 50 01 13

Centre Médico-Pyscho-Pédagogique Universitaire, 28 rue Mazarine. Tel: 42 38 54 03

Médecine Préventive, Cité Les Gazelles, avenue Jules Ferry. Tel: 42 26 13 57 (free treatment on presentation of a student card, but long queues are likely)

Hospital: Centre Hospitalier, chemin des Tamaris. Tel: 42 23 98 00

Chemists: the late night and weekend rota is published every month in a free guide, *Le Mois à Aix* and is also available at the Commissariat de Police, 10 place Jeanne d'Arc. The following are near the centre of town:

- Ganter, 3 cours Mirabeau. Tel: 42 26 12 15
- Stratigeas, 16 avenue Victor Hugo. Tel: 42 26 24 93

Local student insurance offices:

- MNEF, 6 rue Espariat. Tel: 42 26 38 06
- MEP, 16 avenue Jules Ferry. Tel: 42 26 73 75

Travel

Railway station

Avenue Victor Hugo. Tel: 42 27 51 63. A local train service links Aix with Marseille and main-line routes. There is a regular TGV service to Paris from Marseille. London-Aix (via Newhaven-Dieppe) £140 return; (via Dover-Calais) £144 return (Eurotrain)

Coach station

1 rue Lapierre. Tel: 42 27 17 91. London-Aix, £92 return; £56 single (Eurolines)

Airport

Marseille-Marignane. Tel: 42 89 09 74. There is an hourly coach service between the airport and Aix

Taxis

- Les Artisans. Tel: 42 26 29 30
- Taxi Mirabeau. Tel: 42 21 61 61
- Taxi SNCF. Tel: 42 27 62 12

Emergencies

Police: 8 place Jeanne d'Arc. Tel: 42 26 04 81
SOS Médecins. Tel: 42 26 24 00
SAMU. Tel: 42 26 24 00 *or* 91 49 91 91
SOS Amitié. Tel: 91 76 10 10

2 Amiens

The university and its disciplines

Université de Picardie-Jules Verne: droit et sciences économiques, lettres et sciences humaines.
Rue Solomon Mahlangu, 80025 Amiens Cedex 1. Tel: 22 82 72 72. Fax: 22 82 75 00
SUIO: same address. Tel: 22 82 72 00
● Sciences exactes et naturelles, sciences appliquées.
33 rue Saint-Leu, 80039 Amiens Cedex 1. Tel: 22 92 34 54
SUIO: same address. Tel: 22 82 76 66
● Faculté de Pharmacie, 3 place de Dewailly, 80037 Amiens Cedex 1. Tel: 22 91 38 40.
SUIO: same address. Tel: 22 82 77 52
● Faculté de Médecine, 12 Frédéric Petit, 80036 Amiens Cedex 1. Tel: 22 91 76 83
SUIO: 3 rue des Louvels, 80036 Amiens Cedex 1. Tel: 22 82 77 19
IUT: avenue des Facultés, Le Bailly, 80025 Amiens Cedex 1. Tel: 22 53 40 40
SUEE: Présidence de l'Université, Chemin du Thil, 80025. Tel: 22 82 72 51

University libraries
● (Campus) chemin du Thil, 80025 Amiens Cedex 1. Tel: 22 82 73 09
● (Médecine-Pharmacie) 12 rue Frédéric Petit, 80036. Tel: 22 82 77 80
● (Sciences) 33 rue St Leu, 80000. Tel: 22 82 75 42

Courses for languages undergraduates

Amiens offers courses in *Lettres Modernes*, LEA and LVE at DEUG, *licence* and *maîtrise* level. Modern foreign languages include English, German, Spanish and LEA is offered in combinations of English with German or Italian or Spanish.

Courses for foreign students

Vacation courses
Centre de Liaison et d'Echanges Internationaux, Université de Picardie-Jules Verne, 33 rue de Minimes, BP 0339, 80003 Amiens Cedex

1. Tel: 22 91 47 54. Fax: 22 92 96 84

Classes are held daily, for three weeks only in early July. Students are placed in one of three groups, according to their level of attainment. Courses include grammar, civilisation, theoretical and practical classes. Accommodation (full-board) is arranged in halls of residence. Candidates must be at least 16 years of age.

CROUS

25 rue Saint-Leu, 80038 Amiens. Tel: 22 91 84 33 *or* 22 91 90 33. Fax: 22 92 98 89

OTU: same address. Tel: 22 97 95 44

SAEE: same address. Tel: 22 91 84 33

CROUS-controlled accommodation

Amiens has 2,709 beds in the town and on the campus.

● Saint Leu, rue Tagault, 80039 Amiens. Tel: 22 92 01 25
● Le Castillon, rue du Général Frère, 80044. Tel: 22 43 38 07
● Le Bailly Est, avenue P Claudel, 80044. Tel: 22 95 34 41
● Le Bailly Ouest, avenue P Claudel, 80044. Tel: 22 95 38 83
● Le Thil, avenue des Facultés, 80044. Tel: 22 95 24 29
● Le Beffroi, 29 rue au Lin, 80044. Tel: 22 80 83 64

CROUS restaurants

● La Veillère, rue Fernel, 80000. Tel: 22 91 87 67
● La Hotoie, 4 rue de la Hotoie, 80000. Tel: 22 91 30 35
● Le Bailly, avenue des Facultés, 80000. Tel: 22 95 12 47

The town and its surrounding area

Amiens sits astride the River Somme, 150 km north of the capital. A town of some 130,000 inhabitants, it is the *chef-lieu* of the Picardie region, and host to a rapidly-expanding university which was founded in the late 1960s.

It has a long and venerable history. It occupies one of the most important prehistoric sites in Europe: the area of St Acheul has given its name to the paleolithic period in question, the Acheulean, some 350,000 years BC. In Roman times, Samarobriva – the bridge on the Somme – in the territory of the Gallic tribe, the Ambiani, boasted an arena which could accommodate 15,000 people. The Middle Ages saw the town build its wealth, first on woad, and subsequently on velvet and corduroy. Thirteenth-century merchant prosperity provided the resources to build one of the largest and most impressive Gothic cathedrals in the West. As a bastion defending Paris to the north, Amiens has been the site of numerous conflicts over the ages, as well as providing the setting for the famous peace treaty between Napoleon and England in 1802. The infamous, bloody, First World War battlefield of the Somme was but a few miles away.

Today, Amiens' main claim to historic fame is as the town of Jules Verne. The celebrated author moved there in 1871 and wrote most of his novels in the town, as well as becoming actively involved in local politics. His house, transformed into a Jules Verne documentation centre, and incorporating a reconstruction of his study, serves as a reminder of his association, as do the walks '*Sur les pas de Jules Verne*' organised by the Centre. There are, however, other focuses of interest. The cathedral deserves special mention, and not only because of its size: its rapid constuction, over a period of barely sixty years, ensured a purity and homogeneity of style which it is difficult to match elsewhere. The carving on the west front is rightly world famous, while inside one can admire, among other delights, unique bronze *gisants*, and the magnificent early sixteenth-century choir stalls.

The old quarter of St Leu, which has undergone much renovation in recent years as part of an effort to integrate town and university, offers picturesque views, and still sports the *marché sur l'eau*, to which was traditionally brought the produce from the market gardens (*hortillonnages*) established on the reclaimed marshy ground between the multiple branches of the Somme. The *hortillonnages*, now transformed largely into pleasure gardens, can still be viewed during trips in the same kind of flat-bottomed boats which originally plied the market trade.

Local delicacies include *pâté de canard*, already well known in the days of Rabelais, confectionery, such as macaroons made from almond paste, or the chocolate and almond *tuiles amiénoises*, and the stuffed *crêpe* known as *la ficelle picarde*, which has been introduced largely since the Second World War.

The town is host to a number of special events in the course of the year: the *Réderie*, a kind of vast flea market, in October; an international film festival, *Festival des différences*, in November, when anglophone students are in demand as helpers; the *Carnaval* and *fête des hortillonnages* in May; an international jazz festival in April; and the *fête dans la ville* and *foire exposition de Picardie* in June. A conference centre able to seat 1,000 delegates, and to feed 1,500, offers state-of-the-art facilities.

With its mixture of the old and the new, its lively and rapidly-expanding student population, and its proximity to Paris – barely 1h30 away on a fast line, blessed with a frequent service – Amiens provides a welcome and a setting for study which have met with an enthusiastic response from foreign learners.

Tourist information

Tourist offices
- 12 rue du Chapeau de Violettes, 80000 Amiens. Tel: 22 91 79 28
- rue Jean Catelas. Tel: 22 91 79 28
- Comité Départemental du Tourisme de la Somme: 21 rue Ernest Cauvin, 80000 Amiens. Tel: 22 92 26 39. Fax: 22 92 77 47

Hotels
- Hôtel Victor Hugo, 2 rue de l'Oratoire. Tel: 22 91 57 91 (rooms from 135F to 230F)
- Hôtel Ambassadeur, place de la Gare. Tel: 22 91 64 06 (has its own *brasserie* and bar; rooms from 175F to 250F)
- Rallye Hôtel, 24 rue des Otages. Tel: 22 91 76 03 (rooms from 115F to 278F)

Restaurants
- Josephine, 20 rue St Firmin Leroux. Tel: 22 91 47 38
- La Taverne de Maître Kanter, 2 rue Albert Dauphin. Tel: 22 91 67 15
- Aux Jacobins Gourmands, 43 rue des Jacobins. Tel: 22 92 98 64

Leisure facilities

Museums
- Musée de Picardie, 48 rue de la République, 80000. Tel: 22 91 36 44
- Musée d'Art Local et d'Histoire Régionale, 36 rue Victor Hugo. Tel: 22 91 81 12
- Centre d'Exposition du Costume, 3 rue de Condé. Tel: 22 92 51 30
- Centre d'Expositions et de Congrès, parc des Expositions. Tel: 22 52 26 26
- Musée Jules Vernes, 2 rue Charles Dubois. Tel: 22 45 37 84

Theatre

- Théâtre Municipal, 62 rue des Jacobins.
- Maison du Théâtre, 8 rue des Majots.
- La Comédie de Picardie, 62 rue des Jacobins. Tel: 22 92 94 95

Cinema

- Le Paris, 42 rue des Trois Cailloux. Tel: 22 92 21 21 (6 screens)
- Le Picardie, 10 rue Ernest Cauvin. Tel: 22 92 15 15 (6 screens)
- Le Région, 36 rue de Noyon. Tel: 22 91 61 23 (3 screens)

Maison de la Culture

2 place Léon Gauthier. Tel: 22 97 79 79

Sports facilities

FNSU: IUT, avenue des Facultés. Tel: 22 53 40 08
SUAPS: Campus, présidence de l'Université. Tel: 22 82 73 74
Direction Départementale de la Jeunesse et des Sports, 56 rue Jules Barni, 80040. Tel: 22 91 53 41
Service des Sports de la Mairie. Tel: 22 97 40 40
Swimming pools:
- Pierre de Coubertin, rue Caumartin. Tel: 22 97 41 66
- Georges Vallerey, rue Alexandre Dumas. Tel: 22 89 48 00
Skating rink: Pierre de Coubertin, rue Caumartin. Tel: 22 97 41 66

Useful addresses

Post office: 7 rue des Vergeaux, 80000
Branch office on campus: outside Résidence Bailly-Ouest, *Bâtiment C*
CAF: 9 boulevard Maignan Larivière. Tel: 22 97 44 00
CRIJ: 56 rue du Vivier. Tel: 22 91 21 31
Town hall: place de l'Hôtel de ville. Tel: 22 97 40 40
Préfecture: 51 rue de la République. Tel: 22 97 80 80
Commissariat: 1 rue du Marché de Lanselles. Tel: 22 92 08 81
Municipal libraries:
- Louis Aragon, 50 rue de la République. Tel: 22 97 10 10
- Edouard David, place du Pays d'Auge. Tel: 22 43 07 79
- Hélène Bernheim, rue G. Guynemer. Tel: 22 52 23 92
- St Leu, 14 rue Gaudissart. Tel: 22 91 12 63
Bookshops:
- Librairie Martelle, rue des Vergeaux
- Librairie Poiré-Choquet, 7 rue de Noyon. Tel: 22 91 55 51

- Librairie Poiré-Choquet, 4 rue Lamartine. Tel: 22 92 82 50
- Librairie Evrard Brandicourt, 6 rue Albert Dauphin. Tel: 22 91 61 80

Nearest British Consulate-General (Paris): 9 avenue Hoche, 75008 Paris. Tel: (1) 42 66 38 10. Fax: (1) 40 76 02 87

Nearest US Consulate (Paris): 2 avenue Gabriel, 75382 Paris Cedex 08. Tel: (1) 42 96 12 02. Fax: (1) 42 66 97 83

Health care

Hospitals:
- Hôpital Nord, place Victor Pauchet, 80054 Cedex 1. Tel: 22 66 80 00
- Groupe Hospitalier Sud, avenue René Laënnec, Salouel, 80054 Cedex 1. Tel: 22 45 60 00
- Centre Saint Victor, 342–363 boulevard de Beauvillé, 80054 Cedex 1. Tel: 22 82 40 00
- Centre de Gynécologie-Obstétrique, 124 rue Camille Desmoulins, 80054 Cedex 1. Tel: 22 53 36 00

SUMPPS: Chemin du Thil, 80025. Tel: 22 82 72 33

MNEF: 6 rue Dusevel, 80044 Cedex. Tel: 22 92 01 37

SMENO: 18 rue Jean Catelas. Tel: 22 91 02 81

Travel

Railway station
Place Alphonse Fiquet. Tel: 22 92 50 50. London-Amiens (via Dover-Calais) £74 return (Eurotrain)

Coach station
Place Alphonse Fiquet. Tel: 22 92 27 03. London-Amiens, £49 return; £33 single (Eurolines)

Airport
The nearest international airport is Roissy-Charles de Gaulle which is 1 hour 30 minutes' drive from Amiens.

Local bus services
SEMTA, rue le Tintoret, 80080 Amiens. Tel: 22 43 84 00. Local buses radiate from the railway station. Tickets may be purchased singly or in books of ten; there is also a concessionary monthly pass.

Taxis
Taxi-Radio. Tel: 22 91 30 03

Emergencies

Police: rue des Jacobins. Tel: 22 92 08 81
SAMU 80: Tel: 15 *or* 22 44 33 33
Duty doctors (24-hour service):
● SOS Médecins. Tel: 22 92 55 55
● PUMA (Permanence Urgence Médecins Amiénois). Tel: 22 92 92 92
All-night chemists. Tel: 22 91 35 15
All emergency numbers and the chemists' duty roster can be found every Saturday in the local newspaper *Le Courrier*.

3 Besançon

The university and its disciplines

Université de Franche-Comté: droit et sciences économiques, lettres et sciences humaines, sciences exactes et naturelles, sciences médicales et pharmaceutiques, technologie.
Hôtel de la Présidence, 3 rue Claude Goudimel, 25030 Bescançon Cedex. Tel: 81 66 50 34. Fax: 81 66 50 36
IUT: 30 avenue de l'Observatoire, 25042 Besançon Cedex. Tel: 81 66 68 99
SUIO: 30 avenue de l'Observatoire, 25030 Besançon Cedex. Tel: 81 66 60 60

University libraries
● Section Lettres, rue Mégevand
● Section Sciences, avenue de l'Observatoire

Courses for languages undergraduates

LEA offers the following modern foreign languages: English, German, Spanish, Italian and Russian.
Lettres Modernes offers Comparative Literature in addition to French literature; a fairly wide range of options is available. Choosing courses and making contact with tutors can, as elsewhere, be difficult early in the session, and administrative arrangements sometimes confuse new-comers (particularly since the adoption of the DEUG *rénové*). Do not be surprised if you are confronted by a (usually short) strike, either by students or the administrative staff.
Arts courses are taught in old buildings in the centre of town; the

Sciences, Law and Commerce, for example, are taught on the modern campus at La Bouloie (which also contains the CROUS and SAEE offices and a Resto-U); the IUT is situated close by. For those interested in the theatre from a practical point of view, there is ample opportunity for participation in plays (in English), a useful way of making contact with French students.

Courses for foreign students

Centre de Linguistique Appliquée (CLA), 6 rue Gabriel Plançon, 25030 Besançon Cedex. Tel: 81 66 52 62 (foreign languages); Tel: 81 66 52 00 (FLE). Fax: 81 66 52 25

The CLA organises summer courses, year-long and short courses in term-time for foreign students.

Vacation courses

Courses range from beginners' to advanced; summer courses of four weeks' duration can be followed from June to September (inclusive). They include *Cours de langue générale (niveaux 1, 2, 3)*. The DALF and DELF are available, as are courses in the following specialisms: *français des affaires, français juridique, français scientifique et technique, français du tourisme, de l'hôtellerie et de la restauration*. There are modular courses for teachers of FLE *(français langue étrangère)* whilst the Centre also offers a *Maîtrise d'été de FLE*, organised over two consecutive summers. Accommodation can take different forms: a room in a hall of residence, *logement individuel* in a *centre de séjour*, board and lodging with a family, a *studio* under the control of the CROUS. Hotel accommodation can be arranged through the CLA.

Term-time courses

Courses range from *stages courts* to year-long courses. Diplomas and certificates on offer are: the *Certificat Pratique de Langue Française*, the *Diplôme d'Etudes Françaises*, the *Diplôme Supérieur d'Etudes Françaises*, the DELF, the DALF, the *Certificat pour l'Enseignement du Français aux Etrangers* (1 semester), and the *Diplôme Supérieur de Professeur de Français à l'Etranger* (2 semesters).

CROUS

38 avenue de l'Observatoire, 25030 Cedex. Tel: 81 50 26 88. Fax: 81 53 14 36

OTU: same address

SAEE: same address and telephone. Fax: 81 53 15 81

CROUS-controlled accommodation

Besançon has 2,280 beds in the *résidences universitaires*. A formula which tends to be used by foreign students, however, is a room in an HLM at Planoise, a suburb well served by buses to the centre of town (the CROUS has an office there and students taking up rooms are not obliged to go to the main office at La Bouloie in order to complete formalities). The HLM have four or five bedrooms (one student per room); shared facilities are a kitchen (two hot-plates), toilet and bathroom and a generously-proportioned lounge. Some flats are in need of redecoration but a major refurbishment programme is under way. You will need to provide all your own cutlery, crockery, etc.; spare bed linen is also a good idea. Students occupying a room in an HLM pay 'residence tax' (*taxe d'habitation*).

- HLM flats: 11 rue de Champagne, Planoise. CROUS Office. Tel: 81 52 21 77
- Cité Canot, 73 quai Veil Picard. Tel: 81 81 10 90 (214 beds)
- Foyer Central, 36 rue Mégevand (71 beds)
- Résidence Universitaire de La Bouloie, 38 avenue de l'Observatoire. Tel: 81 50 26 88; for residents, tel: 81 50 38 55 (12 *pavillons* and 1,754 single rooms; two rooms for disabled students)

Furnished accommodation is available in new apartments of varying size at Planoise (place de l'Europe), La Bouloie and Clairs Soleils.

CROUS restaurants

All offer *à la carte* and set meals (with a choice of five different dishes); cafeteria service is available in all restaurants, as is breakfast.

- Brasserie-Cafétéria, 36 rue Mégevand. Tel: 81 82 12 44
- Restaurant Universitaire Canot (see above).
- Restaurant Universitaire La Bouloie (see above).

Privately-run hostels

- Forum, 1 rue Léonard de Vinci. Tel: 81 52 25 72
- Foyer de Jeunes Filles, 18 rue de Cassotte. Tel: 81 80 90 01
- Foyer Saint François Xavier, 12 rue du Lycée. Tel: 81 81 10 11

The town and its surrounding area

Besançon, with a population of 120,000, is the regional capital of Franche-Comté which is composed of several *départements*: Doubs, Jura, Haute-Saône and the *territoire de Belfort*. Situated some 390 km south-east of Paris, the town can be reached easily by rail (there is a direct TGV link to Paris), by motorway or by air (Lyon, Mulhouse and Geneva airports are not too far away).

The town is both small and beautiful and is rich in history: dominated by *la boucle*, a lyre shape formed by the meandering of the river Doubs, Besançon boasts an ancient Hôtel de Ville (1573), a Palais de Justice (1585) and the Palais Granvelle (1534–40) which houses the Musée Historique de la Franche-Comté. Other places of interest include the theatre and the Citadelle, which stands some 350 feet above the river Doubs and which houses a folk museum, a museum of the Resistance, a zoo and an aquarium. The Horloge Astronomique is well worth a visit (Besançon is famous for its major contributions to the watch and clock industry). Victor Hugo and the Lumière brothers were born in Besançon.

Those interested in outdoor pursuits will particularly enjoy Besançon and the surrounding area which offers beautiful scenery: hiking and skiing are activities which are especially favoured in the region.

There is a good selection of bars, nightclubs and restaurants for a town of Besançon's size, and one factor particularly appreciated by students is the local bus service, which continues to run until about midnight. As Besançon is a small and friendly town, contact with fellow students and with local inhabitants tends to be easier than in many other provincial French towns.

Tourist information

Office du Tourisme, 2 place de la 1ère Armée Française, 25000 Besançon. Tel: 81 80 92 55

Hotels
For short stays or for visiting parents, etc., there are three hotels within walking distance of the railway station:
- Hôtel Florel, 6 rue de la Viotte. Tel: 81 80 41 08 (inexpensive)
- Hôtel Urbis, 5 avenue Foch. Tel: 81 88 27 26
- Hôtel Foch, 9 avenue Foch. Tel: 81 80 30 41

Nearer to the town centre, there are:
- Hôtel du Nord, 8–10 rue Moncey. Tel: 81 81 34 56
- Hôtel Granvelle: 13 rue Lecourbe. Tel: 81 81 33 92 (situated between the river and the theatre)
- Hôtel Regina, 91 Grande Rue. Tel: 81 81 50 22

Youth hostel

Centre International de Séjour, 19 rue Martin du Gard. Tel: 81 50 07 54

Restaurants
- Brasserie Granvelle, place Granvelle. Tel: 81 81 05 60
- Crep Corner (*crêperie*), 1 rue Mégevand (adjacent to the Arts Faculty). Tel: 81 81 81 49
- Le Levant, 9 rue des Boucheries
- Le Poker d'As, square St-Amour. Tel: 81 81 42 49
- La Boîte à Sandwiches, 21 rue du Lycée (sandwiches and salads)
- La Régale 'in' (*Salon de thé, crêperie, glacier*), Centre Saint-Pierre (10% reduction for students)
- L'Emiliana (*pizzas, raviolis, lasagnes*), 12 rue des Frères Mercier. Tel: 81 82 23 64

Leisure facilities

Museums and art galleries
- Musée Historique de la Franche-Comté, Palais Granvelle, 96 Grande Rue
- Musée des Beaux Arts, place de la Révolution
- Citadelle, rue des Fusillés de la Résistance
- Horloge Astronomique, Cathédrale Saint-Jean, rue de la Convention

Theatre

Rue Mégevand (opposite the Arts Faculty)

Cinema
- Building, 26 rue Proudhon. Tel: 81 81 17 18 (2 screens)
- Plaza Victor Hugo, 6–8 rue Gambetta. Tel: 81 82 09 44 (3 screens, including 1 *art et essai*)
- Plaza Lumière, 59 rue des Granges. Tel: 81 83 17 67 (5 screens)
- Styx, 11 rue Battant. Tel: 81 81 29 13 (1 screen: *art et essai*)
- Vox, 62 Grande Rue. Tel: 81 81 36 18 (4 screens)

Sports facilities

FNSU: 30 avenue de l'Observatoire. Tel: 81 50 57 67

SUAPS: same address. Office: Gymnase de la Bouloie. Tel: 81 50 47 56

Stade Léo-Lagrange, avenue Léo-Lagrange. Tel: 81 50 44 16

Palais des Sports, 1 avenue de l'Observatoire. Tel: 81 50 60 87

Complexe Sportif Universitaire de la Bouloie, rue Laplace. Tel: 81 50 60 96

Swimming pool: 13 rue Mallarmé

Useful addresses

Main post office: 19 rue Proudhon (off rue de la République). Tel: 81 82 23 12

Office des Services Etudiants: Point Logement, 24 rue Ronchaux. Tel: 81 81 36 38

Bookshops:
● Librairie à la Page, rue Ronchaux (close to the Arts Faculty in rue Mégevand)
● Librairie Universitaire, Grande Rue (opposite the 'Quick')

Municipal library: rue de la Bibliothèque

CIJ: 27 rue de la République. Tel: 81 83 20 40

Nearest British Consulate-General (Lyon): 24 rue Childebert, 69002 Lyon. Tel: 78 37 59 67. Fax: 72 40 25 24

Nearest US Consulate (Lyon): 45 rue de la Bourse, Lyon. Tel: 72 40 59 20. Fax: 72 41 71 81

Health care

SUMP: avenue de l'Observatoire, BP 1535

Duty chemist. Tel: 81 82 03 67

Hospitals:
● Jean Minjoz, Châteaufarine. Tel: 81 52 33 22
● Centre Hospitalier Régional, 2 place St-Jacques. Tel: 81 52 33 22

There is a dispensing chemist in the Planoise shopping centre, conveniently situated for the flats, rue de Champagne.

Local student insurance offices:
● MNEF, 43 Grande Rue. Tel: 81 82 23 67.
● SMEREB, 22–24 rue Ronchaux. Tel: 81 81 36 38

Travel

Railway station
Rue Viotte. Tel: 81 53 50 50. London-Besançon (via Newhaven-Dieppe) £112 return; (via Dover-Calais) £116 return (Eurotrain).

Bus/coach station
9 rue Proudhon. Tel: 81 83 06 11. A return coach journey from London to Dijon (the nearest direct service) costs £82 (Eurolines); single fare £51.

Local travel in Besançon
Monthly student passes are available on the buses (which offer an excellent service) as are single tickets and *carnets* of 10 journeys and *carnets* of 12 journeys (within a week).
- Compagnie des Transports Bisontins (CTB), 46 rue de Trey
- CTB INFO. Tel: 81 48 12 12
- Société des Autocars Monts-Jura, 4 rue Bethelot. Tel: 81 88 11 33
- Régie Départementale des Transports du Doubs, 32 faubourg Rivotte. Tel: 81 81 14 58.

Taxis
Tel: 81 88 80 80

Emergencies

Hôtel de police, avenue de la Gare d'Eau. Tel: 81 82 03 67
Poste de police de Planoise, 5 rue de Champagne. Tel: 81 52 22 66
SAMU. Tel: 81 81 13 12 *or* 81 52 15 15
AUMB (Urgence Médicale et Médecine de Nuit). Tel: 81 52 11 11
SOS Médecins (24 hour service). Tel: 81 52 36 36

4 Bordeaux

The universities and their disciplines

Bordeaux I: sciences économiques et juridiques, sciences exactes et naturelles, technologie.
351 cours de la Libération, 33405 Talence Cedex. Tel: 56 84 60 00. Fax: 56 80 08 37
IUT: Domaine Universitaire, 33405 Talence Cedex. Tel: 56 84 57 20
SUIO (droit, sciences économiques): Hall Amphi 400, avenue Léon

Duguit, 33604 Pessac. Tel: 56 84 85 49
SUIO (sciences): 351 cours de la Libération, 33405 Talence Cedex.
Tel: 56 84 63 98
Bordeaux II: lettres, arts, sciences sociales et psychologiques, forma-
tions de santé, formations en éducation physique et sportive.
146 rue Léo Saignat, 33076 Bordeaux Cedex. Tel: 57 57 10 10. Fax:
56 99 03 80
SUIO: same address. Tel: 57 57 13 81
Université Michel de Montaigne (**Bordeaux III**): lettres, langues,
sciences humaines, technologie.
Domaine Universitaire, esplanade Michel de Montaigne, 33405
Talence Cedex. Tel: 56 84 50 50 Fax: 56 84 50 90
IUT: rue Naudet, BP 204, 33175 Gradignan Cedex. Tel: 56 84 44 44
SUIO: Domaine Universitaire, esplanade Michel de Montaigne, 33405
Talence Cedex. Tel: 56 84 50 23

University libraries
- Bibliothèque Interuniversitaire, Direction et Service Général,
Domaine Universitaire, avenue des Arts, 33405 Talence Cedex. Tel:
56 84 86 86
- Section Lettres, same address. Tel: 56 84 86 66
- Section Droit et Sciences Economiques, Domaine Universitaire,
allée Maine de Biran, 33405 Talence Cedex. Tel: 56 84 86 66
- Section Sciences et Techniques, Domaine Universitaire, allée
Baudrimont, 33405 Talence Cedex. Tel: 56 84 89 89
- Section Socio-Psycho-Odonto, 3 place de la Victoire, 33076
Bordeaux Cedex. Tel: 56 91 35 26
- Section Santé, 146 rue Léo Saignat, BP 4, 33035 Cedex. Tel: 56 98
45 93
- Section Pluridisciplinaire, 125 cours d'Alsace Lorraine, 33000
Bordeaux. Tel: 56 52 33 02

Courses for languages undergraduates

At Bordeaux III, options for LCE include English, Spanish, Portuguese, Arabic, Chinese, Italian, Russian and Slavonic Languages. LEA
offers a similar range; however, English must be taken as one of the two
languages in every case. The DEUG in English/Serbo-Croat and
English/Czech may lead to a *Diplôme d'Université Bilingue*. For all other
combinations there is a Licence LEA. A wide range of other languages
may traditionally be taken as complementary units: Romanian, Swedish,

Basque, Catalan, Occitan, Korean, Japanese, Polish and Ukrainian.

The DEUG in *Lettres Modernes* consists of 12 UV, six of which are normally taken in each year. A Latin course is compulsory in the first year, but not in the second, when it is possible to take a modern foreign language instead. The obligatory literature courses tend to be rather traditional: in Year 2, these comprise *Littérature Française Classique* and *Littérature du Moyen Age*. A UV of either Comparative Literature, or History or Art History, a UV of Latin or a modern language, and two *options libres* complete the pattern. There is a wide and interesting range of options, including Theatre Studies, Music, Francophone Literature, and other languages at beginners' or advanced levels.

The Arts Departments of Bordeaux III are located on the huge campus at Talence, which is a half-hour bus ride from the town centre. With its vast open spaces, the campus can appear quite forbidding at night and at certain periods of the year. Fears have been expressed about personal security, and some students may prefer to forgo the chance of cheaper accommodation in the CROUS *villages* in favour of a more reassuring, if costly, room in the centre. The campus is, however, well served by buses (Route F), and there is a late night service.

Courses for foreign students

Département d'Etudes de Français-Langue Etrangère (DEFLE), Université Michel de Montaigne, Bordeaux III, Domaine Universitaire, 33405 Talence Cedex. Tel: 56 84 50 44. Fax: 56 84 51 05

Full-year or semester-based courses
In each semester (October-February, February-June) there are intensive audio-visual language programmes (16–20 hrs per week) in groups of 25 students, for beginners, intermediate courses, and more advanced courses in language, civilisation and culture, for groups of about 30 students, leading to the *Certificat Pratique de Langue Française* (*1er degré*), the *Diplôme d'Etudes Françaises* (*2e degré*) and the *Diplôme Supérieur d'Etudes Françaises* (*3e degré*). There is also instruction in Commercial French, and in the methodology of teaching French as a foreign language. In all cases, candidates must have a qualification which is recognised as equivalent to the *baccalauréat*. The CROUS helps students to find rooms in town. Participants enjoy the benefits of the campus sporting facilities and in the evening there are video screenings. The civilisation course is backed up by moderately-priced

visits and excursions.

Vacation courses
Courses of four weeks' duration are available in July, August and September. Twenty-five hours' instruction per week in groups of 20 is offered at various levels, ranging from beginners' and elementary audio-visual language units, to more advanced provision in language and culture. A complementary programme of films is open to all students following the courses. In addition to a free excursion once a week, there are optional inexpensive visits and outings which seek to explore the culture of the region. Candidates must be over 18 years of age, or hold an end-of-secondary-education qualification recognised as equivalent to the *baccalauréat*.

CROUS

18 rue du Hamel, BP 63, 33033 Bordeaux-Midi Cedex. Tel: 56 33 86 86. Fax: 56 92 86 65 (*Directeur*) or 56 91 77 11 (Cités)
SAEE: same address and telephone
OTU: next to Resto-U no. 2 (see below). Tel: 56 80 71 87
CROUS-controlled accommodation
There are 4,270 rooms available in halls of residence, most of which are in the six so-called *villages* on the campus at Talence; all *villages* are mixed except for no. 2, which is for women only:
- Village 1, Domaine Universitaire, 33405 Talence. Tel: 56 80 67 68 (716 rooms)
- Village 2, same address. Tel: 56 04 01 30 (445 rooms)
- Village 3, same address. Tel: 56 80 67 10 (900 rooms)
- Village 4, same address. Tel: 56 04 30 70 (620 rooms)
- Village 5, same address. Tel: 56 80 74 34 (909 rooms)
- Village 6, same address. Tel: 56 80 48 65 (298 rooms)
In terms of distance, nos 1 and 2 are the most convenient for students of Science, nos 2 and 3 for Law and Economics, nos 4 and 5 for Arts and Law, and no. 6 for the IUT. In addition, there is a single-sex hall in the centre of Bordeaux:
- Maison des Etudiantes, 50 rue Ligier. Tel: 56 96 40 30 (102 rooms)
Various 'new-style' residences have recently been completed. All qualify for APL:
- Résidence Budos, 17 rue de Budos. Tel: 56 96 24 35
- Résidence Tauzin, rue de Tauzin
- Résidence La Boétie, cours Victor Hugo

- Résidence de la Marne, cours de la Marne
- Résidence Clairefontaine, rue Francisco Ferrer, Mérignac
- Résidence Bellegrave, Pessac

CROUS restaurants
Of the four main student restaurants in Bordeaux, three are on the campus at Talence and the other is in the centre. All serve the *menu traditionnel* in addition to the alternatives indicated below:
- Restaurant 1 (near to Village 1), Domaine Universitaire, 33405. Tel: 56 80 67 67 (*brasserie*: five different counters, wide choice)
- Restaurant 2 (near to Village 2), same address. Tel: 56 80 67 55 (*steak/frites/salade; plats du jour avec entrées et desserts en supplément; brasserie-cafétéria*; open at lunch-time only)
- Restaurant 3 (near to Village 6), same address. Tel: 56 80 79 62 (*spécialité/grill/friterie avec possibilité de suppléments; brasserie-cafétéria*).
- Cafétéria Le Forum (near the Lecture Theatres for Law, Politics and Economics). Tel: 56 37 26 00. Open 7.30–18.30
- Cafétéria Vera Cruz (in Village 3). Tel: 57 96 94 18. Open from 7.00–22.00
- Restaurant Central, 42 rue Sauteyron. Tel: 56 92 75 30 (five service points, offering a wide choice of meals, desserts and drinks)
In addition, the CROUS runs a *Brasserie-Cafétéria* in Bordeaux II-Médecine, Domaine de Carreire, 146 rue Léo Saignat. Tel: 56 96 24 35 *or* 56 98 69 36 (*plats du jour, hors d'oeuvres, desserts, pâtisseries, sandwichs, pizzas, quiches, glaces . . .)*

Private-sector residences

- Les Lauréades de Bordeaux, 35 rue Pauline Kergomard, 33000 Bordeaux. Tel: 56 91 25 01
- Les Lauréades de Talence, 340 cours de la Libération, 33400 Talence. Tel: 56 84 40 00
- Les Résidences de Bissy-Mérignac, 83 avenue Bon Air, 33700 Mérignac. Tel: 56 47 03 67

Privately-run hostels

For details, write to the *Directeur/Directrice*:
- Foyer Doctrine Chretienne (70 places for women), 9 rue Bigot, 33000 Bordeaux. Tel: 56 91 53 45
- Foyer Saint-Joseph de Cluny (100 places for women), 54 boulevard Godard, 33000. Tel: 56 50 24 97

- Foyer l'Eveil (25 places for women), 19 rue des Etuves, 33000 Bordeaux. Tel: 56 44 37 55
- Foyer Saint-Pierre (100 places for women), 4 rue Peydevant, 33400 Talence. Tel: 56 80 69 69
- Foyer Sévigné (75 places for women), rue du Hâ, 33000 Bordeaux. Tel: 56 52 10 89
- Foyer SNCF: Foyer des Acacias-Bordeaux, rond-point des Acacias, 194 ter boulevard Albert ler. Tel: 56 33 19 96

The town and its surrounding area

Bordeaux, formerly capital of the old province of Guyenne, is today the *préfecture* of the Gironde. It stands on the left bank of the Garonne some 100 km from the point at which it flows into the Atlantic, and about 25 km south of the confluence with the River Dordogne. Good motorway links and fast trains (including a TGV service) link it with Paris, some 565 km away to the north-east. There are direct flights to London.

The modern city developed from the prosperous Gallo-Roman town of Burdigala. It is steeped in history: occupied by the English from the twelfth to the fifteenth century, it had its heyday in the eighteenth century by virtue of its trade with the Indies, while in more recent times it has been on several occasions the seat of the French government, when the latter has been obliged to leave Paris (1870–71, 1914 and 1940). Famous names connected with the town include the Latin poet Ausonius (*c.* 310–95); the sixteenth century *moraliste*, Michel de Montaigne, who served two terms as Mayor (1581–85); the painter Francisco de Goya (1746–1828), who died in the town after spending his last four years there; the musician, Eugène Goossens (1867–1958); and modern writers like François Mauriac (1885–1970) and Jean Anouilh (1910–87).

There are many relics of this glorious past. The ruins of a third-century amphitheatre, the Palais Gallien, are a reminder of centuries gone by. The Middle Ages and the Renaissance are represented by churches: Cathédrale St André (twelfth–fifteenth century), St-Seurnin (mainly twelfth–fourteenth century), Ste-Croix (twelfth–thirteenth century), St-Pierre (fifteenth–sixteenth century), St-Michel (fifteenth–sixteenth century); and by monuments such as the Porte de la 'Grosse Cloche' and the Porte Cailhu. The 'Golden Age' of the eighteenth century lives on in the architecture of the place de la Bourse, the place Gambetta, the Grand Théâtre, the impressive *portes* that rear up at various points in the town, in buildings like the Hôtels de Poissac, de

Pierlot and de Lalande, and the waterfront facades. A great deal of work has been done to restore buildings in the historical central area, which was made a 'protected sector' (*secteur sauvegardé*) in 1967.

Everyone associates Bordeaux with the wine trade and it is still its most important commercial activity. However, in recent times it has expanded into new areas, such as the space and aeronautics industries, and other sectors of high technology (bio-technological, bio-medical, etc.). If the port is not what it was two centuries ago, the river is still host to pleasure boats and race craft of all shapes and sizes.

Within easy reach lie the vineyards, the fine sandy beaches of the Atlantic coast, and the pine forests of the Landes.

Tourist information

Maison du Tourisme: 12 cours du XXX Juillet, 33080 Bordeaux Cedex. Tel: 56 44 28 41. Fax: 56 81 89 21 (with outposts at the main railway station (Tel: 56 91 64 70) and the airport. (Tel: 56 34 39 39)).

Hotels

- Hôtel Arcade, 60 rue Eugène-le-Roy, 33800. Tel: 56 91 40 40 (convenient; a typical modern chain hotel; a single room with shower, WC and television will cost around 300F, without breakfast)
- Les Relais Bleus, 14 place de la Victoire
- Hôtel Gambetta, 66 rue Porte-Dijeaux. Tel: 56 51 21 83

Youth hostel

22 cours Barbey. Tel: 56 91 59 51

Restaurants

- Restaurant Breton-Crêperie La Fromentine, 4 rue du Pas Saint-Georges. Tel: 56 79 24 10 (pleasant; good atmosphere; inexpensive)
- La Pyramide, rue Ste Catherine (fairly central)
- Bistrot Johnathan, avenue Charlionnet (between campus and town; lunchtime menu, about 50F)

Leisure facilities

Museums and art galleries

- Musée d'Aquitaine, 20 cours Pasteur. Tel: 56 10 17 50
- Musée d'Arts Contemporains, 7 rue Ferrère. Tel: 56 44 16 35
- Musée des Arts Décoratifs, 39 rue Bouffard. Tel: 56 10 15 62
- Musée des Beaux-Arts, Jardin de la Mairie, 20 cours d'Albret. Tel: 56 10 17 49

- Musée des Douanes, 1 place de la Bourse. Tel: 56 52 45 47
- Muséum d'Histoire Naturelle, Jardin Public, cours de Verdun. Tel: 56 48 29 86
- Musée Militaire, 192 rue de Pessac
- Centre National Jean Moulin, place Jean Moulin. Tel: 56 10 15 80
- Maison des Métiers de l'Imprimerie, 10 rue Fort-Louis. Tel: 56 92 61 17
- Galerie des Beaux-Arts, place Colonel Raynal. Tel: 56 44 88 69
- Galerie l'Ami des Lettres, 5 rue Jean-Jacques Bel. Tel: 56 52 58 84

Theatre
- Grand Théâtre de Bordeaux, place de la Comédie. Tel: 56 81 90 81
- Théâtre du Port de la Lune, 3 place Renaudel. Tel: 56 91 99 44
- Théâtre Barbey, 22 cours Barbey. Tel: 56 91 59 51
- Théâtre Fémina, rue Grassi. Tel: 56 52 45 19
- Compagnie Dramatique d'Aquitaine, rue Montgolfier. Tel: 56 52 66 74
- Centre André Malraux-Conservatoire National, 22 quai Sainte-Croix. Tel: 56 92 96 96

Cinema
- UGC, 20 rue Judaïque. Tel: 56 44 34 94
- Français, rond-point de l'Intendance. Tel: 56 48 17 55
- Gaumont, 9 cours Georges Clemenceau. Tel: 56 48 13 38
- Saint-Genès, 6 boulevard du Président Roosevelt. Tel: 56 92 57 31
- Trianon Jean Vigo, 6 rue Franklin. Tel: 56 44 35 17

Sport
FNSU: Domaine Universitaire, 33405 Talence Cedex. Tel: 56 80 14 25
Palais des Sports, place de la Ferme-de-Richemond. Tel: 56 90 91 60
Athletics: Stade Municipal de Thouars, 33400 Talence. Tel: 56 80 51 20
Football:
- Les Girondins de Bordeaux FC, Stade Municipal, place Johnston. Tel. (bookings): 56 93 25 83 (the professional club)
- District Bordeaux Foot, 13 rue Soubiras
Rugby: Stade Delphin Loche, Bègles. Tel: 56 85 94 01
Skating: Patinoire Olympique Bordeaux-Mériadek, 100 cours du

Maréchal Juin. Tel: 56 93 11 11

Swimming:

- Piscine Olympique du Grand Parc, rue G. Duché. Tel: 56 50 31 97
- Piscine du CREPS, Domaine Universitaire, allée Pierre de Coubertin, Talence. Tel: 56 80 75 80

Tennis: Antennes Sportives, Plaine des Sports de Bordeaux-Lac. Tel: 56 50 92 40

As regards student sport, the SIUAPS is based on the main campus at Château Roquencourt, Stadium Universitaire, esplanade des Antilles, 33600 Pessac. Tel: 56 80 17 49. Well known, too, is the Bordeaux-Etudiants-Club (BEC), 38 rue de Cursol, which enters teams in non-university sports competitions.

Useful addresses

Main post office: 52 rue Georges Bonnac. Tel: 56 48 87 48

Municipal library: La Nouvelle Bibliothèque Municipale, 85 cours du Maréchal Juin, 33075. Tel: 56 24 32 51

Bookshops:

- Chez Mollat, rue Porte Dijeaux
- FNAC, St Christoly, rue des Trois Conils
- Mon Livre, Domaine Universitaire, avenue Albert Schweitzer

CIJA: 5 rue Duffour Dubergier and 125 cours Alsace Lorraine. Tel: 56 56 00 56

CAF: rue du Docteur Gabriel Péry, 33078 Cedex. Tel: 56 43 50 00

ANPE: 1 terrasse Front du Médoc, 33000. Tel: 56 00 18 00

Administrative offices:

- Préfecture de la Région Aquitaine, 21 rue Esprit des Lois, 33077 Cedex. Tel: 56 90 60 60
- Préfecture de la Gironde, esplanade Charles de Gaulle, 33077 Cedex. Tel: 56 90 61 30

However, to obtain a *carte de séjour*, students should go, armed with black-and-white photographs, to the Cité Administrative in the rue Judaïque (if they live in the centre of town) or the Commissariat in Pessac (if they live on the campus).

British Consulate-General: 353 boulevard du Président Wilson, 33073 Cedex. Tel: 56 42 34 13. Fax: 56 08 33 12

US Consulate-General: 22 cours du Maréchal Foch, 33080 Cedex. Tel: 56 52 65 95. Fax: 56 51 60 42

Health care

The main hospitals for emergency treatment are:
- Hôpital Saint-André, 1 rue Jean Burguet. Tel: 56 79 56 79
- Hôpital Pellegrin-Tripode, place Amélie Raba Léon. Tel: 56 79 56 79
- Hôpital Charles Perrens, 121 rue de la Bèchade. Tel: 56 56 34 34

SUMP: Domaine Universitaire, avenue Pey Berland, 33405 Talence Cedex (by appointment). Tel: 56 80 71 95. A day-time *infirmerie* is available in Village 2 (Bâtiment C).

Local student insurance offices:
- MNEF, 150 cours Victor Hugo, 33026 Cedex. Tel: 56 31 32 33 Accueil Centre-ville, 24 cours de l'Argonne, 33086
- SMESO, 111 cours du Maréchal Galliéni. Tel: 56 51 56 02

CPAM: place de l'Europe. Tel: 56 39 62 94

Travel

Railway station
Gare St-Jean, 33000. Tel: 56 92 50 50
Reservations, Tel: 56 92 60 60. London-Bordeaux (via Newhaven-Dieppe) £129 return; (via Dover-Calais) £133 return (Eurotrain)

Coach station
25 rue du Col Marchand, 33082 Cedex. London-Bordeaux, £50 single; £89 return (Eurolines)

Airport
Bordeaux-Mérignac, Cedex 4, 33700 Mérignac. Tel: 56 34 84 84. Regular direct flights to Heathrow.

Local buses
CGFTE, 25 rue du Commandant Marchand, 33082 Cedex. Tel: 57 57 88 88. Single journey (one bus only) costs 7F; student monthly bus pass (*Carte Bordeaux Etudiant*) available; *carnets* of 10 tickets available with student card at a reduced rate.

Emergencies

SOS Médecins: 21 rue Croix de Seguey. Tel: 56 44 74 74
SAMU. Tel: 56 96 70 70
SOS Amitiés. Tel: 56 44 22 22

La Porte Ouverte, 2 rue Paul Bert. Tel: 56 52 30 35
Bordeaux I, II, III Accueil, 26 rue Paul Louis Lande. Tel: 56 91 86 38
Duty doctors and chemists. Tel: 56 90 92 75

5 CAEN

The university and its disciplines

Université de Caen: droit et sciences économiques, lettres et sciences
humaines, médecine et pharmacie, sciences exactes et sciences
naturelles, technologie.
Esplanade de la Paix, 14032 Caen Cedex. Tel: 31 45 55 00. Fax: 31
45 56 00
SUIO: same address. Tel: 31 45 55 12
SUEE: same address. Tel: 31 45 55 38
IUT: boulevard du Maréchal Juin, 14032 Caen Cedex. Tel: 31 45 70 00

University library
Esplanade de la Paix, 14032 Cedex. Tel: 31 45 57 70
● Section Droit-Lettres (Campus I, Law Building). Tel: 31 45 55 34
● Section Scientifique (behind the Science Building). Tel: 31 45 55 35
● Section Médecine et Pharmacie (at UFR de Médecine, CHU, Côte
  de Nacre). Tel: 31 06 31 06, ext. 8093

Courses for languages undergraduates

Modern Languages come under the UFR des Langues Vivantes
Etrangères. A DEUG *rénové* in LCE is available in German, English,
Spanish, Italian, Russian and *Fenno-Scandinave*. In each case, it is
possible to proceed to a *Licence/Maîtrise de Langues Vivantes Etrangères* in
the language concerned. A DEUG *rénové* in LEA is offered in the
following combinations: English/German, English/Spanish, English/
Italian and English/Russian. All except English/Russian can lead into a
Licence LEA and a *Maîtrise* LEA (*Mention 'Affaires et Commerce'*).

The Departments of Littérature Française et Littérature Générale et
Comparée, Linguistique Française and Arts du Spectacle form part of
the UFR des Sciences de l'Homme. Under the DEUG *rénové*, *Lettres
Modernes* is divided into four strands after the *semestre d'orientation*: I
Enseignement, II *Formation Littéraire Générale* (begins in second year
only), III *Arts du Spectacle*, and IV *Linguistique*. Some courses are common to two or more strands, while others are related to the specialism
chosen. All students are required to take at least one year of Latin (more

if they start as beginners) and to include a modern foreign language in the programme in the second year. DEUG II *Enseignement* is obviously the more 'traditionally'-based course, and contains elements of Medieval Literature, Comparative Literature and Historical Linguistics. The *Formation Littéraire Générale* option consists of two compulsory courses in common with strand I: *Méthodes d'Explication et de Commentaire* and *Description du Français Contemporain*, plus a free choice of DEUG II *Lettres Modernes* offerings.

The programme is strong on methodologically-based courses. Foreign students who wish to enter the course other than in year one may find that their *aménagement d'études* requires them to take a mixture of elements from different years.

The university was totally destroyed in 1944. It was rebuilt on a hillside campus site (Campus I) in a residential area not far from the town centre. Some of the residences, the sports facilities and the CROUS headquarters stand at the top of the hill on the same site.

Courses for foreign students

Centre d'Etudes Françaises pour l'Etranger, SUEE, Université de Caen, 14032 Caen Cedex. Tel: 31 45 55 38. Fax: 31 93 69 19

Full-year courses
During the academic year, which is divided into semesters, instruction is offered at various levels. There are intensive audio-visual programmes for beginners, proficiency courses for the more advanced learner. Teaching is organised mainly in units representing three hours per week of classes, and the normal diet is five units per semester. One semester's study at the appropriate level can lead to either the *Certificat Pratique de Langue Française* (*1er degré*) or the *Diplôme d'Etudes Françaises* (*2e degré*) or the *Diplôme Supérieur d'Etudes Françaises* (*3e degré*). The more advanced courses contain the following options: *lecture et rédaction de textes*, Economics, Economic and Commercial French, Translation Techniques, Contemporary Literature, History, European Studies, *didactique du FLE*, Art and Architecture, Theatre Studies. Candidates must present certified copies of their birth certificate and qualifications and take a placement test on arrival. A very lively and varied programme of evening socio-cultural activities is organised for those enrolled on the courses. A range of accommodation possibilities is available.

Summer courses

The *Cours Internationaux d'Eté* (address as above) operate in four 18-day sessions and offer, on the basis of 45 hours per session, language classes at all levels. Cultural activities are organised in the evenings and there are optional, modestly-priced excursions.

CROUS

23 avenue de Bruxelles, 14040 Cedex. Tel: 31 94 73 37
OTU: same address. Tel: 31 93 70 17
SAEE: same address and telephone

CROUS-controlled accommodation

There are 3,423 rooms in five halls of residence.
- Résidence des Peupliers, Campus I, 23 avenue de Bruxelles 14040 Cedex. Tel: 31 94 73 37
- Résidence des Tilleuls, Campus I, 23 avenue de Bruxelles, 14040 Cedex. Tel: 31 94 73 37
- Résidence de Lébisey, 114–116 rue de Lébisey, 14040 Cedex. Tel: 31 93 06 59
- Résidence de la Côte de Nacre, Campus II, boulevard du Maréchal Juin, 14040 Cedex. Tel: 31 43 80 60
- Résidence d'Hérouville, Quartier de la Cité, 14202 Hérouville-Saint-Clair Cedex. Tel: 31 47 61 23
- Résidence Edmond Bacot, Campus II, 2 boulevard du Maréchal Juin, 14000 Caen. Tel: 31 43 80 60 (*studios* which attract APL)

In addition, some single (furnished) rooms are available in HLM flats in Hérouville-Saint-Clair, as well as furnished HLM flats of different sizes for student families.

CROUS restaurants

There are four restaurants, each with adjoining *cafétéria*. The Faculté de Médecine and the Résidence d'Hérouville-Saint-Clair also have *cafétérias*. In Restaurant A, a 'credit badge' system operates instead of the usual *tickets de restaurant*. Credit is bought in advance, the student selects a meal and the cost is deducted from the 'badge' at the till.
- Restaurant A, Campus I, 23 avenue de Bruxelles. Tel: 31 94 73 37
- Restaurant B, same address. Tel: 31 94 73 37
- Restaurant C, rue du Recteur Daure (near to the Résidence Lébisey). Tel: 31 94 77 35
- Restaurant D, Campus II, boulevard du Maréchal Juin (near to the Résidence de la Côte de Nacre). Tel: 31 43 80 60

Private-sector accommodation

Le Jardin des Sciences de Caen, place Wurzbourg, La Folie
  Couvrechef, 14000. Tel: 31 85 45 45 (138 flats)

Privately-run hostels

For details write to the *Directeur/Directrice*:
CIS, 1 place de l'Europe, 14200 Hérouville-Saint-Clair. Tel: 31 95 41
  00 (costs between 76F and 122F per night for a single room)

The town and its surrounding area

Situated 14 km from the coast, and some 230 km west of Paris, Caen is
the *préfecture* of the Calvados and the capital of its region (Basse-
Normandie), a prosperous agricultural area. It is easily reached by rail
from Paris or by boat direct from Portsmouth (Brittany Ferries to
Ouistreham). The town suffered massive destruction during the
Second World War, but has been tastefully rebuilt around gardens in
the French style.

Miraculously, some of its architectural heritage survived and has
been restored, in particular the huge château, still almost surrounded by
its twelfth-century walls, the Abbaye-aux-Dames and the Abbaye-aux-
Hommes. The *abbayes* were built according to the wishes of Queen
Matilde and William the Conqueror respectively and house their
remains. The Abbaye-aux-Dames is now the seat of the Conseil
Régional, while the Abbaye-aux-Hommes, with its fine Romanesque
architecture, has become the Hôtel de Ville. There are a number of
interesting churches: Saint-Pierre (fourteenth–sixteenth century),
Saint-Nicolas (built in 1083) and Saint-Jean. Buildings such as the
Hôtel d'Escoville (1540), the Maison des Quatrans and the half-
timbered sixteenth-century houses in the rue Saint-Pierre are but some
of the fine examples of civil architecture from the medieval period
onwards to be found around the town.

Among personages of note connected with the town are the poet
François de Malherbe (1555–1628), the printer Christophe Plantin
(1520–1589), the artists Jean Restout le Vieux (1663–1702) and Robert
Tournières (1668–1752), and George Bryan ('Beau') Brummell, who
was appointed Consul in 1830.

Since the war, Caen has seen major expansion, and now has some
120,000 inhabitants. It has developed into a major commercial and
industrial centre, and a thriving port, thanks to the long canal which

links it to the coast. It also has the reputation of being a lively 'young' town, for about 45 per cent of the population is under twenty-five. It enjoys an active cultural life, with its theatres, cinemas and concert halls, and there are ample recreational facilities catering for some sixty sports.

It is at the heart of a region which has much to offer. Bayeux and the Mont Saint-Michel are within easy reach, while for those with interests in more modern 'history' there are the nearby D-Day landing beaches, and the Musée du Débarquement at Arromanches. Inland lies the rural peace of the Normandy countryside or the Gorges de la Vire, ideal territory for exploration on foot, by bicycle or on horseback. There are organisations to promote all these activities (cf. the brochure *Randonnées dans le Calvados et dans la Région*, available from the offices of the Comité Départemental de Tourisme du Calvados, address below). Pre-planned circuits introduce explorers to the delights of local produce, activities and landmarks: *la route du fromage, la route du cidre, la route des traditions, la route des moulins*, etc . . .

Tourist information

Office du Tourisme, place Saint-Pierre. Tel: 31 86 27 65
Comité Départemental de Tourisme du Calvados (CDT), place du Canada, 14000. Tel: 31 86 53 30

Hotels
- Au Départ, 28 place de la Gare. Tel: 31 82 23 98 (warm, inexpensive and convenient for the station; a single room with shower and WC will cost about 230F, including breakfast)
- Hôtel des Cultivateurs, 21 quai de Juillet. Tel: 31 84 64 57 (about the same price as the above, but a little nearer the town centre)
- Auto-Bar, 40 rue de Bras. Tel: 31 86 12 48 (centrally situated; rooms from about 60F)

Youth hostel
Located in the Résidence Robert Rème, 68 rue E Restout, 14300. Tel: 31 52 19 96

Restaurants
- Restaurant Chantegrill, 17 place de la République. Tel: 31 85 23 52 (centrally situated)
- Les Balladins, Hôtel-Grill, avenue du Général de Gaulle, 14200 Hérouville-Saint-Clair (a little way out of town)

In the area near the station, there are a number of inexpensive restaurants offering menus at about 50F, midday and evening, e.g. Super-Mamie Restaurant-Crêperie, 42 rue d'Auge. Tel: 31 83 80 70

Leisure facilities

The Bureau de l'Animation Culturelle in the university (located in the Galerie Vitrée, next to the entrance to the Bâtiment Droit) is responsible for organising and co-ordinating artistic activities on the campus. Events take place mainly in the Amphi Paule Daure and include films, theatre clubs, the university choir, concerts and lectures.

A useful source of information are the monthly magazines, *Le Mois à Caen*, and *Caen Informations: Bulletin d'Informations Municipales* which are available free in various outlets in town.

Museums and art galleries
- Musée des Beaux-Arts (Enceinte du Château). Tel: 31 85 28 63
- Musée de Normandie (Enceinte du Château). Tel: 31 86 06 24
- Musée de la Poste, 52 rue Saint-Pierre. Tel: 31 50 12 20
- Musée d'Anthropologie, 24 place Reine-Mathilde. Tel: 31 86 06 24
- Musée de la Nature (Enceinte de l'Hôtel de Ville). Tel: 31 30 43 27
- Mémorial, un Musée pour la Paix, esplanade Eisenhower. Tel: 31 06 06 44

Theatre
- Théâtre de Caen, 135 boulevard Maréchal Leclerc. Tel: 31 30 76 20
- Comédie de Caen, 32 rue des Cordes. Tel: 31 46 27 27
- Salle George Brassens, promenade Madame de Sévigné. Tel: 31 84 57 49
- Centre Chorégraphique National de Caen-Basse-Normandie, 10 rue Pasteur, 14000. Tel: 31 85 73 16
- Espace Puzzle, 28 rue de Bretagne. Tel: 31 50 04 52
- Théâtre d'Ostreland, 9–18 quartier du Grand Parc, Hérouville. Tel: 31 95 56 00
- Théâtre du Gros Caillou, 5 rue de l'Arquette. Tel: 31 34 40 40
- Théâtre d'Hérouville, square du Théâtre, Hérouville. Tel: 31 95 65 00
- Conservatoire National de Région de Caen (Petit Auditorium and Grand Auditorium), 1 rue du Carel, 14027 Caen Cedex. Tel: 31 86 42 00
- Chants, Danses, Musiques Traditionnels de Basse-Normandie et d'Ailleurs, Centre d'Animation du Calvaire St-Pierre, 7–9 rue de la Défense Passive (for details tel: 31 93 37 58 *or* 31 50 20 46 *or* 31 74 42 75)

Maisons des Jeunes et de la Culture
- Chemin-Vert, 1 rue d'Isigny. Tel: 31 73 29 90
- La Prairie, 11 avenue Albert Sorel. Tel: 31 85 25 16
- La Maladrerie, 25 rue du Général Moulin. Tel: 31 74 41 02
- Grâce-de-Dieu, 1 place Lavoisier. Tel: 31 52 11 09
- La Guerinière, 6 rue des Bouviers. Tel: 31 82 22 25
- Saint-Pierre, 7–9 rue de la Défense-Passive. Tel: 31 93 11 08
- Venoix, 19 rue Gallieni. Tel: 31 73 72 51

Cinema
- Pathé-Cinémas, 17 boulevard Maréchal Leclerc. Tel: 36 68 20 22
- Lux, Studio du 7ème Art, avenue Sainte-Thérèse. Tel: 31 82 29 87
- Pathé-Cinémas, 55 rue des Jacobins. Tel: 36 68 20 22 (7 screens)

The CROUS also runs a ciné-club, the CORAC, which meets roughly once a fortnight in the Foyer du CROUS.

Sport
FNSU: CSU, esplanade de la Paix. Tel: 31 45 55 54
Football: Stade Malherbe Caennais (the professional club), 74 boulevard Detolle. Tel: 31 74 69 91
Ice hockey: Hockey Club de Caen (the professional side), Patinoire Municipale, rue de la Varende. Tel: 31 85 66 60
Skating: Patinoire Municipale, avenue Albert Sorel. Tel: 31 86 04 12
Swimming: Piscine Municipale, avenue Albert Sorel. Tel: 31 86 04 12
Rugby: rue d'Alsace. Tel: 31 74 44 32
The SUAPS offers facilities in some 30 types of activity. Details of times and places may be obtained from the Bureau d'Accueil, Bâtiment Lettres, Campus I. Tel: 31 45 55 94

Useful addresses

Main post office: place Gambetta. Tel: 31 39 35 78
Municipal library: place Guillouard. Tel: 31 86 22 01
Bookshops:
- FNAC, Centre Commercial Paul Doumer, rue Demolombe. Tel: 31 50 20 50
- Maxi-Livres, rue Demolombe
- Librairie Universitaire Au Brouillon de Culture, 29 rue St Sauveur. Tel: 31 50 12 76

CAF: 8 avenue du 6 Juin. Tel: 31 30 90 90
CIJ: 104 boulevard du Maréchal Leclerc, 14000. Tel: 31 85 73 60

Préfecture: rue Saint Laurent. Tel: 31 30 41 00
Two organisations catering specifically for newcomers:
- Caen-Accueil, 45 rue Ecuyère. Tel: 31 86 02 60
- Bienvenue à Caen (introductions to French families), Service des Affaires Culturelles, Porte B, Hôtel de Ville. Tel: 31 30 43 85

Information on opportunities for voluntary work may be obtained from:
Le Centre de Volontariat de l'Agglomération Caennaise, 5 place de la Résistance, 14300. Tel: 31 85 74 08
Nearest British Consulate: 9 quai Georges V, 76600 Le Havre. Tel: 35 42 27 47
Nearest US Consulate (Paris): 2 avenue Gabriel, 75382 Paris Cedex 8. Tel: (1) 42 96 12 02. Fax: (1) 42 66 97 83

Health care

CHU: Côte de Nacre, 14032 Cedex.
Nearest chemist to halls on Campus I is in the rue de Gaillon.
SUMP (Campus I, near to the Résidence Universitaire des Peupliers, Tel: 31 93 18 64) is open from 9.00 to 17.00 hours and offers treatment by appointment.
Local student insurance offices:
- MNEF, Résidence Universitaire Les Tilleuls, Pavillon D, Campus I, 14034 Cedex. Tel: 31 86 00 58
- SMENO, 40 avenue de la Libération, 14000. Tel: 31 94 41 53

Travel

Railway station
Place de la Gare, 14300. Tel: 31 83 50 50 (information) *or* 31 34 11 64 (reservations). London-Caen (via Newhaven-Dieppe) £98 return; (via Dover-Calais) £103 return (Eurotrain)

Coach station
Next to the Gare SNCF. The cost of a youth return London-Caen by coach (Eurolines) is £40. The single fare is £34. Higher fares apply during the peak period (July–September).

Airport
Caen-Carpiquet. Tel: 31 26 58 00

Taxis
Abbeilles (24h service). Tel: 31 52 17 89

Local buses

- Syndicat Mixte des Transports en Commun de l'Agglomération Caennaise (CTAC), 14000. Tel: 31 85 42 76. Individual tickets are valid 1 hour; there are concessions on a *carnet* of 10 tickets with a student card. For journeys further afield, there are the Bus Verts:
- STDC, 11 rue des Chanoines, 14000. Tel: 31 44 77 44. Concessionary rates are available.

Emergencies

CHR-CHU. Tel: 31 44 81 12
Ambulances (24-hour service). Tel: 31 34 35 36
SOS Amitié, BP 78, 14014 Cedex. Tel: 31 44 89 89
Details of the duty chemist and of the roster of night chemists are published in the monthly bulletin of the municipal tourist office.

6 Clermont-Ferrand

The universities and their disciplines

Université d'Auvergne (**Clermont-Ferrand I**): droit et sciences économiques, formations de santé, technologie.
49 boulevard Gergovia, BP 32, 63001 Clermont-Ferrand Cedex. Tel: 73 35 55 20. Fax: 73 35 55 18
SUIO: 36 bis boulevard Côte Blatin, 63000 Clermont-Ferrand. Tel: 73 93 64 46
IUT: Ensemble Universitaire Cézeaux, 63170 Aubière. Tel: 73 26 41 10
Université Blaise Pascal (**Clermont-Ferrand II**): lettres et sciences humaines, sciences exactes et naturelles, technologie, activités physiques et sportives.
34 avenue Carnot, BP 185, 63006 Clermont-Ferrand. Tel: 73 40 63 63. Fax: 73 40 64 31
SUIO: 36 bis boulevard Côte Blatin, 63000 Clermont-Ferrand. Tel: 73 93 64 46
SUEE: same address

IUT: avenue Aristide Briand, BP 408, 03107 Montluçon. Tel: 70 29 36
55

University libraries
- Section Lettres, 29 boulevard Gergovia. Tel: 73 34 65 92
- Section Droit et Sciences Economiques, 41 boulevard Gergovia. Tel:
  73 43 42 90
- Section Médecine, Pharmacie, Odontologie, 28 place Henri Dunant.
  Tel: 73 26 60 54
- Section Sciences et Techniques, Campus des Cézeaux, Aubière.
  Tel: 73 40 74 90

Courses for languages undergraduates

LEA offers the following modern foreign languages: Arabic, English,
German, Italian, Portuguese, Russian and Spanish.

In *Lettres Modernes* there are core courses on the French language
(grammar, morphology and phonetics) and on French literature from
the medieval period to the twentieth century. Optional courses include
Latin, Greek, Comparative Literature, Communication Skills, History,
History of Art, Literature and Stylistics, Civilisation, Occitan, Linguistics, Media Studies, and a choice of modern foreign languages (English,
German, Italian, Portuguese, Russian, Spanish and Esperanto).

Courses for foreign students

Term-time courses
Service Interuniversitaire des Etudiants Etrangers (SIEE), Université
  Blaise Pascal, 34 avenue Carnot, 63000 Clermont-Ferrand. Tel: 73
  40 64 97. Fax: 73 40 64 31
Full- and half-year courses are available. Students are taught in small
groups for 14 hours per week. For beginners, there are audio-visual
courses sanctioned by an attendance certificate. For more advanced
students there are half-year courses leading to a *Certificat Pratique de
Langue Française (1er degré)* or a *Diplôme d'Etudes Françaises (2ème degré)*,
and for a full-year's successful study a *Diplôme Supérieur d'Etudes
Françaises (3ème degré)*. All students should be over 18 and have the
equivalent of the *baccalauréat*. Accommodation is arranged in halls of
residence or in private hostels. Extra-curricular activities include music,
theatre and cinema, as well as archaeology and sport.

Vacation courses
The SIEE (for address and telephone see above) also organises four-

week courses in September for students of all levels. Teaching is in groups of 15 for 20 hours per week. The programme of study focuses on practical aspects of French language and civilisation. Participants are usually housed either in university halls of residence or in privately-run hostels. Leisure activities include excursions to the extinct volcanoes of the Auvergne and archeological sites as well as the more traditional visits to local theatres, cinemas and concert halls.

CAVILAM, 14 rue du Maréchal Foch, 03200 Vichy Cedex. Tel: 70 32 25 22. Fax: 70 97 99 80

During the months of July, August and September, study-programmes are jointly mounted by the University of Clermont and the town of Vichy. Students must be at least 16 years of age and take a placement test on arrival. Teaching is in groups of 15. There are courses of one week or more for beginners in the French language, with twelve options including Contemporary French Civilisation, Literature, and Commercial French. For the more advanced student there are courses which prepare modules in the DALF and DELF programmes. There is also the *Certificat Pratique de Français Commercial et Economique* and the *Diplôme Supérieur de Français des Affaires*. For practising teachers of French there are two courses: *formation théorique* (from mid-July to early August) and the complementary *stage pratique* (which follows on in August). Various forms of accommodation are organised by CAVILAM. An extensive and wide-ranging programme of cultural, leisure and social activities is provided.

CROUS

25 rue Etienne-Dolet, 63037 Clermont-Ferrand Cedex. Tel: 73 34 44 00. Fax: 73 35 12 85
OTU: same address and telephone, ext. 513
SAEE: same address and telephone

CROUS-controlled accommodation
There are some 2,400 rooms available in halls with additional accommodation in HLM for married couples.
- Résidence Amboise, 11 rue d'Amboise. Tel: 73 92 54 86 (females; 135 rooms)
- Résidence des Céseaux, BP 146, rue Roche-Genès, 63173 Aubière Cedex. Tel: 73 26 41 81 (males: 306 rooms; females: 306 rooms; and 115 *studios*).
- Résidence du Clos St-Jacques, 25 rue Etienne-Dolet. Tel: 73 34 44

00 (mixed; 1,156 rooms and 4 for disabled students)
- Résidence Philippe Lebon, 28 boulevard Côte Blatin. Tel: 73 91 79 09 (females; 485 rooms)

CROUS-controlled restaurants

There are four self-service restaurants offering a variety of facilities.
- Restaurant du Clos St-Jacques, 25 rue Etienne-Dolet, Bât. A (first floor, traditional menu with choice of dishes; ground floor, cafeteria and grill)
- Restaurant Philippe Lebon, 28 boulevard Côte Blatin (traditional menu with some choice of dishes)
- Restaurant La Rotonde, rue de la Rotonde, UFR de Droit (traditional menu and grills)
- Restaurant Les Cézeaux, Campus des Cézeaux, 63170 Aubière (three choices are offered: the set menu, a single course with sweet, or a *brasserie* menu)

Privately-run hostels

- Foyer Notre Dame, 8 rue de Lezoux, 63000. Tel: 73 91 41 10 (females; 85 rooms)
- Foyer Home Dôme, 12 place de Regensburg, 68038. Tel: 73 93 07 82 (mixed; 480 rooms)
- Foyer Sainte Marguerite, 15 rue Gaultier-de-Biazat, 63000. Tel: 73 37 23 62 (females; 140 rooms)

The town and its surrounding area

With a population of 150,000, Clermont-Ferrand is the thriving industrial capital of the Auvergne. Most readily associated, perhaps, with Michelin tyres, the town is also a centre for a variety of chemical and metallurgical industries, as well as factories producing such varied goods as jam, chocolate and polished precious stones. Clermont-Ferrand has a rich past reflected in its old districts, with notable buildings such as the cathedral, the romanesque church Notre-Dame du Port, and several fine town houses. The new Musée des Beaux-Arts has works from the Middle Ages to the twentieth century, the Musée Bargoin has important Gallo-Roman collections, while the Musée Lecocq houses the region's geological and natural history exhibits. The city enjoys an active cultural life and its universities, Grandes Ecoles and other institutes of higher education attract some 30,000 students, including 1,500 foreign students. Standing at the foot of the Puys mountain range, with, to the west, the famous Puy de Dôme, Clermont-Ferrand is a good tourist base for hiking in the Parc des Volcans or for enjoying the many forests, rivers and lakes of the Massif Central. Among the famous associated with Clermont-Ferrand are the troubadour Pierre d'Auvergne (c.1130), the scholar Savaron (1550–1622), the philosopher Blaise Pascal (1623–62), Chamfort the moralist (1741–94) and Pierre Teilhard de Chardin (1881–1955). The town is accessible by motorway (A71), has regular trains to Paris, and local services to Lyon.

Tourist information

Office Municipal du Tourisme, 69 boulevard Gergovia, 63000 Clermont-Ferrand. Tel: 73 93 30 20. Fax: 73 93 56 26

Hotels
The price of a single room with breakfast in the following hotels is between 150F and 225F:
- Hôtel Foch, 22 rue Maréchal Foch. Tel: 73 93 48 40 (near town centre)
- Hôtel des Commerçants, 51 avenue de l'Union Soviétique. Tel: 73 92 37 19. Fax: 73 91 87 81 (opposite railway station; restaurant with meals ranging from 50F to 150F)
- Floride II, cours Raymond Poincaré. Tel: 73 35 00 20

Youth hostel
Auberge du Cheval Blanc, 55 avenue de l'Union Soviétique, 63100. Tel: 73 92 26 39 (closed November to March; membership of YHA obligatory)

Restaurants
- Les Commerçants, 51 avenue de l'Union Soviétique. Tel: 73 92 37 19 (menus from 50F to 150F)
- La Crémaillère, 61 avenue de l'Union Soviétique. Tel: 73 90 89 25 (menus 38F and 60F)
- Café Riquier, 11 rue de l'Etoile. Tel: 73 36 67 25 (menus from 49F to 89F)

Fast food
- McDonalds, 51–53 avenue des Etats-Unis. Tel: 73 37 12 05
- Quick Hamburger, Centre Jaude. Tel: 73 93 08 85

Leisure facilities

Office Municipal des Loisirs et de la Jeunesse: rue Lacépède. Tel: 73 92 90 26

Service Interuniversitaire d'Activités Artistiques, 29 boulevard Gergovia. Tel: 73 35 57 47

Theatre and music
- Opéra Desaix, boulevard Desaix. Tel: 73 37 56 88
- Orchestre d'Auvergne, 2 rue Urbain II. Tel: 73 92 39 11
- Musique Université, 28 boulevard Côte-Blatin. Tel: 73 35 57 47
- Maison des Congrès et de la Culture, boulevard Gergovia. Tel: 73 35 50 10
- Maison du Peuple, place de la Liberté. Tel: 73 37 81 50
- Théâtre du Pélican, 49 rue de la Libération. Tel: 73 68 39 61
- L'Oeil Ecoute, 3 rue Gaultier-de-Biauzat. Tel: 73 30 82 00
- Préambule Le Valet de Coeur, 8 rue Antoine-d'Auvergne. Tel: 73 91 20 66

Amateur theatrical groups
- Comédie Gauloise, 31 cours Sablon. Tel: 73 91 76 82
- Théâtre de la Plaine, 1 rue Huguet, Aulnat. Tel: 73 61 26 97
- CRAD, 5 rue Gilbert-Gaillard. Tel: 73 38 22 56.

Cinema
- Pathé Capitole, 32 place de Jaude. Tel: 73 93 55 75 (5 screens)
- Pathé Jaude, Centre Commercial Jaude. Tel: 73 93 27 15 (7 screens)
- Paris, 8 place de la Résistance. Tel: 73 34 19 39 (4 screens)
- Cinémonde, place de la Résistance. Tel: 73 93 54 98

Museums and art galleries
- Musée des Beaux-Arts, place Louis Deteix. Tel: 73 23 08 49 (student rate 11F)
- Musée Bargoin, 45 rue Ballainvilliers. Tel: 73 93 30 20
- Musée du Ranquet, 1 rue Saint-Pierre. Tel: 73 37 38 63
- Musée Lecocq, 15 rue Bardoux. Tel: 73 91 93 78

Sport and recreation
FNSU: Campus Universitaire Les Cézeaux, BP 51, 63173 Aubière Cedex. Tel: 73 40 70 34

Office Municipal des Sports: 121 avenue de la Libération. Tel: 73 93 16 97

Association Sportive Montferrandaise (ASM): Stade de la Gauthière, 84 boulevard Léon-Jouhaux. Tel: 73 24 87 01

ASPTT Clermont: 32 rue Bansac. Tel: 73 27 58 95

SIUAPS: 15 bis rue Poncillon. Tel: 73 93 24 18

Maison des Sports, place des Bughes. Tel: 73 92 17 05

Bowling: 88 avenue du Brézet. Tel: 73 92 17 66 (weekdays before 8 p.m. student rate 14F)

Ice skating: rue Gustave Flaubert. Tel: 73 26 22 96 (closed Mondays)

Swimming:

- Stade Nautique Pierre de Coubertin, place Pierre-Coubertin. Tel: 73 93 06 95
- Piscine de Flamina, chemin de Flamina. Tel: 73 24 64 50

Tennis:

- Tennis Flamina. Tel: 73 24 43 47
- Tennis des Cézeaux. Tel: 73 27 22 71
- Tennis Croix de Neyrat. Tel: 73 24 74 71

Useful addresses

Main post office: 1 rue Louis Renon. Tel: 73 30 63 00

Municipal library: 1 boulevard Lafayette. Tel: 73 92 41 18

Bookshops:

- FNAC, Centre Jaude. Tel: 73 93 22 00
- Librairie Gibert, 42 avenue des Etats-Unis. Tel: 73 37 31 88
- Librairie Les Volcans, 88 boulevard Gergovia
- Librairie Abbé Girard, 13 place du Champgil. Tel: 73 36 60 49

ANPE:

- 67 boulevard Lafayette. Tel: 73 92 20 32
- 87 rue Edith Piaf. Tel: 73 25 21 20

CAF: Cité Administratif, rue Pélissier. Tel: 73 42 80 00

CIJ: 8 place de Regensburg. Tel: 73 35 10 10

CPAM: Cité Administratif, rue Pélissier. Tel: 73 42 81 00

Mairie: 10 rue Philippe-Marcombes. Tel: 73 42 63 63

Nearest British Consulate-General (Lyon): 24 rue Childebert, 69002 Lyon. Tel: 78 37 59 67. Fax: 72 40 25 24

Nearest US Consulate (Lyon): 45 rue de la Bourse, Lyon. Tel: 72 40 59 20. Fax: 72 41 71 81

Health care

Hospital: Hôpital Gabriel Montpied, 30 place Henri Dunant. Tel: 73
62 57 00
Chemists:
- Pharmacie Ducher, 1 place Delille. Tel: 73 91 31 77 (24-hour
service)
- Pharmacie Sarret, 13 place Delille. Tel: 73 92 60 55

SIUMP: 25 rue Etienne-Dolet, Pavillon B. Tel: 73 93 29 88
Local student insurance offices:
- MNEF, 16 boulevard Lafayette. Tel: 73 92 21 96
- SMERRA, 10 rue Kessler, 63038. Tel: 73 35 16 95

Travel

Railway station
Avenue de l'Union Soviétique. Tel: 73 92 50 50. London to Clermont-
Ferrand (via Newhaven-Dieppe) £112 return; via Dover-Calais £116
return (Eurotrain)

Bus/coach station
Boulevard Gergovia. Tel: 73 93 13 61. (8h30–18h30).
There is no direct coach link to Clermont-Ferrand; the nearest towns
served by coach are Lyon and Limoges. The return fares to these
destinations are respectively £82 and £76 (Eurolines).

Local buses
Transports en Commun de l'Agglomeration Clermontoise (T2C),
15–17 boulevard Robert Schuman. Tel: 73 26 44 90. Single tickets 6F.
Day/monthly/annual passes at reduced rates.

Taxis
- Allo Taxi, 18 rue Ballainvilliers. Tel: 73 90 75 75
- Radio Taxi, 7 place de la Victoire. Tel: 73 92 57 58

Emergencies

Police. 73 92 10 17
SAMU. 73 27 33 33

7 Dijon

The university and its disciplines

Université de Bourgogne: droit et sciences politiques, sciences économiques et de gestion, lettres et sciences humaines, sciences exactes,
biologiques, médicales et pharmaceutiques, technologie.
Campus Universitaire de Montmuzard, BP 138, 21004 Dijon. Tel:
80 39 50 00. Fax: 80 39 50 69
IUT: rue du Docteur Petit-Jean, BP 510, 21014 Cedex. Tel: 80 39 64
00
SUIO: Campus Universitaire de Montmuzard, BP 138, 21004 Dijon.
Tel: 80 39 52 40

University libraries
- Bibliothèque Universitaire, rue de Sully (main campus, next to Pa-
villon Lamartine)
- (Town centre): Ancienne Faculté, 36 rue Chabot-Charny

Courses for languages undergraduates

LEA offers the following modern foreign languages: English, German,
Italian, Spanish and Russian.
Lettres Modernes courses tend to be of a fairly 'traditional' nature, and
students who have no qualification in Latin are obliged to follow the
beginners' course. Interesting options include Canadian Literature,
Film and History of Art. Organisation of courses tends to be good; the
campus is modern and is situated to the south-east of the town.

Courses for foreign students

Centre International d'Etudes Françaises (CIEF), Ancienne Faculté
des Lettres, 36 rue Chabot-Charny, 21000 Dijon. Tel: 80 30 50 20
The well-established CIEF, based at the Ancienne Faculté near the
centre of the town, offers a very wide range of term-time and summer
courses whose duration varies from four weeks to a full academic year.
Summer courses are run in July and August only.

Term-time courses
Beginners' courses are available during the academic year and the
following certificates and diplomas are on offer: *Certificat Pratique de*

Langue Française (1er degré) (this corresponds to the DELF), *Diplôme d'Etudes Françaises (2e degré)* (corresponds to the DALF), *Diplôme Supérieur d'Etudes Françaises (3e degré)*. The centre organises cultural visits, excursions and sporting activities.

Vacation courses

Registration can be for four, six or eight weeks. Beginners' courses entail 23 hours per week and groups are of a maximum of 18 students. The Centre offers *Cours de langue générale (niveaux 1, 2, 3)*. At levels 2 and 3 there are *cours de langue, littérature et civilisation françaises*, whilst options include Literature, Linguistics, History, History of Art, French Song, Commercial French and Translation. There are courses for teachers of FLE and options include Literature, Theory of Linguistics, History, History of Art and Economics. The *stages pédagogiques* also include translation (English, German, Italian, Spanish and – August only – Japanese).

CROUS

3 rue du Docteur Maret, 21012 Dijon Cedex. Tel: 80 40 40 40. Fax: 80 58 94 57

SAEE: same address and telephone

OTU: Antenne Montmuzard, 6B Marcel Bouchard, Campus Universitaire Montmuzard, 21000 Dijon. Tel: 80 39 69 33

CROUS-controlled accommodation

Dijon has 2,617 beds in its *résidences universitaires*. The buildings are modern and Montmuzard and Mansard, for example, are situated adjacent to the main campus. All facilities for the working week are therefore close at hand. Rules concerning noise are quite strictly enforced, as they are in French *résidences* generally. It is possible to walk into the town centre (it takes about half an hour). The bus service is good during the day and in the evening.

- Résidence Universitaire Maret, 3 rue du Docteur Maret. Tel: 80 40 40 38
- Résidence Universitaire Montmuzard, 6 rue du Recteur Bouchard. Tel: 80 39 68 01
- Résidence Universitaire Mansard, 94 boulevard Mansard. Tel: 80 66 18 22
- Résidence Universitaire Beaune, 37 rue du Recteur Bouchard. Tel: 80 39 69 51

CROUS restaurants
- Maret (see above). Tel: 80 40 40 32
- Montmuzard (see above). Tel: 80 39 69 01
- Mansard (see above). Tel: 80 66 39 85

Privately-run hostels

- Association Educative Saint Dominique, 21 rue Claude Bouchu, 21000. Tel: 80 71 39 01
- Foyer des Etudiants, 65 rue Saumaise, 21000. Tel: 80 67 18 00
- Foyer International d'Etudiants, 6 rue du Maréchal Leclerc, 21000. Tel: 80 71 51 01
- Foyer Lacordaire, 3 rue Turgot, 21000. Tel: 80 30 09 21

The town and its surrounding area

Dijon, capital city of the old province of Burgundy, is the *chef-lieu* of the Côte-d'Or. Situated some 310 km south-east of Paris, the town is easily accessible by rail (there is a direct TGV link to Paris) and by road.

The town is noted for its high gastronomic standards, and contains countless buildings of outstanding architectural merit. Of particular interest are the Palais des Ducs de Bourgogne (which is now the Hôtel de Ville and houses one of France's finest provincial museums, the Musée des Beaux-Arts), the Palais de Justice and the Cour de Bar (with its Tour de Bar and Tour de Philippe le Bon). There are many churches ranging from the medieval to the modern; the cathedral is that of St-Bénigne. In the summer there is a music festival, a theatre festival and the Fêtes de la Vigne. Wine-tasting in the vineyards of Burgundy is a popular leisure activity amongst tourists and foreign students. The town boasts a theatre and a number of cinemas, which offer a wide choice of films. There is a good bus service. Restaurants vary greatly in price, but it is possible to eat quite cheaply in a self-service restaurant in the centre of town. The shopping centre is good (shops range from department stores to specialist boutiques). The shop which specialises in mustard is well worth a visit.

Tourist information

Tourist office: place Darcy, 21000 Dijon. Tel: 80 43 42 12. Also 34 rue des Forges. Tel: 80 30 35 39

Hotels
- Hôtel Continental, 7–9 rue Docteur Albert Rémy. Tel: 80 43 34 67 (very close to the railway station. Fairly recently refurbished; rooms cost 220F–240F. The restaurant is also good value)
- Hôtel de Paris, 9–11 avenue Foch. Tel: 80 43 41 88 (a single room with shower and toilet costs 190F; breakfast 20F; the hotel has its own grill/pizzeria)
- Hôtel Terminus, 24 avenue Foch. Tel: 80 43 53 78 (rooms cost 200F–300F)
- Hôtel Chateaubriand, 3 avenue Foch. Tel 80 41 42 18 (a single room costs 135F; breakfast 24F)

Youth hostel
Centre de Rencontres Internationales, 1 boulevard Champollion. Tel: 80 71 32 12 (single room with breakfast 120F; self-service dinner 42F)

Restaurants
Pizzerias offer the cheapest meals in Dijon and the only real possibility for vegetarians (pizzas and pasta dishes cost about 30F–40F). The following are typical:
- Version Latine, 16 rue Odebert
- Pizzeria Paolo, 1 bis avenue Foch
- Pizzeria Coppa, 12 rue Audra
- Pizzeria au feu de bois, 41 rue Pasteur

For a more expensive meal the Brasserie du Théâtre, place du Théâtre, is recommended.

Leisure facilities

Theatres/museums
- Théâtre de Dijon, place du Théâtre. Tel: 80 67 20 21 (in the centre of town)
- Nouveau Theâtre de Bourgogne, situated at the Théâtre du Parvis St-Jean, place Bossuet
- Musée des Beaux-Arts, place de la Sainte Chapelle (of interest; entry is free for students)

Sport
FNSU: CRU-UEREPS, BP 138, 21004 Dijon Cedex. Tel: 80 39 67 91
Palais des Sports, rue Léon Mauris.
Swimming pool: Cours du Parc, next to parc de la Colombière (access

via cours Général de Gaulle)

Useful addresses

Post office:
- (town centre) place Grangier. Tel: 80 43 81 00
- (campus) boulevard Mansard

Bookshops:
- Librairie de l'Université, 17 rue de la Liberté
- FNAC, rue de Bourg (in town centre)

CIJ: 22 rue Audra. Tel: 80 30 35 56 (a useful source of general information)

CAF: 8 boulevard Georges Clemenceau. Tel: 80 70 40 40

Nearest British Consulate-General (Lyon): 24 rue Childebert, 69002 Lyon. Tel: 78 37 59 67. Fax: 72 40 25 24

Nearest US Consulate (Lyon): 45 rue de la Bourse. Tel: 72 40 59 20. Fax: 72 41 71 81

Health care

Hospital: Hôpital Général, 3 rue Faubourg Raines. Tel: 80 41 81 41

SUMP: rue du Recteur Bouchard (on campus)

The nearest chemist to the campus is on the corner of boulevard Gabriel/boulevard de l'Université (about 5 minutes' walk from the halls of residence).

Local student insurance offices:
- MNEF, 13–15 rue Berlier (close to place Wilson). Tel: 80 67 15 35
- SMEREB, 11 ter boulevard Voltaire. Tel: 80 65 21 27

Travel

Railway station

Gare Foch, avenue Foch. Tel: 80 42 11 00. London-Dijon (via Newhaven-Dieppe) £112 return; (via Dover–Calais) £116 return (Eurotrain)

Coach station

Adjacent to the railway station. London-Dijon £82 return, £51 single (Eurolines)

Local travel
STRD. Tel: 80 30 60 90. Bus tickets for local travel cost 37F50 for a *carnet* of 12; single tickets 5F. Bus no. 9 runs from the station to the university, as does the no. 12 which goes on to Quétigny. There is an evening bus service every day.

Taxis
Taxi Radio Dijon, cour Gare. Tel: 80 41 41 12

Emergencies

SAMU. Tel: 80 41 12 12
SOS Amitiés. Tel: 80 67 15 15
Police: 2 place Suquet. Tel: 80 41 81 05

8 Grenoble

The universities and their disciplines

Université Joseph Fourier (**Grenoble I**): sciences exactes et naturelles, sciences biologiques, médicales et pharmaceutiques, géographie, éducation physique, technologie.
   621 avenue Centrale, Domaine Universitaire de Saint-Martin d'Hères, BP 53X, 38041 Grenoble Cedex. Tel: 76 51 46 00. Fax: 76 51 48 48
SUIO: Bibliothèque des Sciences, same address. Tel: 76 51 46 21
IUT: Domaine Universitaire, BP 62, 38042 Saint-Martin d'Hères Cedex. Tel: 76 82 53 00
Université Pierre Mendès France (**Grenoble II**): sciences économiques, juridiques et politiques, lettres et sciences humaines, technologie.
   Domaine Universitaire de Saint-Martin d'Hères, BP 47X, 38040 Grenoble Cedex. Tel: 76 82 54 00. Fax: 76 82 56 54
SUIO: same address. Tel: 76 82 55 45
IUT: place Doyen Gosse, 38031 Grenoble Cedex. Tel: 76 46 60 81
Université Stendhal (**Grenoble III**): langues, communications et lettres.
   Domaine Universitaire de Saint-Martin d'Hères, BP 25X, 38040 Grenoble Cedex 9. Tel: 76 82 43 00. Fax: 76 82 43 84
SUIO: same address, Bureau 332. Tel: 76 82 43 11

Main library: Bibliothèque Interuniversitaire de Grenoble, BP 56, 38402 St-Martin d'Hères Cedex. Tel: 76 44 82 18

Courses for languages undergraduates

LEA offers the following modern foreign languages: Arabic, Czech, English, German, Greek, Hebrew, Italian, Japanese, Polish, Portuguese, Romanian, Russian and Serbo-Croat.

In *Lettres Modernes*, there are courses in French language and literature (from the medieval period to the present day), Comparative Literature, the language, civilisation and literature of other countries (see languages listed above), History of Ideas in England and the USA, Latin and Greek, Classical Civilisation, Linguistics, General Linguistics, Phonetics, the Press, the Language of Advertising, Art, Cinema, Theatre and Sport.

ERASMUS Diploma

Students of those institutions with an exchange agreement with Grenoble which is supported by ERASMUS funding may enrol for a *Diplôme d'Université d'Etudes Européennes Intégrées (1er* or *2e cycle)*. Candidates are required to follow two compulsory courses in Translation and Methodology, together with four other modules taken from a wide range offered as part of existing programmes.

Courses for foreign students

Centre Universitaire d'Etudes Françaises (CUEF), BP 25X, 38040 Grenoble Cedex 9. Tel: 76 82 43 27 *or* 76 42 48 37. Fax: 76 82 43 84

Full-year or semester-based courses

Applicants must be at least 17 years of age and there is a placement test on arrival. Students are taught in groups of 15 for 20 hours per week. There are courses on French language, literature and civilisation from beginners' to advanced levels over two semesters, leading to the *Certificat Pratique de Langue Française (1er degré)*, or the *Diplôme d'Etudes Françaises (2e degré)*, or the *Diplôme Supérieur d'Etudes Françaises (3e degré)*. There are also courses for teachers of French leading to the *Diplôme Supérieur d'Aptitude à l'Enseignement du Français Langue Etrangère*. Accommodation is usually with families in town. There are many leisure activities including skiing, tennis, golf and the majority of team sports.

Vacation courses

The CUEF (for address, telephone and fax numbers, see above) organises a general intensive study of French in four-week periods during July, August and September at beginners', intermediate and advanced levels. Applicants must be at least 17 years of age and sit a placement test on arrival. Students are taught in groups of 15–20 for 20 hours per week. There are options in Literature, Civilisation, History of Art and Art. Accommodation is provided in student halls. Leisure activities include walks in the mountains, and tennis.

CROUS

5 rue d'Arsonval, BP 187, 38019 Grenoble Cedex. Tel: 76 87 07 62
   Fax: 76 47 78 03
OTU: same address and telephone
SAEE: same address and telephone

CROUS-controlled accommodation
- Résidence d'Arsonval, 16 rue Casimir Brenier. Tel: 76 87 07 62 (females; 52 rooms)
- Home d'Etudiantes, 2 avenue du Général Champon. Tel: 76 47 13 54 (females; 152 rooms)
- Maison des Etudiants, 6 place Pasteur. Tel: 76 47 13 54 (mixed; 291 single rooms and 72 doubles)
- Résidence Rabot, rue Maurice Gignoux. Tel: 76 87 44 65 (mixed; 600 rooms)
- Cité Olympique, avenue Edmond Esmonin. Tel: 76 23 08 63 (mixed; 798 rooms)
On the campus:
- Résidence Berlioz. Tel: 76 54 35 45 (mixed; 900 rooms)
- Résidence Condillac. Tel: 76 42 00 36 (mixed; 800 rooms)
- Résidence Gabriel Fauré. Tel: 76 54 40 54 (mixed; 300 rooms)
- Résidence Ouest. Tel: 76 54 28 18 (mixed; 993 rooms and 33 rooms for disabled students)

CROUS restaurants on the campus
- Restaurant de Barnave
- Restaurant Diderot
- Restaurant d'Arsonval
All provide the *menu traditionnel* as well as a *cafétéria* service.

Other CROUS restaurants
- Home d'Etudiantes, 2 rue du Général Champon
- Maison des Etudiants, 6 place Pasteur
- Rabot, rue Maurice Gignoux

Private-sector accommodation

The ALEG-CLEF runs a number of *résidences* with 275 *studios* in Résidence Academy, Résidence Cambridge, Résidence Saint-Charles. For details contact ALEG-CLEF: 15 allée du Jardin-Hoche, 38000 Grenoble. Tel: 76 87 22 73.

Privately-run hostels

For further information write to the *Directeur/Directrice*:
- Foyer de l'Etudiante, 4 rue Sainte Ursule. Tel: 76 42 00 84
- Maison Catholique de l'Etudiante, 13 avenue Gabriel Péri, St-Martin d'Hères. Tel: 76 42 42 49
- Foyer des Jeunes, 8 place Lavalette. Tel: 76 42 36 20
- Foyer Le Taillefer, 12 rue du 140e RIA. Tel: 76 51 35 05

The town and its surrounding area

Capital of the French Alps, Grenoble stands close by the confluence of the Isère and the Drac and is surrounded by mountain ranges: to the north the Grande-Chartreuse massif, to the south-west the Vercors and to the east the Belledonne range. The town has a population of 400,000, with over 40,000 students attending its academic institutions. The university was founded in 1389 and is one of the oldest in Europe. The modern campus at St-Martin d'Hères includes halls of residence and is linked to the town centre by regular tram and bus services. Among the famous historical figures associated with Grenoble are the philosophers Abbé Mably (1709–85), Condillac (1777–1832) and Jean-Jacques Rousseau (1712–1778), the author Henry Beyle (Stendhal) (1783–1842), the painter Théodore Fantin-Latour (1836–1904), the mechanical engineer Jacques de Vaucanson (1709–82) and Napoleon Bonaparte (1769–1821). There are several buildings worthy of note: the Palais de Justice (sixteenth–nineteenth century), the modern plate-glass Town Hall (1967) by Maurice Noravina, the Musée des Beaux-Arts, the Musée Dauphinois and, overlooking the town, the Fort de la Bastille, which is accessible on foot or by cable-car. A former host to the

Winter Olympics, Grenoble has a long tradition as a centre for skiing and there are some twenty resorts in the region. Other sporting activities are encouraged with over 250 tennis courts, 20 swimming pools and a covered ice-rink. The mountains provide good walking, rock-climbing and pot-holing. Grenoble is served by two international airports: Lyon-Satolas and Grenoble-St-Geoirs. Mountain cheeses such as Emmental, Beaufort or Reblochon are to be enjoyed, as are Grenoble walnuts. For the thirsty there are Savoy wines, Chartreuse liqueurs, Evian mineral water or the many *sirops* which are manufactured in the region. There is a TGV service to Paris and *autoroutes* give rapid access to the French capital as well as to Geneva.

Tourist information

Maison du Tourisme, 14 rue de la République, 38019 Grenoble. Tel: 76 54 34 36

Hotels

The following are near the station. A room with breakfast will cost between 200F and 250F.
- Hôtel Bastille, 25 avenue Félix Viallet. Tel: 46 43 10 27
- Hôtel Bristol, 11 avenue Félix Viallet. Tel: 76 46 11 18
- Institut Hotel, 10 rue Barbillon. Tel: 76 46 36 44

Youth hostel

La Quinzaine, 18 avenue du Grésivaudan, Echirolles. Tel: 76 09 33 52 (no. 8 bus from cours Jean Jaurès; bed and breakfast 75F for YHA members)

Restaurants

There are several popular pizzerias along the *quais*; however, it would be foolish to miss the many traditional restaurants offering good-value meals.
- Brasserie Anthea, 4 bis rue Lafayette. Tel: 76 63 09 26 (menus 50F–70F)
- Le Jardin de Ville, quai Stéphane Jay. Tel: 76 42 40 06 (menus 59F, 69F, 89F)
- La Petite Ferme, 3 rue Jean-Jacques Rousseau. Tel: 76 54 21 90 (menus 58F and 95F)

Leisure facilities

Listings of films, plays and cultural events are found in *Lumières sur la Ville*, which is free from the Tourist Office.

Theatre
● Théâtre de Grenoble, 4 rue Hector Berlioz. Tel: 76 54 03 08
● Le Cargo, 4 rue Paul Claudel. Tel: 76 24 49 56
● Théâtre 145, 145 cours Berriat. Tel: 76 49 53 39
● Théâtre du Rio, rue Servan. Tel: 76 54 41 83

Cinema
Student reductions are available. These take several forms and are sometimes restricted to particular days or times. Many cinemas offer discounts on season tickets. Programmes change on Wednesdays.
Cinemas showing new releases:
● Gaumont, 17 avenue Alsace-Lorraine. Tel: 76 46 16 45 (6 screens)
● Pathé-Grenette, 17 place Grenette. Tel: 76 43 37 37 (6 screens)
● Les 6 Rex, 13 rue Saint-Jacques. Tel: 76 51 72 00 (6 screens)
● UGC Royal, 2 rue Clot Bey. Tel: 76 46 11 42 (5 screens)
Cinemas showing second runs, classics and foreign language films:
● Centre Culturel Cinématographique (CCC), 4 rue Hector Berlioz. Tel: 76 40 70 38
● Le Club, angle cours Berriat, boulevard Gambetta. Tel: 76 87 46 21 (5 screens)
● Le Méliès, 3 rue de Strasbourg. Tel: 76 47 99 31
● Mon Ciné, 10 avenue Ambroise Croisat, St-Martin d'Hères. Tel: 76 44 60 11
● Le Lux, 15 rue Thiers. Tel: 76 46 46 58
● La Nef, 18 boulevard Edouard Rey. Tel: 76 46 53 25 (5 screens)
● La Cinémathèque Française, 21 rue Génissieu. Tel: 76 24 13 83

Principal museums and art galleries
The admission price indicates student rate, usually half the full rate:
● Centre National d'Art Contemporain, 155 cours Berriat. Tel: 76 21 95 84 (10F; closed Mondays)
● Musée Stendhal, 1 rue Hector Berlioz. Tel: 76 54 44 14 (free; closed Mondays)
● Musée de la Résistance et de la Déportation, 14 rue Jean-Jacques Rousseau. Tel: 76 44 51 81 (free; closed Tuesdays and Sundays)

- Musée Dauphinois, 30 rue Maurice Gignoux. Tel: 76 87 66 77 (10F; closed Tuesdays)
- Musée de Peinture et de Sculpture, place Verdun. Tel: 76 54 09 82 (10F; closed Tuesdays, free Wednesday afternoons)

Sports facilities

FNSU: CSU, Domaine Universitaire, 38400 St-Martin d'Hères. Tel: 76 42 70 51

Office Municipal des Sports, 3 passage du Palais de Justice. Tel: 76 44 75 61

Le Palais des Sports, boulevard Clémenceau. Tel: 76 54 67 80 (includes ice-skating rink)

Mountain Sports:
- CIMES (Centre Information Montagnes et Sentiers), 7 rue Voltaire. Tel: 76 51 76 00
- Club Alpin Français, 32 avenue Félix Viallet. Tel: 76 87 03 73

Swimming pools:
- Chorier-Berriat, 12 rue le Chatelier. Tel: 76 21 05 91
- Clos d'or, 111 rue de Stalingrad. Tel: 76 09 08 51

Tennis: GUC Tennis, Domaine Universitaire. Tel: 76 44 17 33

Useful addresses

Main post office: 7 boulevard Maréchal Lyautey. Tel: 76 76 14 14

Nearest to campus: 2 rue Molière. Tel: 76 54 20 34

Municipal library: Bibliothèque d'Etude et d'Information, 3 boulevard Maréchal Lyautey. Tel: 76 46 01 56

MJC: 2 rue Berthe de Boisseux. Tel: 76 43 10 75 (headquarters' address). Enquire for details of local branches serving your district.

Bookshops:
- FNAC, 26 cours Berriat. Tel: 76 87 27 27
- Librairie Arthaud, 23 Grande Rue. Tel: 76 42 49 81
- Librairie Gibert, 4 rue Béranger. Tel: 76 46 59 05
- Librairie de l'Université, 2 place du Dr Martin. Tel: 76 46 61 63
- La Bouquinerie, 9 boulevard Agutte Sembat. Tel: 76 46 15 32
- Just Books, 1 rue de la Paix. Tel: 76 44 78 81

Préfecture de l'Isère: 2 place de Verdun. Tel: 76 54 81 31

CAF: 3 rue Alliés. Tel: 76 20 60 00

CRIJ: 8 rue Voltaire. Tel: 76 54 70 38

Alliance Française: chez Mme Mutel, 12 avenue Charles de Foucauld, 38700 Corenc. Tel: 76 90 11 65 (contact with French families)

ANPE:
- 17 rue Denfert Rochereau. Tel: 76 87 61 43
- 23 rue Trembles. Tel: 76 40 72 61

Horizon Grenoble International: 24 place Paul Vallier (job opportunities for foreign students; open Mondays to Fridays)

ONISEP: 11 rue du Général Champon. Tel: 76 74 70 27

OSE:
- 15 rue Saint Joseph. Tel: 76 87 88 33
- 11–13 rue Anthoard. Tel: 76 70 98 98

Nearest British Consulate-General (Lyon): 24 rue Childebert, 69002 Lyon. Tel: 78 37 59 67. Fax: 72 40 25 24

Nearest US Consulate (Lyon): 45 rue de la Bourse. Tel: 72 40 59 20. Fax: 88 24 06 95

Health care

Hospitals:
- Hôpital Albert Michallon, 38700 La Tronche. Tel: 76 42 81 21
- Hôpital Sud, avenue Grugliasco, 38130 Echirolles. Tel: 76 09 80 50

Chemists:
- Pharmacie du Campus, 37 avenue Gabriel Péri. Tel: 76 54 49 25
- Pharmacie Foch, 33 boulevard Foch. Tel: 76 87 36 33
- Pharmacie Centrale, 10 rue Lafayette. Tel: 76 44 14 66

Local student insurance offices:
- MNEF, 28 cours Jean Jaurès. Tel: 76 87 38 88
- SMERRA, 15 rue St Joseph. Tel: 76 87 88 33

Travel information

Railway station
8 place de la Gare. Tel: 76 47 50 50. London-Grenoble (via Newhaven-Dieppe) £127 return; (via Dover-Calais) £130 return (Eurotrain)

Coach station
1 place de la Gare. Tel: 76 87 90 31. London-Grenoble, £89 return, £52 single (Eurolines)

Local buses and trams
Transportation de l'Agglomération Grenobloise (TAG). Tel: Allo TAG, 76 09 36 36. Bus or tram: single journey 8F; *carnet* of 10 tickets 47F; monthly student pass available. Bus to campus: no. 22.

Taxis
Taxis grenoblois. Tel: 76 54 42 54

Airports
- Grenoble-St-Geoirs. Tel: 76 65 48 48
- Lyon-Satolas. Tel: 78 52 80 45 (coach link Satolas-Grenoble: 120F)

Student travel
Try OTU at the CROUS or one of the following offices of Voyages Wasteels:
- 20 avenue Félix Viallet. Tel: 76 46 36 39
- 50 avenue Alsace-Lorraine. Tel: 76 47 34 54
- 3 rue Crépu. Tel: 76 47 34 54

Emergencies

SAMU. Tel: 76 42 42 42
SOS Amitié. Tel: 76 87 22 22
Police: boulevard Maréchal Leclerc. Tel: 76 60 40 40

9 Lille

The universities and their disciplines

Université des Sciences et Technologie de Lille (**Lille I**): sciences économiques et sociales, sciences exactes et naturelles, sciences agricoles et alimentaires, technologie.
   Cité scientifique, 59655 Villeneuve d'Ascq Cedex. Tel: 20 43 43 43. Fax: 20 43 49 25
SUIO: same address. Bibliothèque universitaire. Bâtiment A3. Tel: 20 43 43 31
IUT 'A': BP 179, 59653 Villeneuve d'Ascq Cedex. Tel: 20 43 41 72
IAE: 1 bis rue G Lefèvre, 59043 Lille Cedex. Tel: 20 52 32 56
Université du Droit et de la Santé (**Lille II**): droit, sciences politiques et économiques, formations de santé, technologie, sport.
   42, rue Paul Duez, 59800 Lille Cedex. Tel: 20 52 56 29. Fax: 20 88 24 32
SUIO: Faculté des Sciences Juridiques, Politiques et Sociales, Hall 169, 59653 Villeneuve d'Ascq Cedex. Tel: 20 05 74 07
UFRAPS: 9 chemin Latéral, 59790. Tel: 20 52 52 85
Université Charles de Gaulle (**Lille III**): arts et lettres, langues,

sciences humaines, techniques de réadaptation, technologie.
Quartier du Pont de Bois, BP 149, 59653 Villeneuve d'Ascq Cedex.
Tel: 20 33 60 00. Fax: 20 91 91 71
SUIO: same address. Tel: 20 33 62 46. Fax: 20 91 91 71
IUT 'B': 9 rue Auguste Angellier, 59046 Lille. Tel: 20 15 41 00. Fax: 20
15 42 18

Courses for languages undergraduates

LEA offers the following modern foreign languages: Danish, Dutch,
English, German, Italian, Russian, Spanish and Swedish.

In the *Lettres Modernes* programmes there are core courses on French
language and literature from the medieval period to the present day,
Literary History, Phonetics and Linguistics. Arabic, Chinese, Czech,
Danish, Dutch, English, German, Modern Greek, Hungarian, Italian,
Japanese, Polish, Portuguese, Russian, Spanish and Swedish may be
studied, though sometimes only at second year level. There are also
options in such diverse subjects as Contemporary European Society,
European Law, the Press and the Media, Geography, Greek and
Roman Civilisation, Film Studies, Modern and Contemporary Drama,
Jazz, Contemporary Philosophy and Logic.

All the Lille universities have indicated their intention of imple-
menting the most recent reforms. Course structures and their content
are, therefore, under review.

Courses for foreign students

Département des Etudiants Etrangers (Université Charles de Gaulle),
BP 149, 59653 Villeneuve d'Ascq Cedex. Tel: 20 33 62 96, ext. 4296
or 4266. Fax: 20 47 23 62

Full-year or semester-based courses
There are courses at five levels and candidates (who should be 18 or
over) sit a placement test on arrival. The first two levels cater for
beginners and those with only a passive reading knowledge of French.
Level 3 prepares for the *Certificat Pratique de Langue Française*; level 4 for
the *Diplôme d'Etudes Françaises*; level 5 for the *Diplôme Supérieur d'Etudes
Françaises*. There are two examination sessions for the first two diplomas
but for the highest diploma, which is a full-year course for those who
hold the *baccalauréat* or its equivalent, there is only a summer examination.

In addition, upon request, the Department provides preparatory courses for entry into university as well as specialised intensive courses in the teaching of French as a foreign language and Business French.

Vacation courses

There are two three-week general courses in July and August at all levels and two specialised sessions in teaching French as a foreign language (3 weeks in July) and Business French (2 weeks in August). These are organised in Boulogne-sur-Mer. Four hours of courses take place in the mornings with three optional hours in the afternoons, up to a maximum of twenty-four hours per week. There is a supporting programme of cultural events, sporting activities and visits. A range of accommodation is on offer.

CROUS

74, rue de Cambrai, 59043 Lille Cedex. Tel: 20 88 66 00. Fax: 20 88 66 59

SAEE: same address and telephone

OTU: same address. Tel: 20 52 84 00

SCLE (Service Central du Logement Etudiant): same address. Tel: 20 52 84 00. There is a branch office at Villeneuve d'Ascq in the Hall de la Faculté de Droit. Tel: 20 91 83 18

CROUS-controlled accommodation

The following halls are on the campus at Villeneuve d'Ascq and have a common address, namely: Domaine universitaire scientifique, 59650 Villeneuve d'Ascq.

- Résidence Gaston Bachelard. Tel: 20 43 48 71
- Résidence Albert Camus. Tel: 20 43 46 99
- Résidence Evariste Gallois. Tel: 20 43 43 64
- Résidence Hélène Boucher. Tel: 20 43 43 77

The following halls are also at Villeneuve d'Ascq:

- Résidence Quartier du Triolo, 8 rue Trémières. Tel: 20 91 46 19
- Résidence Quartier du Pont de Bois, rue de Fives. Tel: 20 04 91 91 (there are also flats with the possibility of APL)

The following halls are in Lille itself:

- Résidence Bas-Liévin, 48–50 rue du Bas-Liévin, 59045 Cedex. Tel: 20 53 49 63
- Résidence A. Châtelet, rue F Combemale, 59045 Cedex. Tel: 20 53 62 37

- Résidence G Lefèvre, 2 boulevard du Dr Calmette, 59800. Tel: 20 52 59 58
- Résidence Maupassant, 10 rue de Maupassant, 59000. Tel: 20 52 98 66 (405 rooms and 6 for handicapped students; there are also 94 *studios* with the possibility of APL)

CROUS restaurants
All offer a choice between the traditional three-course meal, fast-food and snacks.
In Lille:
- Restaurant Universitaire Cambray, 70 rue de Cambray, 59043 Cedex (*Métro* Porte de Valenciennes)
- Restaurant Universitaire Debierre, 171 rue Charles Debierre, 59000 (*Métro* Mairie de Lille)
- Restaurant Universitaire Châtillon, 24 rue G de Châtillon, 59000 (*Métro* République)
- Restaurant Universitaire Châtelet, rue F Combemale, 59045 Cedex (*Métro* CHR/O Lambret)
- Restaurant Le Meurein, 47 boulevard Vauban, 59800
In Villeneuve d'Ascq:
- Restaurant Universitaire Pariselle, Domaine Universitaire Scientifique (*Métro* Cité Scientifique/4 Cantons)
- Restaurant Universitaire Sully, Domaine Universitaire Scientifique (*Métro* 4 Cantons)
- Restaurant Universitaire Flers, Domaine Littéraire et Juridique (*Métro* Pont de Bois)
- Restaurant Universitaire Flers 2000 (same address and *metro* station).

Privately-run hostels

- Foyer Béthanie, 15 rue Saint-Génois, BP 308, 59026 Lille Cedex. Tel: 20 06 08 57 (females; 140 places)
- Foyer International, 10 rue de la Bassée, 59000 Lille. Tel: 20 93 94 20 (males; 156 places)
- Foyer Notre Dame, 20 rue Lydéric, 59800 Lille. Tel: 20 54 88 82 (females; 60 places)
- Foyer Valentine Charrondière, 68 boulevard Vauban, 59004 Lille Cedex. Tel: 20 30 80 30 (males; 65 places)
- Résidence Teilhard de Chardin, 47 boulevard Vauban, 59000 Lille. Tel: 20 57 63 91 (females; 74 rooms)

The town and its surrounding area

The fifth largest town in France, Lille (including the conurbation) has a population of almost a million, of which some 65,000 are students. Originally a trading post on the River Deûle, the town has retained its lively, commercial atmosphere in its modern transformation while keeping the Flemish character of its old quarters. With Paris just over 200 kilometres away, Lille has long provided an important link between the capital and the Channel ports of Calais and Boulogne and its historical importance as a garrison town is evident from the imposing Citadelle. During both world wars, the town was at the centre of fierce fighting and suffered considerable damage. An important manufacturing base, Lille is perhaps best known as the centre for the French textile industry. Among the famous associated with the city are Charles de Gaulle, General Faidherbe, and the composer Lalo.

The town's architecture is eclectic: there are fine historic buildings such as the fifteenth-century Palais Rihour, the seventeenth-century Bourse, Gothic churches, and several merchants' houses dating from the seventeenth and eighteenth centuries which coexist with more recent constructions such as the unfinished neo-Gothic Cathédrale de Notre Dame de la Treille, the Opéra, the Hôtel de Ville and 'Euralille', a futuristic development which includes a new TGV station. As befits a thriving, youthful city there are numerous cultural activities with music, theatre and cinema to the fore while the Musée des Beaux-Arts houses one of France's finest collections. The Lillois enjoy seafood and there are numerous fish restaurants where *moules*, in particular, are to be enjoyed. The town boasts good transport links with major destinations. The new TGV service puts Paris just an hour away while the Channel port of Calais can be reached in a similar amount of time. For international travellers there is the Lille-Lesquin airport and Lille's favoured position in the motorway network ensures rapid travel between France and her north-eastern neighbours. However, the pride of every Lillois is the fully-automated *Metro* system which symbolises the city's innovative, pioneering spirit and determination to be in the vanguard of modern industrial developments.

Tourist information

Office du Tourisme, place Rihour, BP 205, 59002 Lille. Tel: 20 30 81
  00. Fax: 20 30 82 24
Comité Régional de Tourisme Nord-Pas de Calais, 26 place Rihour.
  Tel: 20 60 69 62

Hotels

There are several modestly priced hotels near the main station. A room with breakfast will cost between 150F and 200F.
- Hôtel du Coq-Hardi, 34 place de la Gare. Tel: 20 06 05 89
- Hôtel Faidherbe, 42 place de la Gare. Tel: 20 06 27 93
- Hôtel des Voyageurs, 10 place de la Gare. Tel: 20 06 43 14

Better grade hotels include:
- Hôtel de France, 10 rue de Béthune. Tel: 20 57 14 78. Fax: 20 57 06 01
- Hôtel Breughel, 5 parvis Saint Maurice. Tel: 20 06 06 69. Fax: 20 63 25 27

Youth hostel

1 avenue Julien Destrée. Tel: 20 52 98 94 (bed and breakfast for YHA members, 60F)

UCRIF (Relais Européen de la Jeunesse): 40 rue du Thumesnil. Tel: 20 52 69 75 (bed and breakfast, 70F)

Restaurants

Good-value restaurants abound in the pedestrianised area of the *rue de Béthune*, such as Le Bureau (50F menu), Entasis (50F menu) or, for those keen on mussels, Aux Moules (40F-60F menus). The area is also well served by fast-food restaurants such as McDonalds, Flunch or Le Quick. The following are also worth trying:
- Brasserie Le Lion des Flandres, 3 place de la Gare. Tel: 20 51 12 22 (menu 65F)
- Les Feux de la Rampe, 23 rue de Tournai. Tel: 20 31 77 00 (menus 66F to 92F)
- Le Napoléon, 17 place de la Gare. Tel: 20 06 80 50 (menus from 45F to 130F)
- Les Brasseurs, 22 place de la Gare. Tel: 20 06 46 25 (menu 60F)

For the homesick British student there is a French-style pub:
- Bar de l'Echo, 20 place Charles de Gaulle. Tel: 20 57 36 28

Leisure facilities

Museums and art galleries
- Musée des Beaux-Arts, place de la République. Tel: 20 57 01 84
- Musée de l'Hospice Comtesse, 32 rue de la Monnaie. Tel: 20 51 02 62 (10F – but free on Saturdays; closed on Tuesdays)
- Musée des Canonniers, 44 rue des Cannoniers. Tel: 20 55 58 90

- Musée d'Histoire Naturelle et de Géologie, 19 rue de Bruxelles. Tel: 20 85 28 60 (closed Tuesdays and Saturdays)
- Musée de Charles de Gaulle, 9 rue Princesse. Tel: 20 31 96 03 (7F)

Theatre
- Opéra de Lille, place du Théâtre. Tel: 20 55 93 06
- Théâtre Le Grand Bleu, 36 avenue Max-Dormoy, Lille. Tel: 20 09 45 50
- Théâtre Massenet, rue Massenet, Lille-Fives
- Théâtre La Métaphore, place du Général de Gaulle. Tel: 20 40 10 20
- Théâtre des Nuits Blanches, rue Brûle Maison, Lille.
- Théâtre Sébastopol, place Sébastopol. Tel: 20 57 15 47
- Théâtre de la Verrière, 28 rue Alphonse Mercier, Lille. Tel: 20 73 75 16
- Théâtre de Marionnettes, Chalet des Chèvres, Centre du Jardin Vauban, Lille. Tel: 20 42 09 95

Cinema
Special rates apply on Mondays and early in the day.
The following are in Lille:
- Les Arcades, 53 rue de Béthune. Tel: 36 68 00 43
- Gaumont, 25 rue de Béthune, Lille. Tel: 36 68 75 55
- Le Métropole, 25 rue des Ponts-de-Comines. Tel: 20 06 63 61
- Le Splendid, 1 place du Mont-de-Terre. Tel: 20 56 08 61
- UGC Cinémas, 40–46 rue de Béthune. Tel: 36 65 70 14
- L'Univers, 14 rue Georges-Danton. Tel: 20 58 14 23
The following are in Villeneuve d'Ascq:
- Kino Ciné, Hall de l'Université de Lille III, rue du Barreau. Tel: 20 33 61 43
- Les Cinq Lumières, Centre Commercial V2. Tel: 20 91 19 73
- Le Méliès, Centre Commercial du Triolo. Tel: 20 91 68 94

Sport
FNSU: CSU, G Berger, 180 avenue Gaston Berger. Tel: 20 52 59 91

Concert halls
- Auditorium Edouard Lalo, place du Concert, Lille. Tel: 20 74 57 50
- Auditorium, 3 place Mendès France, Lille. Tel: 20 12 82 40 (Orchestre National de Lille)

Useful addresses

Main post office: 7 place de la République. Tel: 20 54 70 13
Municipal library: 32–34 rue Edouard Delesalle
Bookshops:
- FNAC: 20 rue St Nicolas. Tel: 21 65 44 46
- Le Furet du Nord, 11 place du Général de Gaulle. Tel: 20 78 43 43 (5% student reduction)
- Librairie Meura, 25 rue de Valmy. Tel: 20 57 36 44 (student reductions)
- Book'n Broc, 17 rue Kolb. Tel: 20 40 10 02 (English books)

ANPE: 63 rue Buffon, 59000. Tel: 20 85 15 40
CAF: 82 rue Brûle Maison. Tel: 20 30 76 30
CPAM: 2 rue d'Iéna. Tel: 20 42 34 00
CRIJ: 2 rue Nicholas Leblanc, 59000. Tel: 20 57 86 04
Fédération des Etudiants: 125 rue Meurein. Tel: 20 30 60 26
Hôtel de Ville: place Roger Salengro. Tel: 20 49 50 50
Préfecture du Nord: 171 bis boulevard de la Liberté (apply here for *carte de séjour*)
British Consulate-General: 11 square Dutilleul, 59800 Lille. Tel: 20 57 87 90. Fax: 20 54 88 16
Nearest US Consulate (Paris): 2 avenue Gabriel, 75382 Paris 08 Cedex. Tel: (1) 42 96 12 02. Fax: (1) 42 66 97 83

Health care

Hospital: Cité Hospitalière, 2 avenue Oscar Lambret. Tel: 20 44 59 62
Student Health Service: CUPS (Centre Universitaire de Promotion de la Santé):
- Lille I: avenue Poincarré, 59650 Villeneuve d'Ascq. Tel: 20 43 65 50 (*Métro* Cité Scientifique)
- Lille II (Santé): 24 rue Jeanne d'Arc, 59000. Tel: 20 54 74 59 (*Métro* République)
- Lille II (Droit) and Lille III: rue de Fives, Parking P3, 59560 Villeneuve d'Ascq. Tel: 20 91 16 08 (*Métro* Pont de Bois)

BAPU (Bureau d'Aide Psychologique Universitaire): 153 boulevard de la Liberté, 59800. Tel: 20 54 85 26 (*Métro* République)
Local student insurance offices:
- MNEF: 142 rue Nationale, BP 144, 59001. Tel: 20 54 95 44
- SMENO: 84–86 rue des Stations, BP 101, 59003. Tel: 20 54 01 47

Travel

Railway station
Place de la Gare. Tel: 20 78 50 50. London-Lille (via Dover-Calais) £74 return (Eurotrain)

Coach station
Place des Buisses. London-Lille, £46 return; £30 single (Eurolines)

Local buses
TCC, rue le Corbusier. Tel: 20 98 50 50 (students should apply for the *Espace Carte* which gives a 25% discount on the weekly travel pass. Apply to the office at the *Métro* station Lille-Gares).

Student travel
- OTU Voyages (see under CROUS)
- Wasteels, 25 place des Reignaux. Tel: 20 06 24 24

Métro
Place des Buisses. Tel: 20 98 50 50. A single ticket costs 7F10; a *carnet* of ten, 50F.

Airport
Aéroport de Lille-Lesquin. Tel: 20 49 68 68

Emergencies

Police: 16 boulevard du Maréchal Vaillant. Tel: 20 62 47 47
SAMU. Tel: 20 54 22 22
SOS Amitié. Tel: 20 55 77 77

10 LIMOGES

The university and its disciplines

Université de Limoges: droit et sciences économiques, lettres et sciences humaines, sciences bio-médicales et pharmaceutiques, sciences exactes et naturelles, technologie.
13 rue de Genève, 87065 Limoges Cedex. Tel: 55 45 76 01 Fax: 55 45 76 34

IUT: allée André Maurois, 87065 Limoges Cedex. Tel: 55 01 53 42
SUIO (known locally as the Bureau Universitaire d'Information- BUI):
13 rue de Genève, 87065 Limoges Cedex. Tel: 55 45 76 40
SUEE: BUI, same address and telephone number

University libraries
● Section Droit/Sciences Eco: 39 C rue Camille Guérin. Tel: 55 01 38 71
● Section Lettres/Sciences Humaines: same address and telephone number
● Section Médecine/Pharmacie: 2 rue du Docteur Marcland. Tel: 55 01 64 82
● Section Sciences: 123 avenue Albert Thomas. Tel: 55 45 72 90

Courses for languages undergraduates

LCE is available in English, German and Spanish, either as the study of a single language and its culture, or as a major/minor bilingual package. LEA is offered in German/English, English/Spanish and German/Spanish. It is possible to incorporate a third language (Italian, Russian or Portuguese).

Lettres Modernes involves elements of French Literature and Linguistics, Comparative Literature, Medieval Language and Literature, a modern foreign language and compulsory courses in Latin and Computing. While there is little choice within the obligatory pattern, about 10 per cent of each year's assessment is on the basis of *options libres*, for which there are many possibilities.

Since 1985, all courses in the *premier cycle* in the Faculté des Lettres et des Sciences Humaines have been of the DEUG *rénové* type, with increased access to academic counselling, careful choice of specialisation in the light of performance in the first semester of the first year, and *préprofessionnalisation*.

The Faculté is located on the campus at Vanteaux, near to the CROUS headquarters, the university library, the Resto-U Camille Guérin and the hall of residence of the same name. Though it is a little way out of town, the campus is well served by buses from the centre (nos 10/17), though the service from the off-campus residences is less frequent (no. 14). However, the distances in each case are not such as to deter a committed walker. The university is small by French standards.

Courses for foreign students

Institut de Français Langue Etrangère, Faculté des Lettres et des
  Sciences Humaines, Campus Universitaire Limoges-Vanteaux, 39
  E rue Camille Guérin, 87036 Limoges Cedex. Tel: 55 01 26 19

Term-time courses
Courses, which are organised on a semester basis, are offered at
beginners', intermediate and advanced levels. There is an intensive
beginners' and post-beginners' course during the first semester
(October-January) based on 10 hours of teaching per week. The intermediate course prepares for the DELF, whilst the Advanced course
leads to a *Diplôme d'Université*. There are also specialist options in the
language of science, law and economics and in the methodology of
teaching French as a foreign language.

Summer course
An intensive three-week refresher course is run in September (27 hours
a week). Accommodation is available in university halls of residence,
and excursions are organised in the region.

CROUS

21 avenue Alexis Carrel, 87036 Limoges Cedex. Tel: 55 43 17 00. Fax:
  55 50 14 05
SAEE: same address and telephone
OTU-Voyages: same address. Tel: 55 05 13 31

CROUS-controlled accommodation
The CROUS has 1,992 beds in the town.
● Résidence Universitaire La Borie (601 rooms, mixed, plus 24 dormi-
   tory places), 185 avenue Albert Thomas, 87065 Cedex. Tel: 55 45 26
   00
● Résidence Universitaire de l'Aurence (two buildings mixed, one
   women only; 453 rooms in all), 24 avenue du Président Vincent
   Auriol, 87065 Limoges Cedex. Tel: 55 01 36 74
● Résidence Universitaire Camille Guérin (353 rooms, mixed), 39 A
   rue Camille Guérin, 87038 Limoges Cedex. Tel: 55 43 16 00
Of the three, Camille Guérin is the most modern and most comfortable,
as it was built to different standards from the others. In addition, the
CROUS controls a number of HLM units, some of which are let to

jeunes ménages étudiants, while others are occupied by groups of students (in twos or threes), each of whom has an individual study-bedroom, with shared common facilities. This accommodation attracts APL.

One 'new-style' residence has been opened:

- Les Hauts de Vanteaux, rue Camille Guérin (206 independent units, let for twelve-month periods only, and qualifying for APL)

CROUS restaurants

The restaurants all offer the *menu traditionnel*. Camille Guérin also has one 'quick-service' counter which serves a single-dish meal together with a dessert or yoghurt. There is a *restaurant médico-diététique* open to students who are referred on medical advice. Only Bernard Palissy is open on Saturdays; on Sundays, provision alternates between Camille Guérin and La Borie.

- Restaurant La Borie, 185 avenue Albert Thomas. Tel: 55 45 26 00
- Restaurant Bernard Palissy, 14 rue Bernard Palissy. Tel: 55 77 39 24
- Restaurant Camille Guérin, 39 B rue Camille Guérin. Tel: 55 01 16 51
- Restaurant-Brasserie La Croustadine, rue Camille Guérin. Tel: 55 01 16 51
- Restaurant de L'IUFM, 209 boulevard de Vanteaux. Tel: 55 50 62 34 (closed evenings and weekends)

Privately-run hostels

For details, write to the *Directeur/Directrice*:

- Foyer Municipal de Jeunes Travailleurs, 44 rue Emile Montégut. Tel: 55 79 64 41
- Foyer de Jeunes Travailleurs, 2 avenue du Président Vincent Auriol. Tel: 55 01 65 61 (rooms can attract APL)
- Foyer de Jeunes Travailleurs de Beaubreuil, 36 allée Fabre d'Eglantine. Tel: 55 35 43 97
- Foyer Limousin de Jeunes Travailleurs, 15 rue Eugène Varlin. Tel: 55 30 39 79 (men only)
- Foyer Nazareth, 2 rue Pierre Brossolette. Tel: 55 34 30 67 (women only)
- Accueil FJT 2000 (Foyer de Jeunes Travailleuses), 20 rue Encombe Vineuse. Tel: 55 77 63 97 (mixed)
- Foyer de l'Institut d'Economie Sociale et Familiale, 5 rue de la Cité. Tel: 55 34 41 25 (rooms must be taken for the full university year)

The town and its surrounding area

Situated some 375km south-south-west of Paris, Limoges is the *préfecture* of the Haute-Vienne. It is a medium-sized, pleasant, fairly quiet town which stands at the heart of Le Limousin, a region renowned for its woods, rivers and lakes. It is about three hours from Paris by train on the fast line which serves the south-west, and constitutes a major junction for the north-south and east-west routes in the region.

There are many remnants of its historic past still in evidence. An impressive Gothic cathedral, begun in the thirteenth century, heads the list of the churches, which includes St-Michel-des-Lions (fourteenth–sixteenth centuries), so named because of the two ancient stone lions which stand guard, and with a 65m tower dating from 1373; and St-Pierre-du-Queyroix, largely rebuilt in the sixteenth century, but sporting an older bell-tower typical of the region. The eighteenth-century Bishop's Palace, with its terraced gardens overlooking the River Vienne, is now the home of the municipal museum. A good deal of restoration work has been put into the 'Village de la Boucherie', the territory of the influential corporation of the butchers which goes back many centuries. Their chapel, St-Aurélien (fifteenth century, but with a later tower and facade), stands near to the stalls which still line the rue de la Boucherie. The Thursday market well deserves a visit.

Famous people associated with the town include the humanist, Jean Dorat (1502–88), the soldier Maréchal Jourdan (1762–1833), and the painters Auguste Renoir (1841–1919) and Suzanne Valadon (1867–1938). The well-known playwright and novelist, Jean Giraudoux (1882–1944), was born at nearby Bellac.

The town has known considerable expansion in recent times, and its industrial base has diversified, in part due to the discovery of uranium in the area. However, it is most famous for its enamels and its porcelain. The manufacture of Limoges enamels was already at its height in the sixteenth century. It died out before the end of the eighteenth century, but was revived in 1875. The discovery of kaolin in the neighbourhood in the 1760s led to the establishment of the porcelain industry and many fine examples of its wares, along with exhibits of chinaware from much further afield, can be seen in the Musée National Adrien Dubouché.

Tourist information

Tourist office
Pavillon du Tourisme, boulevard de Fleurus, 87000. Tel: 55 34 46 87

Hotels
- Hôtel de France, 23 cours Bugeaud. Tel: 55 77 78 92 (near the station; rooms from about 120F, with breakfast)
- Familia, 18 rue du Général du Bessol. Tel: 55 77 51 40 (in town centre; inexpensive)
- Hôtel Royal Limousin, place de la République, 87000. Tel: 55 34 65 30 (a three-star hotel which has the reputation of being the best in town, and good value for the upper end of the market. For those extra-special visitors!)

Restaurants
- La Fringale, 11 rue Aigueperse, 87000. Tel: 55 77 38 41 (inexpensive meals)
- Le Flunch, 5 rue Dalesme. Tel: 55 34 59 00 (part of the chain; meals from 30F)
- Le Paris, 7 place Denis Dussoubs. Tel: 55 77 48 31 (more up-market, but the place to be in Limoges; sells home-made beers)

Leisure facilities

Museums and art galleries
- Musée Municipal de l'Evêché, place de la Cathédrale. Tel: 55 45 61 75
- Musée National Adrien Dubouché, place Winston Churchill. Tel: 55 77 45 58

Centres Culturels et Sociaux Municipaux
- Jean Gagnant, 7 avenue Jean Gagnant. Tel: 55 34 45 49
- Jean Le Bail, rue Jean Le Bail. Tel: 55 45 61 68
- Jean Macé, rue de New York. Tel: 55 45 61 67
- Jean Moulin, 76 rue des Sagnes. Tel: 55 45 61 65
- John Lennon, 41 ter rue de Feytiat. Tel: 55 06 24 83

Theatre
- Grand Théâtre Municipal, 48 rue Jean-Jaurès. Tel: 55 34 12 12
- Centre Dramatique National-La Limousine-Théâtre, 20 rue des Coopérateurs. Tel: 55 79 90 00 (reservations)
- Théâtre de la Passerelle, 4–6 rue du Général du Bessol. Tel: 55 79 26 49

In addition, there are two student theatre groups:

- Théâtre de la Cigale, 1 rue Armand Barbès. Tel: 55 79 84 38
- Théâtre de la Balise, RU La Borie (see above)

There is a university orchestra and choir (Orchestre Universitaire du Limousin, La Chorale 'La Chanterie'). Contact M. Henri Deglane, 11 rue du Grand Treuil. Tel: 55 79 56 79. Concerts are held at L'Auditorium, 41 ter rue de Feytiat. Tel: 55 06 21 11

Other possibilities include:
- Groupe Régional d'Animation Musicale, 37 allée de Villefélix, 87270 Couzeix. Tel: 55 39 27 09
- Ensemble Baroque de Limoges, 7 boulevard de Fleurus. Tel: 55 32 19 98
- Orchestre Symphonique Régional de Limoges et du Limousin, 27 boulevard de la Corderie. Tel: 55 34 12 12

Cinema
- Ciné-Max Les Lidos, 3 avenue du Général de Gaulle. Tel: 55 77 26 71
- Ciné-Max Les Ecrans, 11 place Denis Dussoubs. Tel: 55 77 40 79
- Le Colisée, 13 place Jourdan. Tel: 55 32 41 21 (a 30% reduction is available to students at certain times. Information on programmes is available from the following numbers (24-hour service): Ecrans, Lidos – Tel: 55 79 52 52; Colisée – Tel: 55 32 41 20)

The Ciné-Club Universitaire de Limoges (CCUL), based in the RU la Borie (see above) meets weekly, usually in the Faculté des Sciences. For programme and venue, see posters in the halls and university restaurants.

Sport
Parc Municipal des Sports (swimming, tennis), boulevard de Beaublanc. Tel: 55 77 68 35
Centre Sportif Municipal de Saint-Lazare (golf, swimming, tennis), rue Jules Noël. Tel: 55 30 21 02
Municipal swimming pools:
- Les Casseaux, boulevard des Petits Carmes
- Beaubreuil, ZAC de Beaubreuil
Skating: Patinoire Olympique Municipale, boulevard des Petits Carmes. Tel: 55 34 13 85
FNSU: Gymnase Universitaire de la Borie, 185 avenue Albert Thomas. Tel: 55 77 43 20

The SUAPS (Centre Sportif Universitaire, same address. Tel: 55 77 22 84) organises a wide range of activities and produces a *Guide du Sport Universitaire* which is available from faculty offices or its own secretariat at the beginning of the academic year. Equally, Le Limoges-Etudiants-Club (LEC) enters teams in non-university competitions in a range of sports. Details may be had from its office at the Centre Sportif Universitaire, same address, same telephone number.

Useful addresses

Main post office: 1 rue Daniel Lamazière. Tel: 55 44 44 44
Municipal library: 6 place de l'Ancienne Comédie. Tel: 55 34 11 25
Bookshops:
- Le Plaisir du Texte, 3 rue Jules Guesde. Tel: 55 33 33 98
- Les Yeux dans les Poches, 6 rue de la Boucherie. Tel: 55 32 25 32
- Page et Plume, 4 place de la Motte. Tel: 55 34 45 54
CAF: 25 rue Firmin Delage. Tel: 55 43 40 00
CRIJ: Hôtel de Région, 27 boulevard de la Corderie. Tel: 55 45 18 70
   (publishes the useful brochure *Loisirs à Limoges*)
Administrative offices:
- Commissariat Central de Police, 2 rue des Vénitiens. Tel: 55 77 58 61
- Préfecture de Région, place Stalingrad. Tel: 55 44 18 18
- Mairie, place Léon Betoulle. Tel: 55 45 60 00
Nearest British Consulate-General (Bordeaux): 353 boulevard du Président Wilson, 33073 Bordeaux Cedex. Tel: 56 42 34 13. Fax: 56 08 33 12
Nearest US Consulate-General (Bordeaux): 22 cours du Maréchal Foch, 33080 Bordeaux Cedex. Tel: 56 52 65 95. Fax: 56 51 60 42

Health care

Centre Hospitalier Régional Universitaire (CHRU) Dupuytren: 2 avenue Alexis Carrel. Tel: 55 05 61 23
CPAM: 22 avenue Jean Gagnant. Tel: 55 33 71 20
Local student insurance offices:
- MNEF, 8 bis rue A Dubouché, BP 75, 87002 Cedex. Tel: 55 34 61 35
- SMESO, 1 rue de la Basse Comédie, BP 396, 87010 Cedex. Tel: 55 32 50 60

Local chemists:
- (Mutualistes) Carnot, 65 rue François Chénieux. Tel: 55 77 32 37
- Pharmacie du Théâtre, 5 rue des Combes. Tel: 55 77 32 35

SUMPS: Campus Universitaire de Vanteaux, 21 bis avenue Alexis
    Carrel, 87036 Cedex. Tel: 55 01 56 90 (next to the CROUS)

Travel

Railway station
Gare des Bénédictins, rue Aristide Briand (information, tel: 55 01 50
50; reservations, tel: 55 72 72 34). London-Limoges (via Newhaven-
Dieppe) £112 return; (via Dover-Calais) £116 return (Eurotrain)

Coach station
9 rue Charles Gide. Tel: 55 34 47 77. London-Limoges, £42 single;
£76 return (Eurolines)

Airport
Limoges-Bellegarde. Tel: 55 00 10 37

Taxis
Tel: 55 37 44 33 *or* 55 37 81 81

Buses
The local trolley-buses and buses are operated by the Société des
Transports en Commun de Limoges (TLC), 10 place Léon Betoulle.
Tel: 55 32 46 46. Tickets are expensive if bought individually, but there
are the usual reductions for *carnets*. Prices vary according to the range of
services offered (books of 10 or 12 tickets, with the option of one or even
two changes of bus, etc.). Equally, an annual card is available to students
which enables them to buy a weekly, reduced-price *carnet* which is valid
between their place of residence and of work. Application forms for the
card may be obtained from the TCL or the *activités socio-culturelles*
division of the CROUS.

Emergencies

Duty doctor. Tel: 55 33 53 59
For emergency medical supplies, contact the Commissariat de Police, 2
    rue des Vénitiens. Tel: 55 77 58 91

11 Lyon

The universities and their disciplines

Université Claude Bernard (**Lyon I**): formations de santé, sciences exactes et naturelles, technologie.
43 boulevard du 11 Novembre 1918, 69622 Villeurbanne Cedex.
Tel: 72 44 80 00. Fax: 55 45 72 01
SUIO or CELAIO: same address. Tel: 72 44 80 59
IUT (A): 43 boulevard du 11 Novembre 1918, 69622 Villeurbanne.
Tel: 78 94 88 00
IUT (B): 17 rue de France, 69100 Villeurbanne. Tel: 78 03 43 43
Université Lumière (**Lyon II**): lettres et sciences humaines, économie, droit.
86 rue Pasteur, 69365 Lyon Cedex 07. Tel: 78 69 70 00. Fax: 78 69 56 01
SUIO: 5 avenue Pierre Mendès France, 69676 Bron Cedex. Tel: 78 00 67 04
Université Jean Moulin (**Lyon III**): droit, lettres et sciences humaines, langues, sciences administratives.
1 rue de l'Université, BP 0638, 69339 Lyon Cedex 02. Tel: 72 72 20 20. Fax: 72 72 20 50
SUIO: 15 quai Claude Bernard, 69007 Lyon. Tel: 72 72 20 33

University libraries
● Section Droit, ler cycle Sciences, 43 boulevard du 11 Novembre 1918, 69100 Villeurbanne. Tel: 72 72 45 32
● Section Santé, 8 avenue Rockefeller, 69373 Lyon Cedex 08. Tel: 78 74 19 54
● Section Centrale Droit-Lettres, 18 quai Claude Bernard, 69365 Lyon Cedex 07. Tel: 78 72 36 89
● Section Droit-Lettres, 5 avenue Pierre Mendès France, 69676 Bron Cedex. Tel: 78 00 60 03

Courses for languages undergraduates

LEA offers the following modern foreign languages: Arabic, English, German, Portuguese and Spanish. These are taught mainly at the Bron campus.

In *Lettres Modernes*, courses embrace a study of French language and literature from medieval times to the present day. In addition, there are courses on French Canadian Literature, French African Literature, Stylistics, Linguistics, Comparative Literature, Poetry, Roman and Greek Civilisation, Literary History, History, Art History, Approaches to Literature, Semiology, Cinema, Drama and the Press. English, German, Italian or Spanish can also be studied as a foreign language option. Some of the above courses are taught in the quai Bernard buildings, others at the Bron campus.

Courses for foreign students

Centre International d'Etudes Françaises (CIEF), 18 quai Claude Bernard, 69007 Lyon. Tel: 78 69 71 35

Term-time courses
Year-long and semester courses are run by the Université Lumière. There are semester-based programmes designed for complete beginners. Semester dates are October-February and March-June. The following qualifications may be obtained: *Certificat d'Etudes Pratiques de Français (1er degré)* and *Diplôme de Langue et de Civilisation Françaises (2e degré)*. The year-long courses are geared towards the *Diplôme Supérieur d'Etudes Françaises (3e degré)*. Candidates must be at least 18 and have the equivalent of the *baccalauréat*. Accommodation is provided in student hostels or with families.

Service d'Enseignement du Français aux Stagiaires Etrangers, Bâtiment 601, 20 avenue Albert Einstein, 69621 Villeurbanne Cedex. Tel: 72 43 83 66
The Institut National des Sciences Appliquées (INSA) organises an audio-visual course of three-months' duration for complete beginners. The courses begin in January, April, July and October. Students must be at least 18. For more advanced students, there are courses beginning each month. Accommodation is available in the INSA residences, hotels or with families.

Vacation courses
Centre International d'Etudes Françaises, 18 quai Claude-Bernard, 69007 Lyon. Tel: 78 69 24 45, ext. 435 or 436
In July, courses in French language, literature and civilisation, Commercial French, Drama and the Press are organised for advanced students. Pre-university session courses are arranged for students of all levels and are held in September. Accommodation is usually in student hostels or with families.

Alliance Française, 11 rue Pierre Bourdan, 69003 Lyon. Tel: 78 95 24
72
Courses are organised during July, August and September under the
aegis of the university. There are two levels for candidates who must be
at least 16: (i) four-week courses for complete beginners; (ii) four-week
courses for intermediate or advanced students. The courses lead to a
Certificat de Français Parlé (CEFP) or *Diplôme de Langue Française* (DL).
Accommodation is in student halls.

CROUS

59 rue de la Madeleine, 69365 Lyon Cedex 07. Tel: 78 72 55 47. Buses
12, 35, 47 or *Métro* Jean-Macé
OTU: same address and telephone number

CROUS-controlled accommodation
There are some 3,400 rooms available in mixed halls and a further 100
for females only in Lirondelle. In addition there are some 800 *studios*
which attract APL.
Résidences universitaires:
● Residence La Madeleine (357 rooms), 4 rue du Sauveur, 7e. Tel: 78
72 80 62. Buses 12, 35, 47
● Résidence André Lirondelle (100 rooms), 8 rue Rachais, 3e. Tel: 78
60 13 20. Buses 1, 2, 9, 11, 24, 43
● Résidence Jacques Cavalier (269 rooms), 8 rue Jeanne Koehler, 3e.
Tel: 78 54 08 62. Buses 1, 9, 24, 34
● Résidence Jean Mermoz (584 rooms), 29 rue Pr J Nicolas, 8e. Tel: 78
74 41 64. Buses 34, 39
● Résidence André Allix (1018 rooms), 2 rue Soeur Bouvier, 5e. Tel:
78 25 47 13. Buses 30, 49
● Résidence Jussieu (616 rooms), 3 avenue Albert Einstein,
Villeurbanne. Tel: 78 93 34 21. Buses 26, 38, 69, 27
● Résidence Puvis de Chavannes (528 rooms), 29 rue Marguerite,
Villeurbanne. Tel: 78 89 62 02. Buses 26, 38
Studios/flats:
● Les Antonins (400 units), 30 rue des Antonins, 69100 Villeurbanne
● Le Paradin (300 units), 24 rue Paradin, 69008 Lyon
● Studios 'Bron' (20 units), 3 rue Paul Pic, 69500 Bron
● Studios du 'Vieux Fort' (80 units), 2 rue Soeur Bouvier, 69005 Lyon
● Chambres 'Salengro-Le Beryl' (24 units), 28 rue Salengro, 69100

Villeurbanne
● Quartier 'Le Mas du Taureau' (100 units), Chemin du Pilat, 69120 Vaulx-en-Velin

CROUS restaurants
All serve the traditional meal while snacks, pizzas, etc., are available in adjoining *brasseries* or *cafétérias*.
● La Madeleine, 360 rue Garibaldi, 7e. Tel: 78 72 80 62. Buses 12, 35, 47; *Métro* Jean Macé
● Jean Mermoz, 98 avenue Jean Mermoz, 8e. Tel: 78 74 41 64. Buses 34, 39
● Jussieu, 3 avenue Albert Einstein, Villeurbanne. Tel: 78 93 34 21. Buses 26, 38, 69
● Puvis de Chavannes, 118 boulevard du 11 Novembre 1918, Villeurbanne. Tel: 78 89 62 02. Buses 26, 38
● André Allix, 2 rue Soeur Bouvier, 5e. Tel: 78 25 47 13. Buses 30, 49
● Bron-Parilly, avenue Mendès France, Bron-Parilly. Tel: 78 26 97 04. Buses 38, 91
● Cafétéria Lumière, same address. Tel: 78 75 49 11
● Cafétéria 'La Fac', 15 quai Claude Bernard, 7e. Tel: 72 73 07 02

Private-sector accommodation

There are several privately-run *foyers* and *résidences* in Lyon. A full list can be obtained from the CROUS or OSE. Here is a small selection:
● Foyer de Jeunes Filles (capacity 50; females), 10 place Puvis de Chavannes, 6e. Tel: 78 89 15 52. Buses 4, 27, 36; *Métro* Foch
● Foyer l'Escale Lyonnaise (capacity 140; females), 11 rue Bossuet, 69006 Lyon. Tel: 78 52 08 68
● Union Chrétienne de Jeunes Gens (mixed), 1 rue Charny, 69100 Villeurbanne. Tel: 78 53 21 79
● Résidences Les Tamaris, Le Shakespeare, MNEF, 20 rue François · Garcin, 69003 Lyon. Tel: 78 60 09 59
● Résidence Benjamin Delesert (capacity 366; males), 145 avenue Jean-Jaurès, 69007 Lyon. Tel: 78 61 41 41
● Résidence Bon Accueil (capacity 144; males), 57 rue Longfer, 69005 Lyon. Tel: 78 25 11 66

The town and its surrounding area

Standing at the confluence of the Rhône and the Saône, Lyon, with a population of well over a million, is the third largest town in France. It is a thriving commercial, industrial and academic centre with over 80,000 students. Lyon's rich history is reflected in its varied architecture and notable features include the stone amphitheatres at Fourvière, testifying to its Roman origins; the narrow streets and town houses from the Renaissance period, fine seventeenth-century buildings (the Hôtel de Ville, the Musée des Beaux-Arts, the Musée des Hospices); the civic buildings of the nineteenth century (the Bourse, the Palais de Justice, Théâtre des Célestins and Fourvière Cathedral); and representing the twentieth century the Musée de la Civilisation Gallo-Romaine and the cylindrical Tour de la Part-Dieu. Once the undisputed centre of the silk trade, Lyon is now the home of synthetic fibres and chemical products. The town's changing industrial base is recorded in its excellent museums: the Musée Historique des Tissus, the Musée des Arts Décoratifs, the Maison des Canuts and the Musée de l'Imprimerie et de la Banque.

The town is culturally active with several theatres, most notable of which are the Théâtre des Célestins, the Théâtre National Populaire and the Opera House. Lyon's love of the cinema is reflected in its many cinemas and thriving film clubs. Attractive pedestrianised areas, a modern *Métro* and a good bus service contribute to the pleasant life-style of the town. The two rivers, their bridges, the public squares, notably the tree-lined Place Bellecour, and the magnificent Parc de la Tête d'Or bring beauty to the town. Among the many famous personalities associated with Lyon are the poets Maurice Scève (1515–77) and Louise Labé (1526–66), the novelist Antoine de Saint Exupéry (1900–44), the sculptors Antoine Coysevox (1640–1720), Nicolas and Guillaume Coustou (1658–1733 and 1677–1746), Joseph Chinard (1756–1813), and François-Frédéric Lemot (1772–1827), the artists Jean Pillemont (1728–1808), Hippolyte Flandrin (1809–64), Ernest Meissonnier (1815–91) and Pierre Puvis de Chavannes (1824–98). In the sciences there are Joseph Jacquard (1752–1834) inventor of the power loom, the physicist André-Marie Ampère (1775–1836), Auguste Lumière (1862–1954), optical engineer and pioneer of the cinema, and the botanist Bernard de Jussieu (1699–1777).

Lyon and its region is synonymous with good but simple cooking, complemented by the wines of the Rhône valley (Mâcon and Beaujolais). The *charcuterie* of the region is famous, ranging from rolled pig's head with pistachios, *quenelle* (made with fish or chicken) and *cervelas* with truffles to the gigantic Lyon Jésus sausage. Desserts include *bugnes*, *matefaims* and walnut gâteaux. The town enjoys an excellent rail service with several TGV connections, is served by the motorway network and an international airport at Satolas.

Tourist information

Office du Tourisme, place Bellecour, 2e. Tel: 78 42 25 75
Comité Régional du Tourisme, 5 place de la Baleine, 5e. Tel: 78 42 50 04

Hotels

The following are reasonably priced and close to the main stations (Perrache and Part-Dieu) or the town centre.

- Hôtel Dubost, 19 place Carnot. Tel: 78 42 00 46. Fax: 72 40 96 96 (near Perrache; rooms between 202F and 282F; breakfast 32F)
- Hôtel des Savoies, 80 rue de la Charité, 2e. Tel: 78 37 66 94. Fax: 72 40 27 84 (near Perrache; rooms between 230F and 250F; breakfast 25F)
- Hôtel Columbia, 8 place Aristide-Briand, 3e. Tel: 78 60 54 65. Fax: 78 62 04 88 (near Part-Dieu; rooms from 220F to 270F; breakfast 29F)
- Hôtel Alexandra, 49 rue Victor Hugo, 2e. Tel: 78 37 75 79. Fax: 72 40 94 34 (central area-place Bellecour; rooms from 117F to 224F; breakfast 22F)

Short-term accommodation

- Auberge de Jeunesse de Lyon Vénissieux, 51 rue Salengro, Vénissieux. Tel: 78 76 39 23. Buses 35, 36, 76 (maximum stay 3 consecutive nights)
- Bed and Breakfast, 4 rue Joliot-Curie, 69005 Lyon. Tel: 78 36 37 19
- Centre International de Séjour de Lyon (CISL), 46 rue Cadet Pégout, 69008 Lyon. Tel: 78 01 23 45
- OSE, 78 rue de Marseille 69007 Lyon. Tel: 78 69 62 69

Restaurants

Lyon is famous as a gastronomic centre. Many restaurants will, however, be beyond a student budget. A number of reasonably-priced restaurants with fixed menus are found in rue Mercière and rue Tupin, 2e (*Métro* Cordeliers) such as La Tosca (60F, 70F), Le Bistro Romain (69F, 100F) and Pizzapapa (59F, 79F). The following offer good value with menus as low as 41F, but there are many others to be discovered!

- Les Trois Tonneaux, 4 rue des Marronniers, 1er. Tel: 78 37 34 72 (menus 55F and 100F)
- Le P'tit Comte, 17 rue Auguste Comte 2e. Tel: 72 41 06 09 (menus

41F and 125F)
- Le Patisson, 17 rue du Port-du-Temple 2e. Tel: 78 81 41 71 (menus 49F and 85F; vegetarian dishes)
- Le Relais, 39 rue Sainte-Hélène, 2e. Tel: 78 37 67 50 (menus 80F and 130F)

Homesick British students might like to try:
- The Albion Public House, 12 rue Sainte-Catherine, 1er. Tel: 78 28 33 00 ('Le vrai pub anglais de Lyon')

Leisure facilities

Lyon is second only to Paris in its range of cultural activities. Listings of films, plays, concerts and exhibitions, etc., are published in the weekly guide *Lyon Poche* (7F). Students can obtain a range of reductions on presentation of their student card, and there is also a special student pass (*le Pass-Culture*) which for 125F allows the holder to attend five performances at one or more of the following: l'Opéra, le Théâtre des Célestins, la Maison de la Danse, l'Orchestre national de Lyon and le Théâtre de Lyon. Students from Birmingham (UK), St Louis, Missouri and Montreal should apply to the Hôtel de Ville for a free pass (*le Pass Lyon Cité*) to the city's museums, art galleries, swimming pools and skating rinks. Applications should be made to: Le Bureau des échanges internationaux, Hôtel de Ville de Lyon. Tel: 79 39 07 10.

Museums and art galleries

The following is a selection. Check times of opening before visiting as these can vary throughout the year.
- Musée des Beaux-Arts, 20 place des Terreaux, Lyon 1er. Tel: 78 28 07 66 (20F; closed Mondays and Tuesdays)
- Musée Saint-Pierre d'Art Contemporain, 16 rue Président Edouard Herriot. Tel: 78 30 50 66 (20F; closed Tuesdays)
- Musée Historique de Lyon et Musée de la Marionnette, place du Petit-Collège, 5e. Tel: 78 42 03 61 (20F; closed Tuesdays)
- Musée de la Résistance, 5 rue Boileau, 6e. Tel: 78 93 27 83 (free; closed Mondays and Tuesdays)
- Musée des Arts Décoratifs, 30 rue de la Charité, 2e. Tel: 78 37 15 05
- Musée Historique des Tissus, 34 rue de la Charité, 2e. Tel: 78 37 15 05 (a single ticket for both museums costs 13F; closed Mondays)
- La Fondation de la Photographie et l'Institut Lumière, 25 rue du Premier Film, 8e. Tel: 78 00 86 68 (free; closed Mondays)

- Musée Gallo-Romain, 17 rue Cléberg, 5e. Tel: 78 25 94 68 (20F; closed Mondays and Tuesdays)
- Musée de l'Imprimerie de la Banque, 13 rue de la Poulaillerie, 2e. Tel: 78 37 65 98 (20F; closed Mondays and Tuesdays)

Theatre

There are 15 theatres in Lyon, but not all have programmes throughout the year. The following rank amongst the most important:
- Théâtre Les Ateliers, 5 rue du Petit David, 2e. Tel: 78 37 46 30
- Théâtre des Célestins, place des Célestins, 2e. Tel: 78 42 17 67. Buses 13, 23, 28
- Théâtre Guignol, 2 rue Louis Carrand, 5e. Tel: 78 28 92 57
- Théâtre de Lyon, 7 rue des Aqueducs, 5e. Tel: 78 36 67 67. Buses 2, 31, 44, 84
- Théâtre National Populaire, 8 place Lazare-Goujon, Villeurbanne. Tel: 78 03 30 30. Buses 38, 69
- Théâtre Tête d'Or, 24 rue Dunoir, 3e. Tel: 78 62 96 73. Buses: 4, 18, 26, 28

Cinema

Lyon has nearly 70 screens providing a wide choice of programmes. There are multiscreen cinemas showing new releases in rue de la République and the Part-Dieu Commercial Centre as well as several Art cinemas (*les cinémas d'Art et d'Essai*) which screen subtitled foreign films (*en version originale – V.O.*), established classics and second-run popular films. Reductions are available with a student card on specified days. Programmes are published weekly in *Lyon Poche*.
- Astoria, 31 cours Vitton, 6e. Tel: 36 65 70 45 (5 screens)
- Comoedia, 13 avenue Berthelot, 7e. Tel: 36 65 70 47 (6 screens)
- Pathé, 78 rue de la République, 2e. Tel: 78 37 64 64 (8 screens)
- Les 7 Nef, 20 rue Thomassin, 2e. Tel: 78 92 94 71 (7 screens)
- Pathé Cinéjournal, 71–75 rue de la République, 2e. Tel: 36 68 20 22 (5 screens)
- UGC Part-Dieu 2, CC Part-Dieu, 3e. Tel: 36 65 70 14 (6 screens)
- UGC Part-Dieu 4, CC Part-Dieu, 3e. Tel: 36 65 70 14 (8 screens)
- Les Alizes, 214 avenue Franklin Roosevelt, Bron. Tel: 72 37 20 24 (6 screens)

Art cinema
- CNP Bellecour, 12 rue de la Barre, 2e. Tel: 78 42 33 22 (4 screens)

- CNP Terreaux, 40 rue Edouard-Herriot, ler. Tel: 78 42 33 22 (6 screens)
- Fourmi Lafayette, 68 rue P. Corneille, 3e. Tel: 78 60 84 89 (6 screens)
- Institut Lumière, rue du Premier Film, 8e. Tel: 78 00 86 68
- Odéon-CNP, 6 rue Grolée, 2e. Tel: 78 42 33 22

Sport

FNSU: 43 boulevard du 11 Novembre 1918, Villeurbanne. Tel: 72 44 80 89

SIUAPS: same address. Tel: 72 44 80 95

Ice-skating: Patinoire Charlemagne, 100 cours Charlemagne, 2e. Tel: 78 42 64 55. Bus 8

Squash: 20 rue d'Essling, 3e. Tel: 78 95 13 25. Buses 37, 41

Tennis: 17 rue du Bat-d'Argent, ler. Tel: 78 27 37 97. *Métro* Cordeliers

Swimming pools:
- Bassin nautique de Gerland, 349 avenue Jean Jaurès, 7e. Tel: 78 72 66 17
- Garibaldi, 221 rue Garibaldi, 3e. Tel: 78 60 89 66
- Monplaisir, 19 avenue des Frères Lumière, 8e. Tel: 78 00 74 49.

Useful addresses

Main post office: place Antonin Poncet, 2e. *Métro* Bellecour

Municipal libraries:
- 30 boulevard Vivier-Merle, 3e. Tel: 78 95 40 73
- 10 rue Bourgelat, 2e. Tel: 78 37 21 62. *Métro* Ampère/Victor Hugo
- Palais Saint-Jean, 4 avenue Adolphe-Max, 5e. Tel: 78 92 83 50. Buses: 2, 28, 29, 30, 31, 44

Bookshops: there are bookshops on each campus (Decitre at la Doua; Cartillier and Berthezène at Bron-Parilly; ACEML at the Faculté de Médecine-Rockefeller; Corpo Lyon 3 at La Doua and Quai Bernard). Branches of the major bookshops are situated around place Bellecour (*Métro* Bellecour). The list is by no means exhaustive.
- Decitre, 29 place Bellecour, 2e. Tel: 72 40 54 54
- Flammarion, 19 place Bellecour, 2e. Tel: 78 38 01 57
- FNAC, 85 rue de la République, 2e. Tel: 72 40 49 49
- Gibert, 6 rue de la Barre, 2e. Tel: 78 42 22 22
- Eton, 1 rue du Plat, 2e. Tel: 78 92 92 36 (specialist English bookshop)
- Le Réverbère, 4 rue Neuve, 2e. Tel: 78 28 27 48 (specialist cinema bookshop)

CAF: 23 boulevard Jules Favre, 6e. Tel: 78 65 60 36
CAIO: 15 rue du Dauphiné, 3e. Tel: 78 54 62 55
Centre d'Information Municipal, Mairie Annexe, place Louis Pradel, 1er. Tel: 78 28 56 26
CIES: 16 avenue Berthelot, 7e. Tel: 78 69 28 99. Fax: 78 72 54 42
CLEF: 8 rue Bourgelat, 2e. Tel: 78 38 38 21
CRIJ: 9 quai des Célestins, 2e. Tel: 78 37 15 28
Lost property: 5 rue Bichat, 2e. Tel: 78 42 43 82
Mairie du 8e, 12 avenue Jean Mermoz, 8e. Tel: 78 74 18 38 (provides help for students looking for temporary employment)
ONISEP: 15 place des Terreaux, 1er. Tel: 78 28 66 49
OSE:
- 78 rue de Marseille, 7e. Tel: 76 69 51 24
- 43 rue Jaboulay, 7e. Tel: 78 58 65 83
- 26–28 rue Viala, 3e. Tel: 78 54 68 02
British Consulate-General: 24 rue Childebert, 69002. Tel: 78 37 59 67. Fax: 72 40 25 24. Buses 8, 9, 23, 24, 26, 28, 58
US Consulate: 45 rue de la Bourse. Tel: 72 40 59 20. Fax: 72 41 71 81
Préfecture: 106 rue Pierre Corneille, 3e. Tel: 72 61 60 60. Buses 4, 9, 23, 24, 25, 26, 28
Préfecture du Rhône, 14 bis quai Général Sarrail, 6e.

The following organisations welcome foreign students to Lyon:
ALRESE: 69 rue Jean Jaurès, 69100 Villeurbanne. Tel: 78 58 06 19 (Tuesday and Thursday mornings)
CLALU: 59, rue de la Madeleine, 69007. Tel: 78 72 53 47
Rhône-Accueil: 5 place de la Baleine, 5e. Tel: 78 42 50 03 (Friday at 18h30)

Health care

SUMP (MPU): (open Mondays-Fridays, 8.30–16.30):
- La Doua, 43 boulevard du 11 Novembre 1918, 69622 Villeurbanne Cedex. Tel: 78 93 97 97. Buses 26, 78
- Lumière II, Bron, Bât. L, Porte 25, avenue Pierre Mendès France, 69676 Bron Cedex. Tel: 78 00 60 05
Centre Medico-Sportif: 27 boulevard du 11 Novembre 1918, 69622 Villeurbanne. Tel: 78 94 92 93 (for sports injuries)
Chemists (24-hour service):
- Pharmacie Blanchet, 5 place des Cordeliers, 2e. Tel: 78 42 12 42. *Métro* Cordeliers

- Pharmacie Corrand, 28 avenue Henri Barbusse, 69100 Villeurbanne. Tel: 78 84 71 63. *Métro* Gratte-Ciel
- Pharmacie du Château d'Eau, 19 avenue Jean-Cagne, Vénissieux. Tel: 78 70 26 70. Buses 12, 36, 90
- Pharmacie Perret, 30 rue Duquesne, 6e. Tel: 78 93 70 96. *Métro* Foch or Masséna; buses: 27, 36

Hospitals:
- Centre Hospitalier Lyon-Sud, 69495 Pierre Bénite Cedex. Tel: 78 86 10 00
- Hôpital Edouard Herriot, 5 place d'Arsonval, 8e. Tel: 78 53 81 11. Buses 1, 9
- Hôpital de la Croix Rousse, 93 Grand rue de la Croix Rousse, 4e. Tel: 72 07 10 00
- Hôpital de l'Hôtel Dieu, 1 place de l'Hôpital, 2e. Tel: 78 92 20 00

Local student insurance offices:
- MNEF, 20 rue François Garcin, 69423 Lyon Cedex 03. Tel: 78 60 09 59 Buses 4, 18, 26; *Métro* Guichard
- SMERRA, 43 rue Jaboulay, 69349 Lyon Cedex 07. Tel: 78 58 65 83. *Métro* Jean-Macé

Travel

Discount travel tickets can be obtained from student organisations such as OTU (see under CROUS); MNEF; SMERRA; OSE or CRIJ. Alternatively try Voyage Wasteels at one of the following addresses:
- Centre d'Echange de Perrache
- 5 place Ampère, 2e
- 40 cours de Verdun, 2e
- Campus de la Doua

Railway stations
- Gare de la Part-Dieu, boulevard Vivier Merle, 3e. Tel: 78 92 50 50
- Gare de Perrache, 2e. Tel: 78 92 50 50

London-Lyon (via Newhaven-Dieppe) £127 return; via Dover-Calais £130 return (Eurotrain)

Coach station
Centre d'Echanges, Perrache. Tel: 72 41 09 09. *Métro* Perrache. London-Lyon, £82 return; £51 single (Eurolines)

Airports
- Lyon-Satolas. Tel: 72 22 72 21 (Coach Colibri from Perrache or Part-Dieu; 42F)
- Lyon-Bron. Tel: 78 26 81 09. Bus 65

Bus/Métro
Société Lyonnaise de Transports en Commun (TCL). Head Office: boulevard Vivier Merle, Part-Dieu, 69003 Lyon. Tel: 78 60 25 53. For information about routes, timetables and fares, tel: 78 71 70 00. Fares: for a single journey by bus or *Métro*, 7F. A book of 6 tickets with student reduction, 32F; 20 tickets, 95F. Monthly pass 213F, after obtaining a Carte Orange (15F). This card also allows a 20% reduction on standard ticket prices.

Taxis
- Allo Taxi. Tel: 78 28 23 23
- Taxi Lyonnais. Tel: 78 26 81 81
- Taxi Radio. Tel: 78 30 86 86

Emergencies

Ambulance. Tel: 72 33 15 15
Centre anti-poisons. Tel: 78 54 14 14
Police: place Antonin Poncet. Tel: 78 28 92 93
SAMU. Tel: 72 33 15 15
SOS Amitiés. Tel: 78 29 88 88 *or* 78 85 33 33
SOS Médecins: 10 place Dumas de Loire, 9e. Tel: 78 83 51 51
Urgence dentaire. Tel: 72 04 68 68

12 Montpellier

The universities and their disciplines

Montpellier I: droit et sciences économiques, formations de santé, sciences alimentaires, sport.
   5 boulevard Henri IV, BP 1017, 34006 Montpellier Cedex 1. Tel: 67 41 20 90. Fax: 67 41 02 46
SUIO: same address. Tel: 67 54 17 37
Université des Sciences et Techniques du Languedoc (**Montpellier II**): droit, sciences économiques, sciences et technologie.

place Eugène Bataillon, 34095 Montpellier Cedex 5. Tel: 67 14 30
30. Fax: 67 14 30 31
SUIO: same address. Tel: 67 14 30 60
IUT: 99 avenue d'Occitanie, 34096 Montpellier Cedex 5. Tel: 67 63 38
86
Université Paul-Valéry (**Montpellier III**): lettres, langues, sciences
humaines, droit et sciences économiques.
route de Mende, BP 5043, 34032 Montpellier Cedex. Tel: 67 14 20
00. Fax: 67 14 20 52
SUIO: same address. Tel: 67 14 23 42

University libraries
● Bibliothèque Interuniversitaire, 4 rue Ecole Mage. Tel: 67 84 77 77
● Section Lettres, route de Mende. Tel: 67 61 00 66
● Section Médecine, 2 rue école de Médecine. Tel: 67 66 27 77
● Section Pharmacie, 11 avenue Charles Flahault. Tel: 67 61 01 55
● Section Science, place Eugène Bataillon. Tel: 67 63 28 31

Courses for languages undergraduates

LEA offers the following modern foreign languages: Czech, English,
German, Modern Greek, Italian, Portuguese, Romanian, Russian and
Spanish.
Lettres Modernes courses include a wide choice of options. It is pos-
sible to study the language and civilisation of France, Germany, Greece,
Italy, Portugal, Russia and Spain. There are also language-only options
in Czech and Slavonic tongues, Hebrew, Romanian, Turkish, Catalan
and Occitan. Courses in Comparative Literature, Approaches to
Literature, Linguistics, Cinema, Theatre, History, Philosophy,
Sociology and Ethnology, Psychology, Art History and Egyptology,
Geography, Music and Sport complete a generous range of possibilities.

Courses for foreign students

Full-year or semester-based courses
Institut Montpelliérain d'Etudes Françaises (IMEF), 21 avenue Professeur Grasset, BP 4202, 34092 Montpellier Cedex 5. Tel: 67 52 30
40. Fax: 67 41 39 09

There are courses for beginners, intermediate and advanced students who are taught in groups of 8 to 15 for approximately 21 hours per week. There is a placement test on arrival and students must be at least 17 years of age. *Certificats de stage* validate attainment. Accommodation is usually in single rooms with half-board. Cultural activities are organised throughout the year.

Vacation courses

Centre Universitaire de Vacances, Université Paul Valéry, BP 5043, 34032 Montpellier Cedex 1. Tel: 67 14 22 29. Fax: 67 41 29 75

During July, August and September the centre organises courses at beginners', intermediate and advanced levels in discrete programmes, each lasting three or four weeks. Applicants must be at least 17 years of age and take a placement test on arrival. A *diplôme d'université* may be awarded at the end of the course. There is a generous programme of leisure activities both in Montpellier and further afield. These include cinema and theatre evenings, swimming, team sports and walking tours.

Cours Intensifs de Français (CIF), 87 rue de la Chênaie, 34090 Montpellier. Tel: 67 52 32 20. Fax: 67 04 18 23.

The CIF offers month-long courses during July and August which are taught exclusively by university staff. The programmes cater for students at the following levels: beginners', intermediate and advanced. Applicants must be at least 17 years of age. A *certificat d'assiduité* is awarded to successful candidates at the end of the course. Accommodation is provided, and extra-curricular activities include visits to Mediterranean resorts, Nîmes, Avignon, Carcassonne, Arles and the Camargue.

CROUS

2 rue Monteil, BP 5053 Montpellier Justice, 34033 Montpellier Cedex. Tel: 67 63 53 93. Fax: 67 04 26 96. Buses: 2, 5, 6

OTU: same address. Tel: 67 41 10 29

SAEE: 11 rue Baudin. Tel: 67 58 27 43

CROUS-controlled accommodation

There are six *cités universitaires* with a total of 5,710 rooms.

- Boutonnet, 119 rue Faubourg Boutonnet, 34053 Montpellier Cedex 1. Tel: 67 61 11 31 (797 rooms). Buses 2, 5, 6
- Les Arceaux, 61 boulevard des Arceaux, 34053 Montpellier Cedex. Tel: 67 58 17 00 (435 rooms). Bus 9

- La Colombière, 570 route de Ganges, 34096 Montpellier Cedex 5. Tel: 67 04 28 48 (890 rooms). Buses 2, 6, 10
- Le Triolet, avenue Augustin Fliche, 34096 Montpellier Cedex 5. Tel: 67 04 10 80 (1,000 rooms; opposite the Université des Sciences et Techniques du Languedoc). Buses 2, 6
- Vert-Bois, 192 rue de la Chênaie, 34096 Montpellier Cedex 5. Tel: 67 04 02 62 (981 rooms; next to the Université Paul Valéry). Bus 5
- Voie Domitienne, 259 voie Domitienne, 34096 Montpellier Cedex 5. Tel: 67 04 03 05 (991 rooms; next to the UFR Pharmacie). Buses 3, 6, 7, 10
- Résidence Logement, 6 rue du Colonel Marchand, 34000 Montpellier Cedex (55 *studios* with APL).
- Résidence Minerve, avenue de l'abbé Paul Parguel (200 *studios* with APL; adjacent to **Montpellier II**).

Addresses of approved, privately-rented accommodation can be obtained from the CROUS between 2 and 4.30 p.m. CROUS accepts no legal responsibility for this service. Usually two months' rent is payable in advance together with the equivalent of another two months' as a *caution*. Insurance is obligatory.

CROUS restaurants

There are four *restaurants universitaires*, all serving traditional three-course meals, located as follows:

- RU des Arceaux, rue Gustave. Tel: 67 58 17 00
- RU de Boutonnet, 2 rue Emile Duployé. Tel: 67 63 52 06 (next to the CROUS)
- RU de Vert-Bois, 205 rue de la Chênaie. Tel: 67 63 48 96
- RU du Triolet, rue du Professeur Anglada. Tel: 67 63 50 16

Boutonnet and Vert-Bois also serve single-course set menus; Triolet caters for special dietary needs.

Private-sector accommodation

The following *résidences* are run for students by organisations other than the CROUS. For details write to the Association des Résidences Internationales (ARI), Résidence Agropolis, avenue d'Agropolis, 34000 Montpellier. Tel: 67 54 79 13

- Résidence Cambaceres, Quartier de la Paillade
- Résidence Internationale d'Agropolis, Domaine de Lavallette, avenue d'Agropolis
- Résidence Olympique, place Marcel Godechot

● Tour Monge, Quartier de la Paillade

Privately-run hostels

For further details, write to the *Directeur/Directrice*:
● Foyer Claire Joie, 14 rue de la Merci. Tel: 67 92 62 71
● Foyer Sainte Famille, 22 bis rue Carré du Roi. Tel: 67 63 47 09
● Foyer International Theresanium, 6 rue des Carmélites. Tel: 67 63 55 49
● Institut Protestant de Théologie, 13 rue Louis Perrier. Tel: 67 92 34 68
● Couvent des Dominicains, 8 rue Fabre. Tel: 67 66 02 00
● Centre St Guilhem, 4 rue abbé Montels. Tel: 67 60 76 66

The town and its surrounding area

In origin a medieval city, Montpellier has been subsequently graced with rich merchants' town houses dating from the seventeenth and eighteenth centuries and fine public works. It also has several examples of the best of twentieth-century architecture. The Peyrou gardens, the *Aqueduc* with its magnificent Château d'Eau, the Jardin des Plantes, the Arc de Triomphe, the Place de la Comédie (*l'Oeuf*) with its well-proportioned theatre, all contribute to the beauty of the city. The old quarters with their narrow, twisting streets are particularly attractive. Among the more striking modern creations is the imposing Antigone development designed by the Catalonian architect Ricardo Bofill. Now the prosperous regional *préfecture* of Languedoc-Roussillon with over 200,000 inhabitants, Montpellier is an important administrative, commercial and cultural centre and, with the nearby Mediterranean beaches of Palavas and Carnon, an important tourist area. Inland, the striking Causse region offers several cave systems, including the Grotte de Clamouse, and the picturesque village of Saint Guilhem-le-Désert. The university, founded in 1289, is one of the oldest in Europe and counts among its former students François Rabelais. Montpellier now has three universities which attract some 55,000 students, and the town is geared to cultural activities, with many theatrical groups, over thirty cinema screens, regular concerts and several good bookshops. Among the famous associated with Montpellier are Auguste Comte (1798–1857), the founder of Positivism; Pierre Magnol (1638–1715), the botanist credited with plant classification; the artists Sebastien Bourdon (1616–71), Jean Ranc (1674–1735), F.-X. Fabre (1766–1837) and Frédéric Bazille (1841–70); and the organ builder Aristide Cavaillé-Coll (1811–99). The wines of Languedoc-Roussillon are enjoying increasing esteem and the nearby *bassin de Thau* provides oysters and mussels. The region is known for its fresh fruit and confectionery made from honey and liquorice. There are good travel connections with the rest of France and Spain. A TGV service links Montpellier to Paris and the A9 gives access to the motorway system. There are regular flights serving London and New York from the international airport.

Tourist information

Tourist office: L'Office du Tourisme, le Triangle, allée du Tourisme. Tel: 67 58 67 58. Fax: 67 58 67 59

Hotels
The following are near the station and convenient for the town centre (rooms with breakfast cost between 190F and 290F).
- Hôtel d'Angleterre, 7 rue Maguelone. Tel: 67 58 59 50. Fax: 67 58 29 52
- Hôtel Le Mistral, 25 rue Boussairolles. Tel: 67 58 45 25
- Hôtel France, 3–4 rue de la République. Tel: 67 92 68 14

Youth hostel
Rue des Ecoles Laïques. Tel: 67 60 32 32. Fax: 67 60 32 30

Restaurants
- Le Feu Follet, 10 rue du petit St-Jean. Tel: 67 66 01 63 (menus between 45F and 120F)
- La Tomate, 6 rue du Four des Flammes. Tel: 67 60 49 63 (menus between 50F and 80F; Tuesdays-Saturdays)
- Le Provençal, 18 rue du Petit St-Jean. Tel: 67 60 52 13 (menu at 65F; Mondays-Fridays)
- Romulus, cour de la Bobote. Tel: 67 66 17 03 (open every day; pizzas at about 45F, salades 22F, meat dishes 75F)

Leisure facilities

Details of cinema, concert and theatre programmes are published in the free listings magazine *Sortir*.

Theatre

- Opéra Berlioz, le Corum. Tel: 67 61 67 61
- Opéra de Montpellier, place de la Comédie. Tel: 67 66 31 11
- Théâtre de Grammont, route de Maugio. Tel: 67 64 14 42
- Théâtre du Chai, Château d'O, 857 rue St Priest. Tel: 67 61 06 30
- Théâtre Iséion, 18 rue Fouques. Tel: 67 58 38 15
- Théâtre Lakanal, 20 rue Lakanal. Tel: 67 79 65 51
- Nouveau Théâtre, 19 rue Chaptal. Tel: 67 58 64 76
- Théâtre des Treize Vents, avenue A. Einstein. Tel: 67 64 14 42

Cinema

- Gaumont, place de la Comédie. Tel: 67 52 72 00 (7 screens; reductions with student card)
- Capitole, 5 rue de Verdun. Tel: 67 58 44 74 (6 screens)
- Royal, 13 rue Boussairolles. Tel: 67 58 04 03 (5 screens)

Cinémas d'art et d'essai:

- Diagonal Campus, 5 avenue du Dr Pezet. Tel: 67 52 32 00
- Diagonal Celleneuve, place P. Renaudel. Tel: 67 75 41 90
- Diagonal Paillad', 418 avenue de Barcelone. Tel: 67 75 75 20
- Ciné-Club Jean Vigo, 6 rue de la Vieille Aiguillerie. Tel: 67 66 36 36

Music

- Le Corum, Esplanade Charles de Gaulle. Tel: 67 61 67 61. (Orchestre philharmonique de Montpellier)
- Conservatoire National de Région, 14 rue Eugene Lisbonne. Tel: 67 60 79 33

Museums and art galleries

- Musée Fabre, boulevard Sarrail. Tel: 67 66 06 34 (free on Wednesdays; otherwise, students 16F)
- Musée Atger, rue Ecole de Médecine. Tel: 67 66 27 77 (free; open in the afternoons, Monday to Friday, October to May)
- Musée du Vieux Montpellier, Hôtel de Varenne, place Pétraque. Tel: 67 66 02 94 (open in the afternoons, Monday to Friday)
- Musée Languedocien, 7 rue Jacques Coeur. Tel: 67 52 93 03 (open in the afternoons, Monday to Friday)

Sports

Direction Municipale des Sports, 18 avenue Frédéric Mistral. Tel: 67 34 72 73

FNSU: 532 rue du Professeur Emile Jeanbreau. Tel: 67 14 39 18
STAPS: 700 avenue du Pic St Loup. Tel: 67 54 62 62
- Centre Sportif Universitaire, avenue Triolet. Tel: 67 63 48 42 (apply here to obtain your card for all university sports facilities)
- Palais des Sports, avenue du Val-de-Montferrand. Tel: 67 54 00 07
- Complexe Sportif de Grammont, avenue A. Einstein. Tel: 67 64 29 55
- Stade de la Mosson, avenue Heidelberg. Tel: 67 40 04 36
Swimming pools:
- ASPTT, route de Vanguière. Tel: 67 65 40 70
- La Motte Rouge, avenue Pr E Jeanbreau. Tel: 67 63 48 42
- CREPS, 2 avenue Charles Flahaut. Tel: 67 61 05 22
- Centre Nautique de la Paillade, avenue de Heildeberg. Tel: 67 75 34 93 (summer only)
- Piscine Aude Maurin, 1933 avenue de Maurin. Tel: 67 27 74 79
Squash: Diabolo Squash, 104 faubourg Boutonnet. Tel: 67 54 64 54
Ice-skating: Patinoire Olympique, 669 avenue de Vert-Bois. Tel: 67 63 32 28
Bowling: 662 avenue de la Pompignane. Tel: 67 65 80 08
Tennis:
- Complexe Sportif de Grammont, avenue A. Einstein. Tel: 67 64 29 55
- Stade Universitaire, avenue Pr E Jeanbreau. Tel: 67 14 31 70

Miscellaneous
Jardin des Plantes, 163 rue A Broussonnet. Tel: 67 63 43 22
Zoo: parc de Lunaret, avenue du val de Montferrand. Tel: 67 54 45 23

Useful addresses

Main post office: PTT, place Rondelet, rue Rondelet. Tel: 67 34 50 00
Other offices in the centre of Montpellier:
- Avenue Buisson Bertrand. Tel: 67 54 02 88
- PTT Préfecture, place des Martyrs de la Résistance.
- Avenue de la Justice (nearest to the Faculté). Tel: 67 63 49 91
Mairie: 1 place Francis Ponge. Tel: 67 34 70 00
Prefecture: 1, rue de Pilory. Tel: 67 61 61 61
Commissariat Central: avenue Professeur Grasset. Tel: 67 22 78 22. (for residence and work permits). Buses 2, 5, 7
Commissariat de Police: 10 rue Flaugergues. Tel: 67 22 78 77 (lost property)

Municipal library: 37 boulevard Bonne Nouvelle. Tel: 67 60 77 06
American library: 11 rue St-Louis. Tel 67 58 13 44 (student sub-
    scription 100F per year)
Bookshops:
- FNAC, Centre Commercial Le Polygone, Niveau 1. Tel: 67 64 14 00
- Sauramps, Le Triangle. Tel: 67 58 85 15
- Librairie Gibert, 3 place des Martyrs de la Résistance. Tel: 67 66 27
  20
- Librairie Gibert, 6 rue de l'Université. Tel: 67 52 85 15
- La Bouquinerie du Languedoc, 12 rue de l'Université. Tel: 67 60 67
  57
- Book Shop, 4 rue de l'Université. Tel: 67 66 09 08 (English books
  and periodicals)
- Arcane, 13 rue des Ecoles Laïques. Tel: 67 60 30 25
Centre Culturel Britannique, 23 rue du Général Riu. Tel: 67 64 07 86
Centre Culturel Celtic: 10 rue de Berger. Tel: 67 66 22 66
Centre Culturel Irlandais: 273 rue du Mas de Portaly. Tel: 67 92 95 98
Centre International des Etudiants et Stagiaires (CIES): 4 rue Jules
    Ferry. Tel: 67 58 92 12
French-American Centre: 4 rue St-Louis. Tel: 67 92 30 66
ANPE:
- 3 rue Dubreuil. Tel: 67 84 51 00
- quai Louis Le Vau, Zac de la Fontaine, Celleneuve. Tel: 67 84 78 70
CAF: 8 rue Chaptal. Tel: 67 92 48 78
Chambre de Commerce: 32 rue Jean Moulin. Tel: 67 55 91 55
CPAM: 29 cours Gambetta. Tel: 67 22 86 00
CRDP: allée de la Citadelle. Tel: 67 60 74 66
Nearest British Consulate-General (Marseille): 24 avenue du Prado,
    13006 Marseille. Tel: 91 53 43 32. Fax: 91 37 47 06
Nearest US Consulate-General (Marseille): 12 boulevard Paul Peytral,
    13286 Marseille Cedex. Tel: 91 54 92 00. Fax: 91 55 09 47

Health care

Hospitals:
- Hôpital Saint-Eloi, 2 avenue Bertin Sans. Tel: 67 33 90 50. Buses 2,
  10
- Hôpital Saint-Charles, 300 rue Broussonnet. Tel: 67 33 67 33.
  Buses 2, 3, 4, 5, 6, 7, 9, 11, 14
- Hôpital Lapeyronie, 555 route de Ganges. Tel: 67 33 90 50. Bus 2

Chemists:
- Centre Commercial du Pré aux Clercs (opposite Résidence Boutonnet)
- place Albert ler, boulevard Pasteur

Local student insurance offices:
- MNEF: 13 rue de Ratte. Tel: 67 66 18 10
- MEP: 3 place de la Canourgue. Tel: 67 66 06 50

Travel

Students can obtain cut-price tickets from OTU at CROUS. Other outlets are:

Voyages Wasteels:
- 6 rue de la Saunerie. Tel: 67 58 74 26
- 1 rue Combacérès. Tel: 67 66 20 19

Council Travel: 20 rue de l'Université. Tel: 67 60 89 29

Railway station
Place Auguste Gilbert. Tel: 67 58 50 50. London-Montpellier (via Newhaven-Dieppe) £140 return; (via Dover-Calais) £144 return (Eurotrain)

Coach station
Place du Bicentenaire. Tel: 67 92 01 43
Eurolines (tel: 67 58 57 59) and Iberbus (tel: 67 64 35 42) have London-Montpellier services: £99 return; £58 single (Eurolines)

Local bus services
- Société Montpelliéraine de Transports Urbains (SMTU), 27 rue Maguelone. Tel: 67 22 87 87. Single tickets: *trajet court*, 6F; *trajet long* 8F50; with bus pass 6 tickets cost 20F.
- SERNAM: 28 rue du Grand St Jean. Tel: 67 92 29 09

Taxis
- Taxis Radio Artisans Montpellier (TRAM). Tel: 67 92 04 55
- Radio Taxis, Gare SNCF. Tel: 67 58 74 82 (24-hour service)

Airport
Aéroport Montpellier-Méditerrannée. Tel: 67 20 85 00
Courrier du Midi Coach Service no. 120 runs between Montpellier and the airport. Air France/British Airways have direct flights London-

Montpellier (Air France, tel: 67 92 48 28; British Airways, tel: 67 65 88 88)

Emergencies

Gendarmerie. Tel: 67 54 61 11
Duty Doctors. SOS Médecins Hérault, 21 avenue du Jeu de Mail, Castelnau-le-Nez. Tel: 67 72 22 15
SAMU. Tel: 67 63 00 00
SOS Amitiés. Tel: 67 63 00 63

13 Nancy

The universities and their disciplines

(Académie de Nancy-Metz) **Nancy I**: formations de santé, sciences exactes et naturelles, technologie, sport.
  24 rue Lionnois, BP 3069, 54013 Nancy. Tel: 83 32 81 81. Fax: 83 32 95 90
IUT: Le Montet, 54600 Villers-lès-Nancy. Tel: 83 91 20 00
SUIO: Campus Scientifique, boulevard des Aiguillettes, BP 239, 54506 Vandoeuvre-lès-Nancy Cedex. Tel: 83 91 20 00
Nancy II: sciences juridiques, économiques et commerciales, lettres et sciences humaines, sciences administratives, technologie.
  25 rue Baron Louis, BP 454, 54001 Nancy Cedex. Tel: 83 34 46 00. Fax: 83 30 05 65
IUT: 2 bis boulevard Charlemagne, 54000 Nancy. Tel: 83 91 31 31
SUIO: 14 rue de la Ravinelle, Case officielle 26, 54035 Nancy Cedex. Tel: 83 36 72 30
Institut National Polytechnique de Lorraine: agronomie, électricité, énergétique, métallurgie, géologie.
  2 avenue de la Forêt de Haye, ZAC de Brabois, BP 3, 54501 Vandoeuvre-lès-Nancy Cedex. Tel: 83 59 59 59. Fax: 83 59 59 55
SUIO: same address. Tel: 83 59 59 30

University libraries
Bibliothèques Interuniversitaires
● Section Lettres, 46 avenue de la Libération, BP 3408, 54015 Nancy Cedex. Tel: 83 96 12 59
● Section Droit, 11 place Carnot, 54042 Nancy Cedex. Tel: 83 37 02 13

- Section IUT, 2 bis boulevard Charlemagne, 54000. Tel: 83 27 30 85, ext. 250
- Section Sciences, rue du Jardin Botanique, 54600 Villers-lès-Nancy. Tel: 83 91 22 90
- Section Médecine, 9 avenue de la Forêt de Haye, 54500 Vandoeuvre. Tel: 83 54 01 60
- Section Pharmacie, 30 rue Lionnois, 54000. Tel: 83 36 45 76
- Section Dentaire, 96 avenue Maréchal de Lattre de Tassigny, BP 3034, 54012 Cedex. Tel: 83 36 74 62

Courses for languages undergraduates

LEA offers the following modern foreign languages: English, German, Italian and Russian.

Lettres Modernes offers a DEUG course which is usually to the liking of British undergraduates. Latin is not compulsory and a number of interesting literature courses are on offer. A distinctive feature of the Faculté des Lettres is the Bibliothèque Sonore which is run by the languages departments and which provides up-to-the-minute information on current affairs in the countries of the target languages.

Courses for foreign students

Vacation courses
Cours d'Eté pour Etudiants Etrangers, Université de Nancy II, 23 boulevard Albert ler, BP 33–97, 54015 Nancy Cedex. Tel: 83 34 36 00. Fax: 83 96 23 47

Courses run in July from beginners' to advanced levels (approx. 25 hours per week over 2, 3 or 4 weeks). There is a placement test on arrival, and students are taught in groups of approximately 15. In addition there are *séminaires de pédagogie et de didactique* for intending foreign teachers of French. Optional couses include French Literature, Civilisation, the Press, Current Affairs, and Commercial French. Candidates must be over 18, and accommodation is in university halls of residence.

CROUS

75 rue de Laxou, 54042 Nancy Cedex. Tel: 83 91 88 20. Fax: 83 27 47 87
OTU: same address

CROUS-controlled accommodation

There are some 5,307 beds in halls of residence, HLM and *studios* in the town. The hall of residence where most foreign students registered at the Faculté des Lettres are housed is Boudonville, which is situated barely five minutes' walk away.

Mixed residences (general telephone number: 83 91 88 00)

• Résidence de Monbois, 2 rue Ludovic Beauchet, 54052
• Résidence de Saurupt, 26 rue de Saurupt, 54052
• Résidence de Vandoeuvre-Monplaisir, rue Jacques Callot, 54500 Vandoeuvre
• Résidence du Charmois, allée du Charmois, 54500 Vandoeuvre
• Résidence de la Haute-Malgrange, rue Jean Lamour, 54500 Vandoeuvre
• Résidence du Placieux, boulevard Maréchal Lyautey, 54600 Villers-lès-Nancy
• Résidence de Boudonville, 61 rue de Boudonville, 54000
• Résidence de Médreville, 28 rue Aristide Briand, 54524 Laxou
• Résidence le Provençal, rue Marie Leszczynska, 54000
• Résidence la Batelière, 7–15 route de Metz, 54320 Maxeville.

Women's hall (no male visitors allowed):

• Résidence Notre Dame de Lourdes, 3 rue Notre Dame de Lourdes, 54000. Tel: 83 91 88 00

CROUS restaurants

• RU de Brabois, 9 avenue de la Forêt de Haye, 54500 Vandoeuvre. Tel: 83 91 88 00 (two outlets for *menus traditionnels* and *brasserie* at lunchtime. Cafeteria with snacks from breakfast to late afternoon)
• RU de Médreville, 73 rue de Laxou. Tel: 83 91 88 00 *(menu traditionnel, brasserie, rotisserie,* Greek *cuisine* in the evening)
• RU de Vandoeuvre, rue Jacques Callot, 54500 Vandoeuvre. Tel: 83 91 88 00 (two outlets for *menus traditionnels, brasserie, viennoiseries.* Cafeteria service. Also caters for *régime médico-diététique)*
• RU de Saurupt, 26 rue de Saurupt. Tel: 83 91 88 00 *(menu traditionnel* at lunchtime and in the evening, and *brasserie)*
• RU du Cours Léopold, 16 cours Léopold. Tel: 83 91 88 00 (three outlets for *menus traditionnels,* one with extra dishes for cash, plus *brasserie,* cafeteria and sandwich bar)
• RU de Monbois, 138 avenue de la Libération. Tel: 83 91 88 00 (*menu traditionnel* and *brasserie*; reservations accepted)

Privately-run hostels

- Foyer de l'Assomption Etudiantes, 37 rue Raymond Poincaré. Tel: 83 40 22 45
- Foyer Desilles, 13 rue de la Craffe. Tel: 83 32 20 52
- Groupe des Etudiants Catholiques de Nancy, 35 cours Léopold, 54042. Tel: 83 35 48 67
- Maison Sainte-Marie, 28 rue Primatiale. Tel: 83 35 09 03

The town and its surrounding area

Nancy is situated some 310 kilometres to the east of Paris and is easily accessible by road and rail from the capital. There is a small local airport with flights to Paris, but flights from the UK to Luxembourg offer the best service for British students. Nancy is the historical capital of the Duché de Lorraine. The *vieille ville* is what remains of the town which was developed in the Middle Ages by the Dukes of Lorraine. Charles le Téméraire, Duke of Burgundy, met his death there in 1477 when he was defeated by René II, Duke of Lorraine, in an unsuccessful attack on the refortified town. In 1725, ex-king Stanislas of Poland married his daughter to Louis XV of France and received the Duchy of Lorraine in 1737. He was the last Duke and Lorraine became French on his death in 1766. Le Palais Ducal (only one part of the original façade still stands) now houses the Musée Historique Lorrain which has an outstanding collection. L'Eglise des Cordeliers, adjacent to the Palais, was consecrated in 1487 and contains the tombs of several of the Ducs de Lorraine. The *ville neuve* goes back to the end of the sixteenth century and Charles III; there still remains the Porte de la Graffe, the Porte Notre Dame, the Porte Saint Georges and the Porte Saint Nicholas. The most outstanding architectural feature of the town is undoubtedly the magnificent Place Stanislas (formerly Place Royal) which dates from 1750–55 and is the work of the local architect Emmanuel Héré (1705–63) and of the famous iron-master, Jean Lamour. The shopping centre is excellent and contains a wide range of shops from boutiques to department stores. The local buses and trolley-buses offer a good service. The cultural life of the town has a lot to offer: cinemas, theatre, opera, ballet, jazz clubs, dance, classical concerts and a whole range of sporting activities. A most useful publication on current cultural activities is entitled *Spectacles à Nancy* and can be obtained free of charge (for information, ring 83 35 30 20).

Tourist information

Office du Tourisme, 14 place Stanislas, 54000. Tel: 83 35 22 41

Hotels
- Hôtel Foch, 8 avenue Foch. Tel: 83 32 88 50 (near town centre and railway station)
- Hôtel Ibis, 3 rue Crampel. Tel: 83 32 90 16 (single rooms up to 290F)
- Hôtel Les Portes d'Or, 21 rue Stanislas. Tel: 83 35 42 34 (50 metres from place Stanislas; rooms 195F-280F)

Restaurants
- La Bolée, 47 rue des Ponts. Tel: 83 37 17 53 (a *crêperie* popular with students)
- Pub des Arts, 21 bis rue Saint Dizier (cours des Arts; a *brasserie-restaurant*, open every day from 9.00 till the early hours)
- Le Vesuvio, 17 rue Stanislas. Tel: 83 32 22 05 (French and Italian *cuisine*)
- Pizzéria chez Moretti, 14 rue de l'Armée Parron. Tel: 80 40 34 16 (close to the Faculté des Lettres; offers a typical Italian menu, with prices to suit most pockets)
- La Petite Marmite, 8 rue Gambetta. Tel: 83 35 25 63 (offers excellent value for those more special occasions; advance booking essential; menus 85F-145F)

Leisure facilities

Museums/art galleries/churches
- Palais Ducal et Musée Lorrain, 64 Grande Rue. Tel: 83 32 18 74 (reduction for students)
- Musée des Arts et Traditions Populaires, Couvent des Cordeliers, 66 Grande Rue. Tel: 83 32 18 74
- Eglise des Cordeliers et Chapelle Ducale, 66 Grande Rue. Tel: 83 32 18 74 (visits leave daily from the Musée Lorrain)
- Musée de l'Ecole de Nancy, 36–38 rue Sergent Blandan. Tel: 83 40 14 86 (contains works which are characteristic of the French contribution to Art Nouveau (Daum, Gallé, Majorelle, etc.); reduction for students)
- Musée des Beaux-Arts, 3 place Stanislas. Tel: 83 85 30 72 (free to students on Wednesdays)

Cinema
- UGC Saint Jean, 3 rue Bénit, et rue saint Jean. Tel: 36 65 70 45
- UGC Saint Sebastien, 6 rue Léopold Lallement. Tel: 36 65 70 44
- Caméo Art et Essai, 16 rue de la Commanderie. Tel: 83 28 83 28
- Cinémathèque et Vidéothèque de Lorraine, 9 rue Michel Ney. Tel: 83 37 43 55 (reduction for card-holders)

Cafe-theatre
29 rue de la Visitation. Tel: 83 32 71 97. Programme and information: tel: 83 32 71 99

Sport
FNSU: Gymnase Universitaire A. Lefebvre, 1 bis boulevard Albert 1er. Tel: 83 41 10 23
SIUAP: 1 bis boulevard Albert 1er. Tel: 83 96 53 23
Gymnasium: same address
Swimming pools:
- Piscine Louison Bobet Nancy-Thermal, rue du Sergent Blandan. Tel: 83 40 08 51
- Piscine Olympique de Gentilly, avenue Pinchard. Tel: 83 96 15 46
- Piscine et gymnase universitaire, rue de Verdun.

Useful addresses

Préfecture: 1 rue Maurice Barrès. Tel: 83 34 26 26
Hôtel de police: 38 boulevard Lobau. Tel: 83 32 72 35
Chambre de Commerce: 40 rue Henri Poincaré. Tel: 83 36 46 43
CAF: 21 rue de Saint Lambert. Tel: 83 28 99 30
Post Offices:
- Rue Pierre Sémard
- Rue Pierre Fourrier
Municipal library: 43 rue Stanislas, 54042. Tel: 83 37 38 83
American library: 14 rue du Cheval Blanc, 54000. Tel: 83 36 78 13
Bookshops:
- Librairie Didier, 6 rue Gambetta. Tel: 83 32 00 63 (student reduction available)
- Hall du Livre, 38 rue Saint-Dizier. Tel: 83 35 53 01
CIJ Lorraine: 20 quai Claude Le Lorrain. Tel: 83 37 04 46
Nearest British Consulate (Luxembourg): British Embassy, 14

boulevard Roosevelt, PO Box 87C, L-2018, Luxembourg Ville. Tel: (352) 22 98 64/65/66. Fax: (352) 22 98 67 (Group 2)
Nearest US Consulate (Luxembourg): 22 boulevard E Servois, 2535 Luxembourg. Tel: (352) 46 01 23. Fax: (352) 46 14 01

Health care

Hôpital Central, 29 avenue du Maréchal de Lattre de Tassigny. Tel: 83 57 61 61
SIUMP, 13 place Carnot. Tel: 83 32 43 06
Local student insurance offices:
- MNEF, 2 rue Désilles. Tel: 83 35 00 23
- MGEL, 44 cours Léopold. Tel: 83 32 21 98

Travel

Railway station
3 place Thiers. Tel: (information) 83 56 50 50; (reservations) 83 35 08 08. London-Nancy (via Newhaven-Dieppe-Paris) £117 return; (via Dover-Calais-Paris) £121 return (Eurotrain)

Coach station
Place Monseigneur Ruch. London-Nancy £83 return; £44 single (Eurolines)

Local buses and trolley-buses
CGFTE, 11 avenue de Boufflers. Tel: 83 40 29 65. Agencebus, 3 rue du Dr Schmitt. Tel: 83 35 54 54 (for tickets, travelcards, information, advice and lost property)

Taxis
Taxis radio-gare. Tel: 83 37 65 37

Emergencies

Service Médical d'Accueil et d'Urgence (Hôpital Central). Tel: 83 57 61 61
Centre Anti-Poisons (Hôpital Central). Tel: 83 32 36 36
Police: Hôtel de Police. Tel: 83 32 72 35
SAMU. Tel: 83 32 85 79

14 Nantes

The university and its disciplines

Université de Nantes: sciences juridiques et économiques, lettres et sciences humaines, formations de santé, sciences exactes et naturelles, technologie.

1 quai de Tourville, BP 1026, 44035 Nantes Cedex 01. Tel: 40 99 83 83. Fax: 40 99 83 00

SUIO: chemin de la Censive du Tertre, 44072 Cedex 03. Tel: 40 29 07 39

SUEE: Centre d'Enseignement du Français Langue Etrangère, Ensemble Administratif 'L', chemin de la Censive du Tertre, BP 1025, 44036 Cedex 01. Tel: 40 14 10 40

IUT: 3 rue du Maréchal Joffre, 44041 Cedex 01. Tel: 40 30 60 90

University library
Domaine Universitaire du Tertre, chemin de la Censive, 44072 Cedex. Tel: 40 74 01 34 *or* 40 74 72 52 *or* 40 74 75 21

Courses for languages undergraduates

The UFR de Langues offers a DEUG *rénové* called the DEUG *Trilingue*. It involves the study of two modern foreign languages plus what are referred to as *langages fondamentaux*. There are two strands: (a) *Formation des Formateurs*, where the two foreign languages (including elements of the literature and civilisation of the countries concerned) are studied in a major/minor pattern together with, as *langages fondamentaux*, units of French, History and Linguistics; and (b) LEA, in which the languages (incorporating some civilisation) are of equal weighting, and are taken in conjunction with, as *enseignements d'application*, *langages fondamentaux*, courses in Economics, Law and Accounting plus *techniques d'expression écrite et orale*. The range of languages available includes German, English, Spanish, Italian, Portuguese, Arabic, Russian and Japanese, though the last three of these can only be taken as second languages, and from scratch.

In the *deuxième cycle*, the *Formation des Formateurs* strand becomes *Licence* LCE/LVE in Italian or a *Licence/Maîtrise* LCE/LVE in English, German or Spanish; the other strand proceeds as elsewhere as *Licence/ Maîtrise* LEA.

The DEUG II in *Lettres Modernes*, which comes under the UFR des

Lettres et Sciences Humaines, consists of two courses in French Literature, two courses in Comparative Literature, one course each in Linguistics, a modern foreign language, Latin (at beginners' level if necessary) and an *option libre*. As regards the literature courses, there has not been much choice available in recent years: on occasion, students have been allocated to courses on the basis of an alphabetical distribution. The *options libres* are known as *formations*, and there are some interesting options on offer, including some *pré-professionnalisation* courses: *Enseignement Elémentaire, Enseignement Secondaire, Littérature et Communication, Théorie et Pratique du Théâtre, Littérature et Histoire, Questions sur l'Art*.

The UFR de Langues and the UFR de Lettres et Sciences Humaines are housed in relatively modern buildings on the campus, which is not far from the largest of the residences (Fresche Blanc and La Bourgeonnière) and close to the Resto-U du Tertre, the CROUS headquarters and the SUAPS. The SUIO is on the same site.

Courses for foreign students

UFR-SUEE, Centre d'Enseignement du Français Langue Etrangère, Ensemble Administratif 'L', chemin de la Censive du Tertre, BP 1025, 44036 Nantes Cedex 01. Tel: 40 14 10 26/27

Term-time courses
Courses are run throughout the academic year to cater for all levels from beginners' to advanced, including language and civilisation courses of 15 hours per week leading to the award of the *Certificat d'Etudes Pratiques de Langue Française (1er degré)*, the *Diplôme d'Etudes Françaises (2e degré)* and the *Diplôme Supérieur d'Etudes Françaises (3e degré)*, the last of these being available only after a full year's study. Candidates must be over 18 years of age and there is a placement test on arrival.

Vacation courses
There is an intensive, three-week course (50 hours) run in June and September at beginners', intermediate and advanced levels, after a placement test on arrival.

CROUS

2 boulevard Guy Mollet, 44072 Nantes Cedex 03. Tel: 40 37 13 13. Fax: 40 37 13 00

OTU: at the CROUS headquarters and at 14 rue Santeuil, 44000. Tel: 40 74 70 77 *or* 40 73 99 17

CROUS-controlled accommodation
Nantes has over 3,364 places in halls of residence. It also has access to a number of flats.

- Chanzy, 1 rue H Lasne, 44041 Cedex. Tel: 40 74 15 32 (women only)
- Casterneau, rue André Baugé, 44042 Cedex. Tel: 40 52 12 24 (mixed)
- La Bourgeonnière, rue des Renards, 44072 Cedex. Tel: 40 76 70 56 (mixed)
- Launay Violette, chemin de Launay Violette, Le Petit Port, 44072 Cedex. Tel: 40 76 43 93 (mixed)
- Fresche Blanc, rue de la Bourgeonnière, 44072 Cedex. Tel: 40 76 62 91 (mixed)
- Berlioz, 81 rue de la Gaudinière, 44042 Cedex. Tel: 40 76 83 89 (mixed)
- Santeuil, 14 rue Santeuil. Tel: 40 73 73 84 (mixed)
- Cité Internationale, 2 place de la Manu, rue de Coulmiers. Tel: 40 74 61 86 (mixed; lets rooms only on a short-term basis; it is advisable to enquire in advance)

La Bourgeonnière and Fresche Blanc seem to be the most popular halls for foreign students.

CROUS restaurants
There are six main restaurants scattered throughout the town. Most of them offer snack and sandwich facilities in addition to the traditional meal:

- Ricordeau, place A Ricordeau. Tel: 40 89 34 41
- Le Rubis, 2 route de la Jonelière. Tel: 40 74 96 34
- Le Tertre, route de la Jonelière. Tel: 40 74 96 34
- La Lombarderie, rue de la Haute Forêt. Tel: 40 74 84 50
- Ecole Vétérinaire, route Gachet, BP 3013. Tel: 40 68 72 27
- Grill Chanzy, rue H Lasne. Tel: 40 74 40 22

Private-sector accommodation

- Le Jardin des Sciences de Nantes *and*
- Les Lauréades de Nantes, 13–15 rue Pitre Chevalier, 44000. Tel: 40 41 35 40

Privately-run hostels

For details, write to the *Directeur/Directrice*:

- Foyer Mondésir, 5 rue Mondésir. Tel: 40 73 53 00 (women only, aged between 18 and 23)
- Foyer de l'Edit de Nantes (FJT), 1 rue de Gigant. Tel: 40 73 41 46
- Foyer Sainte-Geneviève, 91 rue Paul Bellamy. Tel: 40 20 41 47 (women only, aged 16–22)
- Foyer Catholique, 13 rue du Chapeau Rouge. Tel: 40 48 50 75
- Résidence Pont du Cens, 28 avenue José de Hérédia
- Résidence Julienne David, 85 rue Félix Ménétrier. Tel: 40 93 28 30

The town and its surrounding area

Situated some 390 kilometres to the south-west of Paris, Nantes can be reached easily by rail (a TGV service was introduced in late 1989), by air, or indeed by road, via Le Mans and the A11, or along the picturesque route north of the Loire. It is the *préfecture* of the Loire-Atlantique, a bustling modern town of 240,000 or so inhabitants. It has long been one of France's principal ports and its position at the eastern end of the Loire estuary meant that it was prominent in trade with the colonies across the ocean, especially in sugar and slaves. Today the Port Autonome de Nantes Saint-Nazaire is the biggest such development on the Atlantic coast, and the fourth most important in France.

In recent times, the town has diversified and extended its industrial base. To traditional activities such as shipbuilding, smelting and food processing, themselves transformed and revitalised, have been added the aeronautics, electronics and nuclear industries. It has developed into an important financial and administrative centre, too. Yet it remains a very pleasant, if somewhat congested, town, with interesting parks and gardens, and a marked cultural heritage. The Cathédrale Saint-Pierre et Saint-Paul (begun in 1434), the Château des Ducs de Bretagne (late fifteenth and early sixteenth century) and the architecture of the Ile Feydeau, for example, attract a constant flow of tourists. Distinguished figures connected with the town's past include Peter Abélard (1079–1142), theologian and philosopher; the politician Aristide Briand (1862–1932); the Napoleonic general, Pierre Cambronne (1770–1842); and the writer Jules Verne (1828–1905). The Duchesse Anne, twice Queen of France, was crowned for the second time in the Château in Nantes, and bequeathed her heart to her birthplace.

Nantes is well situated for access to both *château* country to the east,

and to the south Brittany coast. La Baule, with its excellent sandy beaches, is only a good hour's drive away, while in the hinterland there is Guérande and the Parc National de Brière.
Cultural and sports facilities are good. There are special opportunities for water and marine sports in the area, and the local Association France–Grande-Bretagne welcomes students to its meetings; though it caters for a rather different age-group, it can prove a useful initial point of contact. Equally, the Accueil Familial (see notices in the halls and elsewhere in late September or early October) is very efficient at putting foreign students in touch with local families. Keen musicians should find no difficulty in joining one of the local bands or orchestras.

Tourist information

Office du Tourisme-Syndicat d'Initiative, Maison du Tourisme, place du Commerce, 44000 Nantes. Tel: 40 47 04 51

Hotels
There are a number of convenient two- and three-star hotels near to the station.
● Hôtel de Bourgogne, 9 allée du Commandant Charcot. Tel: 40 74 03 34
● Hôtel de la Gare, 5 allée du Commandant Charcot. Tel: 40 74 37 25
● Hôtel Terminus, 3 allée du Commandant Charcot. Tel: 40 74 24 51
● Hôtel des Trois Marchands, 26 rue Armand Brossard. Tel: 40 47 62 00 (quiet, near the cathedral)
However, the most economical option for short-term student accommodation is the Cité Internationale (for details, see above). Advance booking, with deposit, is essential.

Youth hostel
During the summer months, the Cité Internationale (see above, *CROUS-controlled accommodation*) operates as a youth hostel.

Restaurants
● La Ciboulette, 9 rue Saint Pierre. Tel: 40 47 88 71 (lunchtime menu – four courses – 39F50)
● Les Boucaniers, 28 rue Kervégan. Tel: 40 47 68 83 (menus 55F to 95F)
● Le Tram, 21 boulevard de Stalingrad. Tel: 40 74 00 28 (near the station; convenient and good value; the 69F three-course menu

offers as a starter a *buffet de salade à volonté*).

The combination of an abundant range of local seafood and local Muscadet (or Gros Plant, if you prefer it) offers real gastronomic delights in the restaurants in the pedestrian streets around place du Bouffay.

Leisure facilities

Museums and art galleries

- Musée des Beaux-Arts, 10 rue Georges Clémenceau. Tel: 40 41 65 65
- Musées du Château des Ducs de Bretagne, 1 place Elder. Tel: 40 41 56 56 (Musée des Arts Décoratifs; Musée d'Art Populaire Régional; Musée des Salorges (commercial, colonial and industrial history of Nantes since the eighteenth century))
- Musée Thomas Dobrée, place Jean V. Tel: 40 71 03 50
- Musée d'Histoire Naturelle, 12 rue Voltaire. Tel: 40 41 67 67

Theatre

- Théâtre de Poche Graslin, 5 rue Lekain. Tel: 40 89 36 78
- Maison de la Culture de Loire-Atlantique (reception: 10–12 passage Pommeraye. Tel: 40 48 70 06), with performances in Espace 44, 80 rue du Général Buat. Tel: 40 48 70 06
- Petit Théâtre des Marionnettes, rue de Jemmapes. Tel: 40 47 66 96
- Le Globe, Présidence de l'Université, 1 quai de Tourville. Tel: 40 89 73 16
- Opéra de Nantes, place Graslin. Tel: 40 20 90 60
- Auditorium du Conservatoire, rue Gaëtan Rondeau. Tel: 40 89 40 00
- Salles Paul Fort et Boris Vian, rue Basse-Port. Tel: 40 20 31 17
- Orchestre Philharmonique des Pays de Loire, 15 boulevard de Launay. Tel: 40 69 33 17
- Jeunesses Musicales de France, 9 chemin Guilbaud. Tel: 40 46 34 06

In addition, there are a number of *cafés-concerts*, *cafés-théâtres* and Centres Sociaux et Culturels. Full details are available from the Office du Tourisme.

Several arts festivals are held in the town, in particular a Festival of International Student Theatre: Carrefour International du Théâtre Universitaire, which takes place in March under the aegis of the university's cultural organisation Le Globe.

Cinema
- UGC Apollo, 21 rue Racine. Tel: 40 20 15 31 (7 screens)
- Bonne-Garde, 20 rue du Frère Louis. Tel: 40 75 11 08
- Cinématographe, 12 bis rue des Carmélites. Tel: 40 47 94 80
- Concorde, 79 boulevard de l'Egalité. Tel: 40 46 25 29 (4 screens)
- Gaumont, 12 place du Commerce. Tel: 40 48 29 95 (6 screens)
- Katorza, 3 rue Corneille. Tel: 40 73 37 31 (6 screens)
- Olympia, 1 rue Franklin. Tel: 40 89 42 73

Sport
Complexe Sportif du Petit Port, rue de la Censive du Tertre.
Halle des Sports Universitaires, 3 boulevard Guy Mollet, 44300. Tel: 40 74 87 34
Palais des Sports de Beaulieu, rue André Tardieu. Tel: 40 47 70 00
Salle du Champ de Mars, place du Champ de Mars.
Stade Marcel Saupin, quai Malakoff.
Football: Stade de la Beaujoire, boulevard de la Beaujoire (the home pitch of the professional club, FCN). Seats may be reserved at 13 rue du Maréchal de Lattre de Tassigny. Tel: 40 73 63 63
Skating: Patinoire du Petit Port, chemin de la Censive du Tertre. Tel: 40 74 01 77
Swimming:
- Piscine Léo-Lagrange, quai de Tourville. Tel: 40 47 68 44
- Piscine de la Roche, boulevard de Sarrebruck. Tel: 40 20 93 47
A local directory of sports clubs may be consulted at the Office Municipal des Sports, Mairie de Nantes. Tel: 40 20 90 00
FNSU: 1 rue Douarnenez, 44300. Tel: 40 94 49 50
The SUAPS (3 boulevard Guy Mollet. Tel: 40 74 87 34) organises a comprehensive programme of activities at various levels covering some twenty-five sports. It is possible to take a sports option in Science, Arts and Law. The Association Sportive de l'Université de Nantes facilitates entry into the various championships organised by the FNSU.

Useful addresses

Main post office: place de Bretagne, 44038 Cedex. Tel: 40 20 60 00
Municipal library: rue Gambetta, 44041 Cedex.
CRIJ: 28 rue du Calvaire. Tel: 40 48 68 25
CAF: 32 place Viarme. Tel: 40 41 33 33
Chambre de Commerce: 16 quai Ernest Renaud. Tel: 40 20 90 00

Mairie de Nantes: 64 rue de l'Hôtel de Ville. Tel: 40 41 90 00
Préfecture: 6 quai Ceinery, 44035 Cedex. Tel: 40 41 20 20
Association France–Grande-Bretagne: 7 rue de Gigant. Tel: 40 86 98
 12
Nantes Accueil: 11 allée Duguay-Trouin. Tel: 40 08 22 02
British Consulate: L'Aumarière, 44220 Couëron. Tel: 40 63 16 02
Nearest US Consulate-General (Paris): 2 avenue Gabriel, 75382
 Cedex 08. Tel: (1) 42 96 12 02. Fax: (1) 42 66 48 27

Health care

Hospitals:
● Hôtel-Dieu, place Alexis Ricordeau. Tel: 40 48 33 33
● Saint-Jacques, 85 rue Saint-Jacques. Tel: 40 48 33 33
● Hôpital Laënnec, 44800 Saint-Herblain. Tel: 40 48 33 33
CPAM: 9–11 rue Gaëton Rondeau, 44200. Tel: 40 35 88 88
SUMPPS: 5 rue du Maréchal Joffre, 44000. Tel: 40 74 62 38 *or* 40 74
 14 49. Free medical treatment is available by appointment, as well as
 the usual range of specialist consultation and counselling services.
Local student insurance offices:
● MNEF, 30 rue Jean Jaurès, BP 628, 44017 Cedex 01. Tel: 40 48 66
 63
● SMEBA, 11 ter rue du Maréchal de Lattre de Tassigny, BP 3313,
 44033 Cedex. Tel: 40 73 00 01

Travel

Railway station
27 boulevard de Stalingrad, 44041 Cedex. Tel: 40 08 50 50. London-
Nantes (via Newhaven-Dieppe) £125 return; (via Dover-Calais) £129
return (Eurotrain)

Coach stations
Allée Baco; Champ de Mars; allée Duquesne

Airport
Nantes-Atlantique. Tel: 40 84 80 00 (about 10 kilometres from the
centre of town). There are regular direct flights to London.

Taxis
Tel: 40 63 66 66 *or* 43 69 22 22

Buses

Local buses and the efficient and practical trams (now two lines) are operated by the Tramways et Autobus Nantais (TAN). Tickets may be bought individually for 7F (validity one hour) or in *carnets* of 10; students may obtain a cheap monthly pass (*Billet Campus*).

Emergencies

The dispensing chemist nearest to La Bourgeonnière and Fresche Blanc is in rue de la Bourgeonnière.
Duty doctor *or* chemist. Tel: 40 76 43 93 *or* 40 74 21 21
SAMU. Tel: 40 48 33 33 *or* 40 48 35 35
SOS Amitié. Tel: 40 04 04 04

15 Nice

The university and its disciplines

Université de Nice-Sophia Antipolis: sciences économiques et juridiques, sciences humaines, médecine, odontologie, sciences exactes et naturelles, technologie, sport.
Parc Valrose, 28 avenue Valrose, 06034 Nice Cedex 2. Tel: 93 52 98 98. Fax: 93 51 91 91
SUIO:
- Section sciences/médecine/dentaire, same address, same telephone number, ext. 98 75
- Section droit et économie, Bureau 309, 7 avenue Robert Schuman, 06005 Cedex. Tel: 93 97 70 75, ext. 72 75
- Section lettres, Bureau 125, 98 boulevard Edouard Herriot, BP 362, 06200. Tel: 93 37 53 53
IUT: 41 boulevard Napoléon III, 06041 Cedex. Tel: 93 21 79 00

Courses for languages undergraduates

For *Lettres Modernes* students, the package includes compulsory French Literature (poetry, drama and prose fiction from the medieval period to the twentieth century), Comparative Literature (including *le genre romanesque*) and French Language (including grammar, historical phonetics and linguistics). Courses are offered in LEA, LVE and FLE from DEUG to *maîtrise* level. Modern languages on offer include: English, German, Italian, Russian and Spanish.

Courses for foreign students

Term-time courses
Alliance Française, 2 rue de Paris, 06000 Nice. Tel: 93 62 67 66.
The Alliance Française provides tuition leading to the *Diplôme de Langue Française* and the *Certificat de Français Pratique*. At advanced level, there are courses leading to the *Diplôme Supérieur d'Etudes Françaises Modernes*, and the *Diplôme de Hautes Etudes de Français*. Students, who must be at least 16 years of age, are taught in groups of about 15. Accommodation can be with local families, in private hostels or hotels.

Vacation courses
There are several institutions providing tuition during the summer months, including the following:
● Institut d'Enseignement du Français Langue Etrangère de Nice.
  Institut Blanche de Castille, 17 avenue des Chênes, 06300 Nice. Tel: 93 85 24 76 *or* 93 67 65 97. Fax: 93 62 46 65 *or* 93 67 39 56
The Institut offers courses in July and August for beginners, inter-mediate and advanced learners (*Diplôme de Langue Française, niveaux 1,2,3*). Courses, which take place in the mornings, focus on language development. Students are taught in groups of 15 and audio-visual methods figure prominently. Among specialist options there are courses in translation techniques. The afternoons and evenings are given over to recreational and cultural activities. Full board and lodging is arranged for participants.
● Université Internationale d'Eté. Faculté des Lettres, 98 boulevard Edouard Herriot, 06200 Nice. Tel: 93 37 53 94. Fax: 93 37 54 66
Courses lead to the award of the *Diplôme de Langue et Civilisation Françaises de l'Université de Nice*. Groups are composed of about 15 students; audio-visual methods are used and disciplines include grammar, literature and civilisation (*niveau 2*), translation and art and literature (*niveau 3*). Accommodation is provided in university halls or in furnished rooms in the town. Students have free access to the univer-sity's excellent sports' facilities, which include tennis courts, a swim-ming pool and a gymnasium.
● Alliance Française (for address and telephone, see above)
Tuition is offered at beginners' to advanced level and may lead to the following certificates: *Diplôme de Langue Française, Certificat Elémentaire de Français Pratique (CEFP), Diplôme Supérieur d'Etudes Françaises Modernes (DS)*. Courses, normally of four weeks' duration, take place in July and August. Class size ranges from 8–16 students; the mimimum

age is 16 and there are placement tests on arrival. Accommodation may take a variety of forms (with families, in halls of residence, furnished rooms, hotels, etc.).

CROUS

18 avenue des Fleurs, 06050 Nice Cedex 1. Tel: 92 15 50 50. Fax: 93 86 89 42
SUIO: same adddress and telephone number
OTU: Restaurant Carlone, 80 boulevard Edouard Herriot, 06200. Tel: 93 96 85 43

CROUS-controlled accommodation
- Résidence de la Baie des Anges, 55 chemin de St Antoine de Ginestière, 06200. Tel: 93 86 76 74 (mixed; 461 rooms)
- Résidence St Antoine, 69 route de St Antoine de Ginestière, 06200. Tel: 93 86 37 19 (mixed; 350 rooms)
- Résidence des Collinettes, 3 avenue Robert Schuman, 06000. Tel: 93 97 10 63 (females; 247 rooms)
- Cité Universitaire Montebello, 96 avenue Valrose, 06100. Tel: 93 84 19 81 (mixed; 408 rooms)
- Cité Universitaire Jean Médecin, 25 rue Robert Latouche, 06200. Tel: 93 83 34 61 (mixed; 899 rooms)

CROUS restaurants
Five self-service restaurants with fixed opening hours are backed up by cafeterias open all day. The full choices of *la restauration diversifiée* exist alongside the *menu traditionnel.*
- Restaurant Nice Carlone, 80 boulevard Edouard Herriot. Tel: 93 86 58 05 (near the Faculty of Arts and Social Sciences)
- Restaurant Nice Centre, 5 avenue Robert Schuman. Tel: 93 97 10 20 (also provides vegetarian meals and is near the Faculty of Law and Economics)
- Restaurant Montebello, 96 avenue Valrose. Tel: 93 84 19 81 (near the Science campus)
- Restaurant de la CU Jean Médecin, 25 avenue Robert Latouche. Tel: 93 83 34 61
- Restaurant de l'EPIAR, 20 avenue Stephen Liégeard (midday only)
- Cafétéria de l'IUT, 41 boulevard Napoléon III. Tel: 93 21 79 00
There is also a *restaurant agréé*:
- Cercle d'Etudes Juives, 31 avenue Henri Barbusse

Private-sector accommodation

Résidence Persepolis, Passage Gioffredo. Tel: 93 62 16 37 *or* 93 72
   05 08 (furnished *studios*)

Privately-run hostels

There are three hostels for women:
- Foyer Adriana Mt Carmel, 22 avenue Gravier. Tel: 93 84 42 83
- Le Foyer de France, 2 boulevard François Grosso. Tel: 93 44 50 64
- Maison Blanche, 14 boulevard Carabacel. Tel: 93 62 15 70

The town and its surrounding area

With over three miles of beaches, the beautiful Baie des Anges and an
exceptional climate, Nice is well known as an attractive holiday centre.
However, it is also a town with an interesting history, a rapidly
expanding university and a commitment to adding new business ven-
tures to the horticultural and tourist industries in which it has long been
pre-eminent. The local roses, in particular, have a world-wide reputation. The town of Nice only became definitively French by the treaty of
1860 which ceded the territories previously held by the Dukes of Savoy.
The first settlers were Greek traders and though little of their influence
remains there are several vestiges of their Roman successors such as the
Arènes de Cimiez. Now among the largest of French towns with a
population approaching 450,000, Nice, prosperous and cosmopolitan,
has over 23,000 students contibuting to its lively atmosphere. There are
several museums of note as well as an opera house, theatres and
cinemas, not to mention the various cultural activities which take place
throughout the year. No visitor should miss the renowned Jazz Festival,
the colourful Carnival, nor indeed the spectacular *Bataille des Fleurs*.
The architecture of the town reflects its fashionable past with elegant
Belle Epoque buildings, the Opera, landscaped parks and gardens such
as the Espace Masséna, the *jardin* Albert 1er or the Place Ile de Beauté.
Amongst the town's famous personalities are the two military geniuses
Garibaldi (1807–82) and Masséna (1756–1817), the artist Carle Vanloo
(1705–65), and the celebrated economist Auguste Blanqui (1805–81).
The food and wine of the region are particularly distinctive: the Bellet
wines are increasingly appreciated, while amongst other regional
delights for the palate are *salade niçoise, pissaladière, pan pagnat, socca,
soupe au pistou, estocaficada* and *gnocchis*. The town is well served by rail,

road and air with a TGV service, the A7 motorway, and the international airport, Nice-Côte d'Azur.

Tourist information

Office du Tourisme: Acropolis 1, Esplanade Kennedy, 06058. Tel: 93 92 82 82. Fax: 93 92 82 98
There is also an office at the station: Accueil de France Gare SNCF. Tel: 93 87 07 07

Hotels
Nice has a rich assortment of hotels. The following are among the more modestly-priced in the central area:
● Hôtel Astrid, 26 rue Pertinax. Tel: 93 62 14 64 (rooms from 80F to 150F; breakfast 15F; closed in November)
● Hôtel de France, boulevard Raimbaldi. Tel: 93 85 18 04 (rooms from 60F to 160F; breakfast 11F)
● Hôtel Lyonnais, 20 rue de Russie. Tel: 93 88 70 74 (rooms from 90F to 180F; breakfast 16F)
Better grade hotels: (a single room with breakfast will cost between 200F–250F).
● Hôtel de l'Europe, 24 avenue Malausséna. Tel: 93 62 22 55. Fax: 93 13 41 32
● Hôtel des Flandres, 6 rue de Belgique. Tel: 93 88 78 94

Youth hostel
Route Forestière du Mont Alban. Tel: 93 98 23 64 (a short bus ride – No. 14 – from boulevard Jean Jaurès; 80F for bed and breakfast)

Restaurants
Cheap restaurants are around the station; more expensive ones by the *vieux port.* Here is a selection:
● Le Faubourg Montmartre, 32 rue Pertinax (menu, 65F)
● Flunch, avenue Thiers (popular self-service cafeteria next to the station, dishes from 20F)
● Restaurant de Paris, 28 rue d'Angleterre (menus between 45F and 70F)
● Le Démodé, 18 rue Benoît Bunico. Tel: 93 85 70 86 (the cheaper menus are between 100F and 150F)
● La France, 5 rue Halévy. Tel: 93 87 12 71 (the cheaper menus are between 120F and 150F)

Leisure facilities

Weekly listings of all cutural activities – films, plays, concerts and exhibitions – are found in the *Semaine des Spectacles* (8F).

Museums and art galleries

All are free except the Musée National Marc Chagall.

- Musée des Beaux-Arts, 33 avenue des Baumettes. Tel: 93 44 50 72 (closed on Mondays)
- Musée Masséna, 65 rue de France. Tel: 93 88 11 34 (closed on Mondays and during November)
- Musée International de Malacologie, 3 cours Saleyea. Tel: 93 85 18 44 (closed on Sundays and Mondays and during November)
- Musée Naval, Tour Bellanda, parc du Château. Tel: 93 80 47 61 (closed on Tuesdays and mid-November to mid-December)
- Musée Matisse, 164 avenue des Arènes. Tel: 93 53 17 70
- Musée Archéologique, 160 avenue des Arènes de Cimiez. Tel: 93 81 59 57
- Musée Aléxis et Gustav-Adolf Mossa, 59 quai des Etats Unis. Tel: 93 62 37 11 (closed on Mondays)
- Musée d'Art Moderne et d'Art Contemporain, promenade des Arts. Tel: 93 62 61 62 (closed on Tuesdays)
- Musée National Marc Chagall, avenue du Docteur Ménard. Tel: 93 81 75 75 (closed on Tuesdays; 8F)

Theatre

- Théâtre du Cours, 5 rue de la Poissonnerie. Tel: 93 80 12 67
- Théâtre de l'Alphabet, 10 boulevard Carabacel. Tel: 93 13 08 88
- Théâtre de Nice, Promenade des Arts. Tel: 93 80 52 60
- Nice Opéra, 4 rue St François de Paule. Tel: 93 85 67 31
- Théâtre Municipal du Vieux Nice, rue St Joseph. Tel: 93 62 00 03
- Théâtre de l'Artistique, 27 boulevard Dubouchage. Tel: 93 85 60 68
- Théâtre de la Tour, 63 boulevard Gorbella. Tel: 93 13 13 12
- Théâtre de l'Ariane, 168 boulevard de l'Ariane. Tel: 93 27 37 37
- Théâtre de Verdure, Jardin Albert 1er, promenade des Anglais. Tel: 93 82 38 68

Cinema

- Cinémathèque de Nice, 3 Esplanade Kennedy. Tel: 92 04 06 66 (foreign language films)

- Gaumont, 31 avenue Jean Médecin. Tel: 93 82 25 08
- Mercury, 1 place Garibaldi. Tel: 93 55 32 31 (foreign language films)
- Balzac, 60 avenue Jean Médecin. Tel: 93 62 00 00
- Pâthé, 54 avenue Jean Médecin. Tel: 93 85 18 03
- Rialto, 4 rue de Rivoli. Tel: 93 88 08 41
- Variétés, 7 boulevard Victor Hugo. Tel: 93 87 74 97

Sport

FNSU: CSU Valrose, 65 avenue de Valrose. Tel: 93 84 99 17

Swimming pools: for opening times and entrance charges contact the pools directly. The following are indoor and heated:

- Jean Bouin, Palais des Sports, Esplanade de Lattre de Tassigny. Tel: 93 13 13 13 (Olympic sized)
- Jean Médecin, 178 rue de France. Tel: 93 86 24 01
- St François, place St François. Tel: 93 85 53 08

The following are open air pools:

- Ariane, rue Guiglionda de Sainte Agathe. Tel: 93 54 94 30
- Centre Aéré de Falicon, 13 boulevard Comte de Falicon. Tel: 93 84 21 96
- Piol, 36 avenue Paul Arène. Tel: 93 96 92 07

Skating rink: Jean Bouin, Palais des Sports, Esplanade de Lattre de Tassigny. Tel: 93 13 13 13

Bowling alley: Bowling Acropolis, Esplanade Kennedy. Tel: 93 55 33 11

Squash: Club Vauban, 18 rue Maréchal Vauban. Tel: 93 26 09 78

Tennis: Ligue de la Côte d'Azur, 5 avenue Suzanne Lenglen. Tel: 93 96 92 98

Useful Addresses

Post offices:
- 22 avenue Thiers. Tel: 93 88 55 41
- 18 rue des Postes. Tel: 93 85 98 63
- 2 rue Clémenceau. Tel: 93 88 72 88

Municipal libraries:
- 21 bis boulevard Dubouchage. Tel: 93 62 17 60
- 15 rue Lamartine. Tel: 93 80 29 16

English American library: 12 rue de France. Tel: 93 97 23 54 (check opening times)

Bookshops:
- FNAC, 24 avenue Jean Médecin
- Nouvelle Librairie Française, 111 rue de France. Tel: 93 44 67 47
- La Sorbonne, 23 rue Hôtel des Postes. Tel: 93 62 11 21
- Riviera Bookshop, 10 rue Chauvain. Tel: 93 85 84 63
- Home de la Presse, 27 avenue Jean Médecin. Tel: 93 88 84 16 (sells English books)

Chambre de Commerce: 20 boulevard Carabacel. Tel: 93 55 91 55
CIJ: 19 rue Gioffredo. Tel: 93 80 93 93
MJC: Magnan, 31 rue Louis de Coppet. Tel: 93 86 28 75
Commissariat Central de Police: 1 avenue Maréchal Foch. Tel: 93 92 62 22
Préfecture des Alpes-Maritimes: route de Grenoble. Tel: 93 72 20 00
Mairie de Nice: 5 rue l'Hôtel de Ville. Tel: 93 13 20 00
British Consulate: 2 rue du Congrès. Tel: 93 82 32 04
US Consulate: 31 rue du Maréchal Joffre. Tel: 93 88 89 55. Fax: 88 24 06 95

Health Care

Hôpital Saint Roche, 5 rue Pierre Devoluy. Tel: 92 03 33 33 (24 hour emergency cover)
SUMP: 81 rue de France. (A nurse based at the CROUS provides basic care and advice for students in CROUS-controlled accommodation.) Address: RU Les Collinettes, 3 avenue Robert Schuman. Tel: 93 97 09 79
Chemists:
- 7 rue Masséna
- 58 boulevard Carlone
- 11 avenue de Californie

Local student insurance offices:
- MNEF, 107 rue de France. Tel: 93 44 66 48
- MEP, 81 rue de France. Tel: 93 88 65 67

Travel

Railway station
Nice Ville, avenue Thiers. Tel: 93 87 50 50. London-Nice (via Newhaven-Dieppe) £154 return; (via Dover-Calais) £158 return (Eurotrain)

Coach station
Promenade du Paillon. Tel: 93 85 61 81. London-Nice, £99 return; £59 single (Eurolines)

Airport
Nice-Côte d'Azur. Tel: 93 21 30 30 (the airport bus leaves every 20 minutes from place Leclerc)

Local bus station
The TN (Transports Urbains de Nice) operate out of 10 avenue Félix Faure, near place Général Leclerc and place Masséna. Tel: 93 62 08 08 (single tickets 8F; a 5-ticket *carnet* costs 28F from *tabacs*; daily and weekly passes can be bought on the bus)

Taxis
Tel: 93 80 70 70

Student travel
● Council Travel, 37 bis rue d'Angleterre. Tel: 93 83 23 23
● OTU Voyages, Restaurant Carlone, 80 boulevard Edouard Herriot. Tel: 93 96 85 43
● USIT Voyages, 10 rue de Belgique. Tel: 93 87 34 96
● Wasteels, 32 rue de l'Hôtel des Postes. Tel: 93 92 08 10

Emergencies

Police. Tel: 93 92 62 22
SOS Médecins. Tel: 93 85 01 01
Nice Médecins. Tel: 93 52 42 42
SOS Dentaire. Tel: 93 80 38 40
Duty doctor. Tel: 93 53 03 03
All-night chemist, 7 rue Masséna. Tel: 93 87 78 94
SAMU. Tel: 93 92 55 55

16 Paris

The universities and their disciplines

(Académie de Paris) Université Panthéon-Sorbonne (**Paris I**): droit et sciences politiques, droit des affaires, droit comparé, droit africain, sciences économiques, administratives et de l'information, sciences humaines, art et archéologie, mathématiques.

12 place du Panthéon, 75231 Paris Cedex 05. Tel: (1) 46 34 97 00. Fax: (1) 46 34 20 56

SUIO: Centre Mendès France, Bureau B7–10, 90 rue de Tolbiac, 75634 Paris Cedex 13. Tel: (1) 40 77 18 36

(Académie de Paris) Université Panthéon-Assas (**Paris II**): droit et sciences politiques, sciences économiques, administratives et de l'information.

12 place du Panthéon, 75231 Paris Cedex 05. Tel: (1) 46 34 97 00. Fax: (1) 46 34 98 52

SUIO: Centre Assas, Bureau 508, 92 rue d'Assas, 75006 Paris. Tel: (1) 43 20 12 24, ext. 471

(Académie de Paris) Université de la Sorbonne Nouvelle (**Paris III**): langues, lettres et civilisation du monde moderne.

17 rue de la Sorbonne, 75230 Paris Cedex 05. Tel: (1) 40 46 22 11. Fax: (1) 43 25 74 71

SUIO: Centre Censier, Bureaux 2 et 6, 13 rue de Santeuil, 75231 Paris Cedex 05. Tel: (1) 45 87 40 01

(Académie de Paris) Université Paris Sorbonne (**Paris IV**): lettres et arts, civilisations, langues.

1 rue Victor Cousin, 75230 Paris Cedex 05. Tel: (1) 40 46 22 11. Fax: (1) 40 46 25 88

SUIO: same address, Galerie Richelieu, Salle 12. Tel: (1) 40 46 26 14 *or* (1) 40 46 26 16

(Académie de Paris) Université René Descartes (**Paris V**): formations de santé, sciences humaines, biologie, droit, technologie.

12 rue de l'Ecole de Médecine, 75270 Paris Cedex 06. Tel: (1) 40 46 16 16. Fax: (1) 40 46 16 15

SUIO: same address. Tel: (1) 40 46 16 50

IUT: 143 avenue de Versailles, 75016. Tel: (1) 45 24 46 02

(Académie de Paris) Université Pierre et Marie Curie (**Paris VI**): sciences exactes et naturelles, médecine.

4 place Jussieu, 75252 Paris Cedex 05. Tel: (1) 44 27 44 27. Fax: (1) 44 27 38 66

SUIO: same address, Inter-Amphi 15/25 – niveau Jussieu. Tel: (1) 44 27 33 66 *or* (1) 44 27 39 70

(Académie de Paris) **(Paris VII)**: médecine, odontologie, sciences exactes et naturelles, lettres et sciences humaines.

2 place Jussieu, 75251 Paris Cedex 05. Tel: (1) 44 27 44 27. Fax: (1) 44 27 69 64

SUIO: same address, Bât 45–55, niveau J. Tel: (1) 44 27 52 08

(Académie de Créteil) Université Vincennes-Saint-Denis **(Paris VIII)**: sciences humaines, lettres, informatique, urbanisme.

2 rue de la Liberté, 93526 Saint-Denis Cedex 02. Tel: (1) 49 40 67 89. Fax: (1) 48 21 04 46

SUIO: same address, Hall Central. Tel: (1) 49 40 67 14

(Académie de Paris) Université Paris Dauphine **(Paris IX)**: sciences de gestion, économie, informatique, mathématiques appliquées.

Place du Maréchal de Lattre de Tassigny, 75775 Paris Cedex 16. Tel: (1) 45 05 14 10. Fax: (1) 47 04 76 71

SUIO: same address (Bureau C102) and telephone, exts. 2475 *or* 2156 *or* 2160

(Académie de Versailles) Université Nanterre **(Paris X)**: droit et sciences économiques, lettres et sciences humaines, langues, technologie, sport.

200 avenue de la République, 92001 Cedex 01. Tel: (1) 40 97 72 00. Fax: (1) 47 21 67 44

SUIO: same address, Bât C, Salle C20. Tel: (1) 40 97 73 15 *or* (1) 40 97 75 42.

IUT: 1 chemin Desvallières, 92410 Ville d'Avray. Tel: (1) 47 09 05 70

IUT: allée des Chênes Pourpres, 95000 Cergy-Pontoise. Tel: (1) 34 25 42 95

(Académie de Versailles) Université Paris-Sud **(Paris XI)**: sciences exactes et naturelles, médecine, pharmacie, sciences juridiques et économiques, technologie.

15 rue Georges Clemenceau, 91405 Orsay Cedex. Tel: (1) 69 41 67 50. Fax: (1) 69 41 61 35

SUIO: Centre Scientifique d'Orsay, Bât 333, 1er étage, same address. Tel: (1) 69 41 72 77 *or* (1) 69 41 73 63

IUT: 8 avenue Cauchy, 92330 Sceaux. Tel: (1) 46 60 06 83

IUT: plateau du Moulon, BP 23, 91406 Orsay Cedex. Tel: 69 41 00 40

IUT: 9 avenue de la Division Leclerc, 94230 Cachan. Tel: (1) 46 64 10 32

(Académie de Créteil) Université de Val de Marne **(Paris XII)**: sciences bio-médicales, sciences exactes et naturelles, technologie, sciences

humaines, sciences juridiques et économiques.
　Avenue du Général de Gaulle, 94010 Créteil Cedex. Tel: (1) 48 98 91 44. Fax: (1) 42 07 70 12
SUIO: same address and telephone, ext. 87
IUT: same address and telephone, ext. 2270
(Académie de Créteil) Université Paris Nord (**Paris XIII**): sciences exactes, juridiques, économiques, médicales, humaines, technologie.
　Avenue Jean-Baptiste Clément, 93430 Villetaneuse. Tel: (1) 49 40 30 00. Fax: (1) 49 40 33 33
SUIO: same address, Salle F110. Tel: (1) 49 40 30 30
IUT: same address. Tel: (1) 49 40 31 18 *or* (1) 49 40 31 29
(Académie de Créteil) Université de Marne-la-Vallée: lettres, sciences et techniques.
　2 allée Jean Renoir, 93160 Noisy-le-Grand. Tel: (1) 45 92 30 87. Fax: (1) 45 92 15 04
SUIO: same address
(Académie de Versailles) Université de Versailles-Saint-Quentin-en-Yvelines: sciences et techniques, droit, lettres et sciences humaines.
　23 rue du Refuge, 78000 Versailles. Tel: 30 97 21 04
SUIO: same address. Tel: 30 97 21 14
(Académie de Versailles) Université de Cergy-Pontoise: sciences humaines, sciences et techniques.
　8 Le Campus, 95033 Cergy-Pontoise Cedex. Tel: 34 25 49 49 *or* 34 25 49 04
SUIO: same address
(Académie de Versailles) Université d'Evry-Val d'Essonne: sciences et techniques, sciences juridiques, économiques et sociales.
　Boulevard des Coquibus, 91025 Evry Cedex. Tel: 69 47 70 10
SUIO: same address

Courses for foreign students

In addition to the courses run by the Institut Britannique (see below), there are summer and term-time courses available which are so numerous that we do not have room to list them all here. Amongst the most well-known are those mentioned below.

Term-time courses

Centre Expérimental d'Etude de la Civilisation Française associé à l'Université de Paris-Sorbonne, 47 rue des Ecoles 75005 Paris.
　Secrétariat: 17 rue de la Sorbonne, 75005 Paris. Galerie Richelieu, porte 9. Tel: (1) 40 46 22 11, exts. 2664 to 2672

Institut Britannique de Paris (Universities of London and Paris)

9–11 rue de Constantine, 75007 Paris. Tel: (1) 45 55 71 99. (*Métro* Invalides; buses 28, 49, 63, 69, 83, 93)
The Institute is divided into the Département d'Etudes Françaises and the Département d'Etudes Anglaises. The former offers a variety of courses for native English-speakers in French language, literature and civilisation. Students are given a language test prior to their arrival and are assigned to language groups at the appropriate level. Commercial French courses are available, as are advanced courses in translation. The Institute offers its own certificates and diplomas; the commercial qualifications bear the *imprimatur* of the Chambre de Commerce et d'Industrie de Paris. Examination fees are charged on enrolment for these certificates and diplomas and students should also note that 'British' fees are charged for full-time enrolment at the Institute.

Courses take full advantage of the cultural facilities on offer in Paris. Popular non-literary courses include those on French Art, the French Press, the French Cinema and the introductory course on *la bande dessinée*. Courses on nineteenth- and twentieth-century French prose fiction are also very popular.

The Institute has well-appointed classrooms, a projection room, two language laboratories, two libraries and a snack bar in the basement where students can relax in a most friendly atmosphere. One relative disadvantage for some students is the large 'English' presence and the amount of English spoken outside the classroom.

Vacation courses
Cours de Civilisation Française de la Sorbonne. Address for correspondence as above. Tel: (1) 40 46 26 70
Alliance Française, 101 boulevard Raspail, 75270 Paris Cedex 06. Tel: (1) 45 44 38 28. Fax: (1) 45 44 89 42
Chambre de Commerce et d'Industrie (DRIDE): Relations Internationales, 42 rue du Louvre, 75001 Paris. Tel: (1) 45 08 37 34. Fax: (1) 45 08 37 29

CROUS

39 avenue Georges Bernanos, 75231 Paris Cedex 05. Tel: (1) 40 51 36 00. Fax: (1) 40 51 36 99
SAEE: same address and telephone
OTU: 137 boulevard St Michel. Tel: (1) 43 29 12 88 (*Métro* Port-Royal).

CROUS-controlled halls and restaurants in Paris are too numerous to list here; we have included only the restaurants which are on the site of the Cité Internationale. The Latin Quarter continues to offer a wide variety of menus and of prices in the cosmopolitan, narrow streets close to the boulevard Saint-Michel. For recommended restaurants, see below.

There are also some seventy privately-controlled hostels and a full list of them is to be found in the *Guide OSE du logement étudiant* (see *Bibliography*).

Cité Internationale Universitaire de Paris

- Fondation Nationale (Pavillon Administratif) boulevard Jourdan, 75690 Paris. Tel: (1) 45 89 68 52
- Collège Franco-Britannique (Fondation E and H Nathan), 9B boulevard Jourdan. Tel: (1) 44 16 24 00. Fax: (1) 44 16 26 99
- Fondation des Etats-Unis, 15 boulevard Jourdan. Tel: (1) 45 89 35 79. Fax: (1) 45 89 41 50
- Maison des Etudiants Canadiens, 31 boulevard Jourdan. Tel: (1) 40 78 67 00. Fax: (1) 40 78 68 50

Composed of 37 *maisons*, the Cité Internationale is situated in a park of some 40 *hectares* close to the Porte d'Orléans *Métro* station and the Cité Universitaire RER station. Created in 1925, the Cité is a truly international community for which the participating countries built a hall of residence in a style which typifies national architectural characteristics. It is popular with English-speaking students in Paris. Even though rooms there cost more than double the price of a CROUS-controlled room in the provinces, they are cheaper by far than comparable private accommodation in the capital. The Collège Franco-Britannique offers spacious accommodation; security and discipline are much tighter than in provincial residences. Facilities include microwaves, fridges and telephones in rooms. Other halls not mentioned above of particular interest to Modern Languages students include the Maison Heinrich Heine, the Collège d'Espagne and the Maison de l'Italie. The Cité has its own library, Service des Activitiés Culturelles and hospital. It has its own CROUS-controlled restaurants and 'fast-food' cafeteria.

Other addresses at the Cité Internationale:

- Hôpital International de l'Université de Paris, 42 boulevard Jourdan. Tel: (1) 45 89 47 89
- Restaurant du Parc Ouest, 16 avenue Davis-Weill
- Restaurant de la Maison Internationale

Tourist Information

Bureau d'Accueil Central, 127 Champs Elysées. Tel: (1) 47 23 61 72

Hotels
- Hôtel du Parc Montsouris. Tel: (1) 45 89 09 72 (adjacent to the Cité Internationale; has rooms for a little over 300F per night including shower and toilet)
- Grand Hôtel de l'Europe, 74 boulevard de Strasbourg, 75010 Paris. Tel: (1) 46 07 76 27 (has moderately-priced rooms, with shower; toilets in the corridor adjacent to rooms; close to the Gare de l'Est)
- Viator Hôtel, 1 rue Parrot, 75012 Paris. Tel: (1) 43 43 11 00 (more expensive – approx. 360F per night – but well appointed and very close to the Gare de Lyon)
- Hôtel Kuntz, 2 rue des Deux Gares, 75010 Paris. Tel: (1) 40 35 77 26 (*Métro* Gare du Nord *or* Gare de l'Est; rooms from about 180F)

Youth hostel
Auberge de Jeunesse Jules Ferry, 8 boulevard Jules Ferry, 11e. Tel: (1) 43 57 55 60. Fax: (1) 40 21 79 92. (*Métro* République; 86F bed and breakfast)

Restaurants
- Le Drouot, 103 rue de Richelieu, 75002 Paris (convenient for the Bibliothèque Nationale)
- Flunch, Les Halles (Porte Berger), 75001 Paris
- Restaurant Végétarien, 2 place du Marché Ste Catherine, 75004 (closed on Sundays)
- Bar-Restaurant 'Jacky', 32 rue Traversière, 75012 Paris (moderately priced meals)
- Le Parrot, 5 rue Parrot, 75012 Paris (very close to the Viator Hôtel and the Gare de Lyon; customers can cook their own steaks at their table on pre-heated granite slabs)
- Le Tramway de Lyon, 6 rue Michel Chasles (very close to the Gare de Lyon; *formule express* 65F, set meal 78F)

Leisure facilities

Museums and art galleries
They are too numerous to list here, but it is worth bearing in mind that the Louvre, rue de Rivoli, offers free entry on Sundays. The Musée

d'Orsay (quai d'Orsay) is well worth an extended visit.

Theatres
Again they are too numerous to list, but cheap tickets for the Théâtre
National de l'Opéra (place de l'Opéra) can be purchased at the Cité
Internationale.

Cinema
Student reductions on Mondays.

Sport
Sporting facilities in Paris are, of course, excellent and stadia include
the Parc des Princes (football and rugby) and the Bercy (multisport)
complex. *L'Officiel des Spectacles* and *Pariscope* both form useful guides to
cultural and sporting events in Paris.

Useful addresses

For students residing at the Cité Internationale, there is a post office at
Parc Montsouris and at the Cité itself. A whole range of bookshops
(including the very large Gibert shops) are to be found in the Latin
Quarter of Paris, along the boulevard Saint-Michel; FNAC has
branches in the rue de Rennes (*Métro* Saint-Placide) and at Les Halles
(*Métro* Châtelet/Les Halles), for example.
Libraries:
• Bibliothèque Nationale, 58 rue de Richelieu 75002. Tel: (1) 46 03 81
  26
• Centre Culturel Britannique, 9–11 rue de Constantine, 75007
• British Council, 9–11 rue de Constantine, 75007
• Centre Georges Pompidou, plateau Beaubourg. Tel: (1) 42 77 12 33
  (*Métro* Rambuteau *or* Châtelet/Les Halles)
There are many other libraries listed in the various tourist guides.
FNSU: 2 place Jussieu, 75251 Paris Cedex 05. Tel: (1) 44 27 51 86
CAF: 18 quai Austerlitz. Tel: (1) 45 82 29 65
CIDJ: 101 quai Branly, 75740 Paris Cedex 15. Tel: (1) 45 66 06 67
CIDJ Informations Jeunes, 120 quai Branly. Tel: (1) 45 67 35 85 (for
  employment)
Chambre de Commerce: 27 avenue de Friedland. Tel: (1) 42 89 70 00
British Consulate-General: 9 avenue Hoche, 75008 Paris. Tel: (1) 42
  66 38 10. Fax: (1) 40 76 02 87
US Consulate-General: 2 avenue Gabriel, 75382 Paris Cedex 08. Tel:
  (1) 42 96 12 02. Fax: (1) 42 66 97 83

Canadian Consulate: 16 rue d'Anjou, 8e. Tel: (1) 47 23 01 01
Australian Consulate-General: 4 rue Jean Rey, 15e. Tel: (1) 40 59 33 00
Association Nationale pour l'Information sur le Logement (ANIL). Tel:
(1) 42 02 65 95
ANPE:
- Section Départementale de Paris, 4 place Félix Eboué, 75583 Paris
Cedex 12. Tel: (1) 43 41 71 10
- Centre Régional Paris Ile-de-France, 23 rue Taitbout, 75436, Paris
Cedex 09. Tel (1) 42 40 32 47
CROUS-Placements Etudiants, 39 avenue Georges Bernanos, 5e. Tel:
(1) 43 29 12 43 (for employment)

Health care

The Cité Internationale offers good health care provision centred
around the Hôpital International de l'Université de Paris, 42 boulevard
Jourdan. Tel: (1) 45 89 47 89
- Hôpital Franco-Britannique de Paris, 48 rue de Villiers, Le Vallois
Perret. Tel: (1) 47 68 13 12. (*Métro* Anatole France)
- Hôpital Américain de Paris, 63 boulevard Victor Hugo, Neuilly. Tel:
(1) 46 41 25 25. (*Métro* Sablon)
Local student insurance offices:
- MNEF, 137 boulevard St Michel, 75258, Paris Cedex. Tel: (1) 30 75
08 20
- MNEF, 27 rue Linné, 75240 Paris Cedex 05. Tel: (1) 30 75 08 20
- SMEREP, 6 bis rue Bezout, 75675 Paris Cedex 14. Tel: (1) 43 20 13
73

Travel

Rail
London-Paris St Lazare (via Newhaven-Dieppe) £70 return; (via
Dover-Calais) £74 return (Eurotrain)

Coach
London-Paris return £49; single £33 (Eurolines)

Local travel in Paris
Métro tickets cost 39F per *carnet* of 10 tickets; the *Carte Orange* (*Métro/*
buses/RER) costs 208F per month for zones 1 and 2.

Train information
SNCF, Tel: (1) 42 61 50 50

International flights
Roissy-Charles de Gaulle. Tel: (1) 48 62 50 50

Taxis at the Cité Internationale
Borne d'appel, Porte d'Orléans. Tel: (1) 45 40 52 05

Student travel
- Council Travel, 51 rue Dauphine, 6e. Tel: (1) 43 26 79 65
- Council on International Educational Exchange (CIEE), 1 place de l'Odéon, 6e. Tel: (1) 46 34 16 10

Emergencies

SOS Amitiés. Tel: (1) 46 21 31 31 *or* (1) 42 96 26 26 *or* (1) 43 64 31 31
SOS Help. Tel: (1) 47 23 80 80
All-night chemists:
- Les Champs Elysées, Galerie des Champs, 87 des Champs Elysées. Tel: (1) 45 62 02 41 (*Métro* George V)
- Drug Store St Germain, 149 boulevard St Germain. Tel: (1) 42 22 80 00 (*Métro* St Germain des Prés *or* Mabillon)
American Student and Family Service (ASFS): American Church, 65 quai d'Orsay. Tel: (1) 45 50 26 49 (*Métro* Invalides *or* Alma Marceau)

17 Poitiers

The university and its disciplines

Université de Poitiers: droit et sciences économiques, lettres et sciences humaines, sciences exactes et naturelles, médecine, pharmacie, technologie, sport.
 15 rue de Blossac, 86034 Poitiers Cedex. Tel: 49 45 30 30. Fax: 49 45 30 50
SUIO: Centre du Forum Droit-Lettres, 93 avenue du Recteur Pineau, 86000 Poitiers. Tel: 49 45 33 81
SUEE: same address and telephone
IUT:
- chimie, génie électrique et informatique industrielle, génie

thermique et énergie, génie mécanique et productique.
6 allée Jean Monnet, 86034 Cedex. Tel: 49 46 34 00
• gestion des entreprises et des administrations (GEA).
Rue des Carmes. Tel: 49 88 28 16

University libraries
• Bibliothèque Universitaire, Section Centrale (Droit-Lettres), 95 avenue du Recteur Pineau. Tel: 49 45 33 05
• Section Médecine-Pharmacie, rue du Jardin des Plantes. Tel: 49 41 69 31
• Section Sciences, 40 avenue du Recteur Pineau. Tel: 49 45 30 60
• Centre de Documentation Médicale La Gentilhommière, 350 avenue Jacques Coeur. Tel: 49 45 15 17
• Section Communication, Lycée Pilote Innovant, Parc du Futuroscope, Jaunay-Clan. Tel: 49 62 05 75

Courses for languages undergraduates

DEUG/*Licence/Maîtrise* LCE are available in German, English, Spanish, Italian, Portuguese and Russian. All students must take a second modern foreign language in both years of the DEUG, at either beginners' or more advanced levels, together with an element of textual analysis in French and one of Latin, Linguistics, General and Comparative Literature or Cinema.

DEUG/*Licence/Maîtrise* LEA (*Mention Affaires et Commerce*) are available in combinations of the same languages; Law is the major area of study in the *domaines d'application* during the first two years. The university also has a DEUG in *Langages, Images, Communication* (LIC), where courses in the Social Sciences are combined with Cinema, Communications and Language, Literature and Linguistics. This may be followed by a *Diplôme d'Université: Filmer l'entreprise*, or an MST *Information, communication d'entreprises*.

At DEUG level, *Lettres Modernes* is divided into two 'sub-strands': 1 has a heavier Latin component, while 2 involves more General and Comparative Literature and a weightier modern language element; however, Latin in some form remains compulsory. Courses remain fairly 'traditional', with significant elements of Romance Philology and Linguistics, and French Philology and Linguistics. Poitiers is in any case strong in Medieval Studies; its well-known Centre d'Etudes Supérieures de Civilisation Médiévale (Hôtel Berthelot, 24 rue de la Chaîne, Poitiers, Tel: 49 41 03 86) is an important research institute specialising in various aspects of the history, civilisation, literature and art of the period.

Most of the teaching in the UFR de Langues et Littératures (Faculté des Lettres et des Langues) takes place on the campus in the avenue du Recteur Pineau on the edge of town. Some courses, however, are held in the Hôtel Fumé, headquarters of the Faculté des Sciences Humaines (8 rue René Descartes); while the LIC strand is taught at the Université Futuroscope at Jaunay Clan. The campus is well served by buses (nos 1–3, 9 and 10; and the Noctambus).

Courses for foreign students

Full-year and semester-based courses
Département de Français pour Etudiants Etrangers (DEFPE), Université de Poitiers, 95 avenue du Recteur Pineau, 86022 Poitiers Cedex. Tel: 49 45 32 94. Fax: 49 45 32 95

Courses at all levels, from beginners' to advanced in groups of 15 to 25 for some 15 hours per week, as follows:

(a) Semester-based language courses for beginners (leading to a *Certificat d'Initiation 1*) and post-beginners (*Certificats d'Initiation 2 & 3*). Semester-based courses in literature and civilisation prepare for the first level diploma, *Certificat Pratique de Langue Française (1er degré)*. Teaching is based on the use of audio-visual methods and language laboratory exercises alongside the study of a variety of texts and recordings.

(b) Semester-based courses in language, plus either civilisation/ history or literary history/texts, leading to the second level qualification, *Diplôme d'Etudes Françaises (2e degré)*. The language element (*compréhension et expression écrites et orales*) incorporates some grammatical analysis.

(c) Courses in language, literature and civilisation preparing for the third level award, *Diplôme Supérieur d'Etudes Françaises (3e degré)*.

Students may choose to major in either civilisation or literature. Students who have obtained the *Diplôme Supérieur* may be granted the equivalence of the First Year of *Lettres Modernes*. Accommodation is in university halls of residence or hostels or rooms in town. A range of cultural, gastronomic and sporting activities is on offer.

Centre Audio-visuel de Royan pour l'Etude des Langues (CAREL), 48 boulevard Franck-Lamy, BP 219 C, 17205 Royan Cedex. Tel: 46 39 50 00. Fax: 46 05 27 68

Under the aegis of the Université de Poitiers, the centre offers, throughout the year, three- to five-week language courses (25 hours per week) at a variety of levels. Students may attempt the DALF, the DELF and the DEF, which are awarded by the Université de Poitiers. Other possibilities include short intensive courses (a) in audio-visual methods for teachers of French as a foreign language; (b) in French for Business or the Social Sciences, leading to the *Diplôme Supérieur du Français des Affaires* or the *Certificat Pratique de Français Commercial et Economique*; (c) in scientific and technical language, leading to the *Certificat de Français des Professions Scientifiques et Techniques*; (d) secretarial French for the *Certificat de Français du Secrétariat*; and (e) in French for the Tourist and Catering Industries sanctioned by the *Certificat de Français du Tourisme et de l'Hôtellerie*, all awarded by the Chambre de Commerce et d'Industrie de Paris. Accommodation is in hotels, shared flats or with families. An extensive programme of cultural and sporting activities is organised in conjunction with the courses.

Vacation courses

The University of Poitiers provides courses in July and September at a variety of levels. Instruction is in groups of between 15 and 18 for some 20 hours per week. There is a placement test on arrival and applicants should be over 16. A certificat of attendance is awarded. Accommodation is in university halls and there are sporting and cultural activites organised for the evenings and at weekends.

The CAREL also runs courses for three or four weeks in June, July, August and September according to level. Applicants must be at least 17 and there is a placement test or interview on arrival. An *attestation de stage* is provided on the satisfactory completion of the course. Short intensive courses for teachers of French as a foreign language, in Business and Economic French, and in Scientific and Technical French lead to specialist qualifications.

In August and September there is an introductory course in methodology for students from abroad wishing to register in French universities. Priority is given to French Government scholarship-holders, but others may register if places are available.

The same range of accommodation, cultural and sporting activities is available as during the academic year.

CROUS

15 rue Guillaume VII le Troubadour, BP 629, 86022 Poitiers Cedex.

Tel: 49 60 88 00. Fax: 49 41 06 58

OTU: same address, and at the Résidence Universitaire Rabelais on the campus. Tel: 49 44 53 00

SAEE: same address and telephone

CROUS-controlled accommodation

There are 3,354 rooms.

On campus:

- Résidence Rabelais, 38 avenue du Recteur Pineau, BP 637, 86022 Cedex. Tel: 49 44 53 35 (mixed; 660 individual rooms, 9 double rooms)
- Résidence Descartes, 42 avenue du Recteur Pineau, BP 627, 86022 Cedex. Tel: 49 44 52 31 (mixed; 904 individual rooms)

Between the campus and the town centre:

- Résidence Marie Curie, 21 rue Jean-Richard Bloch, BP 617, 86022 Cedex. Tel: 49 01 18 94 (mixed; 720 individual rooms)

In the town:

- Résidence Roche d'Argent, 1 rue Roche d'Argent, BP 607, 86022 Cedex. Tel: 49 88 04 11 (females; 92 in single or double rooms)
- Résidence Jeanne d'Arc, 49 rue de la Cathédrale, 86000. Tel: 49 41 17 79 (females; 15 single, 25 double rooms)
- Résidence Dalesme, rue Guillaume VII le Troubadour, 86000. Tel: 49 60 88 07 (reserved for students of ENSMA; 181 in single or double rooms)

In addition, there are a number of *studios* available, mainly for student families, but some for individuals too.

- Résidence Canolle, 15 rue Guillaume VII le Troubadour, 86000 (94 *studios*)
- Résidence St Eloi, 19–21 avenue le Pelletier, 86000 (76 *studios*)
- Centre de Vie de Jaunay-Clan, rue du Belvédère, 86130 Jaunay-Clan (109 *studios*)

CROUS restaurants

- Roche d'Argent (town centre), 1 rue Roche d'Argent. Tel: 49 88 04 13 (*menu traditionnel, scramble, cafétéria, brasserie, grill*)
- Rabelais (campus), avenue du Recteur Pineau. Tel: 49 44 53 35 (*menu traditionnel* or *plat garni; saladerie, cafétéria* and *pizzéria*)
- Champlain (campus), avenue du Recteur Pineau. Tel: 49 46 26 40 (*menu traditionnel* or *plat garni; brasserie-grill; cafétéria*)
- Cafétéria de l'IUT (campus), 6 place Jean Monnet. Tel: 49 45 33 15
- Marie-Curie, 21 rue Jean-Richard Bloch. Tel: 49 01 18 94 (between

the campus and the town centre; wide choice of menu, *cafétéria, brasserie, tarterie*; breakfast service available).

There is also one *restaurant agréé* to cater for interns and student nurses at the Centre Hospitalier Régional Universitaire at La Milétrie.

Private-sector accommodation

Les Lauréades de Poitiers, 1 avenue Mozart, 86000. Tel: 49 88 18 61

Privately-run hostels

For further details, write to the *Directeur/Directrice*:
- Foyer des Jeunes Travailleurs-MCL, 16 rue St Pierre le Puellier. Tel: 49 41 09 22
- Foyer des Jeunes Travailleurs Kennedy, 1 avenue Kennedy. Tel: 49 47 52 00
- Foyer des Feuillants, 9 rue des Feuillants. Tel: 49 55 19 87
- Foyer du Travailleur Poitevin, 15 rue Dieudonné Costes. Tel: 49 58 36 44

The town and its surrounding area

Lying some 340 km to the south-west of Paris, to which it is connected by a good rail link (the TGV service puts it about an hour and a half away), Poitiers is the ancient capital of Poitou, and the modern *préfecture* of the Vienne. The original town occupied a naturally strong site on a hill above the rivers Clain and Boivre. Today's much expanded city has sprawled well beyond this, with industrial suburbs to the south and east in particular. However, the town centre retains something of the atmosphere and charm of the *ancienne ville*.

Its historic past goes back to at least the Bronze Age, as recent excavations have shown. It subsequently became an important outpost of the Roman Empire, before falling to the Visigoths. In 732, it was at the Battle of Poitiers that Charles Martel turned back the Moorish hordes. In the Middle Ages, the town was subject to the powerful Counts of Poitou and Dukes of Aquitaine, and shuttled backwards and forwards between English and French rule. The university was founded by Charles VII in 1431.

Famous names connected with the town's past include Eléonor (or Aliénor) d'Aquitaine (1122–1204), Queen of France and then of England; Jean Bouchet (1476–*c.* 1557), the *rhétoriqueur* poet and friend

of Rabelais; Guillaume Bouchet (*c.* 1513–93), author and bookseller;
and Michel Foucault (1926–84), the structuralist philosopher.

Important vestiges of the history remain. The Hypogée Martyrium is
a seventeenth-century underground chapel built on a site where 72
Christian martyrs were buried by the Romans. The Baptistère St-Jean
from the sixth century is one of the oldest Christian monuments in
France. The impressive medieval churches include the twelfth-century
Cathédrale St-Pierre, the Romanesque jewel Notre-Dame-la-Grande
(twelfth century) and St Hilaire le Grand, which was rebuilt in the
eleventh to twelfth centuries on the site of a Gallo-Roman edifice. At the
other end of the scale, and just a little to the north of the town, lies
Futuroscope, a science-orientated amusement park which is a show
place for new technology, particularly in the field of communications.

Modern Poitiers is a pleasant town, very manageable in terms of size.
Its bustle is in no small measure due to the presence of some 26,000
students among its 105,000 inhabitants. It is possible to walk to almost
any destination; but, given the nature of the terrain, a love of hills and a
strong pair of shoes are absolute necessities.

Tourist information

Office du Tourisme – Syndicat d'Initiative, 8 rue des Grandes Ecoles.
  Tel: 49 41 21 24

Hotels
- Jules Ferry, 27 rue Jules Ferry. Tel: 49 37 80 14 (near the town
  centre; rooms from about 145F to 175F, including breakfast)
- Modern' Hôtel, 153 boulevard du Grand Cerf. Tel: 49 58 46 72 *or* 49
  58 04 85 (opposite the railway station, a short walk (or rather climb!)
  to the town centre; rooms from about 115F to 185F, including
  breakfast)
- L'Alsace-Lorraine, 6 rue du Petit Bonneveau. Tel: 49 41 25 83
  (rooms between 120F and 185F, including breakfast)

Youth hostel
Auberge de la Jeunesse, 17 rue de la Jeunesse. Tel: 49 58 03 05

Restaurants
- La Pergola, rue Théophraste Renaudot. Tel: 49 41 09 30 (very good
  value; set meals 90F-200F)
- Flunch, 2 rue du Petit Bonneveau (not far from the Hôtel de Ville; a

modern self-service cafeteria, where the food is good and inexpensive)
● Le Poitevin, 76 rue Carnot. Tel: 49 88 35 04 (authentic regional cuisine; generous menu for about 80F)

Leisure facilities

Museums and art galleries
● Musée Sainte Croix, 3 bis rue Jean Jaurès. Tel: 49 41 07 53
● Musée de Chièvres, 9 rue Victor Hugo. Tel: 49 41 42 21
● Ecole des Beaux-Arts, 26 rue Jean Alexandre. Tel: 49 88 96 53
● Hotel Aubaret, 51 place Charles de Gaulle. Tel: 49 88 31 09
● Charles VII, 33 rue Cloche-Perse
● Les Cimaises, 61 Grand Rue
● Des Licearium, 13 rue de la Chaîne
● Galerie Carnot, 37 rue Carnot
● Galerie Diane Grimaldi, 27 place Charles VII
● Arthotèque et Galerie Rivaud, 16 place Henri Barbusse

Theatre
● Les Amis du Théâtre Populaire (ATP), CIJ, 64 rue Gambetta. Tel: 49 88 64 37
● Centre Dramatique: Théâtre Poitou-Charente, 1 place Maréchal Leclerc. Tel: 49 41 28 33
● Théâtre du Kronope, 22 rue Bas des Sables. Tel: 49 88 95 13
● Compagnie Dramatique Universitaire, BP 196, Faculté des Lettres, 95 avenue du Recteur Pineau, 86022 Cedex
● Atelier Théâtre et Pédagogie, UFR de Lettres, same address
Theatrical activities are also to be found in the various *centres culturels* (see below). The organisation Oui, Avec Plaisir: Scène Nationale de Poitiers-Théâtre de Poitiers (1 place Maréchal Leclerc, tel: 49 41 28 33) is responsible for a series of theatrical, musical, cinematographic and dance events, and operates through the subscription scheme Oui, Avec Plaisir. For further details, see the annual brochure *Oui, Avec Plaisir* or ring the above number.

Music
● Jeunesses Musicales de France (JMF), 16 rue des Trois Rois. Tel: 49 60 20 57
● Rencontres Musicales de Poitiers (RMP), 43 rue Carnot. Tel: 49 01 72 96

- Conservatoire National de Région, 5 rue Franklin. Tel: 49 01 83 67
- Ateliers Musicaux Syrinx, 51 boulevard de la Digue. Tel: 49 44 00 00
- Collegium Musicae Antiquae, 2 bis rue René Descartes. Tel: 49 41 37 71
- Ensemble Josquin des Prés (choir and orchestra), 6 rue des Feuillants. Tel: 49 41 41 76
- Compagnons de la Claire Fontaine (traditional music), MCL rue St Pierre le Puellier (see below)
- Jazz Compagnie, 189 rue du Haut des Sables (Friday evenings in the Maison du Puits de la Caille, 36 rue St Simplicien. Tel: 49 41 02 67)
- Chorale A Coeur Joie, MJC Aliénor d'Aquitaine (see below)
- Chorale/Orchestre de l'Université: for information, contact the UFR *secrétariats* or telephone 49 56 70 93

There are six local cultural centres:

- Centre de la Blaiserie, rue des Frères Montgolfier. Tel: 49 58 05 52
- Centre d'Animation de Beaulieu, boulevard Savari. Tel: 49 61 44 50
- Maison de la Culture et des Loisirs (MCL), 16 rue St Pierre le Puellier. Tel: 49 41 09 22 (near to Roche d'Argent)
- Maison des Jeunes et de la Culture Aliénor d'Aquitaine, rue de Nimègue. Tel: 49 44 12 48
- Centre Socio-Culturel des Trois-Cités, le Clos Gauthier, 2 rue de la Vallée Monnaie. Tel: 49 01 29 97
- Maison des Trois Quartiers (Montierneuf), 23 rue du Général Sarrail (Quartier Dalesme). Tel: 49 41 40 33

Le Garage à Vélo... is the cultural centre on the campus. It is administered by the CROUS

Cinema

- Le Rabelais, rue Claveurier, Hôtel de Ville. Tel: 49 88 83 49
- Le Castille, 24 place Leclerc. Tel: 49 41 12 75
- Théâtre, 1 place Leclerc. Tel: 49 41 28 33
- Le Dietrich, quartier Dalesme. Tel: 49 88 88 28

Sport

FNSU: BP 51, rue des Carmélites, 86002 Cedex. Tel: 49 88 33 76

SUAPS, Gymnase Universitaire No. 2, avenue Jacques Coeur, BP 44. Tel: 49 45 37 71 (programmes in some 20 sports)

Association Sportive (ASSU)/Poitiers Etudiants Club (PEC), same address. Tel: 49 45 16 57

Stadium: Stade Poitevin-Stade Municipal Paul Rébeilleau, avenue Jacques Coeur. Tel: 49 46 23 27

Skating rink: avenue Jacques Coeur
Swimming pool: rue de la Ganterie
Salle Omnisport, rue de la Ganterie
Centre Equestre, route de Chavigny

Useful addresses

Main post office: Hôtel des Postes, 16 rue A Ranc. Tel: 49 01 83 80
Municipal library: 43 place Charles de Gaulle. Tel: 49 41 16 86
Branches:
- La Blaiserie, Rond Point de la Blaiserie. Tel: 49 58 05 68
- Les Couronneries, 16 place de Provence. Tel: 49 47 56 05
- Les Trois Cités, 12 place des 3 Cités. Tel: 49 01 29 80
- Médiasud, 23 rue de la Jeunesse. Tel: 49 58 60 06
Bookshops:
- J. Gibert, 7 et 9 rue Gambetta. Tel: 49 41 13 50
- Librairie de l'Université, 70 rue Gambetta. Tel: 49 41 02 05
CRIJ: 64 rue Gambetta, BP 176, 86000. Tel: 49 88 64 37
CAF: 41 rue du Touffenet. Tel: 49 44 55 66
Point Logement OSE: 73 rue de la Cathédrale, 86000. Tel: 49 88 39 79
EDF-GDF: 74 rue de Bourgogne. Tel: 49 45 88 88
Aumônerie des Etudiants (Les Dominos) 10 rue de la Trinité. Tel: 49
    88 02 56 (a meeting place for Christian students)
Préfecture de la Vienne, place A Briand. Tel: 49 55 70 00 (for *carte de
    séjour*)
Nearest British Consulate (Nantes): L'Aumarière, 44220 Couëron.
    Tel: 40 63 16 02
Nearest US Consulate-General (Bordeaux): 22 cours du
    Maréchal Foch, 33080 Bordeaux Cedex. Tel: 56 52 65 95. Fax: 56 51
    60 42

Health care

Centre Hospitalier Régional de Poitiers (La Milétrie). Tel: 49 44 44 44
Centre Anti-Poisons. Tel: 56 96 40 80
SUMPPS: avenue Jacques Coeur. Tel: 49 45 33 54
Local student insurance offices:
- MNEF, avenue Jacques Coeur, BP 159, 86004 Cedex. Tel: 49 46 24
    99
- SMECO, 27 rue du Marché, 86000. Tel: 49 88 38 57
CPAM: 41 rue du Touffenet. Tel: 49 44 55 66

Travel

Railway station
Travel information, boulevard du Grand Cerf. Tel: 49 58 50 50.
London-Poitiers (via Newhaven-Dieppe) £116 return; (via Dover-Calais) £120 return (Eurotrain)

Coach station
Parc de Blossac. Tel: 49 41 14 20. London-Poitiers, £42 single; £76 return (Eurolines)

Airport
Poitiers-Biard (information, tel: 49 58 27 96)
Agence Air France, 11 ter rue des Grandes Ecoles. Tel: 49 88 89 63

Buses
Société des Transports Poitevins (STP), avenue de Northampton (next to the Parc des Expositions). Tel: 49 61 07 71. Student reductions available on *carnets* of five tickets (16F); a travel card for unlimited travel (*Carte Pass Jeunes*) is also available (117F per month; 351F for 3 months). Buses 1 and 3 run between the campus and the town centre and railway station. No. 10 runs to Marie Curie. There is also a night service: Noctambus.

Taxis
● Station Hôtel de Ville. Tel: 49 41 04 06
● Radio Taxi, 650 rue Carnot. Tel: 49 88 12 34
● Station Gare (24 hour service). Tel: 49 58 21 37

Emergencies

Police. Tel: 49 88 94 21
Fire Brigade. Tel: 49 01 41 41
Gendarmerie. Tel: 49 44 02 02
SOS Amitiés. Tel: 49 45 05 73

18 Reims

The university and its disciplines

Université de Reims Champagne-Ardennes: droit et sciences économiques, lettres et sciences humaines, formations de santé, technologie.

23 rue Boulard, 51097 Reims Cedex. Tel: 26 05 30 00. Fax: 26 05 30 98

SUIO:
- Droit et Sciences Politiques, 57 bis rue Pierre Taittinger, 51096 Reims Cedex. Tel: 26 05 38 87
- Sciences et Techniques, Bibliothèque Universitaire, rue des Crayères, BP 347, 51062 Reims Cedex. Tel: 26 05 32 22

SUEE: Bureau 2002, UFR Droit et Sciences Economiques, 57 rue Pierre Taittinger, 51096 Reims Cedex. Tel: 26 04 10 82

IUT: rue des Crayères, BP 257, 51059 Reims Cedex. Tel: 26 05 30 00

University libraries
- Lettres et Sciences Humaines, Droit et Sciences Economiques, avenue François Mauriac, 51100. Tel: 26 08 22 23
- Section Santé, 51 rue Cognacq Jay, 51100. Tel: 26 06 13 68
- Sciences et Techniques, Moulin de la Housse, 51100. Tel: 26 05 32 94

Courses for languages undergraduates

LEA offers the following modern foreign languages: English, German and Spanish. In *Lettres Modernes* there are courses in French language, literature and civilisation as well as in Comparative Literature, Literature and Society, Literature and Cinema, Latin, a modern foreign language, Socio-linguistics, and the Champenois Dialect.

Courses for foreign students

Université de Reims Champagne-Ardennes, CIEF, 8 rue Joliot Curie 51100 Reims. Tel: 26 86 19 38. Fax: 26 49 86 01

Term-time courses
The University of Reims organises semester courses of 14 weeks' duration (15 hours per week) beginning in October and February.

Intending students must be at least 18 years of age. Absolute beginners are taught by audio-visual methods. For students with an elementary level of French, there are more advanced courses, and for those who are suitably qualified there is the possibility of working towards either the *Certificat d'Etudes Pratiques de Langue Française (1er degré)* or the *Diplôme d'Etudes Françaises (2e degré)* with options in French literature, civilisation and translation. A test determines the level of entry. The programme for the *Diplôme Supérieur d'Etudes Françaises (Lettres Modernes, 3e degré)* extends over two consecutive semesters and intending students must have the *baccalauréat* or an equivalent qualification. Accommodation is either in privately-run student hostels or with families. Leisure activities include visits to the local vineyards, Paris and Strasbourg.

Vacation courses

Université de Reims, SUEE, 17 rue de Jard, 51100 Reims. Tel: 26 47 04 11. Fax: 26 47 05 40

During September, there are intensive study programmes at intermediate level for students with a good knowledge of French and at advanced level for university students of French. There is a placement test on arrival. Accommodation is in university halls of residence. Extra-curricular activities include swimming and tennis, visits to the theatre and the cinema, guided tours of Reims and excursions in the Champagne region.

CROUS

34 boulevard Henri Vasnier, BP 2751, 51063 Cedex. Tel: 26 50 59 00. Fax: 26 50 59 29

OTU:
- RU du Moulin de la Housse. Tel: 26 85 67 56 (open 11.30-14.30)
- RU Jean-Charles Prost. Tel: 26 04 08 87 (open 11.00-15.00)

CROUS-controlled accommodation

There are some 3,500 rooms available in CROUS-controlled accommodation. Of these just under 1,300 are in halls, the remainder are in HLM.
- Résidence Evariste Galois/Teilhard de Chardin, rue des Crayères. Tel: 26 85 07 76
  The residence comprises two *pavillons*:
  - Pavillon Evariste Galois, plateau du Moulin de la Housse (300

rooms, cafeteria, TV rooms, table-tennis)
- Pavillon Teilhard de Chardin, rue des Crayères (372 rooms, TV/ cinema room, cafeteria)
- Résidence Paul Fort, boulevard Franchet d'Esperey. Tel: 26 06 06 72 (250 rooms; cafeteria; restaurant (evenings only); games and TV rooms; football team; convenient for Faculté des Lettres)
- Résidence Saint-Nicaise/Gérard Philipe, 2 rue Gérard Philipe. Tel: 26 82 81 39

  This residence comprises two *pavillons*:
  - Pavillon Gérard Philipe (308 rooms; music room; cafeteria and restaurant; TV and games rooms)
  - Pavillon Saint-Nicaise, 34 boulevard Henry Vasnier (251 rooms; cafeteria and restaurant; games and TV rooms)

For details of the rooms available in HLM, contact the Service Logement, 34 boulevard Henry Vasnier, 51100 Reims. Tel: 26 85 50 16, exts. 419/422. These rooms, though more expensive than hall places, attract APL.

CROUS restaurants

There are two restaurants offering the traditional three-course meal and a variety of fast-food single course alternatives. Meals are served between 11.30 and 13.45 and between 18.30 and 19.45, Mondays to Fridays. At the weekend there is only a lunch-time service. However, the cafeteria service is available daily from 8h to 18h or 20h.
- Jean-Charles Prost, rue de Rilly-la-Montagne. Tel: 26 08 04 80
- Moulin de la Housse, plateau du Moulin de la Housse. Tel: 26 85 30 18

Privately-run hostels

For further details, write to the *Directeur/Directrice*:
- Foyer ALEJT, 66 rue de Courcelles. Tel: 26 47 81 42
- Foyer Siegfried, rue Siegfried. Tel: 26 08 04 73
- Maison des Etudiants de l'Aube, 32 rue de Rilly-la-Montagne. Tel: 26 08 20 13
- Foyer de Jeunes Filles, 53 rue du Louvois. Tel: 26 06 09 46

The town and its surrounding area

Now synonymous with champagne, Reims was once more widely known as a textile manufacturing centre. With a population of 185,000, of whom some 20,000 are students, the city has good cultural and sports facilities. A university was first established in Reims by Cardinal Charles of Lorraine in 1548 and this prospered until 1793. The modern university campus dates from the 1960s. The town was badly damaged in the two World Wars, but many architectural monuments have survived including the Porte de Mars, a Roman triumphal arch, and the magnificent Gothic Cathedral, perhaps the finest in France. Among the famous coronations which have taken place in Reims was that of Charles VII, who, in 1429, with the help of Jeanne d'Arc, outwitted the occupying English forces. The Musée Saint-Denis houses paintings by Corot, a rich ceramics collection and fifteenth-century tapestries. Among celebrated figures associated with Reims are Louis XIV's minister Jean-Baptiste Colbert (1619–83); Gilles Gobelin the sixteenth-century tapestry weaver; the artist Jean-Louis Forrain (1852–1931) and the poet Paul Fort (1872–1960). The town will also be remembered as the birthplace of the first French newspaper, the *Gazette de France,* and for the unconditional surrender of the Germans on 7 May 1945. Apart from champagne, Reims is also noted for its biscuits, while the region is associated with bird *pâtés* and bottled vegetables. The town is accessible by the A4, and although it is not on a direct line, it is only about one and a half hours away from Paris by train.

Tourist information

Office du Tourisme, 2 rue Guillaume de Machault, 51100. Tel: 26 47 25 69. Fax 26 47 23 63 (near the Cathedral).

Hotels

The following are near the station and the town centre.

- Ardenn'Hôtel, 6 rue Caqué. Tel: 26 47 42 38. Fax: 26 47 48 82 (rooms 165F to 209F; breakfast 26F)
- Hôtel Le Baron, 85 rue de Vesle. Tel: 26 47 46 24 (rooms 165F–245F; breakfast 26F)
- Hôtel Touring, 17 ter boulevard Général Leclerc. Tel: 26 47 38 15 (rooms 190F to 260F; breakfast 25F)

Cheaper hotels can be found in the rue de Tillois with rooms from 80F and breakfast from 20F:

- Au Bon Accueil, 31 rue de Tillois. Tel: 26 88 55 74
- Hôtel Thillois, 17 rue Thillois. Tel: 26 40 65 65

Restaurants
- La Boule d'Or, 39 rue de Thiers (menus: 44F, 60F)
- Le Danaïde, 12 rue de Thillois. Tel: 26 47 50 42 (menus: 55F, 78F, 98F; closed Mondays)
- La Lorraine, 7 place Drouet d'Erlon. Tel: 26 47 32 73 (menus from 68F to 168F)
- La Moulinière, 4 rue Bertin. Tel: 26 88 64 19 (menus: 68F, 86F)

Leisure and sports facilities

Theatre
- Grand Théâtre de Reims, 9 rue de Chanzy. Tel: 26 47 44 43
- Théâtre de la Comédie, 1 rue Eugène Wiet. Tel: 26 85 60 00
- Espace Malraux, 3–5 chaussée Bocquaine. Tel: 26 47 93 44

Cinema
- Opéra, 9 rue de Thillois. Tel: 26 47 29 36 (6 screens)
- Gaumont, 72 place Drouet d'Erlon. Tel: 26 47 54 54 (7 screens)

Principal museums and art galleries
(Check opening times as these vary throughout the year; free to students, unless otherwise specified)
- Musée des Beaux-Arts, 8 rue de Chanzy. Tel: 26 47 28 44 (a rich collection of French art including Impressionist paintings; closed Mondays and Tuesdays)
- Musée de l'Automobile Française, avenue Georges Clemenceau. Tel: 26 82 83 84 (over 150 different models; open daily during the summer, at weekends in winter; 20F)
- Musée Saint Rémi, 53 rue Simon. Tel: 26 85 23 36 (archeological museum)
- Palais du Thau, next to the cathedral (collection of tapestries and cathedral treasures; students 15F)
- Salle de Reddition, 12 rue Franklin Roosevelt (commemorates the German surrender in the Second World War; closed Mondays)

Miscellaneous
Visits to the famous champagne *caves* take place throughout the year. The following can be recommended:
- Mumm, 34 rue Champ de Mars. Tel: 26 49 59 70
- Pommery, 5 place du Général Gouraud. Tel: 26 61 62 55
- Taittinger, 9 place St Nicaise. Tel: 26 85 45 35

• Veuve Clicquot-Ponsardin, 1 place des Droits de l'Homme. Tel: 26 40 25 42 (by appointment only)
MJC: rue de la Liberté. Tel: 26 55 18 44 (information about other centres in Reims available here)
Maison de la Culture André Malraux, 3–5 chaussée Bocquaine. Tel: 26 47 93 44
Centre Culturel, RU J C Prost rue de Rilly-la-Montagne. Tel: 26 04 15 50
FNSU: UFRS, Moulin de la Housse, BP 347, 51062 Cedex. Tel: 26 05 31 31

Useful addresses

Main post office: rue Olivier Métra. Tel: 26 88 44 22
Municipal library: Carnegie, 2 place de Carnegie. Tel: 26 84 39 60
Bookshops:
• Librairie Clemenceau, 3 ter avenue Clemenceau. Tel: 26 85 43 50
• L'U, 34 rue de Rilly-la-Montagne. Tel: 26 04 67 09
Accueil de Reims: 82 rue Ponsardin. Tel: 26 88 40 04
ANPE: 40 rue de Talleyrand. Tel: 26 40 16 16
CAF: 202 rue des Capucins. Tel: 26 82 25 25
Chambre de Commerce: 30 rue Cérès. Tel: 26 47 15 15
CIJ: 41 rue de Talleyrand. Tel: 26 47 46 70
Commissariat F Mauriac, avenue du Général Bonaparte. Tel: 26 86 31 45 (for *cartes de séjour*)
Mairie: place de l'Hôtel de Ville. Tel: 26 40 54 53
Nearest British Consulate-General (Paris): 9 avenue Hoche, 75008 Paris. Tel: (1) 42 66 38 10. Fax: (1) 40 76 02 87
Nearest US Consulate-General (Paris): 2 avenue Gabriel, 75382 Paris Cedex 08. Tel: (1) 42 96 12 02. Fax: (1) 42 66 97 83

Health care

SUMP: 10 rue des Salines. Tel: 26 85 28 11
Hospital: Hôpital Maison Blanche, 45 rue Cognacq Jay. Tel: 26 40 70 70
Chemist: Pharmacie d'Erlon, 70 place d'Erlon. Tel: 26 47 26 08
Local student insurance offices:
• MNEF, 62 esplanade Fléchambault, BP 245, Cedex. Tel: 26 85 18 45
• MGEL, 49 rue Houzeau Muiron. Tel: 26 88 62 46

Travel

Railway station
Boulevard Joffre. Tel: 26 88 50 50. London-Reims (via Newhaven-Dieppe) £101 return; (via Dover-Calais) £105 return (Eurotrain)

Bus/coach station
Place du Forum. Tel: 26 65 17 07. London-Reims; £62 return, £34 single (Eurolines)

Buses
Transports Urbains de Reims (TUR), 6 rue Chanzy. Tel: 26 88 25 38. Single ticket 5F50, *carnet* of ten tickets 30F. Buses are identified alphabetically, eg Bus D runs from the station to the CROUS.

Taxis
● Les Taxis de Reims, cours de la Gare. Tel: 26 47 05 05
● Taxi Radio Reims. Tel: 26 02 15 02

Emergencies

SAMU. Tel: 26 06 07 08
SOS Amitié. Tel: 26 05 12 12
Centre Anti-Poisons. Tel: 26 78 79 20
EDF. Tel 26 43 33 30
GDF. Tel: 26 47 24 03

19 Rennes

The universities and their disciplines

Université de **Rennes I**: sciences juridiques et économiques, formations de santé, sciences exactes et naturelles, technologie.
2 rue du Thabor, BP 1134, 35014 Rennes Cedex. Tel: 99 25 36 36. Fax: 99 25 36 00
SUIO: same address. Tel: 99 25 36 36, ext 3632
IUT: rue du Clos Courtel, BP 1144, 35014 Rennes. Tel: 99 36 26 51
Université de Haute Bretagne (**Rennes II**): lettres et sciences humaines, langues, technologie, sport.

6 avenue Gaston Berger, 35043 Rennes Cedex. Tel: 99 33 52 52.
Fax: 99 33 51 75
SUIO: same address. Tel: 99 33 52 51
SUEE: same address. Tel: 99 33 51 18

University libraries
● Section Sciences, 18 avenue des Buttes de Coësmes. Tel: 99 36 37 68
● Section Médecine Pharmacie, 5 avenue du Pr L Bernard. Tel: 99 59 15 44
● Section Droit et Sciences Eco, 4 rue Lesage. Tel: 99 38 75 45
● Section Lettres, 5 avenue du Pr L Bernard. Tel: 99 59 19 15

Courses for languages undergraduates

The UFR Langues, Littératures et Civilisations Etrangères mounts a DEUG *rénové* LCE in English, German, Spanish, Italian, Portuguese and Russian. LEA is also available in combinations of the same languages (DEUG *rénové*).

The Second Year of the DEUG in *Lettres Modernes* (in the UFR de Littérature) is in three blocks: I, Literature from the medieval period to the seventeenth century; II, Linguistics (Old French grammar and texts, grammar of the classical period) and Stylistics; III, Comparative Literature and a modern foreign language. Each block includes an option from a restricted list. Among the choices for these are interesting offerings in *littérature maghrébine* and *études québécoises*. More generally, the university teaches a challenging range of Celtic languages.

The UFR de Langues and the UFR de Littérature are situated on the campus at Villejean, near to a number of halls of residence. Buses 8 and 10 run between the campus and the town centre. Rennes has a large student population (35,500 or so). The results of a survey published recently in *Le Monde de l'Education* would suggest that it is one of the most popular university towns.

Courses for foreign students

Term-time courses
SUEE: Université de Haute Bretagne, 6 avenue Gaston Berger, 35043 Rennes Cedex. Tel: 99 33 51 18
Refresher and advanced level courses are provided on an annual basis

(15 or so hours per week over 26 weeks, October to May) leading to the award of the *Certificat Pratique de Langue Française*, the *Diplôme d'Etudes Françaises* and the *Diplôme Supérieur d'Etudes Françaises*. The courses cover language, literature and civilisation. Applicants must hold the equivalent of the *baccalauréat* and pass the grading test. Visits and excursions are proposed in conjunction with courses in civilisation and History of Art. There are no courses at beginners' level during the academic year.

Summer courses
Cours Universitaire d'Eté, Université de Rennes II Haute Bretagne, BP 125, 35402 Saint-Malo Cedex. Tel: 99 40 80 67 (address for corres- spondence until the beginning of the course: 6 avenue Gaston Berger, 35043 Rennes Cedex. Tel: 99 33 52 52)
A language course for beginners runs for four weeks from early July to early August. Over the same period, there are refresher courses in language, literature and civilisation at four levels ranging from inter- mediate to advanced. These may be taken for two weeks or four weeks. Candidates must be over 16 years of age, and are obliged to take a language test which determines their level of study. Accommodation (for those enrolled only) is with families, in hotels or on camp sites. The setting of a very pleasant seaside resort provides many opportunities for extra-curricular activities.

CROUS

7 place Hoches, BP 115, 35002 Rennes Cedex. Tel: 99 36 46 11. Fax: 99 38 36 90
OTU: same address and telephone
SAEE: same address and telephone (organises introductions to French families)

CROUS-controlled accommodation
There are more than 6,000 places available in residences in various parts of the town. These are mainly in single rooms, though there are a few double rooms at Villejean and in the town centre.
Villejean:
● CU, 2 rue d'Alsace. Tel: 99 59 20 48
● CU, square de Guyenne. Tel: 99 59 26 71
● CU, square de Normandie. Tel: 99 59 33 02
● CU, 5 rue du Maine. Tel: 99 54 47 54

- CU, 30 rue Léon Ricottier. Tel: 99 33 70 24
Town centre:
- CU, 94 boulevard de Sévigné. Tel: 99 36 10 21
- CU, rue du Doyen Roger Houin. Tel: 99 38 02 93
- CU, 20 rue Saint Hélier. Tel: 99 30 85 42
Beaulieu:
- CU, 33 avenue des Buttes de Coësmes. Tel: 99 36 38 02
- CU, 29 avenue des Buttes de Coësmes. Tel: 99 36 26 27
Patton:
- CU, rue du Houx. Tel: 99 63 21 91
The CROUS has also built a residence to the 'new' formula, involving some 300 *studios*, on the campus at Beaulieu (rue Mirabeau) and administers 123 HLM flats that it lets to *jeunes ménages d'étudiants*.

CROUS restaurants

- Le Fougères, 46 rue Jean Guehenno (also has a separate *pizzéria*)
- Champ de Mars, 11 bis boulevard de la Liberté (with a *crêperie*)
- Beaulieu I, 37 avenue des Buttes de Coësmes (also caters for *régime médico-diététique*)
- Beaulieu II, allée Jean d'Alembert, Campus de Beaulieu.
- Villejean I, avenue de la Bataille Flandres-Dunkerque
- Villejean II, 36 avenue Winston Churchill (also caters for *régime médico-diététique*)
- RU, 104 boulevard de la Duchesse Anne

Various formulae are available: *menu traditionnel* or a more substantial main course and dessert, in exchange for the standard *ticket de restaurant*: in either case, further dishes may be bought for cash. There are also snack outlets and *brasseries* where payment is in cash. Students who wish to follow the *régime médico-diététique* must arrange this with the Service Social at the CROUS, after having consulted the SUMP.

The town and its surrounding area

The former capital of Britanny, and seat of the Parlement de Bretagne from 1561 until the end of the *ancien régime*, Rennes is still the administrative centre of the Breton peninsula. It is also the *préfecture* of the Ille-et-Vilaine. The inauguration of the TGV service has meant that it is now just 125 minutes away from Paris, in addition to being easily accessible from Normandy by way of Caen.

Its history stretches back to ancient times when Condate, the capital of the Celtic tribe, the Riedones, stood at the confluence of the Rivers Ille and Vilaine. It was a stronghold of the Francs before it fell to the Bretons. However, a great fire in 1720 destroyed much of the centre, after which it was rebuilt in grand eighteenth-century style. The picturesque areas around the *ville neuve* offer numerous examples of buildings from medieval times to the seventeenth century, including half-timbered houses. However, pride of place goes to the more formal developments in reddish granite centred upon two former royal squares, now called the *place de la Mairie* and the *place du Palais*. The sector has been restored and partly pedestrianised, and is host to fashionable shops. Equally, the Jardin du Thabor, consisting in part of the gardens of the former Benedictine abbey of Saint-Melaine, is a very attractive park.

Famous personalities are not legion. However, they include Admiral La Motte-Piquet (1720–91) and the reactionary Général Boulanger (1837–91). It was also in Rennes that, in 1899, Alfred Dreyfus's sentence of deportation was commuted to ten years' imprisonment.

The industrial and commercial activities of the town have much expanded in recent years, including the creation in 1982 of a *zone d'innovation et de recherches scientifiques et techniques*, Rennes Atalante. The construction work which has resulted from this expansion has given the place a distinctly heterogeneous look, which some may find unharmonious. However, it is the administrative and educational sectors which predominate and which establish the tone. A number of important festivals are held in the course of the year: Les Transmusicales (rock music) in December, the Festival des Arts Electroniques in June (every other year) and the Tombées de la Nuit (Breton Arts) in July.

Rennes is about an hour and a half away from the Channel coast and the South Brittany coast. The Mont Saint Michel, Saint Malo, Vannes and La Baule are within easy reach, as also are the great fortresses of the Marches de Bretagne: Châteaugiron, Fougères, Combourg and Vitré.

With its concern for Breton culture, and the impetus provided, in part, by the existence of a large student population, Rennes has proved popular with students who find it a humane and manageable town.

Tourist information

Office du Tourisme – Syndicat d'Initiative, pont de Nemours. Tel: 99 79 01 98
Association Bretonne des Relais et Itinéraires (ABRI), 9 rue des Portes

Mordelaises. Tel: 99 31 59 44

Hotels
- Hôtel Le Magenta, 35 boulevard Magenta. Tel: 99 30 85 37 (near the bus station; rooms between about 140F and 180F, with breakfast)
- Hôtel du Cheval d'Or, 6 place de la Gare. Tel: 99 30 25 80 (convenient for the station; rooms between 140F and 280F)
- Hôtel de Léon, 15 rue de Léon. Tel: 99 30 55 28 (near the R. Vilaine, off quai de Richemont; large, comfortable rooms from about 135F, including breakfast; friendly management)

Youth hostel
10–12 canal St-Martin. Tel: 99 33 22 33 (single 116F, including breakfast and sheets)

Restaurants
- La Toque Rennaise, 9 rue Emile Souvestre. Tel: 99 30 84 25 (in the town centre, near the Champ de Mars; meals at 50F, 82F and 150F)
- Le Bréquigny, 12 boulevard Albert 1er. Tel: 99 31 81 61 (near the Piscine Olympique; meals 44F and 70F)
- Le Descartes, 4 rue Descartes. Tel: 99 30 29 69 (a good, cheap *crêperie*, not far from the centre of town or the station)

Leisure facilities

Museums and art galleries
- Musée des Beaux-Arts, 20 quai Emile Zola. Tel: 99 28 55 85
- Musée de Bretagne, same address. Tel: 99 28 55 84
- Ecomusée du Pays de Rennes, route de Chatillon, La Bintinais

Theatre
- Le Grand Huit, 1 rue Saint-Hélier. Tel: 99 31 55 33 (incorporates the Maison de la Culture and the Théâtre National de Bretagne)
- Théâtre de la Parcheminerie, 23 rue de la Parcheminerie. Tel: 99 79 47 63
- Théâtre de la Ville, place de la Mairie. Tel: 99 28 55 87
- Théâtre de l'Alibi, Eglise du Vieux St-Etienne, rue d'Echange. Tel: 99 30 14 14
- Centre Culturel du Triangle, boulevard de Yougoslavie. Tel: 99 53 01 92

In addition, there are a number of Maisons des Jeunes et de la Culture and of Maisons de Quartier which host socio-cultural activities. For details, see *Spectacles Information* published periodically by the Office du Tourisme, or the weekly magazine *Contact-Le Pub Hebdo*, which is available free from university restaurants, cinemas, shops, etc. For information on the exhibitions, performances, concerts and lectures organised on the campus at Villejean, keep an eye out for the bi-mensual newsletter *R2-Actualités* or contact the Service Culturel de l'Université. Tel: 99 33 52 58 *or* 99 33 52 99 *or* 99 33 52 58.

Cinema
- Arvor, 29 rue d'Antrain. Tel: 99 38 72 40 (2 screens)
- Colombier, place du Colombier. Tel: 99 31 59 75 (6 screens)
- Gaumont, 8 quai Duguay-Trouin. Tel: 99 31 57 92 (8 screens)
- Le Grand Huit, 1 rue Saint-Hélier. Tel: 99 30 88 88

There are a number of university ciné-clubs which meet on Wednesday evenings, including the *Ciné-club de Littérature*. Details are available from the Agence Régionale de Diffusion Culturelle.

Sport
Direction Départementale Jeunesse et Sports, 12 rue Jean Guy.Tel: 99 67 21 33

Service des Sports de la Ville de Rennes, 28 rue de Paris. Tel: 99 28 55 90

Office des Sports, Salle Omnisports, esplanade Charles de Gaulle. Tel: 99 54 22 23

FNSU: Gymnase Universitaire de Beaulieu, avenue des Buttes de Coësmes. Tel: 99 36 77 42

SIUAPS: Complexe Sportif de Beaulieu. Same address. Tel: 99 28 63 87

Football: Stade Rennais, 111 route de Lorient. Tel: 99 59 62 03

Skating rink: Les Gayeulles, rue des Longs Prés. Tel: 99 36 28 10

Swimming pools:
- Piscine de Villejean, square d'Alsace. Tel: 99 59 44 83
- Piscine Olympique de Bréquigny, boulevard Albert 1er. Tel: 99 31 80 33

The brochure *Sports et Loisirs (Rennes et District)*, published in conjunction with the Direction Régionale et Départementale de la Jeunesse et des Sports, gives a full list of sporting activities in the town.

Useful addresses

Main post office: 27 boulevard du Colombier. Tel: 99 31 42 72, with a branch office in place de la République. Tel: 99 79 50 71

Municipal library: BM Centrale, 1 rue de la Borderie. Tel: 99 63 09 09 Amongst many annexes is the one at Villejean: Plate Forme Kennedy, avenue W Churchill. Tel: 99 59 23 82

Institut Franco-Américain, 7 quai Châteaubriand. Tel: 99 79 20 57 (American library and unofficial consulate; Franco-American activities arranged)

Bookshops:
- FNAC, Centre Colombier
- Maxi-Livres, 5 rue d'Orléans. Tel: 99 78 14 95
- Librairie des Facultés Delcourt, 1 rue Maréchal Joffre. Tel: 99 79 36 09

Books are also sold in the foyer of Bâtiment B on the campus at Villejean.

ANPE: 19 boulevard St Conwoin. Tel: 99 35 13 13

CAF: cours des Alliés. Tel: 99 29 19 99

CIJ Bretagne, Maison du Champ de Mars, 6 cours des Alliés. Tel: 99 31 47 48

Mairie: place de l'Hôtel de Ville. Tel: 99 28 55 55

Préfecture: 3 avenue de la Préfecture. Tel: 99 02 82 22

Nearest British Consulate (Nantes): L'Aumarière, 44220 Couëron. Tel: 40 63 16 02

Nearest US Consulate-General (Paris): 2 avenue Gabriel, 75382 Cedex 08. Tel: (1) 42 96 12 02. Fax: (1) 42 66 97 83

Health care

SUMP (some free treatment is available, usually by appointment):
- (Town centre) 3 rue de la Cochardière. Tel: 99 63 19 64
- (Villejean) rue Pierre-Jean Gineste. Tel: 99 54 20 87 (in the UFR Education Physique et Sportive)
- (Beaulieu) avenue des Buttes de Coësmes. Tel: 99 36 39 14

Local student insurance offices:
- MNEF, 29 quai Chateaubriand. Tel: 99 51 65 55
- SMEBA, 4 rue Victor Hugo. Tel: 99 78 33 66

CPAM: Centre de Sécurité Sociale, 1 cours des Alliés. Tel: 99 29 44 44

Travel

Railway station
Place de la Gare. Information, tel: 99 65 50 50; Reservations, tel: 99 65 18 65. London-Rennes (via Newhaven-Dieppe-Paris) £125 return; (via Dover-Calais-Paris) £129 return (Eurotrain). London-St Malo (via Portsmouth) £39 single (Britanny Ferries). Buses connect with Rennes.

Coach station
Boulevard Magenta. Tel: 99 30 87 80. There is no direct Eurolines service to Rennes. Nearest town served is St Malo, £40 single from London. Buses connect with Rennes.

Airport
Rennes St Jacques, St Jacques de la Lande. Tel: 99 31 91 77
Air France: 23 rue du Puits Mauger. Tel: 99 35 09 09

Buses
Service de Transports de l'Agglomération Rennaise, place de la République. Tel: 99 79 37 37. Tickets may be bought singly (on the bus) or in *carnets* of 10 (from most *tabacs* or the above office). There are also weekly travelcards. Night buses run between town and Villejean (the 'green bus').

Emergencies

Police, rue d'Echange. Tel: 99 65 00 22
SAMU. Tel: 99 59 16 16
Hospital: Hôpital de Pontchaillon. Tel: 99 28 43 21
SOS Rennes Médecins. Tel: 99 79 48 33
Centre Anti-Poisons. Tel: 99 59 22 22
SOS Amitiés. Tel : 99 59 71 71

20 Rouen

The university and its disciplines

Université de Haute-Normandie: droit et sciences économiques, lettres et sciences humaines, médecine et pharmacie, sciences exactes et

naturelles, technologie.
1 rue Thomas Becket, BP 138, 76134 Mont Saint Aignan Cedex.
Tel: 35 14 60 00. Fax: 35 14 63 48
SUIO: rue Lavoisier, 76130 Mont Saint Aignan. Tel: 35 14 63 05
IUT: rue Lavoisier, 76821 Mont Saint Aignan. Tel: 35 14 62 10 *or* 35
14 60 00

University library
Section Lettres et Droit, rue Lavoisier, BP 138, 76134 Mont Saint
Aignan Cedex

Courses for languages undergraduates

LEA offers the following modern foreign languages: English, German,
Russian and Spanish. Courses in both LEA and LCE/LVE are offered
up to and including *Maîtrise* level.
   Lettres Modernes courses contain compulsory elements in Lingustics
and History of the Language which British undergraduates often find
difficult. Most DEUG, *Licence and Maîtrise* courses tend not to be
rénovés.

Courses for foreign students

Alliance Française de Rouen, Rencontres Internationales de
   Normandie, 32 rue de Buffon, 76000 Rouen. Tel: 35 98 55 99

Term-time courses
The University of Rouen does not offer foreign students' courses, but
the Alliance Française puts on the following term-time courses:
beginners' courses (minimum period of study one month); 10 and 20
hours weekly. Preparation for the *Certificat Elémentaire de Français
Pratique* and the *Diplôme de Langue Française*. Courses are also offered in
Langue et Tourisme (2, 3 and 4 weeks). Accommodation is with French
families.

Vacation courses
The Alliance Française de Rouen also offers beginners', intermediate
and advanced courses (*niveaux 1, 2 et 3*) in July and August (15 or 25
hours per week, Monday to Friday). Accommodation is provided with
families or in bed-sitters.

CROUS

3 rue d'Herbouville, 76042 Rouen Cedex. Tel: 35 15 74 40. Fax: 35 98
   44 79
SAEE: same address and telephone
OTU: Cité du Panorama, Pavillon Corneille, Mont Saint Aignan. Tel:
   35 70 21 65

CROUS-controlled accommodation
Rouen has 2,529 beds at Mont Saint Aignan. The accommodation
comprises rooms in halls of residence and in single-bedroomed flats
(*appartements, types T1, T2*). Both the Cité du Panorama and the Cité du
Bois are at Mont Saint Aignan in close proximity to the university. The
former is the larger of the two and also contains 32 flats for married
couples. The former Cité d'Herbouville, situated in the centre of the
town, has been transformed into offices and also *chambres d'hôtes* which
are designed for *stagiaires* and teaching staff.
- Cité du Panorama, boulevard Siegfried, BP 218, 76136 Mont Saint
   Aignan. Tel: 35 74 18 68
- Cité du Bois, 35–37 rue du Maréchal Juin, BP 48, 76131 Mont Saint
   Aignan. Tel: 35 74 21 17
- Cité Universitaire la Pléiade, rue du Maréchal de Tassigny, 76130
   Mont Saint Aignan (*appartements/studios: T1, T1 bis, T2*)

CROUS restaurants
- Restaurant du Bois, rue Jacques Boutiolle (*menu traditionnel*; la
   Boiserie offers grills, pizzas and the cafeteria has a snack bar and
   take-away service)
- Restaurant du Panorama, boulevard André Siegfried (range of possi-
   bilities as above)
- Restaurant d'Herbouville, 3 rue d'Herbouville (*menu traditionnel*
   only)

The town and its surrounding area

The historical capital of Normandy, Rouen, with a population of
400,000, is the *chef-lieu* of the *département* of Seine-Maritime. Situated
some 125 kilometres north-west of Paris on the river Seine, it is a town
which suffered greatly in the Second World War but which still has
many outstanding buildings and monuments: the Cathédrale Notre
Dame, which dates from the twelfth to thirteenth centuries and which

was painted on a number of occasions by Monet, l'Eglise Saint-Ouen, the Eglise Saint Maclou (the only remaining charnel-house in France), the Gros-Horloge (sixteenth century) and the Palais de Justice. The town, noted for its art as well as its industry, is the birthplace of the dramatists Thomas and Pierre Corneille, the philosopher Fontenelle, the composer Boiëldieu, the painter Géricault and the celebrated nineteenth-century novelist Gustave Flaubert. The narrow pedestrian streets in the town centre attract large numbers of tourists in summer, as does the place du Vieux Marché where Jeanne d'Arc was martyred and where the modern church which bears her name rises in sharp contrast to the surrounding buildings. The thriving port is situated on the Seine, half-way between Paris and the sea.

The campus is located at Mont Saint Aignan, at the top of a very steep hill and at some distance from the centre of the town. Rouen is only one and a half hours from Paris by train, and is ideally placed for the coastal and inland towns of Normandy.

Tourist information

Office du Tourisme: 25 place de la Cathédrale, BP 666, 76008 Rouen, Cedex. Tel: 35 71 41 77. Fax: 35 98 55 50

Hotels
- Hôtel Morand, 1 rue Morand. Tel: 35 71 46 07 (prices: 150F-250F; will often let rooms, when available, at a discount to students)
- Hôtel du Palais, 12 rue du Tambour. Tel: 35 71 41 40 (right in the centre of town; rooms 110F-200F)
- Hôtel de la Tour de Beurre, 20 quai P Corneille. Tel: 35 71 46 44 (rooms 115F-135F)
- Hôtel de Normandie, 19 rue du Bac. Tel: 35 71 55 77 (less expensive than its rating would suggest: rooms 180F-310F)

Youth hostel
Auberge de Jeunesse, 17 rue Diderot, 76100. Tel: 35 72 06 45 (53F for bed and breakfast)

Restaurants
- La Grillade, 121 rue Jeanne d'Arc. Tel: 35 71 47 01 (prices range from 52F to 130F; closed Sundays)
- Brasserie du Départ, 25 rue Verte. Tel: 35 71 10 11 (meals from 50F-100F)

- Brasserie Paul, 1 place de la Cathédrale. Tel: 35 71 86 07 (meals from 50F-115F)
- Le Dandy, 93 rue Cauchoise. Tel: 35 07 32 00 (meals from 75F-95F)
- Flunch, 60 rue des Carmes. Tel: 35 71 81 81 (inexpensive self-service restaurant)

Leisure facilities

Museums and art galleries

- Musée des Beaux-Arts, 10 square Verdrel. Tel: 35 71 28 40 (free for students)
- Musée de Céramique, Hôtel d'Hocqueville, 1 rue Faucon. Tel: 35 07 31 74
- Musée le Secq-des-Tournelles (*Ferronnerie*), Ancienne Eglise Saint Laurent, rue Jacques Villon
- Musée Flaubert et d'Histoire de la Médecine, Hôtel-Dieu, 51 rue de Lecat. Tel: 35 15 59 95 (former *appartement* of Achille Flaubert, the surgeon and father of Gustave)
- Musée Jeanne d'Arc, place du Vieux Marché. Tel: 35 88 02 70
- Centre d'Art Contemporain, 11 place du Général de Gaulle. Tel: 35 98 06 92
- Musée d'Histoire Naturelle, Ethnographie et Préhistoire, square André Maurois, 198 rue Beauvoisine. Tel: 35 71 41 50
- Maison Natale de Corneille, 4 rue de la Pie. Tel: 35 71 63 92
- Pavillon Flaubert, quai Gustave Flaubert, Croisset-Canteleu
- Musée National de l'Education, 185 rue Eau de Robec. Tel: 35 75 49 70

Theatre

- Théâtre des Arts, rue du Dr Rambert. Tel: 35 98 50 98
- Théâtre du Monde, 303 rue des Quatre Amis, 76230 Bois Guillaume. Tel: 35 15 16 36
- Théâtre des Arts-Opéra de Normandie, quai de la Bourse. Tel: 35 71 41 36
- Théâtre des Deux Rives, 48 rue Louis Ricard. Tel: 35 70 22 82
- Théâtre de l'Echarde, 16 rue Flahaut. Tel: 35 15 33 05
- Théâtre l'Usine, 141 route de Darnétal. Tel: 35 15 54 41
- Théâtre de la Ville, Centre Saint Sever. Tel: 35 62 31 31

Sport

FNSU: Centre Sportif Universitaire (CSU), boulevard Siegfried, 76130 Mont St. Aignan. Tel: 35 74 86 98. Among the sports available are: sub-aqua, canoeing, rugby, pot-holing, flying, archery. For further details, see the sports section of the current edition of *Le Lauréat (Guide Officiel de l'Université de Rouen)*.

- Direction du Sport et de la Jeunesse, Hôtel de Ville. Tel: 35 08 68 00, ext. 4631

Swimming pools:

- 1 rue du Dr Fleury, Centre Sportif des Coquets, Mont Saint Aignan. Tel: 35 74 34 37
- Piscine Duchêne, Ile Lacroix. Tel: 35 70 84 49
- Piscine Salomon, rue Frère Couperin. Tel: 35 60 10 71
- Piscine Diderot, boulevard de l'Europe. Tel: 35 63 59 14
- Piscine Boulingrin, boulevard de Verdun.Tel: 35 98 10 11

Skating: Mont Saint Aignan Roller Skating, rue Nicolas Poussin, 76000.

Useful addresses

Main post office: 45 bis rue Jeanne d'Arc. Tel: 35 08 73 73

Municipal library: 3 rue Jacques Villon (near to square Verdrel; a card costs 33F and can be used in all other local libraries)

Bookshops:

- Plein Ciel, place Colbert, Mont Saint Aignan (5% reduction for students)
- FNAC, rue Ecuyère (close to the place du Vieux Marché)

CIJ: (Haute-Normandie) 84 rue Beauvoisine. Tel: 35 98 38 75

CAF: 4 rue des Forgettes. Tel: 35 52 66 97

Centre Documentation Logement: 70 rue Jeanne d'Arc. Tel: 35 70 33 80

Direction Départementale du Travail et de l'Emploi, Cité Administrative, 2 rue Saint Sever. Tel: 35 62 81 44

Chambre de Commerce: Palais des Consuls, quai de la Bourse, BP 641, 76007. Tel: 35 14 37 37

Maison des Jeunes:

- Rive droite: 11 place du Général de Gaulle. Tel: 35 71 17 07
- Rive gauche: 1 place des Faïenciers. Tel: 35 72 26 51

Nearest British Consulate: Lloyds Register of Shipping, 7 rue Pierre Brossolette, 76600 Le Havre. Tel: 35 42 27 47

Nearest US Consulate-General (Paris): 2 avenue Gabriel, 75382

Cedex 08. Tel: (1) 42 96 12 02. Fax: (1) 42 66 97 83

Health care

SUMP, boulevard Siegfried, Mont Saint Aignan. Tel: 35 74 23 54
Centre Hospitalier Charles-Nicolle, 1 rue de Germont. Tel: 35 08 81
  81
Centre Anti-Poisons. Tel: 35 88 44 00
Chemist: place Colbert, Mont Saint Aignan.
CPAM: 50 avenue de Bretagne, 76039. Tel: 35 03 63 63
Local student insurance offices:
- MNEF, 5 rue Alain Blanchard. Tel: 35 70 20 34
- SMENO, 47 bis rue Bouvreuil. Tel: 35 98 29 06

Travel

Railway station
Rive Droite, place de la Gare (at the top end of rue Jeanne d'Arc). Tel: 35 98 50 50. London-Rouen (via Newhaven-Dieppe) £70 return (Eurotrain)

Coach station
Quai de la Bourse. London-Rouen (via Portsmouth) £63 return; £41.50 single (Eurolines). Peak fares apply during summer months.

Local buses
TCAR (Transports en Commun de l'Agglomération Rouennaise, rue de la Petite Chartreuse. Tel: 35 52 52 52. Student bus pass: an annual card is used in conjunction with individual tickets (available in a *carnet* of ten); the journey from the campus at Mont Saint Aignan to the centre of Rouen requires two tickets. Buses from town to Mont Saint Aignan: nos 10 and 4. (The latter, which stops at Panorama, does not run at weekends.) Buses stop at 21.45.
CNA (Compagnie Normande des Autocars): 25 rue des Charettes. Tel: 35 71 81 71

Taxis
- Radio Taxis Rouen. Tel: 35 88 50 50

• Groupement Taxis Téléphone Rouennais. Tel: 35 61 20 50

Emergencies

Duty Doctor. Tel: 35 88 44 22
Police: 5–6 rue Brisout de Barneville. Tel: 35 63 81 17
Gendarmerie: 39 rue Louis Ricard. Tel: 35 71 80 66
SOS Amitié. Tel: 35 60 52 52

21 Strasbourg

The universities and their disciplines

Université Louis Pasteur (**Strasbourg I**): formations de santé, sciences
exactes et naturelles, sciences humaines, sciences économiques,
technologie.
  4 rue Blaise Pascal, 67070 Strasbourg Cedex. Tel: 88 41 60 00. Fax:
88 60 75 50
SUIO: same address, Institut Le Bel. Tel: 88 41 61 32
IUT: 3 rue St-Paul, 67300 Schiltigheim. Tel: 88 81 24 12
Université des Sciences Humaines (**Strasbourg II**): lettres et sciences
humaines, arts, langues, sport.
  22 rue René Descartes, 67084 Strasbourg Cedex. Tel: 88 41 73 54.
Fax: 88 41 73 54
SUIO: same address. Tel: 88 41 73 52 *or* 88 41 42 40
Université Robert Schuman (**Strasbourg III**): droit et sciences
politiques, sciences économiques, journalisme et techniques de l'in-
formation, technologie.
  1 place d'Athènes, 67084 Strasbourg Cedex. Tel: 88 41 42 00. Fax:
88 61 30 37
SUIO: same address. Tel: 88 61 09 50 *or* 88 41 42 40
IUT: 72 route du Rhin, 67400 Illkirch-Grafenstaden. Tel: 88 67 63 00

University libraries (Bibliothèque Nationale et Universitaire de Strasbourg)
• Section Sciences Humaines, 6 place de la République
• Section Langues Vivantes, Campus de l'Esplanade, Bâtiment IV

Courses for languages undergraduates

LEA offers the following modern foreign languages: German, English,

Arabic, Spanish, Hebrew, Italian and Russian. Greek, Turkish, Hungarian (and some Danish) are also taught.

Lettres Modernes offers a wide range of optional subjects, and French prose fiction (in particular that of the nineteenth century) is taught in a range of interesting courses. Some British undergraduates find Linguistics and Old French difficult (as they do elsewhere) but the staff are sympathetic to the needs and difficulties of the foreign language learner. *Alsacien* can be an interesting option for students of German.

Courses for foreign students

Term-time courses

Institut International d'Etudes Françaises, Palais Universitaire, 9 place de l'Université, 67084 Strasbourg Cedex. Tel: 88 25 97 57. Fax: 88 25 08 63

Candidates must be 18 years of age and courses run from mid-October to mid-June. There are courses at beginners', intermediate and advanced levels. Groups vary between 15 and 25 students; courses entail between 15 and 25 hours per week, depending on the level and range of options chosen. The following qualifications may be obtained: *Certificat Pratique de Langue Française, Diplôme d'Etudes Françaises (2e degré), Diplôme Supérieur d'Etudes Françaises (3e degré)*. A small number of students are housed in halls of residence; others in town. Leisure activities include poetry readings and play productions.

Vacation courses

Institut International d'Etudes Françaises: address, telephone and fax numbers as above

Summer courses (beginners' to advanced) are run in July only and students are given rooms in the Cité Universitaire. Beginners' courses: 15 hours per week in groups of 18 students. Intermediate and advanced levels: 15 hours per week in groups of 20 to 25 students. The Institut issues a *Certificant d'assiduité* to successful candidates. There are also *Séminaires de perfectionnement à l'intention des professeurs de français à l'étranger*. Courses, which take place in July, last for four weeks and include Phonetics, French Literature and Civilisation and European political institutions. Group sizes vary from 30 to 35 and the course is based on 20 to 25 hours per week.

CROUS

1 quai du Maire Dietrich, 67084 Strasbourg Cedex. Tel: 88 36 16 91.
  Fax: 88 36 77 79
OTU: as above (Porte A; opening hours: 9.00–12.00, 13.30–16.00).
  Tel: 88 25 53 99

CROUS-controlled accommodation
Strasbourg has 3,458 beds in the various *cités universitaires* and is also
able to offer 1,251 (more expensive) *studios* which are rented on a
twelve-monthly basis only. They are available to single students over 20
years of age registered for courses in the second and third *cycles* only.
The Alfred Weiss complex is situated closer to the main campus
(l'Esplanade) than the Robertsau complex, but both *cités* offer modern
and well-heated accommodation. Some students find the tower-block
at Weiss rather impersonal but facilities are very much the same as
elsewhere. Rooms are difficult to come by unless your institution has an
ongoing arrangement with the local CROUS. We list below the various
cités universitaires:
● Cité Universitaire Paul Appell, 8 rue de Palerme. Tel: 88 35 66 00
  (mixed)
● Cité Universitaire Alfred Weiss (Neudorf), 7 quai de Bruckhof. Tel:
  88 44 90 22 (mixed; lunch and evening meal available in the cafeteria)
● Cité Universitaire de la Robertsau, 14 route de la Wantzenau. Tel: 88
  31 17 52 (mixed; breakfast and evening meal available in the cafeteria)
● Cité Universitaire Somme, 13 rue de la Somme. Tel: 88 61 12 45
  (mixed)
● Cité Universitaire Gallia, 1 boulevard de la Victoire. Tel: 88 36 16 91
  (female students only)
CROUS studios:
● Studios les Flamboyants, 8 rue Schnitzler (Esplanade)
● Studios les Cattleyas, 2 rue du Vieil Armand (Neudorf)
● Studios les Agapanthes, rue Schott (Robertsau)
● Studios les Héliotropes, route du Rhin (Illkirch)

CROUS restaurants
● RU Esplanade, 32 boulevard de la Victoire (open 11.15–13.15 and
  18.30 to 20.00 Mondays to Fridays; *menu traditionnel* plus 2
  cafeterias)
● RU Paul Appell, 10 rue de Palerme (open 11.30–13.15 and 18.30 to
  19.45 Mondays to Fridays; *menu traditionnel* plus 2 cafeterias)

- RU Pasteur, 5 rue du Faubourg National (open 11.30–13.15 and 18.30 to 19.45 Mondays to Fridays; near to the Faculté de Médecine and to the town centre; *menu traditionnel* plus cafeteria)
- RU Illkirch, 76 route du Rhin-Illkirch (open 11.30–13.15; *menu traditionnel* and cafeteria)

Other, non-CROUS restaurants popular with students are:

- Foyer de l'Etudiant Catholique (FEC), close to the cathedral (17 place Saint Etienne); it offers a variety of formulae including vegetarian dishes and pizzas
- Restaurant Gallia, 1 place de l'Université

Privately-run hostels

- Foyer de l'Etudiant Catholique, 17 place Saint Etienne
- Foyer du Jeune Ouvrier Chrétien, 6 rue de Bitche
- Foyer Jean Sturm, 2A rue Salzmann. Tel: 88 32 45 22
- Foyer Notre Dame, 3 rue des Echasses. Tel: 88 32 47 36
- Foyer Sainte Odile, 8 rue de l'Arc-en-ciel. Tel: 88 35 45 24
- Maison de l'Etudiante, 7 boulevard de la Victoire. Tel: 88 35 32 67

The town and its surrounding area

Strasbourg is the capital of Alsace and the *chef-lieu* of the *département* of the Bas-Rhin, and has a population of around 400,000. Situated on the Rhine some 450 kilometres to the east of Paris and adjacent to the German border, the city is rich in history and has many architectual reminders of its German heritage, particularly those which came in the wake of the Franco-Prussian War (the city was in German hands between 1870 and 1918). Goethe, Metternick and Napoleon are among the more famous graduates of the university. In more recent years Strasbourg has assumed increasing importance at European level (the Council of Europe and the European Parliament) and is now a thriving, cosmopolitan city with easy access to Germany (students often shop in an inexpensive supermarket in Kehl). The town has a busy local airport and good rail connections, including the one to Paris (the journey time is just over four hours (*Train Corail*)). A major pedestrianisation scheme is under way in the city centre and a rapid transit network is being constructed. Cinemas, theatres and music thrive in the city, and there are various festivals: film (March), theatre (May), music (June-July). The city boasts a most unusual cathedral (dating from the eleventh to the fifteenth century) and a whole range of museums and art galleries.

The picturesque suburb known as la Petite France contains some of the most attractive buildings in the local architectural style (*maisons à colombage*) and also a number of the more expensive restaurants. The *Strasbourgeois* are renowned for their ability to consume huge amounts of food and drink. The region has many attractions, from vineyards in the summer to skiing in the winter.

Tourist information

Tourist office: avenue Schutzen-Bayer, 67000 Strasbourg. Tel: 88 35 03 00. There is an additional office in the place de la Gare (Tel: 88 32 51 49)

Hotels
There are a number of hotels in the large semi-circle in front of the railway station; booking is advisable in the tourist season and also when the European Parliament is in session.
- Hôtel Vendôme, 19 rue du Maire Kuss/9 place de la Gare, 67000 Strasbourg. Tel: 88 32 45 23 (this is a small, well-appointed hotel with shower/bath and television in all rooms)
- Hôtel National, 13 place de la Gare, 67000 Strasbourg. Tel: 88 32 35 09 (this is a very large hotel which offers a wide range of prices and facilities)
- Hôtel Arcade, 7 rue de Molsheim
- Hôtel Ibis, 1 rue de Sébastopol

Youth hostel
Auberge de Jeunesse René Cassin, 9 rue de l'Auberge de Jeunesse. Tel: 88 30 26 46 (bed and breakfast 136F; lunch or dinner 43F)

Restaurants
- Au Pont St Martin, 13–15 rue des Moulins. Tel: 88 32 45 13 (lunch menu 52F; *à la carte* 46F-90F)
- Pizzéria: Chez Tony, 9 rue Frères. Tel: 88 35 44 95 (behind the cathedral)

Leisure facilities

Museums/art galleries/buildings of interest
- Le Château des Rohan, completed in 1742 by Robert de Cotte for the

Cardinal-prince-évêque Armand Gaston de Rohan-Soubise, houses the Musée des Beaux-Arts (student tickets cost only 8F), the Musée des Arts Décoratifs and the Musée Archéologique; the entrance is in the place du Château.

- Le Musée Alsacien, 23 quai St-Nicolas (students 5F; open October-March, Mondays and Wednesdays; Saturdays 14.00-18.00; Sundays 10.00-12.00 and 14.00-18.00)
- L'Ancienne Douane (1358), rue de la Douane, has been rebuilt and houses the Maison d'Art Alsacien and the Musée d'Art Moderne (students 15F)
- Palais de l'Europe, inaugurated in 1977, boulevard de la Dordogne, is well worth a visit: meetings with your local MEP can lead to part-time work at the Palais.
- Cathedral: the imposing cathedral houses an *horloge astronomique*. Guided tours start at 12.30. In summer, there is a *son et lumière* performance inside the cathedral, in French, at 21.00.

Theatre/opera houses/concert halls
- Théâtre Municipal-Opéra, place Broglie
- Théâtre National, Conservatoire de Musique, place de la République
- Palais de la Musique et des Congrès, avenue de la Paix

Sport
Centre Sportif Universitaire, rue Gaspard Monge. Tel: 88 61 87 90
Swimming pools:
- Aquadrome, parc du Rhin (has a leisure pool with slides, etc.)
- Piscine de la Kibitzenau, Neudorf (an Olympic-sized pool)
- boulevard de la Victoire (close to the campus)
- Piscine de Wacken, rue Pierre de Coubertin. Tel: 88 31 49 10 (open June to August; 12F)

Useful addresses

Main post office: 5 avenue de la Marseillaise. Tel: 88 23 44 00
Branches:
- place de la Cathédrale
- junction of avenue Jean Jaurès and avenue Aristide Briand (adjacent to the halls of residence at Weiss)
Bookshops:
- FNAC, place Kléber, Maison Rouge

- Librairie Internationale Kléber, 1 rue des Francs-Bourgeois
There is also a (more expensive) bookshop (Librairie des Facultés) close to the main campus.
Municipal library: rue Khun (near to the railway station)
ANPE: 4 rue Sarrelouis. Tel: 88 75 04 50
CAF: 10 rue Soleure. Tel: 88 37 68 00
Chambre de Commerce: 10 place Gutenberg. Tel: 88 32 12 55
CIJ: 7 rue des Ecrivains. Tel: 88 37 33 33
US Consulate-General: 15 avenue d'Alsace. Tel: 88 35 31 04. Fax: 88 24 06 95
Nearest British Consulate-General (Paris): 9 avenue Hoche, 75008 Paris. Tel: (1) 42 66 38 10. Fax: (1) 40 76 02 87
Canadian Consulate: rue du Ried. Tel: 88 96 25 00

Health care

Hospitals:
- Hospices Civils de Strasbourg, 1 place de l'Hôpital. Tel: 88 16 17 18
- Hôpital Hautepierre. Tel: 88 28 90 00
SUMP: 6 rue de Palerme. Tel: 88 36 02 34
Chemist: adjacent to the halls of residence at Weiss, Pharmacie des Tuileries (close to the post office, at the junction of avenue Jean Jaurès and avenue Aristide Briand)
Local student insurance offices:
- MNEF, 24 avenue de la Paix. Tel: 88 35 29 48 (sub-office: 10 rue de l'Abreuvoir, Krutenau 67000 Strasbourg. Tel: 88 25 01 05)
- MGEL: 2 boulevard de la Victoire. Tel: 88 36 61 34

Travel

Railway station
Place de la Gare. Tel: 88 22 50 50. London-Strasbourg (via Newhaven-Dieppe) £117 return; (via Dover-Calais) £121 return; (via Ostend) £111 return (Eurotrain)

Bus/Coach station
Rue du Marché-Gare. London-Strasbourg, £83 return, £44 single (Eurolines)

Air travel
There are direct Air France flights to London; coaches for the airport run from place de la Gare and place Kléber (35F).

Local transport
Compagnie des Transports Strasbourgeois (CTS), place des Halles.
Tel: 88 32 36 97. Single tickets for the buses cost 7F; *carnet* of five
tickets 23F50; there is also a concessionary monthly pass. Buses run into
town from Weiss until 22.45 (weekdays); buses from town to Weiss run
until 23.30.

Taxis
Place de la République. Tel: 88 36 13 13

Emergencies

SAMU: Tel: 88 33 33 33
Police: 11 rue de la Nuée-Bleue. Tel: 88 32 99 08
Late-night chemist: telephone police for details of rota

22 Toulouse

The universities and their disciplines

Université des Sciences Sociales (**Toulouse I**): sciences juridiques et
économiques.
Place Anatole France, 31042 Toulouse Cedex. Tel: 61 63 35 00. Fax:
61 63 37 98
SUIO: 2 rue Albert Lautman, 31042 Cedex. Tel: 61 63 37 30
Université de Toulouse-le-Mirail (**Toulouse II**): lettres et sciences
humaines, langues, technologie.
5 allées Antonio Machado, 31058 Cedex. Tel: 61 50 41 50. Fax: 61
41 56 49
SUEE: Bureau 322, same address and telephone number, ext. 590
SUIO: same address, rue A. Tel: 61 50 45 15/16
IUT: 5 allées Antonio Machado, 31058 Toulouse Cedex. Tel: 61 50 45
03
Université Paul Sabatier (**Toulouse III**): sciences exactes et naturelles,
formations de santé, technologie, sport.
118 route de Narbonne, 31062 Toulouse Cedex. Tel: 61 55 66 11.
Fax: 61 55 64 70

SUIO: same address and telephone number, exts. 7031 and 7032
IUT: 115 route de Narbonne, 31077 Toulouse Cedex. Tel: 61 25 21 17
Institut National Polytechnique (INP) **(Toulouse IV)**: formation
  d'ingénieurs en agronomie, chimie, génie chimique, élec-
  trotechnique, électronique, informatique et hydraulique.
  Place des Hauts Murats, BP 354, 31006 Toulouse Cedex. Tel: 61 25
  54 00. Fax: 61 53 67 21
SUIO: same address. Tel: 62 25 54 32

University libraries
● Section Santé, Bibliothèque de Rangueil Santé, 2 chemin du Vallon,
  31400. Tel: 62 25 59 25; Bibliothèque des allées Jules Guesde, 37
  allées Jules Guesde, 31073 Cedex. Tel: 61 52 63 92
● Section Sciences Sociales, 11 rue des Puits Creusés, 31070 Cedex.
  Tel: 61 15 01 00
● Section Sciences, 118 route de Narbonne, 31077. Tel: 61 52 12 60
● Section Lettres, 12 rue de l'Université du Mirail, 31300. Tel: 61 40
  35 64

Courses for languages undergraduates

DEUG/*Licence/Maîtrise* in LCE/LVE or LEA is available in German,
English, Spanish, Italian, Portuguese and Russian. A much wider range
of languages has, however, traditionally been taught in the university (all
from beginners' level): Arabic, Basque, Catalan, Chinese, Modern
Greek, Guarani, Hebrew, Japanese, Nahuatl, Occitan, Polish,
Romanian, Serbo-Croat and Sanskrit.

For the DEUG in *Lettres Modernes*, courses are divided into three
blocks. In Year Two, this means: I, a unit of Medieval French Language, one of Medieval Literature, and two of Modern Literature; II, a
unit of Comparative Literature, or History, or History of Art, and a
modern language; III, *options libres*. For the options, it is possible to take
interesting courses in Sport, Cinema and Television, Theatre Studies
and Music and Literature. However, the Sports options, in particular,
fill up very quickly.

The Université de Toulouse-le-Mirail is situated on the outskirts of
the town. The low campus buildings, which were thrown together at
considerable speed in the late 1960s/early 1970s, are not an impressive
sight and are joined by draughty walkways. However, the site also
houses the university library, a CROUS restaurant and the Centre de
Promotion Culturel.

Courses for foreign students

Université de Toulouse-le-Mirail, Service Formation Continue, Centre d'Enseignement du Français Langue Etrangère (CEFLE) 5 allées Antonio Machado, 31058 Toulouse Cedex. Tel: 61 50 47 18 *or* 61 50 42 32. Fax: 61 50 42 09

Term-time courses
Semester-based language courses of 12 hours per week in groups of 15 to 18 students at beginners', elementary, intermediate and advanced levels, which focus on communicative skills via an interactive approach. A wide range of materials is used and the courses can be tailored to suit different aims and objectives (October-February, March-June); all candidates must be over 17 and take a language test on entry; there are, however, no formal prerequisites. Certificates specifying the work covered and the level achieved are awarded. Activities exploring the rich cultural and social life of Toulouse and its region may be organised around the courses on request.

Summer courses
The CEFLE (same address and telephone; fax: 61 50 49 62) mounts four-week sessions in July, August and September. Instruction is provided to the tune of 19–25 hours per week at all levels to anyone over 17. Oral and written expression and comprehension are taught using various methods, including audio-visual techniques, language laboratories, films, original texts, etc. At the same time, there are workshops in literature, theatre, civilisation, etc., and options at the more advanced levels in French for Business or the Tourist Industry. Visits and excursions are organised around the course.

CROUS

7 rue des Salenques, 31070 Toulouse Cedex. Tel: 61 21 13 61 Fax: 62 27 24 76
SAEE: same address and telephone
OTU: same address and telephone, exts. 217 and 218

CROUS-controlled accommodation
A total of 6,238 places are available in halls scattered throughout the town.
● Cité de l'Arsenal, 2 boulevard Armand Duportal, 30170 Cedex. Tel: 61 23 00 78 (681 rooms, mixed)

- Chapou, 1 rue Saunière, 31069 Cedex. Tel: 61 23 06 12 (1,182 rooms, mixed)
- Daniel Faucher, allées Camille Saula, 31078 Cedex. Tel: 61 52 84 04 (957 rooms, mixed)
- Ponsan Bellevue, rue Maurice Bécanne, 31078 Cedex. Tel: 61 52 36 89 (606 rooms, mixed)
- Rangueil, 118 route de Narbonne, 31077 Cedex. Tel: 61 52 12 19 (1,931 rooms, mixed)
- Taur, 60 rue du Taur, 31070 Cedex. Tel: 61 21 50 14 (164 rooms, women only)

Of these, Arsenal, by virtue of its central location, and Chapou would seem to be the most popular with foreign students. However, pressure on rooms has led the CROUS to restrict applications from the latter: during the academic year, only *boursiers du gouvernement français, boursiers des états étrangers gérés par le CROUS*, and students covered by an inter-university agreement are entitled to apply. British students in particular have had a hard time finding places in recent years. Because of the large numbers of students in Toulouse, it can be difficult to find suitable accommodation. A number of flats (some qualifying for APL) are reserved for *jeunes ménages d'étudiants*.

There are also *studios* and flatlets (with the possibility of APL) available for allocation to individual students at the following locations:

- Daniel Faucher, allée Camille Soula, 31078 Cedex. Tel: 61 52 84 04 (288 study-bedrooms and 8 flatlets)
- Les Jardins de l'Université, 29 rue Valade, 31000. Tel: 61 23 83 62 (42 flats for 2 people sharing and 15 for 3 people sharing)
- Parc-Bellevue, avenue du Professeur Ducuing, 31400. Tel: 61 25 46 58 (reserved, in theory, for students in the *classes préparatoires aux grandes écoles*)

CROUS restaurants

Some 4 million meals are served each year. All restaurants serve the *menu traditionnel* in addition to the other possibilities indicated below:

- Restaurant de l'Arsenal, 2 boulevard Armand Duportal. Tel: 61 23 98 48 (*section diététique; plat du jour avec possibilité de suppléments payants; brasserie (de 7.00-20h15): pâtes fraîches, salades composées, pâtisseries variées, quiches, pizzas, menu rapide, etc.*, cash payments only)
- Chapou, 1 rue Saunière. Tel: 61 23 06 12 (*formule 'autour d'un plat'; brasserie*)
- Danier Faucher, allée Camille Saula. Tel: 61 25 55 99 (*brasserie*)
- Mirail, Campus de l'Université Toulouse-le-Mirail. Tel: 61 40 36 51

(*restauration rapide*)
- Notre-Dame, 12 rue Notre-Dame. Tel: 61 52 78 82 (*restauration rapide, steak-frites*)
- Rangueil I, 118 route de Narbonne. Tel: 61 52 12 19 (*section diététique*)
- Rangueil II, same address. Tel: 61 52 14 38 (*salle avec suppléments; restauration rapide*)

There are also four *restaurants agréés*:
- Ecole Vétérinaire, chemin des Cappelles. Tel: 61 49 11 40
- Institut du Génie Chimique, chemin de la Loge. Tel: 61 52 92 41
- Lycée Joliment, 44 chemin Cassaing. Tel: 61 10 37 00
- Lycée des Arènes, 4 place Emile Mâle. Tel: 62 13 10 00

Privately-run hostels

For details, write to the *Directeur/Directrice*:
Foyers UNESCO:
- 38 rue Valade. Tel: 61 21 12 83
- 79, allées Charles de Fitte. Tel: 61 42 90 09 (the general secretariat)
- 5 rue Héliot. Tel: 61 62 40 10
- 29 rue de Stalingrad. Tel: 61 63 70 47
- 66 rue Bayard

Others:
- Foyer d'étudiantes-La Présentation, 47 rue des Trente-six Ponts, 31400. Tel: 61 52 91 90 (women only)
- Foyer familial, 23 rue Joly, 31400. Tel: 61 52 93 63 (women only)
- Foyer Garrigou-Desclaux, 13 rue Romiguières. Tel: 61 21 53 44 (women only)
- Foyer de la Gravette, 42 rue de la Gravette. Tel: 61 42 91 90 (women only)
- Foyer de Jeunes Filles Sahuc-Mazas, 11 rue de la Delbade. Tel: 61 52 67 63 (women only)

The town and its surrounding area

Préfecture of the Haute-Garonne, Toulouse is the fourth largest city in France, and is second only to Paris in the number of students it hosts (more than 90,000). It stands on the Garonne some 680 kilometres south of the capital, to which it is connected by fast rail links and motorways.

Known as *la ville rose*, because of the brick of which the old nucleus of the town is built, it has long been a place of great importance. It was successively the Visigothic capital, capital of the Kingdom of South Aquitaine, capital of the independent *comté* of Toulouse and capital of the royal province of Languedoc. Today, it is still proud of its Occitan heritage and its important Spanish connections.

Many relics of its glorious past, both secular and religious, are still to be seen. The Basilique St-Sernin is the largest Romanesque cathedral in France, while Les Jacobins is a magnificent example of *gothique du Midi*. To these should be added the Cathédrale St-Etienne, which was deemed to be following more northern models. The Hôtel de Ville or Capitole, which dominates the square of the same name, dates from the early seventeenth century, though the west front was added in the mid-eighteenth century. *Hôtels* commemorating the prosperous commercial history of the town are dotted throughout Vieux Toulouse. Particular mention should be made of the Hôtel d'Assezat (1558), which today still houses the Académie des Jeux Floraux.

Those of the town who have risen to distinction include: Nicolas Bachelier (*c.* 1485–1557), the sculptor and architect responsible for the design of several surviving buildings in Toulouse; Jacques Cujas (1522–90), the jurist and consul; Guy du Faur de Pibrac (1529–84), the moralist; and the mathematician, Pierre de Fermat (*c.* 1595–1665).

In more recent times, the town has seen a series of massive influxes of immigrants: Spaniards after the Civil War, Jews from Central Europe, North Africans and Portuguese. It has an engaging atmosphere all of its own, with its picturesque squares, bustling cafés, lively markets and inviting parks (Jardin des Plantes, Jardin Royal, etc.). Education has ever played a large part in the town since the university was founded in 1299, as part of a campaign to suppress heresy in the area. The presence of so many students, while it might create accommodation problems on occasion, helps to promote a lively social and cultural environment. The town was recently granted the status of *pôle européen*. Gastronomically, too, there is much on offer: *cassoulet*, cheeses like Roquefort and St-Nectaire, full-bodied regional red wines and sweet white dessert wines.

In recent decades, the town has developed significantly as a centre for research and industry. Electronics and aircraft research and construction lead the way: ARIANE, Concorde and Airbus are names that readily spring to mind in this respect. It is this exciting and successful mixture of the old and the new which gives Toulouse its distinctive stamp.

From Toulouse, there is easy access to the Mediterranean coast, or to the Pyrenees for walking, climbing, skiing or even shopping in the duty-free haven of Andorra! Nearby, too, is Albi and Cathar country, with fascinating churches and fortified towns. The Canal du Midi, which links the principal towns of the region, also makes for interesting exploration.

Tourist information

Tourist office: Donjon du Capitole, square Charles de Gaulle, 31000 Toulouse. Tel: 61 11 02 22

Hotels
There are a number of very cheap hotels near the station.
- Unic Hôtel, 26 allées Jean Jaurès. Tel: 61 62 38 19 (prices in the 65F/165F range)
- Hôtel Pays d'Oc, 53 rue Riquet. Tel: 61 62 33 76 (prices 50F to 90F!)

Rather more expensive but well placed for the town centre:
- Hôtel Saint Sernin, 2 rue St Bernard. Tel: 61 21 73 08 (195F/240F)
- Hôtel de Brienne, 20 boulevard Maréchal Leclerc. Tel: 61 23 60 60 (415F to 750F)

Youth hostel
125 avenue Jean Rieux, 31500. Tel: 61 80 49 93

Restaurants
A cafeteria-style restaurant, popular with students, is Flunch, 28 allée Jean Jaurès. A reasonable meal can be had for 30F-60F. Other possibilities include:
- Le Bengale, 33 rue d'Embarthe (for curry addicts; vegetarian menu available too; 50F-90F)
- Pizzéria Vecchio, allées Jean Jaurès (simple but pleasant; 40F-100F)

Leisure facilities

Museums and art galleries
- Musée des Augustins, 21 rue de Metz. Tel: 61 23 55 07
- Musée Saint Raymond, place St-Sernin. Tel: 61 22 21 85
- Musée Paul Dupuy, 13 rue de la Pléau. Tel: 61 22 21 83
- Musée Georges Labit, 43 rue des Martyrs de la Libération. Tel: 61 22 21 84
- Museum d'Histoire Naturelle, 35 allées Jules Guesde. Tel: 61 52 00 14

- Musée du Vieux Toulouse, 7 rue du May
- Préfiguration du Musée d'Art Moderne et de la Création Contemporaine, 24 rue Croix Baragnon. Tel: 61 55 26 24
- Centre Régional d'Art Contemporain, Labège Innopole, BP126, 31328 Labège Cedex. Tel: 61 39 29 29
- Centre Municipal de l'Affiche, de la Carte Postale et de l'Art Graphique, 58 allées Charles de Fitte. Tel: 61 59 24 64 *or* 61 22 24 64
- Musée de la Résistance et de la Déportation Jean Philippe, 43 bis rue Achille Viadieu. Tel: 61 25 84 81
- Musée de l'Abeille, chemin de Pechebusque, Pouvourville. Tel: 61 27 73 53
- Musée des Transports, 93 avenue Jules Julien. Tel: 61 52 62 06
- Musée des Télécommunications, 45 rue Soupetard. Tel: 61 57 62 26
- Musée des Chefs-d'Oeuvre des Compagnons du Devoir, 28 rue des Pyrénées. Tel: 61 52 84 12
- Galerie Municipale du Château d'Eau, place Laganne. Tel: 61 42 61 72
- Forum des Cordeliers, (Annexe de l'Université Toulouse-le-Mirail), 15 rue des Lois. Tel: 61 22 65 55
- Palais des Arts, 5 quai de la Daurade. Tel: 61 23 25 45

For information on museums, etc., ring 61 22 29 22 (*téléphone général des musées municipaux*). Many of the libraries, *centres culturels* and *centres d'animation* around the town house occasional exhibitions.

Theatre

- Théâtre du Capitole, place du Capitole. Tel: 61 23 21 35
- Le Sorano-Théâtre National de Midi-Pyrénées, 35 allées Jules Guesde. Tel: 61 25 66 87
- Théâtre du Taur, 69 rue du Taur. Tel: 61 21 77 13
- Nouveau Théâtre Jules Julien, 6 avenue des Ecoles Jules Julien. Tel: 61 25 79 92
- Théâtre Garonne, 1 avenue du Château d'Eau. Tel: 61 42 33 99
- Théâtre de la Digue (Association Théâtre Midi-Pyrénées), 3 rue de la Digue. Tel: 61 42 97 79
- Théâtre de Marionnettes-Théâtre de Verdure, Jardin des Plantes, allées Frédéric Mistral.
- Théâtre de la Source, 23 bis rue des Potiers. Tel: 61 63 44 95
- Théâtre du Pavé, 34 rue Maran, 31400. Tel: 62 26 43 66

To the above should be added the many performances that take place in *centres culturels*, *ateliers*, etc. and the *café-théâtre* tradition. As far as music is concerned, there is an orchestra and more than one choir based in the

universities, plus a lot of activity in town:
● Association Départementale pour le Développement des Arts, Musique et Danse, 5 rue Jules Chalande. Tel: 61 21 15 61
● Conservatoire National de Région, 3 rue Labéda. Tel: 61 22 28 62
● Conservatoire Occitan des Arts et Traditions Populaires, 1 rue Jacques Darré. Tel: 61 42 75 79
● Institut de Musique Sacrée, 31 rue de la Fonderie. Tel: 61 36 81 00
● Music-Halle, Ecole des Musiques Vivantes, 23 rue D Casanova. Tel: 61 21 12 25
● Chorale des Compagnons 'A Coeur Joie', 20 rue Demouilles. Tel: 61 52 63 59
● Direction Musicale Régionale, 56 rue du Taur. Tel: 61 29 21 17

Cinema
Archives du Cinéma: Cinémathèque de Toulouse, 12 rue du Faubourg Bonnefoy. Tel: 61 48 90 75 (specialist library). Films are shown at the CRDP, Salle Montaigne, 3 rue Roquelaine.
Commercial cinemas in the town centre include:
● Le Gaumont, 3 place Wilson. Tel: 61 21 49 58
● Les Nouveautés, 56 boulevard Carnot. Tel: 61 62 22 14
● Les Rio, 24 rue Montardy. Tel: 61 23 66 30
● UGC Variétés, 9 allées du Président Roosevelt. Tel: 61 23 36 61
● Alban-Minvelle, allée de Bellefontaine. Tel: 61 40 18 08
This list takes no account of the more adventurous *salles d'art et d'essai*, of suburban cinemas, of the film activities of local MJC and *centres culturels*, or of the numerous ciné-clubs (there are nine or ten listed student clubs, not to mention the clubs run in halls of residence). There are also film festivals in the area.

Sport
FNSU: Université Paul Sabatier, 118 route de Narbonne 31077 Cedex. Tel: 61 25 80 30
Palais des Sports, boulevard Lascrosses. Tel: 61 22 11 00
Direction Municipale des Sports, Parc Municipal des Sports, allées Gabriel Biénès. Tel: 61 52 57 27
Rugby: Stade Toulousain, Sept Deniers (the famous French club)
Skating: Patinoire de Bellevue, 86 chemin de la Salade Ponsan. Tel: 61 52 93 53
Swimming: Piscine Léo-Lagrange, place Riquet. Tel: 61 62 39 01 (student concessions)
A guide to sporting activities – *Toulouse-Sports* – is available from the

Service d'Accueil-Relations Publiques de la Mairie de Toulouse, place du Capitole. Tel: 61 22 29 22. The town has four large sports and leisure complexes: Les Argoulets, La Ramée, Pech-David and Sesquières. For further information, contact the Parc Municipal des Sports. Tel: 61 52 57 27

Toulouse III has a teaching department: Unité de Formation et de Recherche Sciences et Techniques des Activités Physiques et Sportives (STAPS), Université Paul Sabatier, 118 route de Narbonne, 31062. Tel: 61 55 66 34. There are Stades Universitaires at Daniel Faucher (allée Camille Soula, 31400. Tel: 61 52 23 14) and Rangueil (118 route de Narbonne, 31400. Tel: 61 52 11 32). There is a swimming pool at Chapou.

Useful addresses

Main post office: 9 rue Lafayette. Tel: 62 15 30 00 *or* 62 15 33 78
Municipal library: 1 rue du Périgord. Tel: 61 22 21 78
Bookshop: FNAC, Centre Commercial St Georges, place St Georges
Préfecture: place St Etienne. Tel: 61 33 40 00 (four black and white
    photographs required for the *carte de séjour)*
ANPE: 47 rue de la Balance. Tel: 61 62 42 38
CAF: 24 rue Riquet. Tel: 61 29 36 99
Chambre de Commerce: 2 rue d'Alsace Lorraine. Tel: 88 32 12 55
CPAM: 3 boulevard Escande. Tel: 61 58 95 95
CRIJ: 17 rue de Metz. Tel: 61 21 20 20
British Consulate-General: Lucas Aerospace, Victoria Centre, Bât
    Didier Daurat, 20 chemin de Laporte, 31300 Toulouse. Tel: 61 15
    02 02. Fax: 61 15 08 92
Nearest US Consulate-General (Bordeaux): 22 cours du Maréchal
    Foch, 33080 Bordeaux Cedex. Tel: 56 52 65 95. Fax: 56 51 60 42

Health care

The main hospitals are:
● CHU Rangueil, chemin du Vallon. Tel: 61 32 25 33
● CHU Purpan, place du Docteur Baylac. Tel: 61 77 22 33
● Hôpital de la Grave, place Lange. Tel: 61 77 78 33
● Hôtel-Dieu Saint-Jacques, rue Viguerie. Tel: 61 77 82 33
There are dispensaries (*infirmeries*) in the main halls.
The SIMPPS offers various forms of treatment, by appointment, at its three centres:

- Centre de l'Arsenal (Université des Sciences Sociales), 2 rue Albert Lautman. Tel: 61 63 37 26
- Centre du Mirail (Université Toulouse-le-Mirail), 5 allées Antonio Machado. Tel: 61 40 14 11
- Centre de Rangueil (Université Paul Sabatier, INP), Campus Universitaire, avenue de Rangueil. Tel: 61 53 43 57

Local student insurance offices:

- MNEF, 54 rue Bayard. Tel: 61 62 37 05
- SMESO, 16 rue Riquet. Tel: 61 63 17 17

Travel

Railway station
Gare Matabiau, boulevard Pierre Semard. Information, tel: 61 62 50 50; reservations, tel: 61 62 85 44. London-Toulouse (via Newhaven-Dieppe) £137 return; (via Dover-Calais) £141 return (Eurotrain)

Coach station
68–70 boulevard Pierre Semard, 31000 (next to SNCF). Tel: 61 48 71 84. London-Toulouse, £50 single; £89 return (Eurolines)

Airport
Toulouse-Blagnac. Tel: 61 42 44 64/65

Taxis:
- Radio-Taxi-Union. Tel: 61 21 00 72
- Taxis-Radio-Toulousains. Tel: 61 42 38 38
- Taxis-Télé-Bleu. Tel: 61 80 36 36

Buses
SEMVAT operates the local bus services. Individual tickets are quite expensive but there are reductions for students, who may obtain either the *Carte Verte*, which allows unlimited travel in town for a month at a reasonable price, or the *Carte Tarif Réduit Etudiant*, which enables tickets to be bought in *carnets* of ten. The price varies according to the number of zones involved.

Emergencies

SAMU. Tel: 61 49 33 33
SOS Médecins. Tel: 61 49 66 66

All-night chemist: 17 rue de Remusat. Tel: 61 21 81 20
SOS Amitié. Tel: 61 80 80 80
La Porte Ouverte, 20 place du Capitole. Tel: 61 23 56 14

23 Tours

The university and its disciplines

(Académie Orléans-Tours) Université François-Rabelais: droit et
  sciences économiques, lettres et sciences humaines, sciences exactes
  et naturelles, médecine et pharmacie, technologie.
  3 rue des Tanneurs, 37041 Tours Cedex. Tel: 47 36 66 00. Fax: 47
  36 64 10
SUIO: same address. First Floor, Office 110. Tel: 47 36 64 39
SUEE: same address. Tel: 47 36 36 00
IUT: 29 rue du Pont Volant, 37023 Tours Cedex. Tel: 47 36 75 04

University libraries
● Section Lettres et Sciences Humaines, 5 rue des Tanneurs. Tel: 47
  36 64 86
● Section Droit et Sciences Economiques, same address, same
  telephone
● Section Médecine et Pharmacie, 2 bis boulevard Tonnelé. Tel: 47
  36 61 11
● Section Sciences, avenue Monge. Tel: 47 36 70 70

Courses for languages undergraduates

LEA offers the following modern foreign languages: English, German,
Spanish.
   In the *Lettres Modernes* programmes there are courses in French
language and literature from the medieval period to the twentieth
century, but there is a clear emphasis on the early periods. In addition,
there are courses in Linguistics, Latin, Greek, Comparative Literature,
French Literary History, the Cinema and Television. Among the languages on offer are: Arabic, Danish, Dutch, English, German, Hebrew,
Italian, Portuguese, Spanish.

Courses for foreign students

Institut de Touraine, 1 rue de la Grandière, BP 2047, 37020 Tours
  Cedex. Tel: 47 05 76 83. Fax: 47 20 48 98

Term-time courses

Full-year and termly courses are provided by the Institut de Touraine under the aegis of the Université François Rabelais. Students of all levels, from beginners to advanced, are catered for; between 19 and 24 hours per week. There are some courses specialising in business and secretarial French and French for tourism, with the possibility of obtaining a qualification from the Chambre de Commerce de Paris.

Vacation courses

Four-week courses, offering between 19 and 24 hours per week instruction are run in July, August and September. Sporting activities and excursions are available, including visits to the *châteaux de la Loire*. A range of accommodation is on offer in single and double rooms, some of which are at the Cité Internationale.

CROUS

17 avenue Dauphine, 45072 Orléans Cedex 2. Tel: 38 66 28 81. Fax: 38 56 42 02

Tours, however, has its own CLOUS, with its headquarters at the Cité Sanitas, boulevard de Lattre de Tassigny, 37041 Tours Cedex. Tel: 47 05 17 55. Fax: 47 20 46 33

SAEE: same address and telephone

OTU: same address and telephone

CLOUS-controlled accommodation

Tours has well-appointed *résidences universitaires* with a total of 2,343 rooms. For student couples there are 59 flats in HLM. Approved privately-rented accommodation lists are also available through the CLOUS office.

- Résidence du Sanitas, boulevard de Lattre de Tassigny. Tel: 47 20 55 83 (the most centrally-situated of the halls with 406 rooms)
- Résidence de Grandmont, rue François Bonamy, avenue Arsonval (for buildings A, B, C, D, tel: 47 25 13 43; for buildings E, F, G, H, tel: 47 25 14 50). This is the largest complex of halls with 1,152 rooms. It stands in a wooded area in the south east of the town.
- Résidence de Saint-Symphorien, 25 rue du Pont Volant. Tel: 47 54 22 49. This is a modern development with 313 rooms in the north east of the town.

CLOUS restaurants

Traditional meals are served in all restaurants, but there are also

cafeterias and *brasseries* for alternative meals.
- RU du Sanitas (seats 622), 2 rue Hallebardier. Tel: 47 66 85 25 (also Brasserie du Hallebardier with continuous service from 11.45 till 20.30)
- RU de Grandmont (seats 500), parc de Grandmont. Tel: 47 25 14 61 (also cafeteria service (8.00 till 21.30) and *brasserie* (Monday–Thursday 11.45 till 20.45 and Friday till 17.25))
- RU de Saint-Symphorien, 25 rue du Pont Volant. Tel: 47 54 30 58 (seats 530; also cafeteria for snacks)
- Cafétéria de l'Université, 3 rue des Tanneurs. Tel: 47 39 65 20 (snacks from 11.00 a.m. onwards)

Privately-run hostels

For details write to the *Directeur/Directrice*:
- Cité Municipale pour Etudiants, 9 rue Hélène Boucher. Tel: 47 37 04 27
- Cité Internationale, 40 rue des Tanneurs. Tel: 47 39 61 40
- Cité Municipale pour Etudiants, 21 rue Christophe Colomb. Tel: 47 05 23 77
- Foyer d'Etudiantes Saint Thomas d'Aquin, 8 bis place Choiseul, Tours-Saint-Symphorien. Tel: 47 54 47 41 (women)
- Foyer Clair Logis, 159 rue Victor Hugo. Tel: 47 38 19 93 (men). Tel: 47 37 71 78 (women)
- Foyer des Jeunes Travailleuses La Bergeonnerie, 35–37 rue de la Bergeonnerie. Tel: 47 28 64 24 (women)
- Foyer George Sand, 106 rue George Sand. Tel: 47 66 85 81

The town and its surrounding area

Situated between the Loire and Cher rivers, Tours, once the capital of Touraine, is now the thriving *préfecture* of the Indre-et-Loire with a population of 136,500. The town and its region are associated with many celebrated writers, poets and artists, such as the novelists Honoré de Balzac (1799–1850) and Anatole France (1844–1924), the poet Philippe Néricault-Destouches (1680–1754), the poet and historian René Rapin (1621–87), the sculptor François Sicard (1862–1934) and the artists Jean Fouquet (1415–81), Jean Bourdichon (1457–1521) and François Clouet (1510–72). Tours has many fine civic buildings: the Hôtel de Ville with its allegorical statuary; the Palais de Justice; the Musée des Beaux-Arts and the cathedral. The old part of the town is rich in fifteenth-century houses, particularly in the place Plumereau and rue Briçonnet. The university is one of the 67 new institutions created by the 12 November 1968 decree and has some 25,000 students. The region, often known as the Garden of France, has considerable natural beauty and, with its justly famous *châteaux* at Amboise, Chenonceau, Azay-le-Rideau, Chambord, Chinon or Villandry, it attracts many tourists throughout the season. Sports facilities are good and there is a strong theatrical tradition, not to mention the many cinemas which also offer student reductions. The region has many gastronomic delights. Tours is famous for *charcuterie*, especially *rillettes* and game *pâtés*, while local market-garden produce includes such delicacies as asparagus. The Touraine wines are light and fruity, and the *crêpes* and barley sugar associated with Tours are also to be enjoyed. There are good road links with Paris together with fast, regular train connections, including the TGV Atlantique service.

Tourist information

Office du Tourisme, boulevard Heurteloup. Tel: 47 05 58 08

Hotels
The following is near the station with rooms around 300F without breakfast:
● Hôtel de l'Europe, 12 place du Maréchal Leclerc. Tel: 47 05 42 07
The following are near halls of residence with rooms around 170F:
● Hôtel Rosny, 19 rue Blaise Pascal. Tel: 47 05 23 54
● Hôtel Grammont, 16 avenue de Grammont. Tel: 47 05 55 06

Youth hostel
Auberge de Jeunesse du parc de Grandmont, avenue Arsonval. Tel: 47 25 14 45

Restaurants
There are a number of reasonably-priced restaurants, for example:
● Le Petit Patrimoine, 58 rue Colbert. Tel: 47 66 05 81 (menus 75F and 95F)
● Le Tournedos, 94 rue du Commerce. Tel: 47 20 57 81 (menu 50F)
● Le Bouffon, 13 place du Châteauneuf. Tel: 47 61 80 23 (menus at 68F, 92F and 130F; closed Wednesdays)
● Les Trois Canards, 16 rue de la Rôtisserie. Tel: 47 61 58 16 (menus 46F and 68F)

Leisure facilities

Theatre
- Grand Théâtre, 34 rue de la Scellerie. Tel: 47 05 33 87
- Théâtre Louis Jouvet, 12 rue Léonard de Vinci. Tel: 47 20 73 13

Cinema
Various reductions can be obtained, either by buying season tickets, with a student card, or by going on specified days, usually Monday.
- Complexe Olympia, 7 rue de Lucé. Tel: 47 05 71 62
- Pathé-Caméo, 25 rue Michelet. Tel: 47 05 40 62 (5 screens)
- Complexe Rex, 47 rue Nationale. Tel: 47 05 69 59 (5 screens)
- Les Studios, 2 rue des Ursulines. Tel: 47 02 22 80 (6 screens; classic films and recent releases; a student card obtainable from CLOUS for 50F entitles you to a 13F reduction on normal prices for a year.)

Museums and art galleries
There is an all-inclusive ticket issued by the tourist office for 50F which allows entrance to the principal museums.
- Musée des Beaux-Arts, 18 place François Sicard. Tel: 47 05 68 73 (closed Tuesdays; students 15F)
- Musée Grévin, Historial de Touraine, Château Royal de Tours, quai d'Orléans. Tel: 47 61 02 95
- Musée du Compagnonnage, Cloître Saint-Julien, 8 rue Nationale. Tel: 47 61 07 93 (students 10F; check for variable opening times)
- Musée des Vins de Touraine, 16 rue Nationale. Tel: 47 61 07 93 (closed on Tuesdays; students 5F)

Sport and recreation
- Centre Municipal des Sports, 1 boulevard de Lattre de Tassigny (next to Sanitas; swimming, skating, judo, basket-ball; student reductions)
- La Patinoire, rue Georges Thiou. Tel: 47 66 29 94
- Bowling Petite Arche, Centre Commercial Petite Arche. Tel: 47 51 63 27

Useful addresses

Main post office: 1 boulevard Béranger (place Jean Jaurès). Tel: 47 60 34 20
Branch offices:

- Chateaubriand, 10 rue de l'Europe. Tel: 47 54 77 02
- Grammont, 153 avenue Grammont. Tel: 47 05 14 64
- Halles, 67 rue de la Victoire. Tel: 47 37 15 20

Municipal library: 2 bis quai de la Loire. Tel: 47 05 47 33 (subscription 45F for the year for inhabitants of Tours; closed Sundays and Thursdays)

- Sanitas, place Ferdinand Morin. Tel: 47 05 03 37

CAF: 1 rue Alexandre Fleming. Tel: 47 31 55 16

CPAM: 38 rue E Vaillant. Tel: 47 31 54 54

Bookshops:

- Bouquiniste, 20 rue Gambetta. Tel: 47 05 58 30
- Cinémagie, 20 rue du Commerce. Tel: 47 61 50 97
- Le Temps de Vivre, 5 rue de Bordeaux. Tel: 47 20 87 42
- Librairie du Grand Marché, 25 rue du Grand Marché. Tel: 47 05 22 43
- A la Boîte à Livres, 11 rue des Halles. Tel: 47 05 70 39
- A la Boîte à Livres de l'Etranger, 27 rue Marceau. Tel: 47 20 47 80
- Lib. Fac., 104 avenue de Grammont. Tel: 47 05 17 17

Association 'Accueil aux Etudiants Etrangers', 1 rue de la Grandière. Tel: 47 05 48 93

Nearest British Consulate-General (Paris): 9 avenue Hoche, 75008 Paris. Tel: (1) 42 66 38 10. Fax: (1) 40 76 02 87

Nearest US Consulate-General (Paris): 2 avenue Gabriel, 75382 Cedex 08. Tel: (1) 42 96 12 02. Fax: (1) 42 66 97 83

Health care

Hospital: Hôpital Trousseau, rue de Loches. Tel: 47 47 47 47

Chemist: Pharmacie du Sanitas (opposite halls of residence).

Local student insurance offices:

- MNEF, 44 boulevard Heurteloup. Tel: 47 61 04 22
- SMECO, 4 rue Chanoineau. Tel: 47 20 88 17

Travel

Railway station

Place de la Gare. Tel: 47 20 50 50. London-Tours (via Newhaven-Dieppe-Paris) £102 return; (via Dover-Calais-Paris) £106 return (Eurotrain)

Bus/coach station
Place de la Gare. London-Tours £76 return; £42 single (Eurolines).
Higher fares may apply during peak periods in the summer months.

Local airport
Aéroport de Tours, 4 rue Jules Favre. Tel: 47 54 19 46

Local bus service
Société des Transports de Tours (SEMITRAT), place Jean Jaurès.
Tel: 47 66 70 70. Tickets may be purchased singly or in books of ten;
concessionary student monthly passes are also available.

Taxis
- Allo Taxi Radio, 25 rue Bordiers. Tel: 47 54 60 95
- Groupement Taxi Radio Tours, 13 rue de Nantes. Tel: 47 20 30 40
- Taxi, 79 avenue Maginot. Tel: 47 51 58 58
- Taxis Autos Ville de Tours, 14 place Général Leclerc. Tel: 47 05 20 90

Emergencies

Duty doctor: SOS Médecins, 96 boulevard Thiers. Tel: 47 38 33 33
Late night chemist. Telephone police for instructions. Tel: 47 05 66 60
SAMU. Tel: 47 28 15 15
SOS Amitié. Tel: 47 54 54 54
SOS Médecins. Tel: 47 38 33 33
Centre Anti-Poisons. Tel: 47 66 85 11

Glossary and abbreviations

The following glossary contains the most commonly used terms (including acronyms and abbreviations) which you are likely to come across during your period of residence in France. Acronyms in particular need to be mastered so that you can find your way through your preparatory paperwork and complete formalities (including choice of course options where applicable) with the minimum of difficulty. Some terms and abbreviations not contained in this glossary are to be found in the *Index*, as they are explained more fully in the main body of the text.

Académie Administrative division of France for the purposes of education
Accusé de réception Acknowledgement of receipt (of letter, document etc.)
ADPF Association pour la Diffusion de la Pensée Française
AES *Administration Economique et Sociale:* a DEUG/*Licence* 'strand' (*filière*)
AFI Association des Foyers Internationaux
Agréé(e) Officially approved or contracted (as applied to hostels, restaurants, etc.)
Agrèg Abbreviation of *agrégation (qv)*
Agrégation The highest French teaching qualification (for secondary or tertiary education) awarded on the basis of a competitive examination
Agrégé(e) A holder of the *agrégation (qv)*
AIESEC Association Internationale des Etudiants en Sciences Economiques et Commerciales
AJ *Auberge de Jeunesse* (Youth Hostel)
Ajiste Youth hosteller
Ajourné(e) Referred (of exam results)
ALS *Allocation de logement à caractère social*
Aménagement d'études Document granting dispensation from course units, possibly in different years of a given programme
Amphi *Amphithéâtre (qv)*
Amphithéâtre (Large) lecture room/theatre

ANIL   Association Nationale pour l'Information sur le Logement
Année scolaire   Academic year, session
ANPE   Agence Nationale pour l'Emploi (Job Centre)
APL   *Aide personnalisée au logement*: a housing subsidy available to students in certain forms of accommodation
Bac   *Baccalauréat (qv)*
Baccalauréat   Diploma awarded at the end of secondary education studies (in a *lycée*); more broadly-based than A level in the UK, grouping a number of complementary subjects into different strands (A to H). The diploma gives automatic right of entry to first-year university courses (see *Bachelier*)
Bachelier   Someone who has been awarded the *baccalauréat (qv)*
Bachot   A familiar abbreviation of *baccalauréat (qv)*
BAFA   *Brevet d'Aptitude aux Fonctions d'Animateur*: a qualification for intending activity leaders/camp counsellors in a Centre de Vacances
BAPU   Bureau d'Aide Psychologique Universitaire
Bourse   Grant
Boursier/Boursière   Grant-holder
BTS   *Brevet de Technicien Supérieur*: a qualification awarded after two years of specialised, post-*baccalauréat* study in a *lycée*; see STS below
CAF   Caisse d'Allocations Familiales: the local or regional state benefits office, through which e.g. housing subsidies are paid
CAIO   Centre d'Aide Administrative, Information, Orientation
Caisse Primaire d'Assurance Maladie   The office from which beneficiaries of *sécurité sociale* reclaim the State contribution towards medical expenses
CAP   *Certificat d'Aptitude Professionnelle*: a vocational training certificate
CAPEPS   *Certificat d'Aptitude au Professorat d'Education Physique et Sportive*
CAPES   *Certificat d'Aptitude à l'Enseignement Secondaire*: a postgraduate teaching qualification (cf. PGCE in the UK) awarded on the basis of a competitive examination
CAPET   *Certificat d'Aptitude à l'Enseignement Technique*   (cf. CAPES)
Carnet   A 'book' of tickets for local travel/student restaurants, etc.
Carte Bleue   A system in France which covers the use of most major domestic and foreign credit cards
Carte Jeune   Young Person's Railcard, valid in the summer only; offers reductions of 50% for those under 26
Carte Orange   Travel Card in the Paris region; works by 'zones' and covers buses, *Métro*, RER and suburban trains
Caution   **Either**: a deposit (equivalent to one or two months' rent) paid by students entering a *résidence universitaire* or private accommodation, to cover breakages, unpaid rent, etc.
Or: a financial guarantor, an individual or an institution acting as security for accommodation, etc.
CCP   *Compte Chèque Postal*; a post office account (cf. Giro)
CDIA   Centre de Documentation et d'Information de l'Assurance, 2 rue de la Chaussée d'Antin, 75009 Paris. Tel: (1) 42 47 90 00

CEDEX *Courrier d'Entreprise à Distribution Exceptionnelle.* (Where appropriate, this is placed at the end of a postal address; corresponds roughly to P.O. Box but deliveries are to the actual address)

C(E)E Communauté (Economique) Européenne (EC)

CEFI Comité d'Etudes sur les Formations d'Ingénieurs

CES **Either:** *collège d'enseignement secondaire*
Or: *Certificat d'Etudes Spéciales*

CFB Collège Franco-Britannique: the British Hall of Residence at the Cité Universitaire Internationale de Paris

Chambre passagère A room in a hall of residence, let to students on a temporary basis, particularly outside term-time. See also *tarif passager*

CHR Centre Hospitalier Régional

CHU Centre Hospitalier Universitaire

CI(D)J Centre d'Information (et de Documentation) Jeunesse; local or regional information and resource centre for young people; see also CRI(D)J

CIEE Council on International Educational Exchanges

CIES Centre International des Etudiants et Stagiaires

CIO-SUP Cellule d'Information et d'Orientation de l'Enseignement Supérieur

Cité universitaire (A collection of) student halls of residence, run by the CROUS

CLEF Centre pour le Logement des Etudiants de France

CLM *Communication et Langage des Médias*

CLOUS Centre Local des Oeuvres Universitaires et Scolaires (a sub-branch of the Regional Welfare and Accommodation Office; see CROUS)

CM See *cours magistral(-aux)*

CNAM Conservatoire National des Arts et Métiers

CNOUS Centre National des Oeuvres Universitaires et Scolaires (co-ordinates and oversees the work of the various CROUS - see below – and adminsters French ERASMUS awards, for example)

CNR Conservatoire National de Région

CNSM Conservatoire National Supérieur de Musique

Commission des équivalences Validating committee in a university which examines applications by students to be granted the 'equivalence' of certain UV/UC/*modules* or to be allowed to enter a course at a level other than the first year (see also *validation d'acquis*)

Conseil de résidence paritaire Joint committee in halls of residence made up of CROUS officials and student representatives

Contrôle continu Continuous assessment based on assignments and class tests

Conventionné(e) (médecin) Recognised practitioner working within the State Health System

Cours magistral (-aux) (Formal) lectures as opposed to practical classes (TD)

CPAM Caisse Primaire d'Assurance Maladie (*qv*)

CPGE   *Classes préparatoires aux grandes écoles*

CRAPEL   Centre de Recherche et d'Application Pédagogiques en Langues (Nancy)

CRDP   Centre Régional de Documentation Pédagogique (teachers' regional resource centre)

CREDIF   Centre de Recherches et d'Etudes pour la Diffusion du Français

CREPS   Centre Régional d'Education Physique et Sportive

CRI(D)J   Centre Régional d'Information (et de Documentation) Jeunesse (see CI(D)J)

CROUS   Centre Régional des Oeuvres Universitaires et Scolaires (the regional headquarters of the Welfare and Accommodation Services, dependent on the relevant *rectorat*; responsible for the provision of meals throughout the education system at post-*bac* level and for student accommodation. Also responsible for the promotion of social and cultural activities. Administers arrangements for *boursiers du gouvernement français*

CRSU   Comité Régional du Sport Universitaire

CSU   Comité Sportif Universitaire

CU   *Cité Universitaire*

CUFOM   Centre Universitaire de Formation des Maîtres

CUIO   Cellule Universitaire d'Information et d'Orientation (see SUIO)

Cycle   One of three tiers in higher education in France; see *premier cycle, deuxième cycle, troisième cycle*

DALF   *Diplôme Approfondi de Langue Française*

DEA   *Diplôme d'Etudes Approfondies.* A postgraduate diploma (*3ème cycle*) which is indispensable for those who are to prepare a *Doctorat (qv)*

DELF   *Diplôme Elémentaire de Langue Française*

Dérogation   Special dispensation to depart from normal university regulations

DESS   *Diplôme d'Etudes Supérieures Spécialisées*

DEUG   *Diplôme d'Etudes Universitaires Générales* (a two-year diploma; the first university qualification)

DEUST   *Diplôme d'Etudes Universitaires Scientifiques et Techniques*

Deuxième session   Second examination period, normally in September, for students who missed the first session (*première session*) or who are required to resit

Devoir sur table   Class test, written exercise done in class

Doctorat   Doctoral thesis

DOM   Département(s) d'Outre-Mer

DPFE   *Diplôme de Professeur de Français à l'Etranger*

Droits d'inscription   Registration fees paid at the beginning of the academic year

DUFGS   *Diplôme Universitaire de Formation Générale Scientifique*

DUP   *Docteur de l'Université de Paris*

DUT   *Diplôme Universitaire de Technologie.* A two-year diploma awarded in the IUT (*qv*)

ECTS   European Credit Transfer Scheme
EDF   Electricité de France
ENA   Ecole Nationale d'Administration
Enarque   Present or former student of the ENA (*qv*)
ENM   Ecole Nationale de Musique
ENSAM   Ecole Nationale Supérieure des Arts et Métiers
ENSBA   Ecole Nationale Supérieure des Beaux-Arts
ENSEPS   Ecole Nationale Supérieure d'Education Physique et Sportive
ENSI   Ecole Nationale Supérieure d'Ingénieurs
ENSMA   Ecole Nationale Supérieure de Mécanique et d'Aérotechnique
Equivalence   Recognition of a qualification as being of a sufficient standard to be considered as 'equivalent to' a French diploma or university UV/UC/ *module*. Such recognition is granted by the *Commission des équivalences* (see *validation d'acquis*)
Erasmien(ne)   Erasmus grant-holder
ERASMUS   EuRopean (Community) Action Scheme for the Mobility of University Students
ESSEC   Ecole Supérieure des Sciences Economiques et Commerciales
ETE   Emplois Temporaires Etudiants (the section of the CROUS which helps students find part-time jobs)
FFMJC   Fédération Française des Maisons de Jeunes et de la Culture
Fiche pédagogique   Academic record card   .
Filière   A 'strand' or programme of studies leading to an academic award
FLE   *Français Langue Etrangère*
FNAC   Fédération Nationale d'Achat des Cadres (a chain of discount retail outlets specialising in books, records, tapes, compact discs, photographic supplies, etc.)
FNSU   Fédération Nationale de Sport Universitaire
Foyer   A hostel
FSU   *Fonds de Solidarité Universitaire*: offers grants or interest-free loans to students and is administered by the CROUS
GAP   Organisation which arranges work placements abroad for UK sixth-formers intercalating a year prior to higher education
GAPMO   *Gestion Appliquée aux Petites et Moyennes Entreprises*
Gare routière   Bus/coach station
Gare **SNCF**   Railway station
GDF   Gaz de France
GEA   *Gestion des Entreprises et des Administrations*
GEII   *Génie Electrique et Informatique Industrielle*
HAA   *Histoire de l'Art et Archéologie*
HEC   (Ecole des) Hautes Etudes Commerciales
HLM   *Habitation à loyer modéré* (corresponds roughly to 'council flat' in the UK. A number of CROUS let HLM to students)
IAESTE   International Association for the Exchange of Students for Technical Experience

ICP International Cooperation Programme under the ERASMUS scheme (see PIC)

IDHEC Institut des Hautes Etudes Cinématographiques

Inscription Registration

INSEP Institut National du Sport et de l'Education Physique

Institut Britannique de Paris An Institute run jointly by the University of London and by the Paris Universities; contains an English Department and a French Department. Offers a variety of courses, including correspondence courses, and awards diplomas

IPFE Institut des Professeurs de Français à l'Etranger

IRADIF Institut des Recherches et d'Application pour la Diffusion du Français

ISIC International Student Identity Card

ISTC International Student Travel Conference

IUFM Institut Universitaire de Formation des Maîtres

IUP Institut Universitaire Professionnalisé

IUT Institut Universitaire de Technologie

JYA Junior Year Abroad

LCE *Lettres* (or sometimes *Langues*) *et Civilisations Etrangères*: 'traditional' courses for French students of foreign languages

LEA *Langues Etrangères Appliquées*: modern languages courses which include the study of two foreign languages with elements of Economics, Business Studies and Law

Lettres Modernes The study of French language and literature (tends to include linguistics, history of the language; often has some comparative literature)

LIC *Langages, Images, Communication*

Licence Corresponds to the honours degree in Australia and the UK, and to the Master's degree in the USA

Licence ès Lettres Corresponds roughly to BA in Australia and the UK, and to the Master's degree in the USA

Licence ès Sciences Corresponds roughly to BSc in Australia and the UK, and to the Master's degree in the USA

LINGUA An EC programme promoting the exchange of modern languages students; promotes 'minority' languages in particular

LL *Lettres et Langages*

LV *Langues Vivantes*

LVE *Langues Vivantes Etrangères*

Lycée Secondary education establishment in which pupils prepare their chosen strand of the *baccalauréat*; see also CPGE

Lycéen, lycéenne Pupil attending a *lycée (qv)*

MASS *Mathématiques Appliquées et Sciences Sociales*

Médecine Préventive Corresponds roughly to 'Student Health' in British universities; see SUMP

MEL Mutuelle des Etudiants du Languedoc. See also MNEF/USEM
MEP Mutuelle des Etudiants de Provence. See also MNEF/USEM
MGEL Mutuelle Générale des Etudiants de l'Est. See also MNEF/USEM
MIAGE *Maîtrise d'Informatique Appliquée à la Gestion*
Minitel Terminal (private or public) of the French telecommunications system which enables subscribers/users to access information services on a small screen; includes the electronic telephone directory (*annuaire électronique*); available in post offices
MJC Maison des Jeunes et de la Culture. Offers a range of cultural activities; a useful place for meeting French people
MNEF Mutuelle Nationale des Etudiants de France. Most useful as suppliers of insurance to 'top up' either E111 or *Sécurité Sociale Etudiante*, or for help with housing services
Module Course unit; replaces UV under recent reforms. See UV/UC
MPU *Médecine Préventive Universitaire.* See also SUMP
MSG *Maîtrise de Sciences de Gestion*
MST **Either**: *Maîtrise de Sciences et Techniques*
　Or: *Maladies Sexuellement Transmissibles*
MSTCF *Maîtrise des Sciences et Techniques Comptables et Financières*
Mutuelle **Either**: the organisation which provides 'top-up' health policies for students or employees
　Or: the insurance policy itself
OCAU Office de Coopération et d'Accueil Universitaire
ONISEP Office National d'Information sur les Enseignements et les Professions
Option libre A course unit, chosen freely from among the whole range of possibilities on offer, as part of course requirements in a given 'strand'
OSE Office des Services Etudiants: an association dedicated to helping students with practical problems, in particular with accommodation
OTU Organisation pour le Tourisme Universitaire
Partiel(s) Mid-session examination(s) counting towards the assessment of a course unit
PCEM *Premier Cycle d'Etudes Médicales*
PEGASE *Programme d'Echanges avec les Anciens Stagiaires Etrangers*
PIC *Programme International de Coopération* (see IPC)
Pièces justificatives Supporting documentation accompanying application forms, etc.
PMI-PME *Petites et Moyennes Industries-Petites et Moyennes Entreprises*
Première session The main examination period, usually in May/June
Préprofessionnalisation An integral part of the DEUG *rénové* aimed at helping students to decide on their best *orientation professionnelle*
Procès verbal Academic profile
PTT Postes, Télécommunications, Télédiffusion (= post office, and telephone service)
PV See *procès verbal*

RATP Régie Autonome des Transports Parisiens (the Paris transport network)

Recteur/Rectorat The *Rectorat* comprises the administrative offices of the *Recteur*, the representative of central authority at the head of an *académie (qv)*

RER Réseau Express Régional: high-speed underground and suburban rail network in the Paris region

Résidence universitaire Student residence (usually modern blocks) run by the CROUS

Restaurant universitaire Student restaurant run by the CROUS; meals are subsidised and are usually purchased with vouchers (*tickets de restaurant*)

Restau-U Abbreviation of *restaurant universitaire*

Resto-U Abbreviation of *restaurant universitaire*

RIB *Relevé d'Identité Bancaire* (Bank sort code and account number)

Routière See *gare*

RU Abbreviation **either** of *restaurant universitaire (qv)* **or** of *résidence universitaire (qv)*

SAEE Service d'Accueil des Etudiants Etrangers

SAMU Service d'Aide Médicale d'Urgence (ambulance service, etc.)

SATA Student Air Travel Association

Scolarité (Bureau de) Corresponds to the academic registration office in British institutions; registers students with the French university concerned to establish student status and subsequently enrols them for examinations

SCUIO Services Communs Universitaires d'Information et d'Orientation

Sécu See *Sécurité Sociale*

Sécurité Sociale The French health-care scheme which provides cover for up to 70–80% of allowable medical expenses and includes *Sécurité Sociale Etudiante* (that part of the scheme designed specifically for students)

SEM (Union Nationale des) Sociétés Etudiantes Mutualistes

SERNAM Service National des Messageries: a nation-wide delivery service for large parcels, including trunks; it is part of the SNCF (*qv*)

Session Examination period (see *première* and *deuxième*)

SHS *Sciences de l'Homme et de la Société*

SIAPS Service Interuniversitaire des Activités Physiques et Sportives. See also SUAPS

SIEE Service Interuniversitaire des Etudiants Etrangers. See also SUEE

SIUMP Service Inter-Universitaire de Médecine Préventive. See also SUMP and SUMPPS

SL *Sciences du Langage*

SMEBA Société Mutualiste des Etudiants de Bretagne Atlantique. See also MNEF/USEM

SMECO Société Mutualiste des Etudiants du Centre-Ouest. See also MNEF/USEM

SMENO Société Mutualiste des Etudiants de la Région du Nord-Ouest. See also MNEF/USEM

SMEREB Société Mutualiste des Etudiants de la Région de Bourgogne. See also MNEF/USEM

SMEREP Société Mutualiste des Etudiants de la Région Parisienne. See also MNEF/USEM

SMERRA Société Mutualiste des Etudiants de la Région Rhône-Alpes. See also MNEF/USEM

SMESO Société Mutualiste des Etudiants de la Région du Sud-Ouest. See also MNEF/USEM

SMIC *Salaire Minimum Interprofessionnel de Croissance*: the national minimum wage in France

SMUR Service Mobile d'Urgence et de Réanimation

SNCF Société Nationale des Chemins de Fer Français. See also *gare*

SNV *Sciences de la Nature et de la Vie*

Stage Work placement or training course

Stagiaire Trainee, student on a work placement or a course

STAPS *Sciences et Techniques des Activités Physiques et Sportives*

STS *Sections de techniciens supérieurs*

SUAPS Service Universitaire des Activités Physiques et Sportives/Service Universitaire des Activités Physiques, Sportives et de Plein Air

SUEE Service Universitaire des Etudiants Etrangers

SUIO Service Universitaire d'Information et d'Orientation

SUMP Service Universitaire de Médecine Préventive (et de Promotion de la Santé). See also *Médecine Préventive*

SUMPPS Service Universitaire de Médecine Préventive et de Promotion de la Santé

TAMIA *Traducteurs Assistants des Métiers de l'Informatique et de l'Audiovisuel*

Taxe d'habitation Local tax, payable on 1 January, by residents of houses, flats and so on

TD *Travaux dirigés (qv)*

Télécopie/Télécopieur/Telco Fax/Fax machine/Fax number

TGV *Train à grande vitesse*

Ticket(s) de restaurant Meal voucher(s), purchased in books of ten, for use in CROUS-controlled restaurants

TOM Territoire(s) d'Outre-Mer

TP *Travaux pratiques (qv)*

Travaux dirigés Classes in which smaller groups do work in support of large lectures; corresponds to British 'seminars' and 'tutorials' but the groups are much larger

Travaux pratiques Practical classes (as opposed to *cours magistraux*)

Tutorat (System of) tutorial guidance; is being introduced for 'exchange students' in particular; a variation is also being offered to first-year students under the most recent reforms

UC *Unité de compte (qv)*

UER Unité d'Enseignement et de Recherche; replaced the old *facultés* but now superseded by UFR

UFR Unité de Formation et de Recherche (*nouvelle loi de l'enseignement*

supérieur); academic school or department; corresponds roughly to the old *facultés*, subject groupings or disciplines

UFRAPS   Unité de Formation et de Recherche des Activités Physiques et Sportives

UNEF   Union Nationale des Etudiants de France

Unité de compte   Weighting given to individual units within a course programme. See also UV/*module*

USEM   Union Nationale des Sociétés Etudiantes Mutualistes Régionales: an umbrella organisation for local student health insurance provision

UV   *Unité de valeur*: a course unit. UV *obligatoire* is a 'core course' (cf. UV *optionnelle* and *option libre*)

UV *obligatoire*   A core course (cf. UV *optionnelle* and *option libre*)

UV *optionnelle*   An optional course unit chosen from among a limited range of possibilities in a given subject area

Validation d'acquis   Process of ratifying qualifications for *équivalence (qv)*

Appendix

The following letters and CV serve as models: the fictitious name of Butterworth has been used for the CV.

1 Confirming your place at a French university

When you hear that you have been accepted by one of the French universities to which you applied (the *réponse de la première/deuxième université*), you will be required to confirm your acceptance of the offer before 31 July at the latest. Keep this notification as it will be needed when you register at your French university, but return a photocopy with your letter of acceptance (see model below). This letter should be addressed to Monsieur/Madame le Chef du Service de la Scolarité in the UFR in which you are to register.

M/Mlle (your name)
à
Monsieur/Madame le Chef du Service
de la Scolarité
UFR de (full address)

Birmingham, le 10 juin 1994

Monsieur/Madame le Chef de Service,
    J'ai l'honneur de vous accuser réception de votre lettre du 22 mai dernier qui confirme que ma demande d'inscription à l'UFR de ('Faculty' title, name of university) a été acceptée.
    Je suis très heureux/heureuse de vous informer que je m'inscrirai pour l'année 1994–95 et que je me présenterai pendant la période des inscriptions indiquée dans votre communication. Je joins sous ce pli la photocopie de votre réponse à ma demande d'inscription préalable.
    Je vous prie, Monsieur/Madame, de bien vouloir agréer l'expression de mes sentiments respectueux.

Signature
followed by name and forename printed in full

2 Requesting recognition of qualifications

In order to gain admission to a French university, you will need to establish that you have already achieved an equivalent qualification to the *baccalauréat*, and that the qualification that you hold would entitle you to enter a university in your own country (*titres admis en équivalence du baccalauréat*). Chapter 5.1 has already explained what you will need to take for this purpose. However, it may also be the case that you wish to enter the course at a level other than the first year. If this is so, you will need to request that your existing qualifications be recognised as sufficient to excuse you from the relevant part of the course (*validation d'acquis*). To obtain such *équivalences*, you will need to apply for the appropriate form from the *Bureau de Scolarité*. It is advisable to start this process well before you arrive (e.g. at the end of the previous academic year). A normal formula might be:

M/Mlle (your name)
à
Monsieur/Madame le Chef du Service
de la Scolarité
(Full address)

Birmingham, le 12 juin 1994

Monsieur/Madame le Chef de Service
  J'ai l'honneur de solliciter de votre haute bienveillance le dossier qui me permettra de faire une demande d'équivalence ou d'aménagement d'études en vue de mon inscription en (2e année du DEUG, Lettres Modernes *or* 2e année LEA etc, *or* . . .[1]).
  Je vous prie, Monsieur/Madame, de bien vouloir agréer l'expression de mes sentiments respectueux.

Signature
followed by name and forename in full

  When you send back the completed form, with the necessary documents attached, you should append the appropriate version of the letter below. The documentation you will have received will indicate whether you are likely to be granted the *équivalence* of one or more whole years of the course, or whether you will be credited with a certain number of course units from different years (an *aménagement d'études*). In the latter case, this will mean that, to obtain the relevant diploma, you will have to register for, and complete, the outstanding requirements for each of the years specified.

---

[1] The text should be modified according to individual circumstances.

M/Mlle (your name)
à
Monsieur/Madame le Président
de (name of the university)

Birmingham, le 30 juin 1994

Monsieur/Madame le Président,
    J'ai l'honneur de solliciter de votre haute bienveillance *l'équivalence de mes diplômes*[1] or *un aménagement d'études* [2] en vue de mon inscription à l'UFR de . . .
    Je joins sous ce pli la photocopie, et la traduction, des titres britanniques/américains, etc., admis en équivalence du baccalauréat, que j'ai obtenus en 19.. (give year) et qui m'ont permis de m'inscrire à l'Université de . . . (give name), ainsi qu'une attestation détaillée et traduction, certifiées conformes, des cours déjà suivis à l'Université où je suis inscrit(e) depuis un/deux/trois ans.
    Veuillez croire, Monsieur/Madame le Président, à l'expression de ma haute considération.

Signature
followed by your name and forename printed in full

    In all cases, ensure that you include all the documentation specified on the *dossier de demande d'équivalence/d'aménagement d'études.*
    Whenever your correspondance invites a reply, always enclose a self-addressed envelope and at least one international reply coupon.

3   Job application and CV

BUTTERWORTH, Sophie Jane
23 Brunel Street
Birmingham B27 4JT
Royaume-Uni

à

Monsieur le Directeur du Personnel
Société Finesherbes
12, place du Général de Gaulle
59000 Lille
France

Birmingham, le 25 mars 1994

[1] and [2] It is probable that only one of these will apply. The appropriate form will have made this clear. Modify the text accordingly.

Objet: demande d'emploi de programmeur/-euse

Monsieur,

En réponse à votre annonce parue dans *Les Echos du Nord* du 23 mars, je me permets de poser ma candidature au poste de programmeuse dans votre société (emploi été 1994).

Je vous prie de bien vouloir trouver ci-joint mon *curriculum vitae*. Je me tiens à votre disposition pour vous communiquer tout renseignement complémentaire que vous pourriez souhaiter.

Dans l'espoir que vous voudrez bien considérer favorablement ma demande, et dans l'attente de votre réponse, je vous prie de croire, Monsieur le Directeur, à l'assurance de mes sentiments respectueux.

Signature,
(followed by your surname (capital letters) and forenames printed in full).
BUTTERWORTH, Sophie Jane (Mlle)

CURRICULUM VITAE

Nom: BUTTERWORTH

Prénoms: Sophie Jane

Adresse: 23 Brunel Street
Birmingham B27 7JT
Royaume-Uni

Téléphone: 19–44–21–414–5966

Date et lieu de naissance: 03.10.76 à Exeter, Angleterre

Situation de famille: célibataire

Nationalité: Britannique

Langues: Anglais (langue maternelle)
Français (parlé et écrit: niveau supérieur)
Espagnol (parlé et écrit: niveau élémentaire)

Formation:
1990–92 GCE A Levels (diplôme de fin d'études secondaires, équivalent du baccalauréat) en français, histoire, biologie, mathématiques.
1992–93 BA (Licence) en français et informatique, première année. Résultat: reçue.
1993–94 BA (Licence) en français et informatique, deuxième année. Résultat: en cours.

Postes occupés: Employée de bureau (poste temporaire), CHP Secretarial Services, Birmingham, décembre 1992–janvier 1993.
Vendeuse stagiaire, Computerbods plc. Birmingham, été 1993.

Autres renseignements: Permis de conduire.
De nombreux voyages en Europe.

4 Letter of acceptance

BUTTERWORTH, Sophie Jane
23 Brunel Street
Birmingham, B27 4JT
Royaume-Uni.

à

Monsieur le Directeur du Personnel
Socété Finesherbes
12 place du Général de Gaulle
59000 LILLE
France

Birmingham, le 5 mai 1994

Objet: offre d'emploi de programmeuse

Monsieur le Directeur,
Je vous accuse réception de votre lettre du 27 avril. Je suis très heureuse d'accepter votre offre d'emploi en tant que programmeuse dans votre société. Comme convenu, j'arriverai à Lille le 4 juillet 1994, et je me présenterai dans vos bureaux à 8 heures ce matin-là.
Si vous avez besoin de renseignements supplémentaires, vous pourrez me rejoindre à l'adresse citée ci-dessus. Je me permets de vous rappeler aussi mon numéro personnel: (44) 21 414 5966.
Dans l'attente de faire votre connaissance, je vous prie, Monsieur le Directeur, de bien vouloir agréer l'expression de mes sentiments les plus dévoués.

Signature
(followed by your surname (capital letters) and forenames printed in full)
BUTTERWORTH, Sophie Jane (Mlle)

5 Useful addresses (work placements)

Students wishing to place advertisements in French newspapers may contact the following:
● The French Publishing Group, 21–23 Elizabeth Street, London SW1. Tel: 071 730 3477
● The International Herald Tribune, 63 Long Acre, London WC2. Tel: 071 836 4802

The following are recognised organisations which provide information on short-term work placements in France:

- Central Bureau for Educational Visits and Exchanges, 26–37 Seymour Mews, London W1N 9PE. Tel: 071 486 5101
- Concordia, 8 Brunswick Place, Hove, East Sussex
- Centre d'Information et de Documentation de la Jeunesse, 101 quai Branly, 75740 Paris Cedex 15. Tel: (1) 45 66 40 20

Information on opportunities for vacation work may be obtained from:

- Cultural Services, French Embassy, 23 Cromwell Road, London SW7.

Au pair work:

- Accueil Familial des Jeunes Etrangers, 23 rue du Cherche-Midi, 75006 Paris
- Comité Parisien de l'Association Catholique de Services de Jeunesse Féminine, 65 rue Monsieur le Prince, 75006 Paris
- Alliance Française, 101 boulevard Raspail, 75006 Paris

Au pair contracts can be obtained by employers (Paris region) from:

- Service des Stages, 391 rue de Vaugirard, 75015 Paris
- Service de la Main-d'Oeuvre Etrangère, 80 rue de la Croix-Nivert, 75732 Paris Cedex 15

In the provinces, contracts may be obtained from the Direction Départementale du Travail.

Hotel and catering posts:

- The British Hotel, Restaurant and Caterer Association, 13 Cork Street, London W1X 2BH. Tel: 071 499 6641

Information on Social Security arrangements:

- Department of Health and Social Security, Overseas Group, Newcastle-upon-Tyne, NE98 1YX

For general advice on health and welfare abroad, American travellers should contact:

- CIEE, 205 East 42nd Street, New York, NY 10017

BAFA training courses:

- Association Nationale Sciences et Techniques Jeunesse (ANSTJ), 17 avenue Gambetta, 91130 Ris-Orangis. Tel: 69 06 82 20
- Centre d'Entraînement aux Méthodes d'Education Active (CEMEA), 76 boulevard de la Villette, 75019 Paris. Tel: (1) 40 40 43 26
- Comité Protestant des Centres de Vacances (CPCV), 47 rue de Clichy, 75009 Paris. Tel: (1) 42 80 06 99
- Union Française des Centres de Vacances (UFCV), 19 rue Dareau, 75014 Paris. Tel: (1) 45 35 25 26
- Union Nationale des Centres Sportifs et de Plein Air (UCPA), 62 rue de la Glacière, 75640 Paris Cedex 13. Tel: (1) 43 36 05 20

Bibliography

Recent legislation on higher education in France

Loi No 68–978 du 12 novembre 1968 d'orientation de l'enseignement supérieur (Journal Officiel, 13 novembre 1968).
Loi No 84–52 du 26 janvier 1984 (Réforme Savary sur l'enseignement supérieur), Journal officiel, no. 3, 27 janvier 1984.
Loi d'orientation sur l'éducation, Loi No 89–486 du 10 juillet 1989 (B O spécial, no. 4, 31 août 1989).

CNOUS publications

Je vais en France 1993, CNOUS, 8 rue Jean Calvin, 75005 Paris Cedex 05 (published annually). Available from the Service Culturel of French Embassies.
Les Oeuvres de A à Z, 1993, Paris, CNOUS.

CROUS publications

The various CROUS publish their own free guides under a variety of titles such as *Guide de l'étudiant, CROUS en poche, INFOCROUS* or *Labyrinthe*. These can be obtained from the local CROUS offices. See Part III for the addresses of the individual CROUS.

Student publications

Some student groups or associations publish their own guides, under titles such as *Le Dahu* (Grenoble), *L'Indic* (Tours) or *Le Petit Paumé* in Lyon and Montpellier.

Official French Ministry publications

Cours de français pour étudiants étrangers (Année 1992–93).
Cours de français pour étudiants étrangers (Eté 1993).
Both are published annually by the ADPF (9 rue Anatole de la Forge, 75017 Paris) on behalf of the Ministère des Affaires Etrangères.
Cours de français langue étrangère. Stages pour professeurs, 1993, Ministre des Affaires Etrangères, Sous-Direction de la coopération linguistique et éducative.

University publications

Each UFR publishes its own handbook under a variety of titles such as *Guide pédagogique, Guide de l'étudiant* and so on.

Background books on France

Travel and tourist information:
Baedeker's France 1993 (3rd revised edition), Basingstoke, AA publications.
Baillie, K. and Salmon, T. (eds), 1993, *France: The Rough Guide*, London, Rough Guides Ltd.
Knowles, R. (ed.), 1993, *Let's Go 1993. The Budget Guide to France*, London, Pan Books.
Magalaner, J. L., 1992, *Fodor's France*, New York, Fodor.
Michelin France, 1991, Harrow, Michelin Tyre.
Robertson, I., 1991, *Blue Guide: France*, London, A. and C. Black/New York, W.W. Norton.
Les Routiers: The 1993 Guide to France, 1993, Dublin, Gill and Macmillan.
Tucker, A., 1993, *The Berlitz Travellers Guide to France*, New York, Berlitz.

History, culture and society
Aplin, R., 1993, *A Dictionary of Contemporary France*, London, Hodder and Stoughton.
Ardagh, J., 1993, *France Today*, London, Penguin Books.
Braudel, F., 1989, *The Identity of France*, vol. 1, *History and Environment*, London, Fontana.
Cobban, A. (reprinted 1990), *A History of Modern France (1715–1962)*, 3 vols, London, Penguin Books.
Cook, M. (ed.), 1993, *French Culture since 1945*, London, Longman.
L'Etat de la France 93–94, 1993, Paris, Editions La Découverte.
Flower, J., 1993 (7th edition revised), *France Today: Introductory Studies*, London, Hodder and Stoughton.
Frémy D. and M., *Quid 1993*, Paris, Robert Laffont.
Kelly M. and Böck R. (eds), 1993, *France: Nation and Regions*, University of Southampton Press.
Mermet, G., *Francoscopie 1993*, Paris, Larousse.

Articles

Cousins, R., Hallmark, R. and Pickup, I., 'Preparing for the Year Abroad: Savoir-faire or laissez faire?', *French Studies Bulletin*, no. 36, Autumn 1990, pp. 14–16.

Cousins, R., Hallmark, R. and Pickup, I., 'Evaluating Study Residence Abroad', *Higher Education Quarterly*, vol. 36, no. 1, Winter 1992, pp. 124–127.

Firth, K., 'French Universities: The Difficult Road to Reform', *Modern Languages*, vol. 70, no. 1, March 1989, pp. 82–97.

French periodicals

L'Etudiant and *Le Monde de l'Education* are monthly publications which provide invaluable information on the French educational system, reforms, new legislation and the courses available in higher education in France. The following are of particular interest:

L'Etudiant (Spécial Etudes Supérieures), hors série, janvier 1993.

L'Etudiant, nos 143/144, juillet-août 1993. Features include 'Que faire avec ou sans le Bac?' and 'Où s'inscrire en juillet?'.

Le Monde de l'Education, no. 207, septembre 1993. Contains 'Les sujets du Bac 93', 'La rénovation des DEUG' and 'La réforme des IUFM'.

Talents is devoted exclusively to higher education and the following number is especially useful:

Talents, no. 6, octobre-novembre 1993 (Contains a 'Guide de l'année étudiante').

Studying, working and living in France

Bariet, A. and Rollot, O. (adapted by Archer, W.), 1993, *Studying in Europe* (Student Helpbooks), Cambridge, CRAC.

Byram, M., 1992, *The 'Assistant(e) d'Anglais'. Preparing for the Year Abroad*, University of Durham Press.

Carroll, R., 1987, *Evidences Invisibles*, Paris, Seuil.

Franz, D. and Hernandez, L., 1993, (11th edition), *Work, Study, Travel Abroad* (Council on International Educational Exchange), New York, St Martin's Press, .

Fullbright and Other Grants for Graduate Study Abroad, Institute of International Education, 809 United Nations Plaza, New York, NY 10017, USA (a free brochure published annually in May).

Guide OSE du Logement Etudiant, 1993, Paris, Armand Colin.

Hempshell, M., 1993, *How to Get a Job in France*, Plymouth, How to Books Ltd.

Jones, R., 1989, *How to Teach Abroad*, Plymouth, How to Books Ltd.

Prevost Logan, N., 1993, *How to Live and Work in France*, Plymouth, How to Books Ltd.

Woodward, D. (ed.), 1993, *Summer Jobs Abroad 1993*, Vacation Work, Park End Street, Oxford (France pp. 68–102).

Working Holidays 1994, London/Edinburgh, Central Bureau for Educational
Visits and Exchanges (France pp. 98–140).

English reference works

Alexander, C. G., 1992, *Longman English Grammar*, London, New York, Long-
man.
Leech, G., 1989, *An A-Z of English Grammar and Usage*, Walton-on-Thames,
Edinburgh, New York, Nelson.
Shaw, K., 1991, *Collins Cobuild English Grammar Exercises*, London, Collins
ELT.
Sinclair, J. (editor in chief), 1992, *BBC English Dictionary*, London, BBC
English, Harper Collins Publishers.
Sinclair, J. (editor in chief), 1992, *Collins Cobuild English Language Dictionary*,
London and Glasgow, Collins.
Sinclair, J. (editor in chief), 1990, *Collins Cobuild English Grammar*, London,
Collins ELT.

Index

As a general rule, headings and sub-headings which appear in the **Contents** have been excluded from this Index.